ALSO BY HER ROYAL HIGHNESS
PRINCESS MICHAEL OF KENT

Crowned in a Far Country:
Portraits of Eight Royal Brides

Cupid and the King:
Five Royal Paramours

SERPENT and the MOON

TWO RIVALS
FOR THE
LOVE OF A
RENAISSANCE
KING

Her Royal Highness

PRINCESS MICHAEL OF KENT

NEW YORK ... SYDNEY

TOUCHSTONE
Rockefeller Center
1230 Avenue of the Americas
New York, NY 10020

TOUCHSTONE and colophon are registered trademarks
of Simon & Schuster, Inc.

For information regarding special discounts for bulk purchases,
please contact Simon & Schuster Special Sales at 1-800-456-6798
or business@simonandschuster.com

Designed by Ruth Lee-Mui

Manufactured in the United States of America

1   3   5   7   9   10   8   6   4   2

Library of Congress Cataloging-in-Publication Data
Michael, of Kent, Princess.
The serpent and the moon : two rivals for the love of a Renaissance king /
Princess Michael of Kent.
p.   cm.
"A Touchstone book."
Includes bibliographical references and index.
1. Henry II, King of France, 1519–1559—Relations with women.   2. Poitiers,
Diane de, Duchess of Valentinois, 1499–1566.   3. Catherine de Medici, Queen,
consort of Henry II, King of France, 1519–1589.   4. Favorites—France—
Biography.   5. France—Kings and rules—Mistresses—Biography.   6. France—
Court and courtiers—History—16th century.   I. Title.
DC114.5M53   2004
944'.028'0922—dc22
[B]   2004045364

ISBN 0-7432-5104-0

Contents

Author's Note

WHEN I was twenty-one, I traveled from Vienna to London to study history, history of art, and interior design. I decorated my small apartment entirely in black and white, drove a black and white Mini, and acquired a black and white kitten. When my mother heard that I also wore only black and white, she thought it time for her to visit. I had no real reason for adopting my monochrome lifestyle except that I imagined it chic and different. Then my mother told me about Diane de Poitiers, our ancestor, who famously styled her whole life—and her country—in black and white.

Throughout my youth, my mother had always recounted to us children stories from history involving our ancestors—"the Saints and the Sinners," as we called them—but never did she mention Diane de Poitiers. This grand, sixteenth-century French lady was a king's mistress, and although we were descended from her younger daughter by her legitimate union, my religious mama considered Diane an unsuitable subject for chaste bedtime stories. Once she had been informed of my lapse into a chiaroscuro world, it was time for bedtime stories of a grown-up nature.

Now I had a real reason for my black and white lifestyle. Learning about Diane and her use of black and white influenced me so strongly that I even planted a black and white garden in her honor. I searched for and found black flowers—irises, tulips, violas—to put into beds shaped in squares, triangles, or diamonds, all framed in box hedges. I read everything I could find about my heroine. Her character was like her palette—contrasting and uncompromising; there were no gray areas with Diane de Poitiers. I incorporated her story into my second book, *Cupid and the King,* among those of other royal paramours. I have given many lectures about her and the time in which she lived—the Reformation and the French Renaissance, a time of persecution and enlightenment, black and white.

In France, Diane de Poitiers is a household name, but to other readers she is less well known. I hope this book will put that right. Diane's love story is the greatest in French royal history. She lived at a time of giants: François I, the Renaissance king of France; the Holy Roman Emperor Charles V, who ruled more territory than anyone in the known world; Henry VIII, king of England, who would cause bloody schism in his country on account of his passion for Anne Boleyn; the two Medici popes, Leo X and Clement VII, whose machinations swung the delicate balance of power between France and the Holy Roman Empire; and the Infidel Sultan—Suleiman the Magnificent, ruler of the Ottoman Empire. Europe was just emerging from the darkness and superstition of the Middle Ages into the light of the Renaissance, and brave captains of discovery sailed treacherous, uncharted seas to bring home knowledge of the unknown and spoils from the New World. During this time of religious upheaval and brutality, enlightenment and progress, the court of France was the most civilized in the world, and all other rulers strived to imitate it.

Diane's story spans the lives of two French monarchs, father and son. François I was the dashing, heroic "Chevalier King," whose son, the darkly handsome, silent Henri d'Orléans, was a child-prisoner and hostage, unloved by his father and unexpected heir to the throne. Eighteen years Diane's junior, this emotionally deprived warrior-knight would love Diane de Poitiers from the age of six until his tragic death at forty-two, calling out her name. For reasons of state and finance, it was arranged by François and Pope Clement VII that Henri should marry the pope's cousin, the heiress Catherine de' Medici. On the wedding night, Henri did his duty but was not prepared to do more. He retreated to be with his "Lady," Diane. Intelligent but unattractive, Catherine stood no chance of winning the love of a man totally in thrall to a beautiful older woman. It was her tragedy that she fell in love with Henri the moment they met. Catherine de' Medici suffered the jealousy of thwarted passion throughout her married life. Despised and mocked by the French court for her bourgeois origins, she took for her motto the words "Hate and Wait"—and wait she did, like a still, dangerous serpent in the grass.

Diane de Poitiers is popularly known in France as the mistress of two kings, father and son. I hope I have successfully disproved that fantasy. Of course it makes a better story that Diane was the lover of two kings, and many authors have adopted it. Most of the fabrication stems from nineteenth-century histories, and I have tried to dispel these fables whenever I found them. There is a saying that history is "oft-repeated lies." I may have inadvertently included some myself, and for this I apologize.

The nineteenth-century authors who embellished Diane's life didn't let the truth stand in the way of a good story. Much the same can be said of our press today. The sixteenth century, too, had its share of contemporary chroniclers or gossip columnists, who often wrote what their audience wanted to hear and thus are not always reliable. But they give the flavor and mood of the court, and for this reason I have included a number of such stories and annotated their sources. I have also used much of the correspondence from the time, although impersonal subject matter can disguise the writer's true character. Diane de Poitiers instructed Henri to destroy her letters, in line with the chivalric custom of the time. As a result, her own words do not usually show her to be a warm and passionate woman, except in the few poems which her lover did not burn. Her surviving correspondence is factual, to the point, and relates chiefly to her business interests. Her letters concerning the royal children are clearsighted and practical, whereas Catherine de' Medici's voluminous correspondence sheds greater light on her Machiavellian nature.

Diane's character had as many phases as the moon—her alter ego—whereas her rival Catherine de' Medici was famously duplicitous. I have tried to examine both women in detail so that the reader can know them within the kaleidoscopic fabric of their time. I do not seek to exonerate Diane as a partner to the king's adultery, nor from her greed or her support of the king's religious persecutions. She was a woman of her time. But since I descend just as directly from Catherine de' Medici as I do from Diane de Poitiers, I have no personal interest in damning the one while glorifying the other.[1] I simply want to tell the story of a beautiful, cultured, and fascinating woman. Diane de Poitiers lived in a *ménage à trois,* for even at the most intimate moments, there were always three in that royal marriage—the king, his wife, and his mistress.

I am not a qualified historian, but rather a teller of stories from history. My initial inspiration was my late mother who read History, one of the few women admitted to the University of Vienna at that time. We children needed no television; our mother would enthrall us with her tales of the past. She has always been my muse. Later, I had the privilege to be encouraged and advised by Elizabeth (Lady) Longford, to whom I shall always be grateful. There are a number of others I wish to thank: my agents Sam Haskell and Suzanne Gluck for press-ganging me into writing another book when I was content creating and presenting lectures. I am grateful to my editor, Trish Todd, who had faith, gave never-ending constructive criticism, and waited patiently for me to finish. I would also like to thank the rest of the team at Touchstone who have worked so hard to bring this

---

1. See the family tree on page xviii.

book to fruition: my copy chief Martha Schwartz; Joy O'Meara, the designer; Cherlynne Li who designed the cover; and Brett Valley, invaluable assistant to Trish Todd. On the publishing side, I am grateful to Mark Gompertz, my publisher; Chris Lloreda, deputy publisher; and the indefatigable Marcia Burch, publicity director. Thank you all.

In writing this book I have relied on a number of people to help me locate Renaissance texts. I have also had assistance with translations from Old French, especially when the original document is written in script. Much gratitude is due to the conscientious Kate Maxwell for diligently researching many obscure references for me, especially in Old French, and deciphering them. My thanks go to Dr. Alison Adams, Reader in French at the Centre for Medieval and Renaissance Studies, University of Glasgow, for recommending Kate, and for her help with the translations of poetry and mottos from Old French, and especially with unraveling Renaissance devices. I am grateful to Jonathan Spangler, who gave me forty excellent hours of his time for research. Gratitude goes also to Dr. Alexander S. Wilkinson of the *St. Andrews Sixteenth Century French Vernacular Book*. Otherwise, the research and translation work was my own, and I accept full responsibility.

I am greatly indebted to Robert J. Knecht, Emeritus Professor of French History at the University of Birmingham. As one of the acknowledged authorities and authors on Renaissance France, Professor Knecht took time to correspond with me and never failed to reply to my many foolish queries, as well as sending me helpful papers. He also was kind enough to read the manuscript and remove the worst of my mistakes—any that remain are my own.

Many libraries have helped me, especially the Bibliothèque Nationale in Paris, the musée de Chantilly, the château de Versailles, the Metropolitan Museum of Art in New York, the London Library, the British Library, and a number of foreign archives, notably the Niccolini in Florence. I am grateful to Diane de Poitiers' French biographer, the renowned historian Ivan Cloulas, for his generous advice and help. Maximo Gainza-Bemberg deserves my thanks for allowing me access to his deep knowledge of the Age of Chivalry, for helping me to understand many obscure customs and practices of the time, and for his poetic rendering of medieval poetry.

At Anet, Diane de Poitiers' favorite residence, I am once again indebted to the Yturbe family for allowing me into their home to seek and absorb the spirit of Diane and photograph her possessions. The same gratitude goes to the Menier family, who own Diane's other great house, Chenonceau, and who gave me access to their library. I am indebted to Professor Philip Bobbitt for his insights into the wars of the first half of the sixteenth century and for his patient explanations. For Latin translations of mottos and for encouragement, I am most grateful to Claudia Jenkins and to my son, Freddie Windsor. For taking the time to draw all the graphics of the many symbols and devices throughout I would like to thank my cousin Prince Johannes von Auersperg. Another member of my family, my brother Freddy von Reibnitz, was, as always, my first reader. For the maps, accuracy of dates, and all genealogy and tables, I am once again completely in the debt of Leo van der Pas, who tracked down even the most doubtful references I gave him, and read through the text. For illustrations in private collections, I am grateful to Her Majesty The Queen, the Earl of Derby, Baron Guy de Rothschild, the Earl of Spencer, Prince William Lobkowicz, and the Earl of Harewood. Jo Walton and Julia Harris-Voss have been an invaluable help in tracking down the illustrations.

For allowing me to stay for months so that I could write my first draft in her guesthouse, undisturbed, I am indebted to my dear friend Sibilla Clark. Others must be mentioned for their help, advice, and encouragement: Katie Garrod; Emma Kitchener-Fellowes; Julian Fellowes; Leoni Frieda; Nicholas Chance; Prince Michel de Grèce; Princess Mimi Romanoff for advice and anecdotes; and the kind team at SONY in the United States who solved my worst computer crash. I apologize to anyone I have failed to mention.

The person who deserves the most gratitude is my dear husband, who has tolerated my silences, my absences, and all my frustrations. With heroic forbearance he did not complain when I had no time for him, and he never failed to listen and encourage me. Furthermore, he is a stickler for grammar and corrected mine.

To him I dedicate this book.

HRH Princess Michael of Kent
September 25, 2003

POLAND

SAXONY

Danube R.

BAVARIA

AUSTRIA-
HUNGARY

SWITZERLAND

TYROL

VENICE

CROATIA

LOMBARDY
MILAN
Milan
Marignano
Lodi
Po R.
Venice

BOSNIA

SERBIA

OTTOMAN EMPIRE

Turin
Pavia
Boulogne
Genoa
Florence
Arno R.
TUSCANY
SIENA
URBINO
PAPAL STATES
Rome

GENOA

CORSICA

*Adriatic
Sea*

MONTENEGRO

ALBANIA

SARDINIA

Naples

NAPLES

*Tyrrhenian
Sea*

*Ionian
Sea*

SICILY

Mediterranean Sea

© 2004 Jeffrey L. Ward

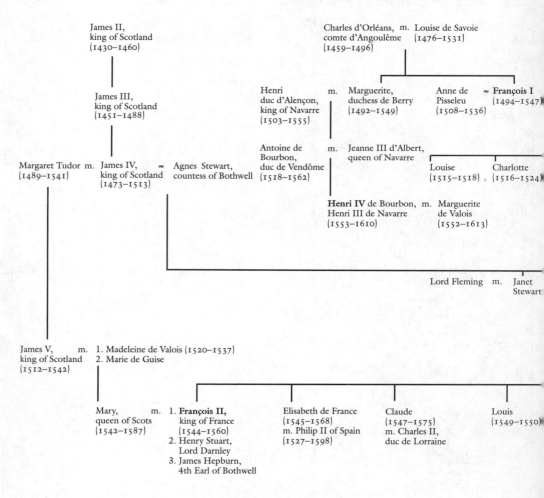

James II,
king of Scotland
(1430–1460)

Charles d'Orléans, m. Louise de Savoie
comte d'Angoulême   (1476–1531)
(1459–1496)

James III,
king of Scotland
(1451–1488)

Henri   m.   Marguerite,   Anne de   ~ François I
duc d'Alençon,   duchess de Berry   Pisseleu   (1494–1547)
king of Navarre   (1492–1549)   (1508–1536)
(1503–1555)

Antoine de   m.   Jeanne III d'Albert,
Bourbon,   queen of Navarre
duc de Vendôme   Louise   Charlotte
(1518–1562)   (1515–1518)   (1516–1524)

Margaret Tudor m. James IV,   ~ Agnes Stewart,
(1489–1541)   king of Scotland   countess of Bothwell
                   (1473–1513)

Henri IV de Bourbon, m. Marguerite
Henri III de Navarre   de Valois
(1553–1610)   (1552–1613)

Lord Fleming m. Janet
                  Stewart

James V,   m.   1. Madeleine de Valois (1520–1537)
king of Scotland   2. Marie de Guise
(1512–1542)

Mary,   m.   1. François II,   Elisabeth de France   Claude   Louis
queen of Scots   king of France   (1545–1568)   (1547–1575)   (1549–1550)
(1542–1587)   (1544–1560)   m. Philip II of Spain m. Charles II,
                     2. Henry Stuart,   (1527–1598)   duc de Lorraine
                        Lord Darnley
                     3. James Hepburn,
                        4th Earl of Bothwell

PRINCIPAL CHARACTERS

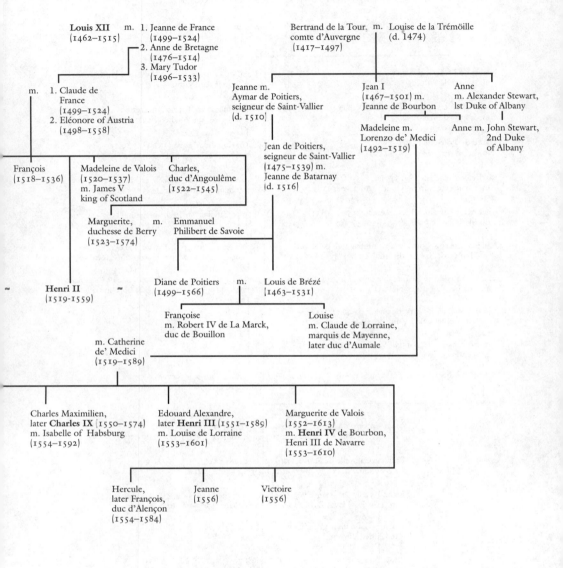

Louis XII (1462–1515) m. 1. Jeanne de France (1499–1524)
2. Anne de Bretagne (1476–1514)
3. Mary Tudor (1496–1533)

Bertrand de la Tour, comte d'Auvergne (1417–1497) m. Louise de la Trémöille (d. 1474)

m. 1. Claude de France (1499–1524)
2. Eléonore of Austria (1498–1558)

Jeanne m. Aymar de Poitiers, seigneur de Saint-Vallier (d. 1510)

Jean I (1467–1501) m. Jeanne de Bourbon

Anne m. Alexander Stewart, lst Duke of Albany

Madeleine m. Lorenzo de' Medici (1492–1519)

Anne m. John Stewart, 2nd Duke of Albany

François (1518–1536)

Madeleine de Valois (1520–1537) m. James V king of Scotland

Charles, duc d'Angoulême (1522–1545)

Jean de Poitiers, seigneur de Saint-Vallier (1475–1539) m. Jeanne de Batarnay (d. 1516)

Marguerite, duchesse de Berry (1523–1574) m. Emmanuel Philibert de Savoie

~ Henri II (1519-1559) ~

Diane de Poitiers (1499–1566) m. Louis de Brézé (1463–1531)

Françoise m. Robert IV de La Marck, duc de Bouillon

Louise m. Claude de Lorraine, marquis de Mayenne, later duc d'Aumale

m. Catherine de' Medici (1519–1589)

Charles Maximilien, later **Charles IX** (1550–1574) m. Isabelle of Habsburg (1554–1592)

Edouard Alexandre, later **Henri III** (1551–1589) m. Louise de Lorraine (1553–1601)

Marguerite de Valois (1552–1613) m. **Henri IV** de Bourbon, Henri III de Navarre (1553–1610)

Hercule, later François, duc d'Alençon (1554–1584)

Jeanne (1556)

Victoire (1556)

Princess Michael of Kent's Descent from Diane de Poitiers and Catherine de' Medici

Bertrand de La Tour, comte d'Auvergne (1417–1497)
m. Louise de La Trémoïlle

Jeanne de La Tour d'Auvergne
m. Aymar de Poitiers

Jean de Poitiers, seigneur de Saint-Vallier (1475–1539)
m. Jeanne de Batarnay

Diane de Poitiers (1499–1566)
m. Louis de Brézé (1463–1531)

Louise de Brézé (1518–1577)
m. Claude de Lorraine, duc d'Aumale (1526–1573)

Charles de Lorraine, duc d'Aumale (1555–1631)
m. Marie de Lorraine (1555–1603)

Anne de Lorraine, duchesse d'Aumale (1600–1638)
m. Henri I de Savoie, duc de Nemours (1572–1632)

Charles Amédée de Savoie, duc de Nemours (1624–1652)
m. Elisabeth de Bourbon (1614–1664)

Princess Maria Giovanna de Savoie-Nemours (1644–1724)
m. Carlo Emanuele II, duc de Savoy (1634–1675)

Vittorio Amadeo II, King of Sardinia (1666–1732)
m. Jeanne Genevieve d'Albert (1670–1736)

Vittoria Francesca di Savoia (1690–1766)   m.

Jean I de La Tour, comte d'Auvergne (1467–1501)
m. Jeanne de Bourbon

Madeleine de La Tour d'Auvergne
m. Lorenzo de' Medici (1492–1519)

Catherine de' Medici (1519–1589)
m. Henri II, king of France (1519–1559)

Elisabeth de Valois, Princess of France (1545–1568)
m. Philip II, king of Spain (1527–1598)

Infanta Catalina Michaella of Spain (1567–1597)
m. Carlo Emanuele I, Duke of Savoie (1562–1630)

Tommaso Francesco de Savoie, Duke of Carignano
(1596–1646) m. Marie de Bourbon (1606–1692)

Emanuele Filiberto de Savoie, Prince of Carignano
(1628–1709) m. Maria Angela Caterina d'Este
(1656–1722)

Vittorio Amadeo de Savoie,
Prince de Carignano (1690–1741)

Luigi Vittorio de Savoie, Prince de Carignano (1721–1778)
m. Landgraefin Christine von Hessen-Rheinfels-Rotenburg (1717–1778)

Princess Gabrielle de Savoie-Carignano (1748–1828)
m. Ferdinand, 6th Prince von Lobkowicz (1724–1784)

Franz Joseph, 7th Prince von Lobkowicz (1772–1816)
m. Princess Maria Karolina zu Schwarzenberg (1775–1816)

Princess Gabrielle von Lobkowicz (1793–1863)
m. Prince Vinzenz von Auersperg (1790–1812)

Prince Vinzenz von Auersperg (1812–1867)
m. Countess Wilhelmine von Colloredo-Mannsfeld (1826–1898)

Princess Gabrielle von Auersperg (1855–1933)
m. Alfred, 3rd Prince zu Windisch-Graetz (1815–1927)

Princess Maria Hedwig zu Windisch-Graetz (1851–1927)
m. Count Frederick Szapary de Muraszombath, Szechysziget et Szapar (1869–1935)

Countess Marianne Szapary de Muraszombath, Szechysziget et Szapar (1911–1988)
m. Baron Guenther Hubertus von Reibnitz (1894–1983)

Baroness Marie Christine von Reibnitz, H.R.H. Princess Michael of Kent
m. Prince Michael of Kent

CHAPTER ONE

The Royal Wedding

*A*S the sun filtered through the autumn mist shrouding the harbor of Marseilles, three hundred cannons boomed from the ramparts of the château d'If and all the bells of the city rang out to announce the arrival of the papal flotilla. It was October 11, 1533. The din must have been deafening, and yet so gratifying to Pope Clement VII to be thus received by the king, François I. This journey would be the apogee of the ailing Medici pope's extraordinary career.

It had taken three years for Clement VII to negotiate the marriage of his fourteen-year-old cousin Catherine[1] to fourteen-year-old Prince Henri d'Orléans, a son of the king of France. The pope was well aware that the Medici, no matter how rich and powerful, were considered no better than glorified merchants by Europe's reigning families. The marriage of this Florentine heiress to the second son of François I would raise his house far higher than he had ever dreamed possible.

The procession of ships was led by a galleon, the *Duchessina,* which

1. The pope was actually the first cousin of Catherine de' Medici's grandfather, but because of her youth, he preferred to call her his niece.

carried the Holy Sacrament, while the pontiff traveled in the second great galleon, the *Capitanesse*. Fourteen cardinals, sixty archbishops and bishops, and countless priests followed in other vessels. The bride was not in the pope's party. To allow the pope to make his own entry into Marseilles in state, for the marriage contracts to be finalized, and the preparations completed, Catherine de' Medici had left the *Capitanesse* shortly before Marseilles to await her summons in the Jardin des Rois. Still, the pope's arrival signaled the beginning of the royal wedding, and dozens of small boats sailed out from the shore, carrying noblemen and musicians to greet and escort the papal flotilla into the ancient Phoenician harbor.

The pope watched the eighteen galleys in his fleet maneuver to dock, each of them draped in his signature red, gold, and purple damask, and manned by hundreds of oarsmen shining bright in crimson satin and orange silk. As Clement VII disembarked, eighty lancers and two companies of infantry stood at attention on the quay and on every bridge. It was a sight worthy of the supreme head of the Christian church.

The pope's party was received on shore by the Grand Master of France, Anne de Montmorency,[2] the senior statesman in the kingdom charged with the court and its residences. He presented Clement VII to several French cardinals and a number of other clerics. The pope then moved into the house prepared for him outside the city to await the next day when he would make his formal entry and complete the final leg of the house of Medici's journey into the French royal family.

On the morning of October 12, the streets were lined with people who had come from every home in the city as well as the surrounding countryside. They were eager to see a pope, but even more eager to see the little bride for whom their lives had been so disrupted. Indeed, the people of Marseilles *needed* to be dazzled since the choice of their city for this grand event had cost them dear. An official entrance into a city by royalty, or indeed a pope, was one of the greatest public spectacles of the time. This one was no exception; the king had ordered a large

---

2. The title "Grand Master of France" is the equivalent of the Court Chamberlain or Master of the Royal Household in England. Montmorency was christened Anne in honor of his godmother Anne de Bretagne, twice queen of France. He pronounced his name "Annay."

swathe of the city demolished to make a wide avenue for the triumphal processions and the ceremonies surrounding this diplomatically important marriage. For the pope's temporary residence, a huge wooden building had been erected next to the old palace of the counts of Provence where the king and his party would lodge. An enclosed "bridge," so large it could be used as an extra reception room, was built to link the dwellings of the monarchs temporal and spiritual.

The pope was preceded in the procession by the Holy Sacrament displayed in a monstrance, mounted on a white palfrey[3] caparisoned in a cloth of gold. As he made his way slowly to the cathedral, Clement VII was carried shoulder-high in his red velvet *sedia,* or papal litter, covered by a large square awning supported at the corners on poles carried by four noblemen. On either side of the pope strode the king's two younger sons, the bridegroom himself, Prince Henri d'Orléans, and Prince Charles d'Angoulême. They were followed by the Italian cardinals and bishops in purple and red, riding on mules. Behind them walked the chanting choir of the Sistine Chapel and a procession of noblemen, prelates, abbots, curates, and monks.

As he heard the gasps of appreciation from the crowd, Clement settled back on his silken cushions beneath the awning of red, green, and yellow damask, nodding benignly and blessing the gaping crowds. He was tired after his sea voyage, and his ten years on the throne of St. Peter had prematurely aged him. All his life he had struggled to increase the glory of his family; finally, through his intervention, the Medici ruled in Florence once again. The French marriage could not come too soon; Catherine was becoming rather attached to his illegitimate nephew,[4] Ippolito de' Medici—brilliant, extravagant, and very, very handsome. But Catherine was the pope's most valuable piece on the chessboard of European politics and could not be wasted for a childish attachment with no possible advantage for the family. Ippolito was promptly dispatched into the church and made a cardinal.

As he passed the royal box, Clement VII caught his first sight of his partner in the Medici–Valois union, King François I. The pope's litter

3. A palfrey is a quiet saddle horse particularly suitable for women to ride.
4. There was no stigma attached to illegitimacy in the sixteenth century, though it precluded dynastic inheritance.

stopped as he blessed the king and his company, then moved on. While the pope was in awe of the French king's power, Clement VII also knew he held the key to the king's heart's desire: Italy.

Ever since France had lost Milan to the Habsburg Emperor Charles V eight years earlier, François I's only thought had been to regain the territory. Patiently, he watched and waited until the moment was right to make his first move. That time came when Henry VIII of England needed a favor from Pope Clement VII and asked the French king for his help. The two monarchs met briefly at Boulogne, where François tactfully explained the need for his son's marriage to Catherine de' Medici, cousin of the pope and Henry's enemy. To soften the blow, François promised he would pressure the pope to annul Henry VIII's marriage to Catherine of Aragon. Desperate to marry Anne Boleyn in church, Henry VIII posed no obstacles to the French proposal.

Pope Clement had his own road to clear to the marriage. By actively endorsing the French match, he risked offending the other great power in Europe, the Holy Roman Emperor Charles V, and France's greatest enemy. For this reason, Clement was obliged to seek the powerful emperor's approval. When the pope asked Charles V's permission to approach the French king, the emperor shrugged and demurred, confident that the royal house of Valois would not accept a mere parvenu Medici girl into its illustrious fold. But the emperor failed to see that, to the king, Catherine represented the coveted duchy of Milan, and that the Valois–Medici marriage would ensure François I achieved his goal. The pope's path was clear, and it had led to this glorious day in Marseilles.

The day after the pope's official entry into the city, The Most Christian King of France, François I, attended by his second son, Henri d'Orléans, and his youngest, Charles d'Angoulême, and flanked by two cardinals, made *his* entrance into Marseilles.

The city was newly decorated with a series of triumphal arches extolling the king's great deeds, real or imaginary. Tableaux with allegorical allusions to the principal guest were staged at various stops on the route. The city's prettiest girls, scantily clad in classical fashion, scattered flower petals in front of the procession. Fresh lavender and rose-mary were strewn before the excited, prancing horses, their hooves crushing the herbs to release heady aromas as they passed. The best tapestries and carpets were hung in a kaleidoscope of color from the balconies overhanging the royal route. Leaning on them were the most elegant and privileged of the citizens, who tossed flowers and ribbons on those below. The king was escorted by his twenty-seven maids of honor, dubbed by his mother Louise de Savoie his "*Petite Bande*," a corps of feminine *aides-de-camp* chosen from the best families for their beauty, vivacity, and superb horsemanship. François saw to it that they were always dressed in matching elegance—furs, cloth of gold and silver, velvets, and scarlet satin—all paid for by him. Their sole duty was to be in constant attendance upon their monarch. Behind these Amazons rode a vast retinue of several thousand nobles glittering in their finery, doffing feathered hats, their horses richly caparisoned with elaborate *aigrettes*[5] bobbing on their foreheads. This dazzling display was accompanied by music, bell ringing, jingling of harnesses, wild cheering, and the crowd's exclamations of joy and admiration to see the king and the princes at close quarters.

Observing tradition, François I and his sons prostrated themselves at the feet of the pope and kissed each of his slippers. The French king was as much a showman as his wily guest and performed the elaborate gestures with panache. A man of exquisite manners, François had allowed the Holy Father to make the first state entrance into the city, though all judged the king's procession the next day the more brilliant.

Feasting continued during the following week, and as the bride had not yet appeared, the pope was the center of attraction. Clement VII reveled in the adulation and was himself overawed by the great honor accorded to his family, despite the surprise and shock of the entire world. "The house of Medici," he said, "has been raised by God's own hand. I know I shall die soon, but I will die happy."

Before the marriage could take place, there were still a number of outstanding negotiations between king and pope that needed to be finalized. No record of their discussions remains other than notes in François' own hand alluding to an offensive alliance with Clement VII

5. A plume or tuft of feathers arranged as an upright head ornament.

against his enemy, the Holy Roman Emperor Charles V. It is probable that the king fulfilled his promise to Henry VIII and discussed the annulment the English king was seeking from his marriage to Catherine of Aragon. Since their meeting in Boulogne, Henry had married Anne Boleyn in a civil ceremony. In May 1533, the new Archbishop of Canterbury, Thomas Cranmer, declared Henry's marriage to Catherine of Aragon invalid and therefore void. A week later, Anne Boleyn was crowned queen. Four months later, on September 7, her daughter, Elizabeth, was born. It is also most probable that the king and the pope discussed the spread of heresy in France; the doctrines of Martin Luther and Jean Calvin were fast gaining followers, and heresy was becoming an issue all Europe's rulers had to confront. As for the contract, it was most generous to France. It had to be. The fabulous heiress that Clement VII had produced for the son of the king of France was small, plain, ungainly, and, worst of all, not of royal blood.

Finally, the marriage negotiations were complete and Catherine de' Medici received word that she could make her entrance into Marseilles. For months, Catherine and her uncle's advisors had planned every detail of this event. Now on October 23 she would make her first official entry into a French city.

Catherine was a child of European politics. She understood that, while this was the day she would meet her bridegroom, it was more important that she impress his father the king and his people. Instead of arriving in her enclosed carriage, she chose to allow the people to catch their first glimpse of her, riding elegantly on a Russian palfrey, an "ambling mare" trained to a smooth, gliding gait. (Catherine did not yet ride well and was anxious should the French people see her jolting in the saddle.) She was escorted by her uncle, the Duke of Albany,[6] and her twelve ladies-in-waiting in chariots (many of them so young they were still accompanied by their governesses). Catherine and her ladies shone in scarlet silk with gold-threaded lace, and behind them rode a dazzling procession of seventy brilliantly attired and bejeweled courtiers. Following her parade came Catherine's empty carriage, the first enclosed, four-wheeler ever seen in France.

6. The husband of her mother's sister.

Just one month younger than Henri d'Orléans, Catherine de' Medici was short and dark; her most beautiful features were her hands and feet. When she dismounted, François I, that connoisseur of women, noticed her lovely legs, surprisingly slender and long on an otherwise awkward body. Her face appeared swollen, with protruding blue eyes under heavy brows, a prominent nose, fleshy lower lip, and a receding chin. Anyone who saw Catherine de' Medici on her first day in France could not have thought her remotely attractive, but her intelligent expression and vivacious manner was commented upon. She had certainly not inherited the famous beauty of her mother; and yet, she had a presence, described years later by La Fontaine as "grace, and grace still more beautiful than beauty."

Arriving at the pope's wooden pavilion, Catherine bowed low before her cousin and was received in his arms. Clement was the nearest she had come to having a parent, but she felt little love for him. With her heritage, she had always known her purpose in his political schemes—and welcomed it. If she could manage it, hers would be an illustrious and secure future within the greatest court in Europe—and Catherine had inherited the Medici confidence. Her powerful uncle had made her destiny possible, and for this her gratitude to her relative overflowed.

Her next greeting was for the king, before whom she prostrated herself, a mark of the modesty she would assume for the next twenty-six years. François raised the girl up and presented her to his wife, his children, and the court. Only then did Catherine de' Medici turn to face the young man whom she would love obsessively—and fear—all her life. As she bowed before him, she caught her breath in awe and admiration.

At fourteen, Henri d'Orléans was tall for his age and his passion for sport had already given him the physique of a young man. He was excellent at tilting, fencing, and tennis, so adept that few at court could beat him. He was most attractive, with the fine straight nose and dreamy dark eyes of his grandmother Louise de Savoie. His hair was dark and his complexion very fair. Catherine had been told her bridegroom was handsome, but she had only had eyes for her cousin Ippolito and could not imagine admiring another. She moved toward Henri as if in a trance, eyes shining, lips slightly parted, and formally embraced him, but he remained grave and silent, giving no reaction or sign of emotion. Not knowing the young prince, Catherine could have mistaken his indifference for shyness, but it was clear to the onlookers it would take a miracle for him to fall in love with her. At least François I seemed pleased with Catherine—and certainly with the secret terms of the treaty signed with Clement VII. King and pope had agreed that once their joint armies had reconquered Milan, the newlyweds would be installed to rule that duchy as well as Urbino.[7]

During the celebrations that followed, king and pope exchanged extravagant gifts. François gave Clement a tapestry woven of silk and gold and silver thread depicting the Last Supper. The pope gave the king a "unicorn" horn two cubits long (the length of two forearms) mounted on a solid gold pedestal. These horns had become an obsession among the nobility and even among the higher clergy. Unicorn horns were said to sweat in the presence of poisoned liquid or food; it was also believed they could detect heresy. The gift, in reality a narwhal tusk, was symbolic, intended to remind François of his duty to detect and expel the poison of heresy from his kingdom.

The French king took advantage of the occasion to rid himself of an unwelcome gift he had received from the Turkish corsair Barbarossa,[8] lieutenant of Suleiman the Magnificent, ruler of the Ottoman Empire. It was customary for great princes to exchange rare or exotic gifts, including animals such as elephants, monkeys, or sometimes deer, but the pirate had recently presented to François I a huge, tame Nubian lion with an insatiable appetite. With considerable relief, the French king passed this gift to Ippolito de' Medici, the pope's nephew and Catherine's dashing favorite cousin. Ippolito was delighted, and on his return to Rome, he commissioned a portrait of himself posing with the lion.

Catherine's marriage portion of cities, gold, and a large income was substantial; the marriage bed alone cost 60,000 gold écus, a formi-

---

7. In the sixteenth century, Urbino was quite a sizable duchy. It is now incorporated in that part of Italy known as The Marches.

8. Barbarossa, or Redbeard, whose real name was Khayr ad-Din, was admiral of the Turkish fleet under the Sultan Suleiman I. He twice defeated the famous Admiral Andrea Doria, and ravaged the coasts of Greece, Spain, and Italy.

Giorgio Vasari painted this fresco of the wedding of Henri d'Orléans and Catherine de' Medici in Florence well after the event, and it bears little resemblance to fact. Henri was tall for his fourteen years, and Catherine was rather small at the same age. The pope did not marry the couple, and the lion, presented to Ippolito de' Medici by François I, was surely not present.

dable sum. In order to pay for her trousseau, the pope pressured Alessandro de' Medici[9] for part of a forced loan he had levied on Florence intended for new fortifications. It was a trousseau worthy of a queen: chests of fine lace; valuable brocades, silks, and velvets; cloth of gold bed hangings; and fashionable black silk sheets to show off the whiteness of the bride's skin. To hold the communion host in her private chapel, the pope gave Catherine a rare crystal casket, its panels engraved with scenes from the life of Christ. Catherine was now the owner of a fortune in jewels, including seven glorious pearls[10] thought

9. Officially Clement VII's nephew, Alessandro was actually his son, installed as ruler of Florence by his father.

10. Catherine de' Medici gave the pearls to Mary, Queen of Scots, when she became her daughter-in-law. Mary took the pearls with her back to Scotland; after her execution, they were kept by Queen Elizabeth I. They were later set into Charles II's state crown and subsequent state crowns. Today, four of them form part of Queen Elizabeth II's crown. Two are known to have been replaced.

at the time to be the most beautiful in Christendom; a gold belt studded with rubies and diamonds; and a parure of diamonds and pearls. Three other fabulous pieces—perhaps the most famous—are mentioned in a number of sources: the "Egg of Naples"—a large pearshaped pearl encircled by rubies; the "Tip of Milan"—a hexagonal diamond; and the "Table of Genoa"—a large, flat-cut diamond. A mystery still surrounds these treasures. In the view of scholars today, their names represented a secret code between the pope and the king, and referred to cities in Italy the young couple would receive once their alliance was victorious. In later inventories of Catherine de' Medici's jewels, the pieces no longer appear under such names.

Finally, on October 27, the marriage contract was signed. The next day the little Medici *duchessina,* whom the French called a grocer's daughter and worse, became the duchesse d'Orléans, wife of the king of France's second son. For her wedding ceremony, Catherine wore a dress of gold brocade, trimmed with ermine; her tight-fitting bodice was of purple velvet, embroidered with gold thread in the Florentine style, edged with ermine and glittering with precious stones. Her thick, dark hair was elaborately dressed and woven with jewels, and on her head she wore her ducal crown. The radiant bride, wearing the pope's enormous pearls, was led to the altar by the king. François was dazzling in a suit of white satin embroidered with silver thread; his great cape, covered in gold-embroidered *fleur-de-lys* and precious stones, hung from one shoulder. Prior to the wedding, the king had knighted his son, a ritual custom dating from chivalric times. The act of bestowing knighthood still held a mystical aura from its roots in medieval mythology, Christianity, and the chivalrous code of warfare. It certainly would have meant much more to Prince Henri than his enforced marriage. The nuptial Mass was conducted by a cousin of the royal family, the cardinal de Bourbon, and the pope blessed the young couple.

Almost everyone who would dominate Catherine's new life attended the ceremony, and she observed each of them shrewdly. She liked her father-in-law immediately, with his bold, handsome face, ready smile, his height and natural air of kingship. Although he could be very authoritarian, François looked at her kindly, and would do so for the rest of his life. His second wife, Queen Eleonore, a good and virtuous lady who had little say at the court, also welcomed Catherine generously. Catherine admired the king's ravishing and beloved sister, Marguerite, queen of Navarre—yes, she would do well to become her friend. The king's new mistress? He had rejected the gracious Françoise de Foix for the vixenish Anne de Pisseleu, another she would try to woo. And, of course, Anne de Montmorency, Grand Master and future Constable of France, was much in evidence—she noted that this grand statesman was Henri's mentor. Catherine might have guessed, though she could not yet know, how strongly Montmorency had opposed her marriage.

And she met for the first time the woman into whose care she had been placed: the beautiful Diane de Poitiers, *dame d'honneur* to Queen Eleonore. Diane had been chosen by the king as Catherine's guide to the court and its intricate ritual because she was the bride's only close relative in France; their mothers had been cousins. Newly widowed, Diane's black and white clothes were in stark contrast to the brilliant colors of the courtiers and their ladies. Diane de Poitiers seemed to tower over Catherine as she greeted her, and her grace and beauty made Catherine appear short and clumsy. She watched as Henri came so naturally to stand at the widow's elbow, noticing that her husband wore black and white plumes on his hat matching those in Diane's hair. Other than making her marriage vows, Catherine had yet to speak a word to her husband.

The festivities were interrupted by an incident that almost marred the proceedings. Emissaries from Henry VIII arrived unannounced in Marseilles, vociferously demanding to know if the pope would withdraw the threat of excommunication from the English king and allow the annulment and Henry's remarriage. All the courts of Europe knew of the king of England's burning desire to sanctify his civil marriage to Anne Boleyn. Catherine, too, would have known of the French king's diplomatic efforts to help Henry. François, who had been proceeding gently and tactfully with the pope on Henry's behalf, was outraged at the emissaries' rude interruption. He dismissed them without ceremony, accusing the English envoys of having greatly harmed their

master's cause. One year later, Henry VIII would break England's ties
with the Holy See, creating the schism that led to the formation of the
Church of England.

The interminable ceremonies did nothing to encourage what little
romance might have survived the bridal couple's first meeting. Both
Henri and Catherine played their parts in the ritual, but were soon forgotten or ignored by their elders, immersed as they were in their power
play and drunken enjoyment of the festivities. According to one of the
guests, the Milanese ambassador Don Antonio Sacco, Henri remained
his dour self throughout the masked ball and the banquet that followed. Catherine, however, was radiant and animated. Then, wrote the
ambassador, the king, the queen and her ladies, including Diane de
Poitiers, accompanied the bride and groom to the nuptial chamber.
François was eager to bring the couple to bed and watch them "joust,"

Pierre de Bourdeille, seigneur de Brantôme, a courtier and chronicler of the courts of François I
and Henri II. He wrote eleven gossipy accounts of the time.

which he later declared they did valiantly. It seems strange to us today that a king of renowned courtesy should subject two shy fourteen-year-olds to such an ordeal. But it was the custom for witnesses to be present during the first amorous exchanges between a newly married couple, and this applied to all classes. The story comes down to us from Pierre de Bourdeille, seigneur de Brantôme, a near contemporary who wrote eleven gossipy volumes of court activities during the reign of François I and of Henri II. Brantôme notes in his journals that anyone not present in the bedroom would be listening outside to the appreciative noises (or otherwise) made by the bridal couple.[11]

According to some observers, when the royal party left with the bride and groom, the festivities grew wilder. A famous local courtesan stripped naked and lay on a banqueting table among the platters of food, to allow the guests to marvel at her perfection. Not to be outdone, some other young ladies undid their bodices and exposed their own assets. By all accounts, a merry evening followed.

The next day, the pope hurried to the bridal chamber, anxious to examine the sheets. He had great plans for the future of the Medici and a consummated marriage could not easily be repudiated. Clement noted that Henri and Catherine slept late and arose looking content, but that morning, a number of the courtiers lamented the speed with which the negotiations had been conducted and the marriage arranged. There were mutterings that the Medici balls had no place on the royal coat of arms among the *fleur-de-lys* of France.[12] In the years to come, Catherine would be made to feel the shame of her *mésalliance* with the house of

11. At the turn of the sixteenth century, it was the custom to rattle or scatter nuts in the next room or even under the marriage bed to stifle the sounds made by the newlyweds.

12. The Medici coat of arms depicts six balls. Some sources claim these represent medicinal pills, referring to the family's alleged origin as apothecaries. Other sources point out that the balls are often painted red and claim they represent the oranges the early Medici grew in huge pots in their extensive greenhouses. (The color orange is not used in heraldry and there is no proof of this theory.) The symbol of the royal house of France is the *fleur-de-lys,* or golden lily. It actually represents a yellow iris said to have been chosen by the medieval French King Clovis. Only under Louis VII in the twelfth century did the symbol become "fleur de Louis" then "fleur de Luce" and finally "*fleur-de-lys*" or lily of France. Florence has been called the city of the Red Lily because it was once ruled by the kings of France and the city arms carry a red *fleur-de-lys.* Certainly, the Medici were merchants and as such most probably also moneylenders, so the Medici balls, often shown as golden, could have represented gold ducats. On some buildings in Florence, the top center ball, and sometimes even the background of the whole escutcheon, can be seen covered in gold *fleur-de-lys* on a blue background. These coats of arms would date from 1465.

The arms of the Medici show the six balls said to represent oranges or pills or, when painted gold, the sign of the moneylender.

Valois. It was the one blot on this great honor of which she was so proud: a mere Medici, married into the oldest royal house in Christendom, and yet scorned by this ostensibly well-mannered assembly, the gracious, smiling, bowing courtiers who laughed at her behind her back. On the day after her marriage, Catherine already knew she must face this opposition and she began to wonder to whom she could turn for support and guidance. Her husband had performed his duty, but had hardly looked at her. She thought of the beautiful widow in black and white. Diane de Poitiers was to be her guide, the woman whose colors her husband wore.

CHAPTER TWO

The King
and the Mistress

FRANÇOIS I was the son of Charles, comte d'Angoulême, a rather pathetic Prince of the Blood,[1] who preferred books and women to statecraft, and Louise de Savoie. Louise went into labor on a hot September 12, 1494, and chose to give birth outdoors. Her bed was placed under a large elm tree in the garden of the *château fort* that loomed defensively over the prosperous little Gascon town of Cognac. A low wall was constructed around the bed to ensure a modicum of privacy. François was a large, lusty baby who hurried into the world and required the services of two wet nurses. With this abundant source of milk, he grew into a giant. His mother declared him her "Caesar"—a title somewhat premature as her husband's claim to the throne of France was remote to say the least.

Louise de Savoie was the daughter of Marguerite de Bourbon and the comte de Bresse, who, in 1496, became duc de Savoie. More important, she was the niece of Pierre and Anne, duc and duchesse de Bourbon. A princess of France, Anne de Beaujeu, as she was known,

---

1. A Prince of the Blood (Royal) is a prince of the ruling house and not just a member of a princely family.

Anne, princesse de France, known as Anne de Beaujeu.
Diane de Poitiers was brought up by her, along with
other scions of French noble houses.

was the eldest daughter of one king, Louis XI, and the sister of another,
Charles VIII. Known as "*Madame la Grande,*" she had twice been regent of France and was a most formidable character, admired for her
authority, stern wisdom, and culture. Taking the reins of government
into her own hands at the age of twenty-two, Anne had succeeded in
destroying the feudal system and centralizing the power of the throne.
Anne's father, Louis XI, called her the most sensible woman in France.
But in giving his daughter her immense properties, Louis XI had stipulated that should she fail to produce a male heir, her properties should
revert to the crown, and not to the collateral branch of her husband's
family, the Bourbon-Montpensier. Louis XI realized that such a huge,
combined estate could well threaten the authority of the crown.

When her brother Charles VIII married Anne de Bretagne in

1491, Anne de Beaujeu retired to Burgundy, which was seen as a state in its own right. Years later, the young Louise de Savoie was sent to Burgundy to live at Anne's two great houses, Chantelles and Moulins. It was the custom for young girls of noble birth to be brought up in the household of an important and learned lady, and it was in Anne's household that Louise joined a privileged group, all scions of noble houses, to be educated in the principles and traditions of life at a royal court.

When Louise was not quite eleven and a half,[2] Anne arranged her marriage to the twenty-nine-year-old Charles d'Orléans, comte d'Angoulême and a Prince of the Blood. Louise was somewhat younger than the brides of most family marriages arranged by Anne de Beaujeu, but she never liked Louise and wished to have her out of the house. Time was to prove her instinct right.

When Louise arrived at her husband's crumbling castle in Cognac, the child bride found two mistresses already in residence. It seems her husband was an avid reader of Boccaccio and shared the libidinous traits of this author's heroes. Intelligent and resourceful, Louise appointed one of his mistresses as her lady-in-waiting and the other as her maid. At fifteen, Louise gave birth to her first child, a daughter, Marguerite, said by poets to have been born of a pearl and known in history as the remarkable "Marguerite of the Marguerites," the "Pearl among Pearls," and future queen of Navarre.[3] François, her "Caesar," was born two years later, in September 1494. In that same summer, the mistresses of her energetic husband each presented him with a daughter. For the next seven, happily bucolic years, the family lived together, until the sudden death of Charles. Louise, a beauty of eighteen, comforted the mistresses, and her husband's young chamberlain comforted the widowed châtelaine. As Louise's father had by then become the ruler of Savoy, she became entitled to use his name.

A series of unexpected events followed, bringing Louise de Savoie's little Caesar closer to the throne. The king of France, Charles VIII, died suddenly at the age of twenty-eight from a blow received

2. According to Erasmus, some girls were women at ten and mothers at eleven. Anne de Beaujeu was fifteen years older than her first cousin, Louise de Savoie (their mothers were sisters).

3. *Marguerita* is the Latin word for pearl.

when he passed under a low stone doorway.[4] The king's heir was his
brother-in-law and cousin, Louis d'Orléans, who, at age fourteen, had
been forced to marry Charles VIII's crippled sister Jeanne. Unlike the
attractive Anne de Beaujeu, this daughter of Louis XI was said to have
the soul of a saint and the body of a monster.[5] The new king claimed
that his marriage had never been consummated, and immediately after
his coronation, Louis XII had this union annulled.[6] He married instead
the pious widow of Charles VIII, Anne de Bretagne, sovereign duchess
of Brittany. Anne de Beaujeu approved her brother-in-law's marriage
on condition he cancel her father's contract by which her territories
would revert to the crown in lieu of a male heir. Little did the new king
realize that with this one stroke of the pen he was creating an independent and immensely powerful Bourbon state.

As Louis XII was often away with his armies and his wife was the
proud ruler of Brittany, he appointed his terrifying sister-in-law Anne
de Beaujeu to act as regent during his absences. As long as Louis XII
had no heirs, François d'Angoulême, Louise's little Caesar, was the
heir presumptive. When François was six, the king created the duchy of
Valois for him. Louise's ambition for her son was growing apace. However, Anne de Bretagne, again queen of France, was charming, and,
worse for Louise, she had proven her fertility by giving birth to three
sons and a daughter. Although childhood illnesses had killed them all,
Anne de Bretagne was young and would surely bear more children.

*L*IKE their mother, Marguerite and François d'Angoulême had a
magical upbringing within the circle of Anne de Beaujeu. Marguerite was the best student among the children and grew to become one
of the sixteenth century's most learned women. Both children studied
well, as their mother took their education very seriously. In keeping with

4. At the king's autopsy it was pronounced that the blow to his head would not have killed
him, and it was noted that he had eaten an orange shortly before the accident, which was thought
to have been sent from Italy. Whispers of poison circulated.

5. Her father, Louis XI, considered Jeanne so ugly that she had to hide behind a screen whenever
he entered the room. She founded a religious order and was canonized by Pope Pius XII in 1950.

6. Jeanne de France solemnly swore that the marriage had indeed been consummated.

her motto "*Libris et liberis*"—"Through books and children," Louise de Savoie commissioned books especially for her children, and taught them Italian. They also learned Spanish and had access to the famous library of their grandfather, Jean d'Angoulême. The New World was opening up through exploration, and François was fascinated by the discoveries being reported from the new continents. With the advent of humanism, the children learned about the heroes of antiquity and made them their own. They were both intelligent and full of *joie de vivre*. François was plainly adored by his mother and sister—a devotion that would last all his life.

While François d'Angoulême was learning to ride fearlessly and hunt with his young companions, the queen, Anne de Bretagne, was praying for an heir. With each of Anne's pregnancies, Louise de Savoie dreaded the loss of her "Caesar's" inheritance. But Louise seems to have cast her ambitious spell over this royal union as well: although they had daughters, the sons of Louis XII and Anne de Bretagne were all stillborn. The queen was so desperate that she wanted to exile the gloating Louise back to Savoy.

In 1509 Louise's daughter Marguerite married the First Prince of the Blood, the duc d'Alençon.[7] Louis XII felt the time had come for François d'Angoulême to be installed with his mother in the château of Amboise, traditional seat of French dauphins, to await their destiny.[8] The king also persuaded Louise to replace her chamberlain with a more suitable mentor and a tutor of his choosing for his heir, and forbade her, for the time being, to remarry. He also decided that his daughter, Claude, would be François' wife.

In 1504, while Louis XII was seriously ill, his queen, Anne de Bretagne—desperate to thwart Louise de Savoie in some way—had tried to take her daughter Claude to Nantes to implement the Treaty of Blois and marry her to Charles of Habsburg, heir to Austria, the Netherlands, and Spain,[9] instead of François d'Angoulême. Her

7. The duke's line belonged to the Valois family, senior to the Bourbon.

8. Although François was the heir to the throne and would be popularly known as "*Monsieur le Dauphin,*" he was never entitled to be so called: only the eldest son or grandson of a king could be dauphin.

9. Spain was not yet united. Technically, Charles was king of Castile, Aragon, Navarre, Leon, Galicia, Algeciras, Jaen, etc. The unification happened in three stages—in 1707, 1715, and 1716. For the sake of simplicity, these countries are referred to here as "Spain."

dowry would have been Brittany. But Marshal Gié, Louis' custodian of his heir, put an end to this plan, which would have jeopardized the unity of France. The Estates-General joined the protest, imploring the king to wed his daughter to a true Frenchman: François, duc d'Angoulême.

Exhausted from bearing and losing so many children, Anne de Bretagne's health began to fail. She loathed Louise and felt sure it was her evil eye that had caused her sons to die. Anne de Bretagne went to her grave on January 9, 1514 in the knowledge that the son of her enemy, Louise de Savoie, would inherit not only France but also her beloved Brittany. Just four months after her death, the gentle, frail, fourteen-year-old Claude de France, daughter of Louis XII and Anne de Bretagne, married François, the eighteen-year-old giant who would surely now become king of France.[10] Louis XII chose to ignore the clause in his own marriage contract, which clearly stated that Anne de Bretagne's *second* child, a daughter called Renée, would inherit Brittany. Instead, the elder child, Claude, was installed as duchesse de Bretagne et de Berry.

Diane de Poitiers accompanied her father to Saint-Germain-en-Laye outside Paris to assist at the royal wedding in her capacity as Claude's *demoiselle d'honneur.* Both girls were almost fifteen. It was a most sinister occasion as all the guests, including the bride and groom, wore black out of respect for the late queen, and no wedding celebration was held.

Other than being the daughter of a king and possessing the sweetest character, Claude was not blessed with many advantages. Her face was considered quite pleasant despite a severe squint. She was very short and had a bad limp. With repeated childbirth she grew "strangely corpulent" and this obesity put her life in danger with each confinement. However, Claude was extremely cultivated, kind, and devout. Quite reasonably, Louise felt that since her son was married to the king's daughter, and the queen was dead, his claim to the throne was guaranteed.

Once again the redoubtable Louise de Savoie was to be thwarted.

---

10. According to the doctors of the time, a girl could only be expected to produce strong, healthy children from the age of seventeen or eighteen. François I himself was almost six feet four inches tall.

Less than a year after Anne de Bretagne's death, despite his age (fifty-two) and the fact that he grieved for his wife (whom he had genuinely loved) Louis XII agreed to wed the young sister of Henry VIII of England, the enchanting, vivacious, eighteen-year-old Mary Tudor.

As yet, Henry VIII had no heirs, and he reasoned that France was a throne worth gambling his sister for. Since she was in love with Charles Brandon, the handsome Duke of Suffolk, Mary Tudor opposed the match. But Henry VIII could not resist the chance that his sister might produce an heir to France, especially as its king had one foot in the grave. The dashing young François d'Anglouême could not resist Mary either, until his mother pointed out that should Mary conceive his son, it would be *this* boy who would inherit the throne of France and not him. Thus chastened, François (assisted by Anne de Beaujeu,

Louis XII married Henry VIII's young sister Mary Tudor in the hope of fathering an heir to the throne. He died shortly after the wedding, it was said, from "kissing her too much."

his mother, and his sister) kept Mary Tudor under close surveillance and well away from any potential indiscretions.

The old king was delighted with Mary and claimed to have "performed miracles" on his wedding night. Mary for her part confided in her new friend Diane de Poitiers how repelled she was by the advances of her old husband. Being queen of France, however, was not so irksome, and after her magnificent coronation at Saint-Denis, Queen Mary Tudor made her state entrance into Paris to celebrate the alliance of France and England. Young, pretty, full of life, Mary flirted outrageously and led the king a merry dance, partying until dawn. Not surprisingly, on New Year's Day 1515, just six weeks after his wedding, Louis XII died; it was said, from "kissing her too much." Mary grieved little and had so enjoyed playing queen that according to the account by Pierre de Bourdeille, seigneur de Brantôme, she prolonged her departure for England by feigning an elaborate pretense of being pregnant—wrapping towels around her waist and fainting in public. Louise de Savoie was not fooled and demanded a physical examination, which exposed the ploy.

*D*IANE de Poitiers was born on the last day of 1499 into a world of privilege, with an ancestry allied to the noblest in France. Her father Jehan de Poitiers' family was one of the oldest in the area known as the Dauphiné in central-southern France, and through her mother, Jeanne de Batarnay, she was connected to the mighty Bourbons. The kings of France and dukes of Burgundy valued the Poitiers family and had made the head of the family comte de Valentinois in 1125. Their device was an upended flaming torch with the Latin motto "*Qui me alit me extinguit*"—"He who inflames me has the power to extinguish me." [11]

In 1275, Diane's grandfather, Aymar III de Poitiers, married Julie de Bourgogne, a direct descendant of King Robert the Pious, whose

---

11. Traditionally, the upturned candle or torch symbolized the end of the pleasures of life. According to Dr. Allison Rawles, this old French saying is a take on the Petrarchan idea of the paradox that love brings both pleasure and pain. It was a commonly expressed Renaissance conceit.

dowry included the town and château of Saint-Vallier in the Dauphiné. As members of the family had always held high office, permission was granted for Aymar to marry the illegitimate daughter of Louis XI. Even though Aymar's bride died in childbirth and Diane's grandmother was his second wife, the connections with the royal house had remained strong.

Historians argue about the exact date of Diane's birth, but the epitaph on her tomb at Anet reads: "Died 26 April 1566, aged 66 years, 3 months and 27 days." As Diane had ordered her own tomb and her daughters carried out all her wishes, it is likely that this information is correct. Historians also debate the place of Diane's birth, but since Saint-Vallier was the family's principal seat and her father, Jehan, and grandfather Aymar were hoping the child would be the heir, it is probable Diane was born at this château. Jeanne de Batarnay's firstborn, a son, had died soon after birth.

The château of Saint-Vallier was situated on a promontory overlooking the town, at the junction of two rivers, the Galure and the Rhône. Originally a monastery dedicated to Saint Valéry, it had been altered into a roughhewn feudal castle, flanked at the corners by four towers. This quiet corner of the Dauphiné on the border of Provence had some of the best forests for the country sport of the time: *la chasse,* hunting deer and wild boar on horseback with hounds.

The baby who heralded the new century was named Diane after the goddess of the chase and the moon that shone at her birth. Although the snow lay deep that winter the villagers and peasants of the Dauphiné followed local custom and came to marvel at the New Year's child born into the great house of Poitiers. Diane's was one of the oldest families of the Dauphiné and much was expected of its scions.

The South of France was well known for its soothsayers, and since the firstborn son of Jehan de Poitiers had died, the villagers brought with them an old woman famous for her prophecies. Gazing at the tiny baby swaddled tightly and wrapped well against the winter chill, the bent old woman announced to them all that this child's star would raise her higher than a queen. At a time when superstition was rife and witches were still burned at the stake, the villagers took note. They never forgot the words uttered on that first day of the new century:

Qui de Jean de Poitiers naîtra
Et qui Diane se nommera
Tête de neige sauvera
Puis tête d'or perdra

Mais, le sauvant comme en perdant,
Pleurs versera icelle enfant
Cependant réjouissez-vous
Pour ce que gouvernera tous
Icelle.

(An enigmatic prediction suggesting that Diane will save a "white head"—perhaps someone old—then lose a "head of gold"—perhaps one wearing a crown. This child will shed tears. Nevertheless rejoice, for she will govern all men.)

Jehan de Poitiers, seigneur de Saint-Vallier, was a proud and ambitious man. At fifteen, he had married Jeanne de Batarnay, and at seventeen he was given a lucrative post in the king's personal entourage. After the death of his father, Poitiers became Grand Sénéchal of Provence, a protégé of the house of Bourbon, and inherited sixteen titles including seigneur de Saint-Vallier, marquis de Crotone, vicomte de l'Etoile, baron de Clérieux, and baron de Sérignan. Jehan was a handsome man, with clear blue eyes, blond beard and mustache, and well-shaped lips, as his pencil portrait (see page 77) by Jean Clouet shows.[12] Since he was a good soldier, popular and charming, Louis XII appointed Saint-Vallier Captain of the King's Guard. Despite such preferment, Saint-Vallier could not forget that when his grandfather had been heavily in debt, he had sold his lands of Valentinois to the king, who raised the estate to a duchy and neglected to pay for them. The new duchy was then bestowed on Cesare Borgia, the illegitimate son of Pope Alexander VI, in gratitude for bringing a papal bull to France. This bull granted Louis XII the annulment from his sadly hideous wife Jeanne and permission to marry Anne de Bretagne. Jehan de Poitiers was helpless against such an act of *force majeure,* but he taught Diane to remember the injustice that had been done to their family.

12. There were two Clouets, Jean and his son François, both painters to the king and the French court.

A French couple on horseback from the first half of the sixteenth century. It was the custom for ladies to wear a mask of black velvet to protect their faces from the elements and from branches when out hunting.

We know remarkably little about Diane de Poitiers' infancy because the baptismal registers and civil archives were destroyed during the Wars of Religion and the pillaging of the Church of Saint-Vallier from 1567 to 1568. We do know she lost her mother at a very early age.

Although she had a surviving brother, Guillaume, and two sisters, it was Diane who captured her father's heart and whom he took riding and hunting with him in the early mornings. All her life she would follow his training to discipline her body. At the age of six she had her own falcon and within a few years she could control any horse in her father's stable. When riding, she wore a black velvet mask to preserve her complexion and protect her face from low branches and dust, as did the other ladies of the time. Like everyone else, she dressed in dark colors and a large cloak to protect her clothes. Wearing the traditional red boots and plumed cap, young Diane was never far behind her father at the front of the mounted hunters. On her gloved fist, Diane—as did most ladies who hunted—held a sparrowhawk or a merlin. It was customary to hunt at least twice a week, and all the grandees had their own packs of hounds.

As we can see from the wonderful tapestries from that time, in the sixteenth century the chase was the greatest excitement, short of war, that life had to offer. It became Diane de Poitiers' passion. When not hunting to hounds, she made it a lifelong habit to take long, energetic rides each morning in all weathers.

After the death of Diane's mother, her education was carefully supervised by her father's family. She was sent to join the household of Anne de Beaujeu, who lived at the time at Chantelles—a great and splendid manor a short distance from Moulins, the capital of her vast

Apart from war, the hunt was the main source of excitement and exercise in sixteenth-century France, and both courtiers and their ladies took part.

domains. Diane could read Latin at seven and Greek by the time she
was nine, and she played the lute and the oboe. Anne de Beaujeu encouraged theatricals, dancing, and games of every kind, indoors and
out. There were dogs large and small, birds of prey to train on one's
arm and those in the many aviaries to teach to talk. Most important,
there were other children like Diane, potential friends for life, including Anne's own disadvantaged daughter, Suzanne, and her father's
young cousin, Charles de Bourbon-Montpensier. None of the children
living in the circle of Anne de Beaujeu had any doubt about the great
role each would inherit, and they relished every moment of their privileged upbringing. It was also clear to anyone who saw Diane de
Poitiers that this highly intelligent, beautiful child with the pale white
skin and red-gold hair would make a dynastic marriage.

As regent, Anne de Beaujeu had served France well; but she
believed unquestioningly that a woman's role was to obey first her elders, then the husband chosen for her, and to produce his heirs. Despite
this conventional attitude, she was convinced that an educated woman
was of greater interest and service to her husband. This cool and
austere lady allowed herself only one passion—politics. From her father, Louis XI, she had inherited the qualities of a great statesman: patience and genius. At her court, she taught her high ideals to the
children of the noblest families; and, while recognizing the different
roles of men and women in society, she insisted that their "virtues
should be the same."

Described by one of her pupils as "tall and severe as a cathedral,"
Anne encouraged them to use her renowned library, which contained
famous works from classical literature as well as beautifully bound, illuminated religious manuscripts. Diane never forgot this library; years
later, she modeled her own on the one she had known and loved at
Moulins.

Madame de Beaujeu's extraordinary influence on her young pupils
could be attributed to her example of chastity, her sense of humor, and
her dedication to duty. Hers had been a varied education, and the children in her care were taught to study the philosophies and logic of
Boethius and Plato as well as the writings of the fathers of the church.
Diane also learned from this wise, highborn lady the true meaning of

the dignity of her rank, nobility of behavior, taste, deportment, and, above all, to despise intrigues. Anne urged her charges to bear in mind that society was still rough and vulgar and had need of their refining influence, to add their gaiety, refinement, grace, and patience to any gathering. She taught them the art of conversation, how to communicate with strangers, and not to discriminate between classes.

The children were taught to avoid unattractive gestures and movements: not to touch their faces, especially not their noses, eyes, or mouths. Young ladies should not jump or run; and, most important of all, they should never encourage young men to make advances. They were to be cool and evasive in all their responses. Anne de Beaujeu prepared the young ladies for marriage by teaching them complete obedience to their husbands, and never to show temper or create jealous scenes.

Despite the seemingly endless receptions, long formal meals, lessons, and hours spent at the duchess' school of manners, Diane still managed her wild gallops through the fields and forests. Only with great reluctance had Jehan de Poitiers allowed his precious daughter to leave his house, and solely on condition that she would be allowed to ride with the same abandon as at home.

When she was around twelve years old, Diane de Poitiers became one of Anne de Beaujeu's *demoiselles d'honneur,* or maids of honor. Any stirrings of ambition in Diane's young heart would not have been unnatural. The purpose of the cultured education and courtly manners taught at Moulins and Chantelles was to strengthen family alliances through a carefully arranged marriage; and the duchess was of the opinion that a girl should marry as young as thirteen or even earlier.

According to the contemporary chronicler Brantôme, there was no lady of a great house in France who was not at some time taught by this remarkable princess. Anne recognized Diane's talents and that her potential was far superior to that of the other girls, even her own daughter, Suzanne, for whom she had written her famous guide to education, *Les Enseignements d'Anne de France à sa fille Suzanne de Bourbon.* This is an extraordinary document, expounding the highest ideals and moral principles—obedience, modesty, chastity, and piety—

all of which Anne de Beaujeu had learned from her pious father, Louis XI. It contained instructions such as: "Always dress well, be cool and poised, with modest eyes, softly-spoken, always constant and steadfast, and observe unyielding good sense. . . . God, who is justice itself, may tarry, but will leave nothing unpunished. . . . Nobles are the kinds of people who must see their reputation go from good to better, as much in virtue as in knowledge, so that they will be known . . . ," and "Another philosopher says that gentility of lineage without the nobility of courage should be compared with the dry tree which has no leaves, no fruit, and which does not burn well." The simplest of all her advice was: "Avoid sin."

The book's final instruction, said to come directly from Louis XI, is: "*En toute chose on doit tenir le moyen*"—"Always keep a balanced view of everything"—a maxim Diane tried never to forget.

Another of Anne de Beaujeu's young pupils at Moulins was Charles de Bourbon-Montpensier,[13] heir of the family's junior branch. Anne de Beaujeu was very fond of this boy, and as she had no son, it was her great wish that the senior and junior branches of the family would unite through the marriage of Charles to her daughter, Suzanne. However, as her husband was adamantly opposed to the idea, she had to wait until his death in 1505[14] to arrange Charles' betrothal to Suzanne. Anne de Beaujeu's brother Louis XII was sufficiently intimidated by her to agree to the union—unwisely, in retrospect as the combined wealth of the young couple represented a formidable challenge to the crown. Further, Louis even allowed the bride and groom to bestow their worldly goods upon one another by law. As eighth duc de Bourbon (he would drop the Montpensier), Charles would become Constable of France, the highest office in the land. Among his titles was dauphin d'Auvergne, and sovereign prince of the Dombes area of eastern France, where he was a vassal of the Holy Roman Emperor, Charles V.

The wedding was as grand as that of royalty, with dukes and princes all wearing their crowns. For the first time, instead of ladies wiping

---

13. Charles de Bourbon-Montpensier was half Italian, as his mother was Claire de Gonzaga.

14. Pierre II de Bourbon suffered all his life from migraines—he was therefore known as *Malatesta*.

(*se moucher*) their noses with their fingers, they used a square of fine fabric, which became known as a *mouchoir* (handkerchief).

 TALL, dark, with flashing black eyes, a large nose, humorous mouth, and ready laugh, François I was as heartily impressive as his contemporary, Henry VIII of England. The French king was extravagant, spoiled, generous to a fault, ebullient, brave, and courteous, a scholar and a lover of women: in a word, a true *Renaissance* gentleman. Always the center of attention, François enjoyed jousting, dancing, and riding to hounds until he dropped with exhaustion. He wore a beard— all his companions did the same. His spurs were made of gold, as were the buttons on his clothes. His scented linen was the finest, and his brushes, goblets, and even his *rebec,* a type of mandolin, were made of silver.

Among François' young companions was Robert III de La Marck, seigneur de Fleurange. Since childhood, Fleurange had called himself "*Le Jeune Aventureux*," and at the age of ten he offered Louis XII his sword, pleading to serve in Italy. The king was charmed, but in view of the extreme youth of the "Adventurer," he sent him to join the group at Amboise growing up with his heir, François. He became an amiable soldier, close friend, and confidant of the young king, who made him Captain of the Swiss Guard. Another of François' youthful friends in his suite at Amboise was Anne de Montmorency, future Constable of France, who was totally devoted to his prince but quick to make enemies by his rough and overbearing ways.

The coronation, or *sacre,* took place on January 25, 1515 at Rheims. François entered the cathedral wearing a long tunic of white damask, edged in ermine, over a white silk shirt and shift. After swearing the oath of office, he replaced the white damask tunic with the coronation robe, a long hyacinth blue cloak covered with golden *fleur-de-lys,* and put on red boots and golden spurs. Then he was anointed with sacred oil from the Holy Ampulla said to have been brought by a dove to the baptism of the Frankish king Clovis in A.D. 497. Anointment with this holy oil ensured that the French king was spiritually su-

The château d'Amboise was traditionally the seat of the French dauphin, and also of the royal nursery. It was François I's favorite château on the Loire.

perior to all other Christian monarchs and was the origin of his title "The Most Christian King." The archbishop, Robert de Lenoncourt, presented François with the sword of Charlemagne, the ring, the royal scepter, and the "hand of justice"—a rod of gold, topped by a carved hand of ivory with the first two fingers and thumb pointing upward as if in benediction, the others curled under. He then placed on the king's head the heavy golden crown of Charlemagne, made of four large golden *fleur-de-lys* covered in rubies, emeralds, and sapphires.

Thus bedecked, François I was led to his throne on a dais in the cathedral, where he turned and faced the congregation in his majesty. Standing, he made a solemn oath on the gospels to give his people peace, to guard them from greed and iniquity, to give them justice and mercy, and to extirpate heresy. At the sound of trumpets, the dignitaries within and the populace outside the cathedral all shouted: *"Vive le Roi!"* Queen Claude watched the ceremony with her imperious mother-in-law, Louise, and Marguerite, François' beloved sister, from above on a stand in the church. It is recorded that both Louise and her

The coronation sword (in its scabbard) of the kings of France belonged to Charlemagne. It was used in the coronation ceremonies of François I and Henri II. It is now in the Louvre.

daughter shed tears of emotion. The choir sang a *Te Deum,* and wearing the heavy gold crown throughout the Pontifical Mass, François I received communion.

At the time of the coronation in the spring of 1515, Diane de Poitiers was just fifteen, the same age as the queen. The favor shown by Louis XII to Diane's father continued under the new monarch, and the whole court noticed his beautiful daughter sitting during the ceremonies according to her rank with the queen's ladies. Like Claude, Diane was modest, conscious of the great occasion and the honor of attending.

Antonio de' Beatis, the contemporary traveler and secretary to Cardinal Luigi of Aragon, described the king's mother, Louise, as "an unusually tall woman, still finely complexioned, very rubicund and lively and seems to me to be about forty years old but more than good, one could say, for at least another ten."[15] Madame Louise,[16] rather than the queen, accompanied her son everywhere, and she played an important part in his government.

The king's sister, Marguerite, was intelligent, animated, and attractive. The contemporary chronicler Brantôme wrote revealingly: "Marguerite's masculine attire suits her well, and her Adonis face is so bewildering you cannot tell if she is male or female. She could as easily be a charming boy as the beautiful lady she is." Other malicious gossips suggested that her close friendship with her brother was incestuous. Sadly, her marriage to the duc d'Alençon was childless and she sought comfort in religion. Marguerite studied religious texts and became a

---

15. Antonio de' Beatis, *The Travel Journal.*

16. Queens and royal princesses are traditionally addressed as "*Madame*" even though Louise de Savoie was not the queen mother because she was never crowned. After the coronation of her son, she was always referred to as "Madame Louise."

The "hand of justice," a scepter, was used in the coronation ceremonies of François I and Henri II. It is now in the Treasury of Saint-Denis.

friend of many of the reformers of the church. Later, after she was widowed and had married Henri d'Albret, king of Navarre, her court became a refuge for Protestants.

Part of the traditional coronation ritual was a pilgrimage by the new monarch to the shrine of Saint Marcoul, a Norman saint credited with the gift of healing. It was commonly believed in France that a monarch who ruled by "divine right" had access to miraculous powers assisted by the saint. François had been transformed by the coronation ceremony and he believed he could indeed cure the sick. A number of people suffering from scrofula were presented to him for ritual "laying on of hands" as he "touched for the king's evil." [17]

From the shrine, François I continued on to Compiègne, to attend a grand reception for all the ambassadors. Here the king granted the request for the hand of his sister-in-law Renée, from a young man of fifteen who would become his lifelong enemy, the future Holy Roman Emperor Charles V.

*W*HEN once a posthumous dauphin succeeded to the throne, it became the custom in France that the royal widow must remain in quarantine for six weeks following the death of her husband the king. Mary Tudor dressed entirely in white and remained in the Hôtel de Cluny for forty days, her darkened room lit only by candles. As soon as her quarantine was over, François I called on the young queen dowager.

---

17. Scrofula was a tubercular infection of the skin of the neck manifested by ugly sores that ulcerated; it was repulsive but not life-threatening. The only other European monarch who traditionally had this alleged gift and "touched for the king's evil" was the king of England.

It seems impossible to imagine, but a number of contemporary accounts allege that he proposed marriage to her. Had not his predecessor, Louis XII, put aside the hideous daughter of the previous king and married instead the attractive royal widow? The dashing young François I was clearly very taken with "*La Reine Blanche,*" as Mary was known, and although he would have lost Claude's dowry of Brittany in a divorce, he pressed his suit.[18]

Marguerite de Navarre was the beloved sister of François I. She married Henri d'Albret, king of Navarre.

To his utter astonishment, he was refused. Mary was still deeply in love with the Duke of Suffolk and determined to marry him instead. Under a portrait of the young dowager-queen, François wrote the inscription: "*Plus folle que reine*"— "more madwoman than queen." Mary had been terrified that either her brother Henry or the new king's dynastic ambitions would force her into the bed of another old man; but she hardly expected François I to woo her himself. After a barely decent interval, the eighteen-year-old dowager-queen cajoled her lover, Suffolk, into marrying her secretly.

Charles Brandon, Duke of Suffolk, had been sent from England by Henry VIII to recover Mary's dowry, as well as the crown jewels King Louis had given her on their marriage. (François I did return some of Mary's dowry but kept the jewels.) A man of Henry VIII's libido should have realized that sending Suffolk to carry out this mission was utter foolishness. His delicious sister would never be able to resist the man with whom she had been in love for so long. Mary had only agreed to marry the old king of France on condition that she could

18. Forty days was the length of strict quarantine imposed on the widow of a king, to ensure she could not conceive a child she could claim was her late husband's. With the exception of some states in Italy, the mourning dress code for Christian queens prescribed white, not black. After the Reformation, only Catholic queens wore white for mourning or during an audience with the pope, which is still the custom today.

After the death of her first husband, Louis XII of France, Mary Tudor, sister of Henry VIII, married Charles Brandon, Duke of Suffolk.

marry Suffolk when Louis died; but Henry VIII never felt himself bound by promises. He was furious when he heard of Mary's clandestine marriage, as she could have been dynastically useful again, perhaps as the wife of Charles of Habsburg. But Mary's charm won Henry round. He forgave his little sister and arranged a sumptuous wedding celebration in London on her return. Suffolk was thirty-one at the time, twice married, widowed, and had two daughters.[19]

AT last, the new king of France could make his solemn entry into Paris. There was a traditional formula for such an event, particularly in the capital, and François' *entrée solennelle* was described

19. With Mary, he would produce a son and two daughters. After her death, he married again and had two more sons.

as the most dazzling ever seen. Alongside tournaments and executions, parades were the principal source of mass entertainment in the sixteenth century, and a new king's entry into his capital was an important event.

To begin the *entrée solennelle,* the religious and civil dignitaries met the king on the outskirts of the city and offered him a handsome gift in return for his confirmation of their privileges. Then the procession began: twelve hundred courtiers—princes, dukes, counts, and noblemen—and in their midst, the king's great warhorse, walking slowly, draped in crimson velvet and carrying on his back the royal seal in a blue velvet coffer sewn with gold *fleur-de-lys* and secured by a large golden lock.

When François I finally rode into public view on February 14, behind endless lines of mounted courtiers and guild representatives, he dazzled as only a twenty-year-old Hercules could. His suit of silver cloth shone in the sunlight, the feathers on his bonnet and on his horse's head bobbing to the steed's excited prancing as the king threw coins to his subjects. He was indeed a worthy sight. The new sovereign was followed on this part of the *entrée* by his courtiers, his nobles all mounted and dressed in white and wearing his symbol of the salamander. The people, overwhelmed by the splendor of it all, could not but notice how sharply the youth, the gaiety, the energy of their new king contrasted with the recently deceased, sober and solemn Louis XII.

When the amazing procession reached the Cathedral of Nôtre-Dame, François I entered to give thanks to God and Our Lady. This was the end of the *entrée solennelle.*

The second part was called the *entrée joyeuse*: it took place outside the cathedral and resembled a carnival parade. There were sideshows, theatrical mime

François I took the salamander as his symbol. This creature was said to have blood so cold it could walk through fire unscathed—a Renaissance conceit implying the opposite, that the king's blood was fiery hot.

routines, street decorations, and the traditional fountains flowing with wine. The anonymous contemporary chronicler of the *Journal d'un bourgeois de Paris* praises the magnificence of François I's entry, although, surprisingly, there is little printed evidence of theatrical performances. Several of the king's biographers point out that the Parisians had only recently staged a most elaborate and expensive entry for Queen Mary Tudor and blanched at the expense of another.

Following the coronation, François indulged in his new status, spending his time in pursuit of pleasure, the chase, jousting, and women. The Venetian diplomat Lorenzo Contarini, who spent three years at the French court, described the new king as most generous, giving out pensions and favors. He tells of François' daily routine at that time: "He rises at eleven o'clock, hears Mass, dines, spends two or three hours with his mother, then goes whoring or hunting, and finally wanders here and there throughout the night, so one can never have an audience with him by day."

As for his mother, Louise, still beautiful at thirty-seven, she had triumphed at last. Having professed humility throughout her life until this moment, Louise de Savoie happily abandoned that virtue until her death. At last the young king was in a position to reward his mother for her devotion to his cause. He created her duchesse d'Angoulême and Anjou, and included her in every royal activity and decision.

*A*FTER the coronation, Diane de Poitiers, as the queen's maid of honor, retired with her to the château of Blois, on the Loire. As a companion to the young queen her duties were largely honorific, but they gave her an entrance into the court and increased her chances of making a good marriage. Diane's beauty made her noticed and the king enjoyed chatting with the attractive ladies of the court. Prior to his reign, it was not customary to have ladies at court, which had been a man's world dedicated to politics and war; François, however, wanted a court dedicated to beauty and pleasure. Queen Claude clearly loved Diane's quiet sense of duty and disciplined intelligence; she fitted so well into the tone of her court. But, apart from her beauty, Diane was not considered sufficiently special at this time to warrant the comments of her contemporaries. Her place at court was merely a consequence of the important appointment held by her father.

Not long after the coronation, Diane was summoned by Anne de Beaujeu and informed of her imminent betrothal (Anne had also arranged the marriage of Diane's parents). At fifteen, Diane knew her time had come to marry, and she had heard whispers that a great match had been planned for her. The husband Anne chose was her Bourbon kinsman, Louis de Brézé, comte de Maulevrier, and Grand Sénéchal[20] of Normandy—the most important province in France. Louis' many titles included baron de Bec-Crespin and de Mauny, seigneur de Nogent-le-Roi, d'Anet, de Brissa, Brévalta et Montchauvet. His most famous ancestor was Pierre de Brézé, first minister under Charles VII, described by one poet as being "courageous as Hector, wise as Nestor and a better captain than Caesar."

The new Constable Charles de Bourbon, husband of Suzanne de Beaujeu, showed his friendship for the house of Poitiers by negotiating the marriage settlement. In 1512, Jehan de Poitiers had been appointed to the government of the Dauphiné, and a year later, Grand Sénéchal of Provence—and he knew he owed it all to his liege lord, Charles de Bourbon.

The bridegroom, Louis de Brézé, was extremely rich and powerful, and famous as a courageous huntsman; in the whole kingdom, only Princes of the Blood held posts higher than his. His mother was Charlotte de France, half sister of Louis XI, the illegitimate daughter of Charles VII and his dazzling mistress Agnes Sorel. Louis de Brézé's father, Jacques, was not best pleased to be forced by King Louis XI (who disliked everything about his late father, including his mistress) to marry his beloved half sister. Even though she had been legitimized, it was a slur on the noble house of Poitiers. Jacques de Brézé and Charlotte loathed one another; but although the marriage was a disaster, they produced five children. Charlotte, who was said—according to witnesses at the subsequent trial—to have been "moved by an inordinate lechery," was discovered by her husband in bed with his master of

20. The king's representative, similar to governor—Louis was made Grand Sénéchal in 1490.

Louis de Brézé, Grand Sénéchal of Normandy, the husband of Diane de Poitiers.

hounds, Pierre Le Vergne. Without hesitation, Jacques de Brézé ran them both through with his sword where they lay—one hundred times, so it was claimed.

Since he had killed the king's sister, albeit with some justification, Jacques de Brézé was stripped of his titles and his estates. Louis XI had loved Charlotte, but he was generous enough to give all Jacques de Brézé's properties to Jacques' son, Louis, and not claim them for the crown. With the death of Louis XI, his successor Charles VIII found Jacques de Brézé's punishment too harsh and restored to him all his titles and properties. (It was rumored at the time that the reinstatement of the famous huntsman had much to do with the decline and subsequent improvement of the king's hunt.) With the elegance of a *grand seigneur,* Jacques left his son in possession of everything the king had returned to him and retired to just one of his castles. He died a few years later.

Louis de Brézé—a famous huntsman like his father—had enjoyed the confidence of Charles VIII's successor, Louis XII, and now shared that of the new king, François. Although he was considered a loyal ser-vant of the crown, perhaps some of the shame of his mother's adultery, or the crime of his father's swift retribution, lingered on in his memory. A union with Diane de Poitiers, a noble girl with illustrious connec-tions, would most certainly help to overcome whatever shame he felt. Brézé's previous wife had died and their marriage had been childless.

Diane inherited the pride and ambition of the Poitiers. She was ac-customed to mixing with the highest in the land, and the value of an al-liance with the powerful and well-connected Louis de Brézé would have been clear to her. However, the bridegroom was fifty-six, which was considered very old at the time, and he was also notoriously short-tempered. Diane reminded herself that her mentor and teacher, Anne de Beaujeu, herself a king's daughter, had obediently married and been happy with the sieur de Beaujeu (later duc de Bourbon), a man twenty years her senior. Anne had arranged Diane's father's marriage to the wealthy Jeanne de Batarnay, and Diane knew Anne had her best inter-ests at heart. Anne had taught the young girl that fortunes were main-tained and great houses formed through marriages that were planned and not impulsive. Diane understood that girls of her status were brought up at their parents' behest and to the benefit of their house. Furthermore, all marriages between important nobility required the approval of the king, and once given, no one dared to disagree with his choice. Diane had the satisfaction of knowing she would become one of the first ladies of France. Through this marriage, Diane's rank would be raised to just one rung below that of a royal princess. Her life would be full and responsible, and she and her husband could share their love of the chase.

Diane had twice caught sight of her intended, first at the cathedral at Rheims during the coronation of François I on January 25, 1515, and again at the king's solemn entrance into Paris on February 14. When in Paris, she had not yet been officially informed of her be-trothal, but she suspected Brézé had been chosen for her. (Her be-trothal to Louis had actually been settled since her tenth year.) She thrilled to see him march in the procession with her father, placed just behind the Princes of the Blood, and surrounded by the most senior courtiers. They in turn were followed by their company of one hundred gentlemen, elegantly attired in outfits of brocaded satin and velvet in various colors. On the tips of their lances and around their thighs they sported narrow taffeta ribbon streamers of white, yellow, and red. They were mounted on splendid chargers, richly caparisoned, some in cloth of gold and others in cloth of silver. Diane could be justifiably proud of the man chosen to become her husband.

Louis de Brézé was most distinguished-looking, with fine features and perceptive eyes. He had the Valois[21] family's large nose, a large mouth, and an air of severity and disdain that inspired fear in some and respect in others. He was stooped—some say humped—and his face bore a strong masculine pride. Contemporary sources agreed that he looked remarkable and alert. Most important, as the bridegroom of a young girl, he seemed to be a man who was interested in pleasing women. In short, he carried his fifties well.

The negative descriptions of Louis de Brézé all come from writers who have trouble understanding the impression such a man would make on a woman. It is even possible that Diane found Brézé attractive and was flattered that such an important, mature man as the Grand Sénéchal of Normandy should take an interest in a fifteen-year-old girl. Did her heart beat faster as she sat with the young queen and watched her future pass in front of her, imagining herself in the front ranks of the kingdom? Brézé's inscrutable nature and ambiguous glances may even have challenged her. There is no doubt Louis de Brézé had charm and the qualities needed to win Diane's affection and respect, if not her love. Whatever impression Mary Tudor's confidences of marriage to an old man may have made on her, or whatever pleasure she had felt at the appreciative glances from the young gentlemen at court, Diane did not hesitate, and agreed to the union.

At the time she left home to marry, Diane de Poitiers' famous beauty was well recorded. Her pale white skin was described as "luminous" and her hair more golden-red than blond. Her forehead was high, and her eyes an indefinite color between green and blue. Her

21. A long nose like that of François I, inherited no doubt from his adulterous Valois mother, Charlotte.

nose was straight; her mouth full and small. Contemporary reports all agreed she had a most aristocratic look and bearing, and carried herself with pride in her tall, slender body.

Anne de Beaujeu and her son-in-law the Constable had made all the arrangements for the wedding. On Easter Monday, March 29, 1515, in the presence of King François, Queen Claude, and the court, the wedding was celebrated at the Hôtel de Bourbon in Paris. The young bride was already considered beautiful, mature for her age, with a face as "solemn as Artemis." [22] Diane's elderly bridegroom was fit and strong; he would remain by her side for the next seventeen years.

Louis de Brézé possessed a number of châteaux, including Bréval, Montchauvet, Rouen, Mauny, and Anet. [23] It was this last, Anet in Normandy, that would become home to the newly married comtesse de Brézé. Anet was a forbidding medieval fortress with four towers, full of old attendants and dark mysteries, that had been left to Brézé by his first wife. The high-vaulted room Diane was to share with her husband contained the wooden four-poster bed in which Charlotte, Brézé's royal and adulterous mother, had been slain by his father. After the fun and laughter of life among Diane's young friends at Moulins, it must have been a shock to come to this house of gloom and decrepitude. Everything around her was old—even the servants. But Diane threw herself into her new life, filling the castle with spring flowers, engaging young women from the village, and soon the chill corridors began to ring with laughter. Fires were lit in every room; silver was brought out from the vaults and cleaned, and candelabra spread light on the highly polished oak furniture.

There were other compensations: country life revolved around the thrill of the chase, at which Diane excelled. Anet had magnificent stables and a vast, wonderful library. When Brézé was away traveling with the king or in Normandy on business, Diane would remain content at Anet, reading her husband's books and riding his horses. There is a legend that while out hunting one day, young Diane, a strong swimmer since early childhood, heard a woman shouting in a swollen river.

22. *Journal d'un bourgeois de Paris.* Edited by Ludovic Lalanne.
23. Pronounced "Annette."

Quickly, Diane rode to the bank and removed her heavy skirts and vel-vet mask. Wearing just her hose and shirt, she swam to the rescue, pulling the half-drowned woman to safety. Diane's groom arrived on the scene and helped avert a tragedy, covering the frozen woman while Diane's companions helped her. In gratitude, the woman gave Diane a small medallion, which she swore would preserve her forever from growing old.

*T*O understand the Valois passion for Italy, and especially Milan, is to understand their reigns. François I considered it his mission in life to retrieve the lost conquests of his predecessors, Charles VIII and Louis XII. They, like him, believed they had a legitimate right to northern Italy through their ancestor, the heiress to Milan, Valentina Visconti.

The city-states of Italy in the sixteenth century were prizes worth winning. Arguably the most powerful and important was the republic of Venice, successfully governed by an elected oligarchy. When the Vis-conti family of Milan died out, the rich duchy was ruled successfully by the Sforzas. The republic of Florence was weaker militarily than Milan or Venice, but it was influential on the peninsula, due to the banking and diplomatic skills of the Medici family. The kingdoms of Naples and the Two Sicilies were controlled by various branches of the Spanish house of Aragon. The Papal States stretched across Italy coast to coast, with Rome as their capital, and the expansion of territory and power was the aim of every pontiff. These various autonomous units within the Italian peninsula all had their own agendas and made their alliances accordingly, often against one another.

French claims, conquests, and reversals in Italy during the late fif-teenth century and the first quarter of the sixteenth are complicated, and require some study in order to understand the seesaw of French and Habsburg rivalries, which dominated the entire reign of François I and spilled over into that of his son. When Charles VIII invaded Italy in 1494, he was following an established pattern of French claims to Milan and Naples. Four years later, it was the turn of his successor Louis XII to invade, accompanied by the pope's son Cesare Borgia and Giuliano de' Medici, son of Lorenzo the Magnificent.

As a result of this French military initiative into various states on the Italian peninsula, Florence took advantage of the general chaos and rebelled against the ruling Medici, who were chased out, Giuliano among them. In the north, Louis XII met with almost no opposition and the Milanese grandees rushed to join his victorious cavalcade into the city, just as they had joined Charles VIII five years earlier. When Naples also fell to France, the peninsula was in French hands and the dream had been realized.

Foolishly, Louis XII had agreed to a coalition with the pope in an expedition against Venice. This succeeded, and the republic was brought to heel. However, in a curious twist, the pope then had the French expelled from the peninsula with the help of the Swiss, whose pikemen formed the strongest mercenary force in Europe at the time. By 1515, the year of the coronation of François I, France no longer had any territory left in Italy. As a very young man, François had traveled to the northern Italian states and visited the studios of some of the great masters. His passion for the art and culture he experienced there made him mourn the loss of Milan more than any other French possession. Throughout his extraordinary life, Italy was never far from François' thoughts. Even at the solemn moment of his coronation he had insisted that "Duke of Milan" be included among his many titles.

After a series of elderly kings, the French nation rejoiced in the youthful *joie de vivre* of François I, and his nobles yearned to prove themselves and gain the spoils of victory. The members of François' court were young, enthusiastic, and daring, and they goaded their young king into reaching for glory by going to war over Milan especially as François had a mighty army and the best captains in memory. While the Spanish army and the pope's forces were engaged in fighting the Venetians, the republic of Genoa asked France for military assistance. The French king knew that Henry VIII of England would not move against him without allies. The time was ripe for François I to strike against the emperor.

Although it was customary for a king of France to appoint his wife as his regent during his absence abroad, Queen Claude felt lost at court

Louise de Savoie, mother of François I and regent of France during his imprisonment in Spain.

and was somewhat frail during her first pregnancy. François installed his undoubtedly more able mother as his regent, and on July 15, 1515, a few months after his coronation, he left for Lyons to assemble his forces there.

Gathering his friends about him, François I rode out at the head of an army of 30,000 men and 370 pieces of artillery—a huge force at the time. While on the march, the king received the news that on August 19, Queen Claude had given birth to a daughter, Louise, a good omen for the forthcoming battle. The Battle of Marignano, near Milan, began on September 13, 1515 and lasted two days. François I fought heroically in the thick of it, like a warrior from ancient times, and emerged the overwhelming victor. He defeated the indomitable Swiss mercenaries, who were employed by the ruler of Milan, Maximilian Sforza, an ally of the Holy Roman Emperor Charles V and of the pope. In a brief ceremony, Pierre du Terrail, chevalier de Bayard, France's most famous warrior, knighted the king on the field as he knelt among the fifteen thousand slain. François wrote to his mother: "There has not been seen so fierce and cruel a battle these last two thousand years. . . ."

On October 13, 1515, François I was declared duke of Milan and Parma. He had begun his reign in glory by regaining France's lost territories in northern Italy, and he could return home to enjoy his kingdom with Milan part of France once more. A medal was struck with the profile of the twenty-two-year-old warrior-king, and his splendid conquest was immortalized in paintings and friezes.

Diane's honeymoon at her husband's château of Anet had been brief. Just three weeks after the wedding, Louis de Brézé and Jehan de Saint-Vallier left for Grenoble to join the king's army heading toward Italy. Brézé and Saint-Vallier each distinguished themselves in the battle of Marignano, and when the king made his triumphal entry into Milan on October 11, the hundred crossbowmen under Brézé and the hundred led by Saint-Vallier, all fully armed and in the liveries of their captains, were much admired. Diane pined for her husband. In a letter she sent him through Florimond Robertet, powerful secretary to the previous king, Diane wrote complaining of having been deserted, and gave the impression of being sincerely attached to Louis de Brézé.

Marignano entered the annals of French history as a great victory, but tragically its gains were short-lived. During her son's absence at war, the regent Louise de Savoie had held back for herself funds that the king had instructed be sent to his troops in Milan. Without pay, the soldiers of the army of occupation in Italy deserted, and the duchy was lost. By May 1522, after the Battle of La Bicocca, all that the French retained were the castles of Milan and Cremona. The territory won by François' dazzling victory at Marignano vanished through the greed of his mother.

Shortly before his coronation, the king had appointed his mother's protégé, Charles de Bourbon, as Constable of France, an office not held for some fifteen years, and thus made him the second most powerful man in the kingdom. (It was common rumor at the time, though it has never been proven, that Louise de Savoie and Charles de Bourbon were lovers.) The Constable de Bourbon acquitted himself superbly at Marignano, and in gratitude, in September following the battle, François appointed the half-Italian Charles lieutenant general in the duchy of Milan. That privilege, together with his vast estates joined to those of his wife, Suzanne de Beaujeu, made the duc de Bourbon a sovereign in all but name. In fact, he was the last great feudal magnate in the style of the old dukes of Burgundy or Brittany, and from his seat of Chantelles, he virtually ruled central France. His holdings were just smaller than today's Belgium.

In 1517, the king, as godfather, with the queen and his mother, Louise de Savoie, attended the almost royal christening of the long-awaited son of Charles and Suzanne de Bourbon. Louis and Diane de Brézé were present at this sumptuous event at Moulins, together with Jehan de Poitiers, Diane's father, whose rank depended on his liege lord, Charles de Bourbon.

It was on this occasion that François I finally appreciated the incredible wealth and power of the Constable de Bourbon. All along the route Bourbon had stationed formations from his own army, dressed in bright costumes, while others staged mock battles on the road. Upon arrival at the château, the royal party was met by the duke, attended by five hundred gentlemen, all dressed in velvet, each wearing a heavy three-strand gold chain. In fact, Charles de Bourbon so loved gold that he would have nothing made of any other metal, whether his plate, his mirrors, cups, or candlesticks. From his own estates he could raise an army of 34,000—and this man was the commander-in-chief of the king's forces. Such wealth and power could rival that of the king of France himself, and perhaps even threaten the security of his realm.

François realized that neither Blois nor Amboise could equal the duke's two great châteaux, Moulins and Chantelles, nor the ducal possessions—his library, paintings, furniture and furnishings, and *objets d'art*—all emblazoned with the arms of their owner. At last the king understood why Anne de Beaujeu's husband had so strongly opposed the marriage of his daughter and Charles de Bourbon. With their combined might and wealth, the peace of the realm would depend on the goodwill of a vassal. Charles de Bourbon, a proud man, easily offended, who kept his own counsel and with unknown ambitions, was someone the king would have to watch carefully.

The magnificent celebrations for the Bourbons' baby, the comte de Clermont, imprudently lavish in the eyes of some, lasted eight days. Tragically, the baby died five months later. The Constable and Suzanne de Beaujeu had been married for twelve years and failed to have another child.

CHAPTER THREE

The Renaissance King

*A*S Louis de Brézé's wife, Diane enjoyed a senior place at court. She had been appointed a matron of honor to Queen Claude and ranked as the third highest placed lady in the land. The queen's court reflected the religious principles, chastity, and austerity of her parents, Louis XII and Anne de Bretagne. But Louise de Savoie, having arranged her son's marriage to the late king's daughter for dynastic reasons, despised Claude for her staunch belief in all the honorable traditions, while she encouraged François in his excesses and his mistresses.

Although the king needed little encouraging in his affairs, he seems to have been genuinely fond of Claude. According to the contemporary Antonio de' Beatis, the king "holds his wife the queen in such honor and respect that when in France and with her he has never failed to sleep with her each night." The result was the birth of three sons and four daughters over a period of nine years. Constantly pregnant or recovering from a birth, Claude did not take part in much of the court ritual, but she did have one glorious moment—her coronation in Saint-Denis on May 10, 1517, and her official entry into Paris three

days later. A queen's coronation and entry into the capital was traditionally celebrated long after the king's—sometimes only after the
birth of an heir. The delay helped to defray the expense of two coronations and state entries so close together. In Claude's case, the ritual had
been postponed for two years due to the queen's pregnancies and slow
recoveries.

It vexed the king that, in order to make the preparations for
Claude's coronation and entry into Paris, he had to remain in the capital for three months. He amused himself by visiting taverns and inns
incognito; according to the *Journal d'un bourgeois de Paris,* he drunk-
enly forced his way into private homes, a diversion that was far from
popular.

During the splendid parade, Diane remained in close attendance
on the queen, who was carried to the cathedral in a litter draped in
cloth of silver. She wore her crown and the crown jewels, including a
necklace of untold value. François watched the coronation ceremony
from a balcony hidden behind a metal grille. The duc d'Alençon stood
behind the queen, holding up Charlemagne's heavy crown. In front of
her, Charles, the Constable de Bourbon, knelt holding the train of her
long cloak of blue velvet lined with ermine. The prince de la Roche-
sur-Yon, who held her scepter, knelt next to her on one side, and on
the other was the comte de Guise, who held the "hand of justice."

As the queen made her state entry into Paris, Diane de Poitiers was
again in attendance and noted that it was as splendid as the king's entry
two years earlier.

Carried in a litter shaded by a canopy gallantly borne in turn by all
the representatives of the city's guilds, Claude was escorted by sixteen
princesses on horseback whose hats were cut to resemble crowns. All
along the processional route, tableaux were staged to demonstrate the
queen's virtues and allegories of her charms. When Claude's litter
reached a fountain, three nymphs burst from a heart, symbolizing the
three kinds of love: divine, earthly, and conjugal. Finally, the celebrations came to a climax in the evening with a sumptuous banquet at the
Palais de Justice. This was served on an immense marble table, draped
in cloth of gold and covered with gold and silver plate. The royal trumpeters announced the serving of each course.

The ermine, symbol of Brittany, was used by Queen Claude of France, who was also the sovereign Duchess of Brittany in her own right.

The next day, François organized a tournament under the patronage of the *fleur-de-lys* of France and Claude's symbol, the white ermine of her duchy of Brittany.[1] The Knights of the Night, dressed in black and led by the comte de Saint-Pol, competed in the tournament against the Knights of the Day, dressed all in white and led by the king.

The queen's coronation was the occasion for the king to take her on a "progress," or journey, through the kingdom, setting in motion an immense royal cavalcade of some ten thousand people. Passing through Picardy, the monarch and the court arrived at Rouen. On August 2, wearing his chain of office and magnificently dressed in cloth of gold, his charger caparisoned in the same, the king made his official entry. François I was met by Louis de Brézé, who presented him with the keys to the city. The next day was the turn of the queen's official entry.

The king and queen were received in the city by Diane at the château de Rouen, and then again at the Brézé country château de Mauny. While the king hunted with his hosts, his ministers negotiated with the Norman elders for a sizable loan.

1. In winter, the ermine has a white pelt, its tail ending in a black tip; its fur was the most prized in Europe.

François I was one of the most attractive and exciting personalities ever to sit on the throne of France—tall, dark, well built, he was thought most handsome (despite rather spindly legs), and very regal. He also had great charm and blind courage, and neither he nor anyone at his court believed there was a woman living who could resist him. He saw the court as a font of pleasure, his own and that of his courtiers. This was an era when tales of chivalry exerted a powerful influence on the young courtiers around the new king. The costly pageantry and *joie de vivre* which enveloped this smiling monarch and his court wherever he went were in stark contrast to the simple ideals of royalty maintained in the reign of Louis XII. François loved women, their spirit as well as their beauty. Gathering the charmers of the court about him at one of his châteaux, he told his enchanted listeners: "A court without ladies 'tis like a year without springtime, and a springtime without roses." Brantôme writes: "Although he held the opinion that they [women] were highly inconstant and variable, he would never hear anything said against them in his Court and required that they should be shown every honor and respect." Although François encouraged his courtiers to take mistresses—he called them fools if they did not— he himself had exquisite manners and never forced a conquest he could not achieve by gentle persuasion. The court soon realized that Diane, the lovely Grande Sénéchale of Normandy, took her marriage vows seriously and the *chevalier* in François admired her the more for that.

$\mathscr{A}$S no children had been born to Louis de Brézé in his first marriage, his joy was complete when in the spring, exactly two years after her marriage, his seventeen-year-old wife gave birth to a daughter. She was named Françoise in honor of the king. The queen produced a son at the same time, the dauphin François. At Claude's request, Diane was soon back at her side at Blois in the Loire, the queen's favourite château and childhood home.

The gentle queen was constantly mocked for her motto *"Candidior candidis"*—"Whiter than the lilies"—by her husband's daring sister, Marguerite (praised by the poet Clément Marot as having *"corps feminin, coeur d'homme et tête d'ange*"—"the body of a woman, the heart of a man and the head of an angel") as well as by his *maîtresse en titre*,[2] the beautiful brunette Françoise de Foix, comtesse de Château-briand. There was also an English girl called Anne Boleyn at the queen's court at this time; she had accompanied Mary Tudor to France when Mary married Louis XII, and she remained behind when Mary returned to England. Anne Boleyn stayed in France for seven years and made it known she found the court in which she served exceedingly dull. Claude, however, had conviction in her principles and ignored the court's excesses. She needed Diane to comfort her and much appreciated her presence.

*L*IFE for Diane continued with its round of official events and private pleasures in their various estates. When she was not at home at Anet or in Normandy, Diane was almost constantly in attendance on Queen Claude. Naturally, the comtesse de Brézé's beauty did not escape the notice of the king or his courtiers, but her reputation was pure. Diane's portrait was one in a wonderful album of drawings of the ladies of the court gathered in 1520 by Madame de Boisy. It is called *Recueil du crayon d'Aix*—and has several remarks noted in the king's hand. François' only comment beneath Diane's portrait was "*Belle à voir, honnête à hanter*"—"Pleasing to look at, honest to know." We see a strong young woman, with ample shoulders and chest, and the coloring of someone who takes a great deal of outdoor exercise. Her gaze is level and confident, her demeanor self-assured and discreet. Although most attractive, her face indicates more nobility and dignity than sensuality. As yet, it does not show the great beauty she would acquire with maturity.

Diane was at Amboise when the queen's second son, Henri, duc d'Orléans, was born there on March 31, 1519. She held him tenderly before placing the tightly swaddled baby into his mother's arms. Both Claude and Diane were eighteen years old.

2. Official mistress.

The Children of France often resided at the château de Blois on the Loire.

Queen Claude liked to spend most of her day in the nursery with the children, particularly as constant childbearing was wearing out what little stamina she had for the activities of the court. She stayed with them predominantly in three palaces, Saint-Germain-en-Laye,[3] Amboise, and Blois. In these châteaux the royal children had the happiest of childhoods; they were joined by a number of others from noble families who were known as *"enfants d'honneur,"* and they received salaries as companions to the royal children. The dauphin and Henri's domestic arrangements in the royal nursery were lavish: in 1523, 240 people were employed at all the palaces to attend to them alone.

Admiral Guillaume Gouffier, seigneur de Bonnivet, was the children's first governor before he left to command the Italian campaign. He then passed the post to his brother-in-law, René de Cossé-Brissac, whose wife had been governess to the dauphin for five years. The Brissac sons were *enfants d'honneur,* who lived with the princes and remained close friends. Bonnivet and Brissac were respected warriors, included in the nursery household to supervise the princes in rough

3. This château is now a museum about twenty miles northwest of Paris.

sports such as wrestling, riding, and hunting to hounds—all essential attributes for a Valois. The dauphin and Henri loved their hunting dogs but did not really enjoy falconry, although the king and court had more than five hundred birds of prey. The English ambassador reported that in 1522, Louise de Savoie told him she had never seen a bigger child than Henri at just three years old.

In 1523, the princes met their new tutor, Benedetto Tagliacarno, a well-known Italian humanist. François I chose him for his knowledge of Latin and Greek—a sign that the king wanted his sons to be well versed in the culture of the Italian Renaissance. One of the *enfants d'honneur*, Gaspard de Coligny, who was the same age as Henri, wrote to his own tutor that "the majority of my time is spent reading Cicero and the study of the tables of Ptolemy under Guillaume du Maine [Henri's second tutor] who, adopting a different method from Tagliacarno, adds cosmography at the same time, especially the part relative to the longitude and latitude of places with the additions of meridians and parallels."

François' sister, Marguerite d'Angoulême, who was celebrated by the humanists for her love of the classics and knowledge of Greek, Latin, Hebrew, and Italian, probably also had some say in their education. Marguerite wrote to François that "Monsieur the dauphin is doing wonders at his studies. . . . Monsieur d'Orléans is glued to his books and says that he wishes to be wise; but Monsieur d'Angoulême knows more than the others." It is interesting that already when so young, Henri was being compared unfavorably with his younger brother, Charles. Accounts show that Henri was intensely physical and loved vigorous sports and exercise. Later in life he would become fluent in Latin, Italian, and Spanish.

*J*UST as Claude preferred Blois, François liked to be at Amboise, the château which dominated the town below. Both châteaux, so near to one another, had unlimited possibilities for *la chasse*. Often, during the long gallops of the hunt, the king would stop at the little redbrick château de Cloux next to Amboise, better known today as Le

Clos Lucé. In 1516, Leonardo da Vinci accepted François' invitation to come to France and adorn his court. François called him "maestro" and installed him in the charming manorhouse. Leonardo had suffered a slight stroke and his right hand was partially paralyzed, leaving him unable to paint. He continued to draw his machines of mass destruction and designs for dams to prevent the flooding of France's rivers. Leonardo died three years later, on May 2, 1519, at Le Clos Lucé while François was hunting at Saint-Germain-en-Laye.[4] The maestro's death greatly affected the king, who recognized his genius. In gratitude for his enlightened patronage, Leonardo willed several paintings to François, who also bought others from Leonardo's heirs, including the *Mona Lisa*.

Life at the court of François I was a constant progress of pleasure from one château on the Loire to another, from feast to festivity and hunt to hunt. The ever restless and curious king would move around his large kingdom to see conditions for himself, display his authority, and be seen by the populace. On the move, the court numbered about twelve thousand mounted members, accompanied by many carriages and caravans of mule wagons which dealt with the baggage. In the first half of the sixteenth century, the court was not yet bound to a rigorous protocol; rather, this was improvised from reign to reign. Benvenuto Cellini wrote in his memoirs: "We had to journey through places where sometimes there were scarcely two houses to be found; and then we had to set up canvas tents like gypsies, and suffered at times very great discomfort." The Venetian ambassador, Marino Giustiniani, complained that "my mission as ambassador lasted forty-five months. Never during the whole time was the court in the same place for forty-five days." In effect, France had two capitals, Paris, and wherever the king happened to be. As he *was* the state, foreign ambassadors or petitioners were obliged to find him to present their credentials or requests.

4. In a journal entry by Antonio de' Beatis, dated October 10, 1517, he states that Leonardo was overcome by a certain paralysis of his right hand and "one can no longer expect fine things of him. . . . Messer Leonardo can no longer paint with the sweetness of style that he used to have, and he can only make drawings and teach others." As the cardinal Luigi of Aragon's secretary, it is likely that Beatis was an accurate observer. The famous painting by Ingres of Leonardo's death in the arms of François is apocryphal.

According to Cellini, at times the court moved with as many as eighteen thousand horses, and another witness gave the figure as twenty-four thousand horses and mules. Ladies were carried in litters or wagons. Grand courtiers rode, and servants walked. The king's châteaux on the Loire were as empty as we see them today. All the furnishings, carpets, tapestries, and plate were packed up and transported with the peripatetic court. Only those palaces regularly used were permanently furnished. When possible, this vast caravanserai would travel by river, as the roads were often in poor condition. For these boat journeys, the king kept a magnificent barge on the Seine; it even contained a kitchen.

Meals at court were served on tables piled high with assortments of food; plates and scented napkins were discarded after each course. Everyone in France ate with just a knife, a spoon, and their fingers; no fork as yet.[5] Napkins were always placed around the neck because eating with one's fingers was never tidy. Ladies would sometimes place a small piece of meat on a slice of bread to make it easier to eat. Pâtés were popular and often spread on bread. Different sorts of meat and game were always part of a court buffet, as were sweetbreads, dressed crab, quenelles, and truffles, which were very popular. The sideboards groaned under the weight of assorted vegetables, wild mushrooms, even codfish. For dessert there were endless sweetmeats, fresh and jellied fruits, some in pastry, and many kinds of mousse. In the main, the food was heavy and rather indigestible. Wines, often spiced, flowed in great quantity and helped to loosen tongues.

Housing ten or twelve thousand was never easy. If the king stayed in one of his own châteaux, only the most privileged would be given rooms; the rest would have to find accommodation locally or in the tent city that sprang up wherever the king halted. The need to feed such a number of people meant that the court could not remain long in one place. Rather than transporting its food, the court was provisioned locally and supplies were soon exhausted.

The population of the court fluctuated. If the king was at war, all the able-bodied men left with him, and only the women, children, and

5. Three-pronged forks, known at the Italian courts, only came into use at the French court with the reign of Henri III, grandson of François I.

the elderly would remain. At other times the total varied according to the number of local nobles who joined the king's progress about the countryside. For a nobleman, life at court was very expensive. He would have to pay for an extensive wardrobe, personal staff, horses, and entertainments; but his chief expense was gambling.

Foreigners, including many Italians when France dominated their peninsula, came to join the French court either to visit and admire its splendor, or to obtain positions and preferment. When François I traveled in northern Italy as a young man, he observed and approved of the role of women in court society. When he became king, he decided to bring that tradition to France. Civility, manners, and elegant customs were all introduced by François, and he permitted his nobles to join some of the Italian courts as well. The king employed many Italians in his household, kitchens, and stables. He also imported horses from the Italian courts; his friend, Federigo Gonzaga, sent him several of his own breed as gifts. Horses were so prized at Gonzaga's court in Mantua that his palazzo has a large room dedicated to his favorites, with a life-size portrait of each frescoed on the walls.

Fashion was also imported from Italy. At François I's request, Isabella d'Este sent him dolls dressed in the latest styles, which were copied and worn at his court. The French king had a true appreciation of art and persuaded great painters and scholars of the humanities to come to France and embellish his kingdom to the greater glory of his name. He told his courtiers: "I can create a noble, only God can make a great artist." The king's love of literature, philosophy, and art stemmed from his youthful travels to the Italian courts and his meetings with renowned artists. When François and his companions returned from their first tour of northern Italy,[6] they looked with distaste at their gloomy castles. The use of gunpowder and cannons had already rendered castellated walls obsolete, and they replaced their forbidding towers with flower-decked terraces and colonnaded walks. The cultured world had long admired the architecture of the French Gothic cathedrals; François planned to take the lead in bringing the classical grace of the Renaissance to his own country. He dreamed of

---

6. François never went farther south than Pavia or farther east than Bologna.

building a new palace that would be the wonder of Europe, where he could summon the greatest artists and philosophers in the world to grace and enhance his Renaissance court.

*T*HERE is a charming legend that when one of the king's most prized hounds, called Bleau (or Bleu), ran into the forest in pursuit of a stag and was lost, François insisted that no one of his hunting party should rest until the dog was found. Deeper into the forest they rode until eventually they reached a large clearing and saw the tired Bleau drinking from a spring near a ruined keep. (Some of the group were so worn out they imagined they saw a beautiful nymph resting by the hound on the grass, her arm around the neck of an exhausted stag.) The weary party dismounted, and the king found the spot so agreeable that thereafter he would often halt there to picnic during a hunt. When François was ready to choose a site for his new palace, he picked the beautiful meadow by the spring in the forest and named it in memory of his hound: Fontainebleau.

In 1528, François began building onto his father's old keep in the meadow with the spring. To its two towers he added a gallery, which joined the ruined keep with a nearby monastery. Much of François I's original Fontainebleau is now destroyed, but the famous gallery still stands to remind us of the wonder of the Renaissance château. It was in this great palace that François I established his school of painting, importing such masters as Giovanni-Battista Rosso, a Florentine known as Il Rosso in 1531; Francesco Primaticcio in 1533; and Cellini soon afterward. Il Rosso had been influenced by Michelangelo, and together with Primaticcio, he invented a style of flat, scrolling stucco decoration called strapwork, which he combined with painting.[7] The Galerie François I is the best example of this art. Unable to visit his beloved northern Italy, François imported all he could of it to France, creating a "French Italy" of marble and statues, precious woods for

---

7. Il Rosso suffered at the hands of the imperial forces during the Sack of Rome, and a later fall from a roof affected his head and probably his brain. After a quarrel with a friend, he fatally poisoned himself.

The stucco strapwork in the Galerie François I at Fontainebleau was created by Giulio Romano in a style known as Mannerism.

paneling, stucco and gilding, Venetian glass and mirrors,[8] and allegorical paintings by Italian masters.

Primaticcio was sent to Italy by the king to buy "antiquities"— sculptures for his fabulous gallery—and the great connoisseur and bon vivant Pietro Aretino was commissioned to buy art for Fontainebleau. The king's gallery there boasted, among other works, Bandinelli's *Mercury Holding a Flute* and Tribolo's statue *Nature*. François himself added Michelangelo's *Leda and the Swan* and Bronzino's *Venus and Cupid,* which became the symbol of his era. An early Michelangelo sculpture, *Hercules,* formed part of a fountain at Fontainebleau. When he could not buy a sculpture, Primaticcio had a plaster cast of it made; cast in bronze in France, these were displayed in the king's gallery to great admiration. While in Italy, Primaticcio was impressed with the paintings of Parmigianino, and on his return to France he brought with him the elongated style of painting—especially nudes—that came

8. Until that time, mirrors in France were made of polished metal.

to represent the School of Fontainebleau. Often combined with stucco, the style became known as Mannerism.

The greatest masterpiece to hang in Fontainebleau was indisputably the *Mona Lisa,* which François I bought from Leonardo da Vinci's heir and installed in his library.

Another of the artists lured to Fontainebleau by the king was Benvenuto Cellini, a "character" who drove everyone mad with his jokes and japes. He disliked the pretensions of the king's mistress, the duchesse d'Etampes, and went out of his way to annoy her—and succeeded. The duchess tried to have the king send him away, but François laughed and kept him at court. Cellini called the château "Fontana Belio." His sketches and wax models always delighted the king, and in his diaries he tells us quite frankly how he would feel the need to make love to his models in order to best portray their long-limbed beauty. Cellini clearly went too far and was tried by jury for using his mistress "after the Italian manner."

Cellini is probably responsible for the greatest *objets d'art* in the royal collection. During his two long visits to the French court, he cre-

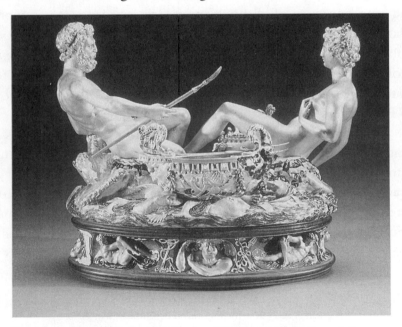

The famous golden saltcellar by Benvenuto Cellini was made for François I.

ated the famous golden saltcellar, depicting a long-legged, reclining nude figure of a nymph with an open shell for holding the salt.[9] Several nineteenth-century writers claim the model was Diane de Poitiers, but in fact the model was Cellini's mistress. The artist planned twelve life-size silver figures of gods and goddesses intended to be used as candelabra, but only one, the Jupiter, was finished. Among his other works for François I was a bronze lunette in demirelief depicting the *Nymph of Fontainebleau,*[10] another long-legged nude beauty mistakenly identified as Diane de Poitiers, this time with her arm protectively around a stag—the Valois kings had always used the stag as their family emblem.

François I established an impressive library at Fontainebleau, with over fifteen hundred books, including forty-one in Greek, four in Hebrew, and two in Arabic. The king sent several learned men to Italy on book-buying expeditions, and his diplomats in Venice and Rome were instructed to buy (or have copied) all the Greek manuscripts they could find. As François never stayed in one place for any length of time, he had a chest of books which followed him wherever he went. From 1537, the French printers and booksellers were obliged to deliver to the king one copy of all books printed in any language. Imported books had to be screened by the Sorbonne[11] before being sold to the public, and one copy had to remain at Blois. In 1544, the library was moved to Fontainebleau, and two years later it was opened to visitors. In twenty years the library was bursting with 3,560 titles. It was moved to Paris, where it formed the basis of the Bibliothèque Nationale.

A charming anonymous miniature from about 1530 shows the king and his three sons listening to Antoine Macault reading from his translation of Diodorus of Sicily. Also present are courtiers and François' pet monkey. Of the three children, only Henri appears to be listening. When Henri became king, the ordinance concerning books printed was stretched to two copies for the king; the second was for Diane's library at Anet.

Fontainebleau is a monument to François I, the patron of human-

9. Cellini's saltcellar, almost unanimously considered the most beautiful small work of all Renaissance art, was stolen in 2003 from the Kunsthistorische Museum in Vienna.

10. Now in the Louvre. A replica has replaced the original at Anet.

11. The Faculty of Theology of the University of Paris, commonly referred to as the Sorbonne.

François I, his three sons, and the court listen to a reading from Diodorus. Of the three boys, only Henri d'Orléans appears to be listening.

ism, scholars, and artists. Of all his many châteaux, it was the closest he came to having a home: he referred to the house as "*chez moi*" and continued improving it for the rest of his life. Brantôme wrote: "What a building is Fontainebleau, where out of a wilderness has been made the finest house in Christendom . . . so rich, so fair a building and so big and spacious that one might house a small world in it, and so many lovely gardens and groves and beautiful fountains, and everything pleasing and delightful."

The greatest pastime of the court was the hunt. Although a noted scholar, the king was primarily a man of action, and when not at war, jousting in tournaments or chasing the stag, bear, wild boar, or wolf was the favorite occupation of courtiers. François I was heroically brave and his lack of concern for his own welfare resulted in many a nasty accident. Idleness was scorned by society. But the only other alternative to scholarship and sport for the nobility was attending festivities, performing in masques, dancing, and for some, even *sinning*.

It has always been said by contemporary as well as later writers that the inspiration for the lifestyle at Fontainebleau came from Baldassare Castiglione's book *The Courtier*. The king had read it in the original Italian and commissioned a French translation for the court. It reached cult status among the *cognoscenti* and was adopted by many other European courts as well. François loved to talk—conversation was one of his greatest joys, and there was no greater book for teaching the art of conversation than *The Courtier*. Castiglione wrote that "all inspiration must come from women. . . . Without women nothing is possible, either in military courage, or art, or poetry, or music, or philosophy, or even religion. God is truly seen only through them." This thinking was at the core of the doctrine for François I's court at Fontainebleau.

Other contemporary writers on art history such as Giorgio Vasari give more credit for the multicultural impact of Fontainebleau to the king's contemporary, François Rabelais, the chief poet of the day. Rabelais studied to become a prior, but he left the monastery in disgust when the old learning became transformed into envy of the new, and great classical books were being banned and even burned. He studied medicine and went to Lyons to practice, where he soon joined the literary circle around the great printer Andreas Gryphius. Rabelais wrote *Pantagruel* as a sequel to the original *Gargantua,* and then composed a *Gargantua* of his own.

Rabelais' books were read to François I during meals. It seems the king laughed until he cried over both books, and called Rabelais "the merriest devil in his realm." Naturally, Rabelais' books were banned by the Sorbonne as seditious, but that did not prevent the king from giving them his royal imprimatur. Lytton Strachey wrote of *Gargantua* that the "whole vast spirit of the Renaissance is gathered within its pages." It has been said that the riotous mirth and wisdom of Rabelais made him "as many friends as enemies," and that his works remain "the most astonishing treasure of wit, wisdom, common sense and satire that the world has ever seen."

Rabelais also wrote erotic verse, very much to the taste of François I and his licentious court. Some of the stories told about the king's womanizing seem hard to believe. Contemporary sources claim that François had an incestuous relationship with his sister, Marguerite, and enjoyed a mistress from the age of ten. If he was capable of such precocity, one must remember that his mother, Louise de Savoie, married at the age of eleven and no one thought that too young. François' love of women was legendary; even Queen Claude's stepmother, Mary Tudor, had complained of his forced attentions. Nonetheless, the French court was the envy of all others in Europe and was viewed as the most scintillating on earth.

CHAPTER FOUR

Treachery and Treason

*A*FTER his triumph at Marignano, François I soon learned that winning northern Italy was one thing, but holding on to it was quite another. The French king needed Pope Leo X's cooperation on the peninsula as there was a real danger of the Habsburg forces joining with Henry VIII and attacking France. The king also had his eye on the title of Holy Roman Emperor, and for that Pope Leo X's endorsement of the imperial crown was essential. There were other territorial gains that an alliance with the pope would help facilitate. As the feudal suzerain of the Kingdom of Naples, the crown was in his gift, and as the senior Medici, the duchy of Florence was also his to bestow.

On December 8, 1515, pope and king met in Bologna and signed a concordat of friendship. François I ensured the Vatican's authority over the Catholic Church in France, and Leo X promised to support François' claims to the Kingdom of Naples. The usual manner of cementing such an arrangement was a wedding. In 1518, the king of France offered the hand of his cousin Madeleine de La Tour d'Auvergne to the pope's nephew, Lorenzo de' Medici, Duke of Urbino and head of the Florentine republic.[1]

For the Medici to marry into the royal house of France was a gigantic elevation, and the family was suitably awed. The origin of the Medicis is unclear. According to legend, they began their rise with a certain Alverado, a knight of Charlemagne. Other sources claim the family's origins rest with two unidentified Florentine apothecaries in the thirteenth century. As the family increased in wealth, it began to infiltrate the political and financial circles of the city. By the fourteenth century, the Medici concentrated on banking and the acquisition of steadily more important appointments within the republic. The aristocratic dynasties and the grand old families of weavers—Florence produced the most elaborate and finely woven fabrics in all Europe—despised the "nouveaux riches" merchant bankers and excluded them from society. Thereafter, the Medici made themselves the champions of the working class, and by the first quarter of the fifteenth century, a Medici had risen to become the head of the republic.

Once at the helm of power, they never let go again, but continued to control politics and finance in Florence for three hundred years. By the fifteenth century, the wealth and power of the Medici was such that they were in a position to make enormous loans to Louis XI of France. It was due to the French king's inability to repay that he permitted the *fleur-de-lys* to be placed on the city's coat of arms and on the central ball of the Medicis' own armorial shield.

The wedding arranged by François I and the Medici pope Leo X would bring their families even closer together. The willing victim of this arrangement was seventeen-year-old Madeleine de La Tour d'Auvergne, comtesse de Boulogne, daughter of a Princess of the Blood, a substantial heiress, and an acknowledged beauty. Since the king had negotiated the marriage contract between the ravishing Madeleine and the Duke of Urbino, he also presided over the magnificent, almost-royal festivities at Amboise, just days after the baptism of his heir the dauphin, on February 28, 1517. It was here that François met Leo-

---

1. Lorenzo, Duke of Urbino, was a grandson of Lorenzo the Magnificent. Pope Leo X was the latter's son.

nardo da Vinci (who was among the pope's suite of representatives) and invited the artist to come to France.

For both occasions—the wedding and the christening—the court-yard of the château was covered and transformed into a huge banqueting hall. The castle walls were hung with rich tapestries, and the awning's ceiling was decorated with garlands of box and flowers. Diane de Poitiers was a cousin of the bride through her mother, as well as the confidante of the queen, and she played a significant part in the joint ceremonies.[2] The first of these was the christening of the dauphin François.

Lorenzo, Duke of Urbino, standing proxy for the pope, who was godfather, held the dauphin at the font during the ceremony, and presented the king of France with a number of gifts, including two paintings by Raphael. The king, for his part, gave the bridegroom a company of men-at-arms and the chain and Order of Saint-Michel, as well as a handsome allowance for his French bride. This double celebration pleased all parties—the king was able to fortify his links with Rome and Florence; the duke felt himself nearer the realization of his ambition to hold sway over more of the Italian peninsula than just his native Urbino; and the bride's family was delighted to come within the illustrious sphere of the pope. The joint christening and wedding celebrations lasted for several days of feasting and dancing, but no festivity was complete without a tournament. The king and the bridegroom distinguished themselves at the joust and no one was unduly disturbed when several of the combatants were killed during the mock battle that followed.

Tournaments were held to enhance the prowess of the warriors by staging competitions. "Jousts," as they were called, included single combat or teams taking part against one another. Once the trumpets had sounded the start, the audience was bound to total silence. Neither coughing nor hand signals or gestures were permitted. Jousting was carried out in "lists"[3] in an enclosed area, with riders charging at one another on either side of a barrier, their lances poised to knock their

2. A pencil sketch of Diane at this time shows a face of classic symmetry and calm, more striking for its strength than its beauty.

3. The term "lists" refers to the long barrier placed lengthwise in the center of a wide aisle. Two contestants galloped toward one another on opposite sides. Leveling a long, blunt wooden lance (tipped with metal to prevent it splitting) across the neck of his horse, the rider aimed at the shield or armor of his opponent, hoping to unseat him with the force of the blow.

When Renaissance cavaliers were not at war, they practiced their
skills and honed their courage by jousting in tournaments.

opponent off his horse. Both riders and horses wore armor, but injury
was still commonplace.

After touring his wife's considerable estates in the Auvergne, the
Duke of Urbino brought his duchess home to Tuscany, where they
spent an idyllic three months before he fell ill. Unlike his famous for-
bear, this Lorenzo de' Medici had only succeeded in mastering dissipa-
tion and drunkenness during his short life. If the pope and the king
knew about it, neither had mentioned the "bad blood" of the Medici,
which carried tuberculosis, and worse. Lorenzo was a victim of the
so-called *mal français* or *mal de Naples,* which had been brought from
the New World allegedly by the Spanish: syphilis.

All the well-laid plans of the Medici pope and the French king
came to nothing. Lorenzo took to his bed with consumption. On

April 13, 1519, one year after her wedding, Madeleine gave birth to a
daughter, but Lorenzo was already too weak to go to his wife's room
to see her. The frail child was immediately baptized Catarina[4] Maria
Romula. Two weeks after the birth, Madeleine de La Tour d'Auvergne
died of puerperal fever and complications from her husband's double
wedding gifts of syphilis and tuberculosis. One week later, Lorenzo,
Duke of Urbino, ruler of Florence, and master wastrel, joined her in
the tomb. He was twenty-eight years old. Although François I and
Pope Leo X may have thought their dynastic alliance ended with these
two deaths, no one could have foretold the intertwining of the des-
tinies of François' second son, the one-month-old Henri d'Orléans,
with Catherine de' Medici—and with Diane de Poitiers.

*P*EACE at home did not prevent the king's mother from plot-
ting another campaign. Why should not François become Holy
Roman Emperor? With the death of the past incumbent, Maximilian, an
election was due soon. Despite its grandeur, the title was largely honorific; it conferred nominal sovereignty over a "mosaic" of principalities,
duchies, free cities, margravates, baronies, the many small kingdoms
that now comprise modern Germany, and the sizable duchy of Savoy.

By ancient tradition, the emperor was chosen by seven German
Electors, although some of them could be bribed. Louise, determined
to add the crown of Charlemagne[5] to her son's glory, noted that there
were really only three contenders: François I; Henry VIII (although he

---

4. Hereafter I will call her Catherine. "Romula" was in memory of Romulus, legendary
frounder of Rome and Florence.

5. The first "crown of Charlemagne" was probably made for Emperor Otto I, crowned in
962. It was used by all the Holy Roman Emperors and later for the German kings, until 1804,
when it was replaced by the crown of the Austrian Empire. French kings were crowned with another "crown of Charlemagne"—a tiara that was said to date from 1180 but was perhaps made in
the thirteenth century. It was reputed to have been used to crown twenty-three kings of France
and was kept in the Treasury of Saint-Denis. As it was destroyed in 1590 and its replacement was
destroyed during the Revolution, the figure of twenty-three is apocryphal. After the Revolution,
yet another "crown of Charlemagne" was made. The medieval closed "crown of Charlemagne"
used for the ceremony of the Holy Roman Emperor is in the Imperial Schatzkammer in Vienna—
see Richard A. Jackson, *"Vive le roi" 1937: A History of the French Coronation from Charles V to
Charles X* (Chapel Hill: University of North Carolina Press, 1984).

was certainly not rich enough to compete); and the Habsburg Charles, king of Spain.

Five years younger than François I, Charles, son of the Austrian Archduke Philip "the Handsome," was in almost every way his father's opposite. How shrewdly the Venetian diplomat Marino Giustiniani, who had served at the courts of both François and Charles, observed: "They will hate each other until one of them dies." Where François was dashing and ebullient, Charles was cold and phlegmatic. With his long Habsburg chin and the permanently open mouth of the adenoid sufferer, Charles was far from good-looking. He wore the colors of shadows and hated the ostentation that the French king loved. The excitement of the chase, which occupied so much of the life of the Valois court and of François in particular, was anathema to the calm and curt Charles of Spain. In fact, although his extended jaw made him look stupid, he was blessed with a rare intelligence. Charles was tenacious, possessing total self-control and patience. With the wealth generated by the New World, he could also afford to outbid François for the crown of Charlemagne.

In addition to being king of Spain, and by dint of other inheritances, Charles had the right to be named ruler of "Sicily, Jerusalem, the Balearic and Canary Islands, the Indies, and the Mainland on the Far Side of the Atlantic." He was "Archduke of Austria; Duke of Burgundy, Brabant, Styria, Carinthia, Carniola, Luxembourg, Limburg, Athens and Patras; Count of Habsburg, Flanders and Tyrol; Count Palatine of Burgundy, Hainault, Pfiart, Roussillon; Landgrave of Alsace; Count of Swabia; Lord of Asia and Afric." He was ruler of the Netherlands, the German Franche-Comté, and the Kingdom of Naples. One historian described this nineteen-year-old paragon as a "coalition in his own person," since no Christian monarch, not even Charlemagne whose crown he now coveted, had ever possessed so much territory and so many titles. It was the dearest wish of the emperor Maximilian that his grandson Charles would succeed him in this title as well as all his others.

Inevitably, with the larger financial clout, the Habsburg Charles of Spain won the election on June 28, 1519, and became the Holy Roman Emperor Charles V, although it would be eleven years before

Pope Clement VII placed the heavy gold crown of Charlemagne on his head. From this moment, Charles V would endanger the kingdom of France and peace in Europe; and he remained an implacable enemy of François I for the rest of his life.

With France now encircled on three sides by the borders of the Holy Roman Empire, Louise de Savoie looked across the English Channel for support. By nature a troublemaker, Henry VIII recognized an opportunity for making mischief between Europe's two great powers. In 1520, after some delicate negotiations, François and Henry agreed to meet in a small, sheltered valley near Calais to discuss a possible alliance. As the neighboring castles were in ruins, the French and the English camps erected pavilions of such splendor that the many paintings of the scene would make appropriate illustrations for a fairy tale.

There are enough contemporary reports to make one believe

Henry VIII of England was the contemporary of François I. They died within weeks of each other.

that Henry VIII really did ship a three-story wooden palace to Calais. It arrived in sections and was assembled with windows of leaded, diamond-shaped panes. Canvas painted to look like stone covered the outside. This legendary castle had four great crenellated towers at its corners, and two large fountain statues of Bacchus and Cupid gushed claret for anyone passing to drink.

To house his retinue of over five thousand on his side of the line, François I created a small city of tents and pavilions covered in cloth of gold, all flying pennants. His own pavilion, embroidered all over with gold and silver thread, was sixty feet high and topped by a life-size statue of Saint Michael, bearing the arms of France and spearing a dragon.

The occupants of both camps preened and postured, but achieved little. The two young sovereigns behaved like overgrown schoolboys. Early one morning François, accompanied by only a few attendants, invaded Henry's camp and, to the surprise of the English king, insisted on acting as his valet and helping him to dress. It was a dangerous prank, as Henry could have imprisoned François, but the French king wanted to win the trust "of the most distrustful of men." Henry was charmed and presented generous gifts, reciprocating the gesture by arriving in the French camp unannounced and challenging "my good brother of France" to a wrestling match. Some Bretons and Yeomen of the Guard had been wrestling earlier and a crowd gathered. The French king, according to an eyewitness report by Robert III de La Marck, François' childhood friend Fleurange, was lighter and quicker, and threw Henry with a *tour de Bretagne* grip so that he hit the ground heavily. Henry demanded another bout, but François refused. Although it was June, the atmosphere was icy thereafter, and with cool *politesse* the two monarchs parted.

Henry VIII, however, did not cross the Channel and return to England. He had always planned a second meeting with Charles of Spain, the new Holy Roman Emperor, and now he secretly concluded with Charles a friendly alliance against France.

One of the gentlemen presented to Henry VIII at the Field of the Cloth of Gold—as the extravagant meeting between the English and French sovereigns came to be called—was the rich and powerful Con-

Charles de Bourbon, Constable of France, the most powerful man in François I's kingdom.

stable of France, Charles, duc de Bourbon. When Henry VIII heard that Bourbon sported an immensely valuable pearl during the festivities and discovered the full extent of the power and wealth of the Constable, it is said that the English king remarked shrewdly that had Bourbon been one of *his* nobles, he would not have risked leaving his head on his shoulders.

Charles de Bourbon inspired true loyalty and love among his followers. Serious and reserved, he was another who was the opposite of the French king. His portrait by the court painter Jean Clouet shows us a delicate, well-bred, thin face, with intelligent, sad eyes. King Louis XII said of him: "I wish he had a more open, a gayer, a less taciturn spirit—stagnant water frightens me."

Although François I had no reason to distrust his Constable, who had served him well in Milan, he had appointed Admiral Bonnivet to replace him there as his viceroy. Brantôme wrote that Bonnivet "was so loved and favored by King François that, while he lived, he ruled everything to do with war. . . ." Charles de Bourbon already lacked self-confidence and had a tendency to imagine slights. This was a slight the Constable of France would not forget.

Bourbon adored his wife, Suzanne, and about half of his vast land-holdings came to him with their marriage. Once her son had died and she realized she could have no more children, Suzanne went to enormous lengths to ensure that her inheritance remained with her husband and his family. Suzanne died in 1521, and both she and her mother, who was still alive, willed everything they possessed to Charles de Bourbon.

Nonetheless, Bourbon, the richest man in the kingdom after the sovereign, faced ruin. Because he had no direct heir, it was possible for the crown to make a claim on Suzanne's inheritance: her mother was a Princess of France and part of her property had come to her from her royal father. There were also other properties of Suzanne's claimed for the crown by the avaricious Louise de Savoie, first cousin of Suzanne's mother, Anne de Beaujeu. Time had faded Louise de Savoie's beauty, and power had turned her head; then, at age forty-five, she lost her heart. As the king's mother, Louise had had no shortage of candidates to console her in widowhood, and she took full advantage of her position. Soon after Suzanne's death, the object of her overwhelming desire became none other than the Constable of France—the recently widowed, attractive, and considerably younger Charles de Bourbon.

Darkly handsome at thirty-two, extremely proud, and grieving for his wife whom he had loved sincerely, Charles was not at all interested in the overtures made to him by the king's mother. The duc de Bourbon needed to produce an heir to his vast possessions and title; otherwise, with his death, everything he owned would revert to the crown. Louise was, of course, too old for childen, and she would have realized all this, but she was madly in love and desired desperately to marry the richest and most powerful nobleman in France.

The king pushed his mother's suit, and his chancellor, Antoine Duprat, a mutual friend of their youth at Amboise, made it clear to Bourbon that he really had no choice. If he did not marry Louise de Savoie, then the case concerning his inheritance would go to the *Parlement,* which would surely find in her favor for her claim on his property. Piqued to anger when the king congratulated him on his forthcoming nuptials, Charles is said to have retorted that "having been married to the best of women, he would surely not now marry the worst." Louise went out of her mind with thwarted love and hurt pride (she was reported to have torn her hair), and demanded that her son come to her support against his Constable and put pressure on him to marry her by threatening to seize his property. Naturally, the king wanted to defend his mother's honor as well as her claims, but it is probable that his envy of Charles' wealth was a significant factor in the equation. Were his mother to inherit the Bourbon lands, with her death this vast inheritance would revert to the throne.

Although Louise de Savoie was her cousin and nearest relative, Anne de Beaujeu was deeply shocked by the king's injustice and the avarice of the relation she had nurtured but always mistrusted. This "most sane" grand old lady recalled the ancient pact between the houses of Bourbon and Burgundy, from which the emperor Charles V descended. Before dying, she uttered these fateful last words to her son-in-law, Charles de Bourbon: ". . . I beg and command you to make an alliance with the emperor, then I can die in peace." This was high treason, from the mouth of a daughter of a king of France and the sister of another. The case concerning the Bourbon lands had gone to trial in the summer of 1522, and even before her death, the king granted some of Anne de Beaujeu's lands to his mother.

Anne de Beaujeu died on November 14, 1522, just one and a half years after her daughter, Suzanne. Her position in the country was so elevated that all along the route between her château de Chantelles and the monastery of Souvigny where she would lie in state, the peasants from her lands knelt and prayed as her bier passed. The king immediately seized all the territory Anne de Beaujeu had been granted by her father, Louis XI.

Three months after Anne de Beaujeu's death, Charles de Bourbon asked the king to halt his unjust trial. The king assured him that, should it proceed, the outcome would be just and not to his detriment. Nevertheless, François sequestered a number of the Constable's estates for his mother, and others he placed under royal seal until the outcome of the proceedings.

Even before the treasonous deathbed request of Anne de Beaujeu, the Holy Roman Emperor Charles V had been making overtures to Bourbon, and offered him as wife his sister Eleonore, the twenty-eight-year-old dowager-queen of Portugal, together with a huge dowry. But Bourbon hesitated to accept for fear of offending the king. Nevertheless, from this time, the Constable of France began to have secret talks with the emperor.

FRANÇOIS I had no more loyal subject than Diane de Poitiers' father, Jehan de Saint-Vallier. In July 1521, he had established himself in Lyons to recruit men for the king's army. He then moved these troops in stages to join the main forces in Italy; but on the way, he succumbed to an unknown fever from which he was to suffer for the rest of his life. The famous "Saint-Vallier fever" had begun in a military camp. On his return from Italy the following year, Saint-Vallier heard about the Constable's disagreement with the king over his proposed marriage to Louise de Savoie and called on him several times to comfort and calm him.

As young blades, Saint-Vallier and the duc de Bourbon's father had both ridden to war with Louis XII in Italy

Jehan de Saint-Vallier, father of Diane de Poitiers.

and pledged their loyalty and friendship to each other. Years later, when the duke and his eldest son died of fever in Naples, Jehan de Saint-Vallier transferred his allegiance to the heir, the twelve-year-old Charles de Bourbon-Montpensier. Though much older, Saint-Vallier was proud to be in the boy's entourage, and had no reason not to remain a faithful adherent of his liege lord as he grew into adulthood.[6]

On July 17, 1523, Saint-Vallier visited Charles to discuss his son's marriage. Diane's father also had a problem concerning monies owed to him for his military expenses in the king's service and hoped that the Constable could address the matter with François. The two friends retired to spend the night at Bourbon's house at Montbrison. Without warning, the Constable confronted Saint-Vallier with a relic of the True Cross and insisted he solemnly swear never to reveal what he would hear at Montbrison.

Bourbon then told Saint-Vallier of the emperor's proposal that he

6. Swearing loyalty to one's liege lord was a solemn undertaking to faithfully serve one's feudal superior.

marry his widowed sister, Eleonore. The Constable went further and told Saint-Vallier that if he, Bourbon, joined forces with Henry VIII and the emperor, Bourbon would be given his own kingdom comprising the provinces of Champagne, Lyons, and Provence. This would be on condition that he allowed Burgundy to go to Charles V and the crown of France to Henry VIII, which had been worn, after all, by his predecessor Henry VI. It is true that Jehan de Saint-Vallier was not renowned for his intelligence and was also somewhat naïve, but to suggest that he would not be averse to this treacherous plan is to deny his first loyalty to the king. There can be no doubt that Saint-Vallier was astounded at the prospect of such treachery from his liege lord.

Although Saint-Vallier was in Bourbon's debt, and had also sworn feudal allegiance to him, Saint-Vallier was not aware of the Constable's plot until he arrived at Montbrison to discuss his personal financial concerns. He was astonished to have joined a gathering of conspirators, all loyal to the Constable. Shocked by what he heard unfolding, Saint-Vallier begged Bourbon to reconsider. The next morning, realizing that Saint-Vallier was still alarmed, Bourbon tried to reassure him that he would abandon the plot and begged him to swear again to keep his silence.[7] Having been forced by the Constable to swear on the Cross that he would divulge nothing, the seigneur de Saint-Vallier returned to court without the courage to denounce his liege lord.

THE emperor Charles V was not the only person matchmaking for Charles de Bourbon. Behind Louise's back, some members of the French royal family hoped to encourage the Constable of France to marry Queen Claude's sister Renée, as he was the last of that royal line. The Constable could see the advantage of this marriage. If he were to marry the king's sister-in-law, who was also the daughter of the late king, he would be even more powerful. Bourbon arranged to arrive at court while Queen Claude was dining alone and asked to join her. Claude had always been a favorite of his—her gentle ways and wisdom

---

7. *Procès criminal de Johan de Poytiers, seigneur de Saint-Vallier.*

attracted the taciturn Bourbon, and he trusted her. In the privacy of the queen's small dining room, he discussed with her the subject of possibly marrying her sister. Suddenly, the king entered and the delicate conversation stopped. François had been hunting and drinking and bridled at the intimate scene before him. François' spies had told him of the emperor's offer to wed Bourbon to his sister Eleonore; the king demanded to know if this was true and accused Bourbon of having secret dealings with Charles V.

Rising, the red-faced Bourbon denied it and replied, "Sire, then you menace and threaten me—I have deserved no such cause." In spite of the fact that he was involved much more deeply with Charles V than the king realized, the sensitive duke was outraged and told his friends he would return his Constable's sword of office. News of the discord between the king and Charles de Bourbon spread overseas. Henry VIII told the emperor's ambassador: "There is great displeasure between King François and the duc de Bourbon, perhaps because he will not marry Madame the regent."

Still Bourbon hesitated to make the final move. However, when the *Parlement* ordered the confiscation of his lands on September 7, 1523 for his refusal to marry Louise de Savoie, the Constable of France finally rebelled. Brantôme suggests that Bourbon had no choice other than to pursue his treason and act as he did. Otherwise, "he would have been imprisoned and dishonored for ever."

*T*HE phantom of Italy was haunting the French king and he ached to retrieve his losses. In an effort to increase his power base, François I had succeeded in renewing his treaty with Henry VIII after Mary Tudor had ceased to be queen of France in 1515; but he failed in his efforts to gain the unequivocal support of the Italian states against the emperor Charles V. In the advent of further hostilities, the king believed he could count on Venice and Genoa with whom he had treaties, and that the Swiss would be brought into the French camp. Blinded by his ambition to see the northern Italian states back within his domains, in 1523 François I began to gather a great army at Lyons. Montmorency was dispatched to Switzerland to raise twelve thousand men, while Charles V made alliances with Venice, Lucca, Siena, and Florence. The emperor had more success than the French in gaining allies, adding Venice, Savoy, Tuscany, and lesser Italian states to his side.

Charles de Bourbon planned his revolt carefully, intending to wait until the king had left for Italy. The emperor was to invade France from the Pyrenees in the south, Henry VIII through Normandy in the north, with the Constable instigating guerrilla action in the middle of the country. He would then move north to Paris with an army of *Landsknechte* (literally, "country farmhands")—the rough, wild Germans from Franche-Comté. All three armies would combine and attack the king from behind.

To ensure that Henry VIII's troops could land safely in the north, Bourbon brought two young Norman noblemen into his plot. Shocked by this proposed treachery, they confessed all to their bishop, who promptly informed the Grand Sénéchal of Normandy, Louis de Brézé, husband of Diane de Poitiers.

The king was heading south to join his troops when he received Brézé's letter telling him of the conspiracy. He took the news calmly, increased his escort to five thousand, and turned to ride to the Constable's seat at Moulins. There, François found Bourbon ill in bed. He told Bourbon that the plot had been uncovered and feigned disbelief. The king also assured his Constable that, should the property case go against him in the *Parlement*, he himself would override the decision and restore Bourbon's lands and possessions to him. In his last attempt to retain the loyalty of his Constable, François urged him to admit to his crime and assured him that he would be forgiven, promising that he was surely Bourbon's friend and understood the stress he had been under. François then urged his Constable to ride south with him and be his second-in-command at the front.

But Charles de Bourbon had decided on his path and to confess was the last thing he wanted. Yet if he did not promise to join the king, then François would be sure of his treason. Bourbon malingered and gave his sovereign his word. As soon as François had gone, he fled to Germany with a small escort and his saddlebags full of gold to offer his undoubted military skills in the service of the emperor Charles V.

Jehan de Saint-Vallier was imprisoned in the château de Loches
on the Indre River.

Tragically, Louis de Brézé realized too late that his father-in-law,
Jehan de Saint-Vallier, was unwittingly involved in Bourbon's conspiracy. Nonetheless, Brézé would do his duty no matter how much it hurt
his wife. Diane's head must have been spinning with conflicting emotions: her love and loyalty to her father, to the king, to her husband;
fear of recrimination against her family; worry about the damage done
to their position at court. Her father's failure to expose the treasonous
plot had put them all in a very dangerous position.

THAT year, 1523, all the courtly games and colorful pageantry
of the French court came to an abrupt end as the Habsburg emperor Charles V, aided by Henry VIII and the traitor Bourbon, laid
siege to France. The north would require defending against Henry

VIII, and the Pyrenees against the advance of the emperor's army. The defection of the English king hurt François the most, as the code of chivalry in which he believed had been broken. Never again, he said, would he place his trust in a living prince. With all Europe united against him, and with typical and misplaced courage, the king of France prepared to face his enemies.

The main culprits in the treacherous plot, including the Constable, had escaped, but the king ordered the immediate capture of Jehan de Saint-Vallier. Despite his reluctance to betray his monarch, Saint-Vallier's first loyalty had been to Charles de Bourbon. These traditional bonds stemmed from medieval times and were deeply embedded in the fabric of society. It was not an excuse, just an explanation, and Diane prayed her husband could influence the king to take the family's long and devoted service into consideration. He was arrested on September 5, 1523, and imprisoned first in Tarare, and then in the forbidding castle of Loches on the Indre. The king's men found incriminating letters in Saint-Vallier's possession, as well as proof that there had been several rendezvous with the conspirators at his house. With insurrection all around, an example had to be made. Saint-Vallier, stripped of his lands and titles, was sentenced to death. Although he was famously brave in battle, when faced with the terrible shame of his crime against his sovereign, Saint-Vallier broke down and wept, and his dreadful fever returned.

Louis de Brézé and Diane received letters from her father begging them to visit him and to plead for his life with the king. Diane knew that François was very fond of her and had treated her with much kindness and respect all her life; surely he would take pity on her misery and weaken in his resolve? Educated in the stern school of Anne de Beaujeu, Diane de Poitiers knew her place. She kept her head and did nothing, praying that her husband could influence the king to take the family's long and devoted service into consideration and hoping that Queen Claude would speak for her to the king. Such treachery by Saint-Vallier could ruin her husband in spite of his lifetime of service to the crown. Anxiously, Diane awaited the outcome of the trial, fearing for her father's life and for their own favor with the king.

Louis de Brézé loved his wife and daughters—they were a close-knit family—and he agonized over their situation of divided loyalty—on the one hand to their king, and on the other, to his wife's father. However, Saint-Vallier's guilt was not in doubt. The Grand Sénéchal of Normandy confided to his close friend Anne de Montmorency that he had found no one who could help him save Saint-Vallier, but that he so trusted in "the goodness of his master that I hope all will be well." Louis de Brézé had only one real ace. As war looked imminent, he knew that the king would need the services of his Grand Sénéchal to keep the coast of Normandy defended against an invasion by Henry VIII. When François sent a gift of twenty-five bottles of wine to the prison for the condemned man, Louis and Diane felt there might yet be some hope.

On December 23, 1523, Jehan de Saint-Vallier was transferred to the grim prison of the Concièrgerie in Paris, and on January 8, 1524, he was brought before the *Parlement*. Saint-Vallier had been on hunger strike in the months spent in prison waiting for his trial; he almost collapsed when, on January 17, he was found guilty of *lèse-majesté*. The sentence carried the death penalty, and the loss of all his properties, honors, and titles. In one month, he would be brought to his execution. All Diane's prayers had been in vain, but she and her husband continued to appeal to the king, the queen, and Madame Louise.

Three of the king's courtiers came to Saint-Vallier's cell and ceremoniously stripped him of his chain and Order of Saint-Michel. They then formally announced the withdrawal of all his honors, decorations, and court privileges. Diane's father was permitted to make his last will and testament and, assisted by a local priest, to prepare for his end. Asked once again if he had any further information to give to the crown, Saint-Vallier replied that he had told all he knew and gave permission to the priest to divulge his last confession. At 3 p.m. on February 17, 1524, Saint-Vallier, shaking from his mystery fever, was too weak to stand, let alone walk, to the place of execution. An archer lifted him onto a horse and had to sit behind him to hold him upright for the ride to the scaffold.

It was a bitterly cold day and the condemned man, bareheaded and with hands tied, was wrapped in a fox-fur cloak. With his confessor following behind on a mule, they came to the Place de Grève, where a huge crowd had come to watch the execution. According to that useful chronicler *"Un Bourgeois de Paris,"* Saint-Vallier was hauled onto the platform, his warm cloak was removed, and he was forced to kneel with his head on the block and beg for God's mercy and justice. Stripped to his doublet and shivering with fever, cold, and fear, Saint-Vallier knelt with his head over the execution block for more than an hour, waiting in anguish and confusion for the sword to fall. The audience grew restless—after all, they had come to see a show. Some denounced this senseless cruelty and others objected to the lack of spectacle; there was little else to amuse the Parisians in winter. It was said that Saint-Vallier's hair turned snow white during that fearful hour of waiting.

Suddenly, the muttering from the crowd ceased as a royal courier galloped into the square, waving a letter sealed with green wax and shouting to stop proceedings in the name of the king. Perversely, François had hesitated until the very last moment; the prisoner was semiconscious by the time the royal reprieve arrived. Nevertheless, Brantôme alleged that when the king's courier arrived, the prisoner cried out, thanking "God and his daughter's 'allure' for saving his life."

It seems that the king had never intended to execute Jehan de Saint-Vallier. Diane's father was arguably the least guilty of the conspirators and François would have heard the popular rumor that Saint-Vallier had opposed the Constable's treachery. The pardon commuting Saint-Vallier's sentence to life imprisonment "at the king's pleasure" had been signed by him at Blois the same day, and was read aloud to the mystified, grumbling crowd. It explained that the sovereign's clemency was due to the Poitiers family's long history of service to the crown and to the entreaties of his son-in-law, the Grand Sénéchal of Normandy, Louis de Brézé, who had uncovered the plot.

One month later, Saint-Vallier was moved back to the fortress of Loches, where he was well treated and permitted to receive visitors. He remained there for two years, when he was released, pardoned, and had his lands and privileges restored. Jehan de Saint-Vallier remarried and lived another fifteen years. François continued with the punishment of the Constable's other accomplices, leaving the sentence of death hanging over them like a sword of Damocles. In his absence, Charles de Bourbon was sentenced to death by decapitation.

The suddenness of Saint-Vallier's royal reprieve, and the fact that he had cried out thanking God for his daughter's intercession, began a rumor so often repeated in print that it must be addressed. That inveterate and colorful court gossip and chronicler Brantôme could not resist recording the scurrilous story that a certain highborn traitor, whose head had been on the block for over an hour, had been reprieved because his daughter had given herself to the king. Although Brantôme mentioned no names, this report gave rise years later to the story that Diane had thus saved her father, despite the contrary opinions of other contemporary writers such as Arnoul le Ferron and François Belleforest.

Brantôme's story was later spread by Victor Hugo in his novel *Le Roi s'amuse,* which was subsequently used as the basis of the plot for the opera *Rigoletto.* One of the Italian ambassadors, the Venetian Lorenzo Contarini, a notorious gossip, writing twenty years after the event, devoted one short paragraph to the episode, implying that Diane had been loved and "sampled" by François I.[8] For this to have been true, the king and Diane would have had to meet with extreme discretion—something for which François I was not known at all in his *amours.*

The sixteenth-century historian Belleforest gives some credence to the affair, but as he was born eight years after the supposed incident, it is more likely that he picked up the rumor many years later and embellished it at a time when it was politic to discredit Diane. Her father was said by Belleforest to have been so distressed that he died of "Saint-Vallier fever," no doubt referring to his recorded trembling on the block; but this was a recurring illness; moreover, he did not die for several years. Most historians, including the eighteenth-century Georges Guiffrey, who edited Diane de Poitiers' correspondence, Helen Henderson, and R. J. Knecht, François I's most recent biographer, all discredit the so-called *affaire.* As for the claim that Louis de Brézé turned a

8. Lorenzo Contarini, *"Relazione di Francia"* in E. Alberi, *Relazione degli ambasciatori veneti.* Florence, 1860.

blind eye to the king's lust for his beautiful wife—this would deny the great dignity and honorable nature of the Grand Sénéchal of Normandy.

It was the discovery of seventeen unsigned love letters addressed to the king that was partly responsible for the gossip. These letters were published as having been written by Diane de Poitiers. In fact, they have since been proven to be the work of François I's first *maîtresse en tître,* Françoise de Foix, comtesse de Châteaubriant.[9] The letters were signed with the same endearments she used in her known letters to the king: "the hand of which the whole body is yours."

Diane was probably with the court at Blois at the appointed time of her father's execution and certainly kept abreast of developments. There is no doubt that the comtesse de Brézé would have been highly vulnerable had François I made her virtue the price for her father's head. At the time, she was twenty-four, noble, beautiful, and destined for a royal liaison. The "Chevalier King" was an irresistibly charming rake of twenty-seven, debonair and immensely, almost heroically dissolute. Under the circumstances, a brief affair would have been excused at a court where adultery was commonplace.

The rumormongers suggested that Brézé, moved by loyalty and hopes of preferment, closed his eyes to the king's lust for his young wife. And yet this was a man whose father had killed his own unfaithful spouse without hesitation, even though she was his king's sister, and in the knowledge that retribution was sure to follow. Louis de Brézé would never have allowed his wife to do something so dishonorable to them both, and Diane would not have dared to act without his permission. When the king himself heard the rumor, he replied that the pardon was in no way due to Diane de Poitiers, and demanded whether he was considered to be so cowardly as to exchange the life of a man for the honor of his daughter.

9. Françoise de Foix entertained other lovers besides the king. Hearing him approach her room one day, she hid one of them behind an arrangement of leaves in her fireplace. After making love to her, François urinated "copiously" into the fireplace.

CHAPTER FIVE

Defeat and Capture at Pavia

*J*UST as autumn of 1523 was turning the forests of the Touraine into shades of gold, the fruit that bore the queen's name—a new species of sweet green plum called the *reine claude*—ripened like the six children who played at her feet.[1] With her health failing, Queen Claude spent more and more time away from the court and remained with her children at Blois. After the birth of her youngest, Marguerite,[2] on June 5 that year, the queen had little strength to continue. All she could manage was to be half-carried from one armchair to another, from bedroom to nursery. Claude had married at fourteen, and her still growing body was not strong enough to overcome the inevitable calcium deficiency and onset of osteoporosis after giving birth to seven children in nine years. She had always limped, but after these births her hips became deformed, and walking was a torment. Because she was always modest and self-effacing, no one really noticed her absences from court, assuming her to be once again in childbed.

1. The eldest, a daughter, Louise, had died young.
2. Known in history as Margot, queen of Navarre.

Queen Claude, the daughter of Louis XII, gentle wife of François I, and mother of the future Henri II.

Claude's greatest pleasure had always been to stay with her children at Blois, where she had spent her own childhood, playing in the gardens and enjoying the good air heavy with the scent of wild roses. For some years now, Diane de Poitiers had been in waiting to the queen, and Claude liked to keep her near. Diane's quiet good sense and experience as a mother was a comfort to the frail queen and her children.

In 1523, Claude's eldest child, Charlotte, was eight years old. The dauphin François was a dreamy, gentle child of six, and the energetic and contentious Henri d'Orléans was one year his junior. It was his grandmother Louise de Savoie who had named Henri in honor of the English king, whom she made the baby's godfather in the vain hope that this gesture would help an alliance with England. There was also three-year-old Madeleine (the future queen of James V of Scotland), and little Charles d'Angoulême was just beginning to walk. The baby

Marguerite was still swaddled in her cradle. The nursery at Blois, Amboise, or Saint-Germain-en-Laye was always crowded with the servants traditionally needed to look after royalty of any age. There was no less than forty household staff to attend to the needs of these six Children of France, and seventy domestics just for the nursery quarters.

With the entire court installed at Blois that autumn, the manic round of festivities and hunts did not slacken on account of the queen's illness. At the same time, the news of the Constable de Bourbon's treason traumatized the court. How was it possible that the king's most trusted friend and servant could betray him? Had Bourbon not always been loyal and had he not distinguished himself by his courage fighting at Marignano, and later in defeating the Swiss mercenaries? Had the king not recognized his value and bestowed on him the title of "Constable of France," which had not been used for some fifteen years? Slowly, the whole sordid story emerged. The winter was harsh and the king remained with the court at Blois into the new year.

Nor did the building works at the château halt because of the presence of the court. Not only did François I build a number of new châteaux in the region of the Loire, but he altered and improved many of the existing ones. Possibly the most famous of these alterations is the staircase at Blois: its double helix is an almost feminine touch, for it was indeed built for the queen. As sovereign duchess of Brittany, Claude used the white ermine of that state as her symbol, one of the few creatures in nature that mate for life. As long as she lived, François added her device to his salamander symbol—that mythological lizard with blood so cold it could walk through fire unscathed.

The Renaissance was a time when such conceits were popular: if your blood was hot, as the king's surely was, then take as your symbol the opposite example. Not known for modesty, François I plastered his châteaux in the Loire with these lizards, and became known as the "Salamander King."[3] When the young Federigo Gonzaga, future Duke of Mantua, came to stay at the French court, he admired this device of the king's and took it for his own. The salamander can be seen

---

3. The stag was the traditional device of the Valois, but individuals in the family chose their own symbols as well.

on the ceilings and walls of his Palazzo del Te in Mantua—symbol of another hot-blooded prince of the same name.

*I*N Italy in the late autumn of 1523, another child's life was about to change dramatically. On November 19, Giulio de' Medici, cousin of Pope Leo X, was elected Pope Clement VII.

First and foremost, Clement VII was a Medici. He was industrious and worked hard to achieve his triple ambition: to secure the city of Florence; to secure his new domains, the Papal States; to defend Europe against the infidel Turk. To this end, he supported a royal alliance with France continuing the policy of his Medici uncle and predecessor Leo X, who had promoted the marriage of Clement's first cousin, Lorenzo, Duke of Urbino, to Madeleine de La Tour d'Auvergne, a kinswoman of the French king.

The young Giulio de' Medici had been brought up by his uncle Lorenzo and governed Florence from the time of Lorenzo's death in 1519. Devout, scholarly, interested in the arts, Giulio, together with Catherine de' Medici's grandmother, Alfonsina Orsini, had been appointed by Pope Leo X to take care of the baby Medici heiress. Catherine was the sole legitimate descendant of Lorenzo the Magnificent and heiress to the Medici hegemony of Florence; she had to be preserved. Her only young Medici cousins, Ippolito and Alessandro, were both illegitimate. Alessandro had been born to Giulio when he was still a cardinal by a beautiful black slave girl—hence his dark skin, tight curls, and nickname "*de Maure*," "of the Moor."

After Clement's election, Alfonsina Orsini brought her tiny granddaughter to Rome so that the pope could guard this fragile hope of a Medici succession. Ambassador Marco Minio reported home to Venice that when Clement VII saw the frail baby in the arms of her grandmother, he said with tears in his eyes, "*Recens fert aerumnas*"— "This child bears the sorrows of the Greeks" (in other words, her life will bear the hallmarks of a Greek tragedy).

Alfonsina Orsini died the following year, 1524, and Catherine's Medici aunt Clarissa Strozzi took her place as her guardian. The scholar Eugène Alberi wrote that "an astrologer was called in to draw up little Catherine's horoscope. It was said that he predicted for her a life full of sorrows, agitation, and storms, a life that was to be a perpetual sacrifice for the sake of French unity."

Indeed, once the French king's dream of a strong alliance with the Medici was destroyed with the deaths of the Duke and Duchess of Urbino, François tried to take charge of the orphaned Catherine, but Pope Leo refused him her custody. In 1525, at the age of six, Catherine returned to Florence with her cousin Alessandro, where she lived in the Medicis' Riccardi Palace.[4] While we can assume she spent the summer months at Poggio a Caiano, a Medici villa in the cooler hills surrounding Florence, no further details are known about her early childhood. Clement VII wrote to François I forbidding Catherine's uncle the Duke of Albany from administering her La Tour possessions, and insisting that the papal nuncio in Paris claim for Catherine the pension promised her by François I at her birth. Clement VII took his role as Catherine's guardian seriously!

*I*N December 1523, Emperor Charles V, encouraged by the defection of the Constable of France to his side, began to move into French territory. Outside Milan, he encountered Admiral Bonnivet, the favorite of François I, who had suffered one defeat after another while fever, plague, famine, and cold decimated his troops. Montmorency had raised a relief army of Swiss to come to Bonnivet's aid, but the snow over the Alps prevented him from accomplishing his mission. Bonnivet could have taken Milan with a final assault, but he preferred to negotiate which gave the city time to reinforce its walls and the imperial army of Charles de Lannoy, viceroy of Naples, a chance to relieve its forces. The king was in Paris when he heard the news that his admiral had retreated to await the Swiss reinforcements he had been promised. With the outer corners of his kingdom under attack, François I immediately rode out at the head of his army to defend his

4. It is still there.

most prized possession, Milan. Meanwhile, Bonnivet and Montmorency missed their rendezvous due to being hounded by the Spanish and the duc de Bourbon. A badly wounded Admiral Bonnivet gave up his command, and the French were forced to retreat over the Alps.

Fighting in the French rearguard, the famous Pierre du Terrail, chevalier de Bayard, known as "*Le chevalier sans peur et sans reproche*"— "The knight without fear or blame," who had knighted the king on the field at Marignano, was shot by a Spanish *arquebusier* and lay dying beneath a tree.[5]

According to Guillaume du Bellay, Bayard turned his face toward the enemy lines to await death, which was surely coming. His followers erected a tent over him and he ordered them to leave him as the Spanish were approaching. Bayard saw that the leader of the Spanish troops was the Constable de Bourbon, who approached stiffly and said to the dying hero: "It grieves me to see you in this state, you who have been such a courageous and virtuous knight." "Sir," replied Bayard, "do not pity me, for I die a righteous death. It is I who pity you, to see you serve against your prince, your country, and your solemn oath."[6]

In the spring of 1524, Charles de Bourbon, at the head of an imperial mixed army of Spaniards, Germans, and Italians numbering twenty thousand men, along with three hundred knights and eighteen pieces of artillery—a modest force at the time—invaded Provence, together with the Italian army of the viceroy of Naples, Charles de Lannoy. While Bourbon's troops ravaged the south, the imperial fleet attacked and pillaged along the coast. Town after town fell to the imperial army and Charles de Bourbon took the title "Comte de Provence."

After a most severe winter, the summer of 1524 brought a terrible drought, and bush fires erupted all around the Touraine, putting the harvest in jeopardy. One great fire destroyed the ancient city of Troyes in the northeast, and rumors spread that the agents of Charles V had begun the blaze. Inevitably, after the drought came the floods, high winds, and earth tremors.

While the fires were raging and the king was leading his army to Lyons against the invasion of France by Charles de Bourbon, Queen

5. The arquebus was an early rifle.
6. Brantôme, *Vie des dames illustres françaises et étrangères.* Volume 5 of *Oeuvres complètes.*

Claude died at Blois on July 24. Her many pregnancies had sapped her frail body, and her weakness was complicated, so it was whispered, by a disease she had caught from her husband. The king cried when he heard the news, and mourned his queen sincerely, declaring that he would give his own life to bring her back.

According to François' close friend Fleurange, he went into deep mourning, as did his mother and their entire suite. Fleurange wrote that the king was right to grieve for his wife, as there had never been a "more honest princess on earth, nor one more beloved in all the world, and everyone, young and old, believed that if she had not gone to Paradise, then few would go. . . ."

The superstitions of the Middle Ages still held with regard to royalty, and it was commonly believed that as long as the sovereign's body remained unburied, it could cause miracles. The body of the queen remained exposed for some time in the chapel at Blois, and the saintly little queen inspired pilgrimages to her catafalque. The children were also taken to pray by their mother's coffin, though there were now only five; Louise, the firstborn, who brought a good omen to Marignano, had died at age two in 1517, and eight-year-old Charlotte had died of measles shortly after her mother, on September 8. The king turned to Diane and appointed her to care for the royal children, the greatest honor he had shown her to date.

In view of the greater disaster of the war that had befallen France, the queen's death passed almost unnoticed. There is little to remind us of this gentle queen, "a pearl among women and a clear mirror of her own goodness without a single stain."[7]

While the king of France was in Lyons mourning his queen, he learned that Charles de Bourbon, now the emperor's lieutenant general, was attacking Marseilles. François headed south and arrived to find that the enemy had retreated; the effect of the plague on Bourbon's troops and the fierce resistance of the town forced the imperial army to withdraw. Provence was retaken by the French. As

---

7. Claude's duchy of Brittany, coveted by French kings for more than two hundred years, was not officially joined to France until 1532, when Queen Claude bequeathed Brittany to her eldest son, the dauphin, to be administered by her husband, François, during the boy's minority (until the age of fourteen).

Charles de Bourbon moved his army back to Italy, the king seized his chance to follow and take revenge on his traitorous cousin, and to reverse the losses of Bonnivet.

Louise de Savoie was anxious to prevent her son from making an impetuous advance and hurried to his side in Aix-en-Provence. She was too late, and moved on with speed to Avignon, arriving on October 5, 1524. Again, she missed her son. In Avignon, she heard the news she dreaded: François had pressed on toward the mountains after the Constable.

The French king's army was the best fighting force he had ever raised, and his soldiers had fought well all summer. Although the autumn was advancing, François was loath to lay these troops off for the winter. Against all advice, and with lightning speed, the king pressed home his advantage. By October 20 he had reached Milan, which he invested,[8] and was met by the representatives of the city. He accepted their homage but did not enter because of the plague. François I's approach appealed to the good Milanese, who had been obliged to change masters a dozen times in the past quarter century. Since they had refused to take up arms for the imperial viceroy Charles de Lannoy, they sent the keys of the city to the French king. Lannoy meanwhile moved his men on to the strategically important city of Lodi, which controlled the crossing of the Adda River.

François was further encouraged to hear that the pope, Clement VII, wished to change sides and join with France, possibly bringing Florence and Venice with him. With the promise of such extra force, the king advanced to lay siege to the fortified city of Pavia, which the main imperial army had occupied on leaving Milan. Pavia was the ancient capital of Lombardy, a fabled city of a hundred towers that had once rivaled Milan. It was well fortified, enclosed within thick walls on three sides; the Ticino River protected the fourth.

Bourbon eventually joined Charles de Lannoy and his exhausted troops in Lodi. Faced with the prospect of imminent battle against his former king and countrymen, Bourbon left to recruit more soldiers for the imperial cause. The garrison within Pavia was commanded by a

---

8. A military term for the surrounding or the hemming in of a town or fort by a hostile force.

Spaniard, Antonio de Leyva, whom Blaise de Montluc,[9] one of François I's most valiant marshals, described as the greatest general in Europe, were it not for his severe gout.

Word reached the château of Blois of a victory in Milan, but it was too soon for rejoicing. The king arrived at Pavia on October 24, 1524, and surrounded the city. Then, on November 9, with part of his army laid low by a stomach infection, and winter closing in, François mounted an assault that failed to dent the walls, or the resistance of the Spanish. The French regrouped and planned their next attack from a number of vantage points surrounding the walled and fortified town. The siege continued, and although the town sent word that there was no shortage of food, one of the French officers, Pierre d'Aumout, wrote home to his mother that he had heard the Spanish were beginning to eat their horses.

Winter arrived with its cold, rain, and fog. Still the king did not leave for France to wait to mount a spring offensive. Swiss reinforcements arrived for the French, as did others from Giovanni de' Medici (known as Giovanni della Bande Nere) in Florence. Boredom set in, and the French and Swiss troops complained of the cold. François tried to draw the enemy out by sending ten thousand of his soldiers to Naples. It was an expensive ruse and a mistake. The Spanish were not drawn out—and with reason. On the freezing cold night of February 3, 1525, reinforcements arrived for the besieged of Pavia from Lodi, where Lannoy had waited for Charles de Bourbon. With the emperor's money, the French traitor had succeeded in recruiting fresh troops— thirteen thousand Germans, six thousand Italians, three thousand Spanish, eight hundred lances, and a thousand light cavalry he would command himself. This mighty force, led by the imperialist Charles de Lannoy, the marquis de Pescara (said to be the cleverest of the Spanish generals), and Charles de Bourbon, encircled the French camp. François I found himself caught between the town's garrison and the imperial reinforcements. He decided to wait.

As the troops on both sides were demoralized and deserting, the impasse could not last forever. Charles de Lannoy chose to attack the

9. His full name was Blaise de Lasseran-Massencôme, seigneur de Montluc, Maréchal de France.

French during the early hours of February 24, the emperor's birthday and the Feast of Saint Matthew. His soldiers wore white tunics over their armor to help them recognize one another in the dark, and they set to work, breaching the walls of the park that lay outside the city. At first light, they succeeded: some seven thousand Spanish troops charged through the breached garden wall, cutting off the French line of retreat to Milan. As soon as they reached the city walls, they were able to reinforce their garrison inside.

At the sound of three cannon shots, the imperial troops on one side, and those from the Pavia garrison on the other, attacked the French, who were caught between them. As the fog lifted with the dawn, François saw that his position just north of the city between the Vernavola stream and the eastern wall of the Mirabello Park was still superior to that of the enemy. He held the high ground, and the troops inside Pavia were weak from starvation and taking a battering. The king and his horse wore full armor, and a white plume flowed from his helmet to his shoulders, making him instantly recognizable. The French were more than holding their own on both fronts, and their fortified line fought off the imperialist advance. All was going well until, inexplicably, the king, a chivalrous knight of the old school, decided to lead his heavy cavalry[10] in a wildly courageous but ill-considered charge—a *furia francese* across and in front of his own artillery's line of fire. This was a disastrous move as the French did not dare fire blindly into the mêlée for fear of hitting their own troops.

The heavy winter rains and flooded river had turned the plain around the town into a bog of clinging mud, which pinned down both men and horses. The Spanish light cavalry had a better chance of maneuvering than the French heavy cavalry, their riders' long lances proving useless among the trees in the park. Charging behind their mounted troops, the French infantryman were pelted by clods of mud flying from the horses' hooves. Frenchmen in heavy armor were pulled off their warhorses down into the mud by Spanish infantry hiding behind trees. Unable to move quickly, they were easily knifed through the joints of their armorplates. If the imperial soldiers could not find a gap to stab

10. The heavy cavalry consisted of larger, powerful warhorses known as destriers. Both horse and rider wore full armor.

through, they inserted their rifles into the suits of armor and fired. Grouped together, these primitive, slow-to-load, inaccurate rifles—the arquebus—with a range of four hundred yards, made the imperial soldiers invincible.

When the Swiss mercenaries saw that the situation was hopeless, they fled, abandoning the French cavalry, who fought on with heroic fervor. As his men were driven back in every direction, François' trumpeter could be heard again and again calling for help to come to the king's side. Disregarding the danger he was in, François drew the best of his nobles to surround him and fight. All of them perished, and on that day France lost the flower of its young nobility. The king's horse was shot from under him with twenty bullets. François continued fighting on foot, swiping at all comers with his great gold-hilted battle sword, until there was just one Frenchman left standing with him.

The Spanish *arquebusiers* had torn off his splendid silver surcoat, yet François fought on bravely to the last. Covered in blood and blinded from a gash above his eyebrow, he was wounded in the arm, hand, and leg, and unable to move for the bodies piled around him. His trumpeter, too, had been silenced. Encircled by the enemy aiming their arquebuses at him, the king was finally brought down. He would have been killed had not Charles de Lannoy recognized him by his splendid gold-inlaid armor, and the long plume hanging from his helmet. The viceroy and his bodyguard forced their way through the soldiers surrounding the stricken king. As the viceroy dismounted, François raised his visor in defeat. Charles de Lannoy kissed the king's hand and received his sword. Like jackals, Lannoy's Neapolitan soldiers hacked at François' armor for souvenir pieces—proof that they had been present at the capture of the king of France.

At Pavia on February 24, 1525 the French suffered their most bloody and decisive defeat since Agincourt in 1415. So many of the country's bravest and best lay dead. The Spanish took no prisoners other than those worthy of a great ransom. Eight thousand Frenchmen and mercenaries lost their lives, while only seven hundred of the imperial troops were killed. Among the king's friends, Fleurange and Montmorency were captured. Admiral Bonnivet, a veteran of many battles, declared: "I cannot survive such disaster, such destruction," and opened his visor to face certain death. When the Constable saw the body of Bonnivet, who had been given his command in the French army, he is said to have declared: "Miserable man—you are the cause of France's ruin and my own."[11]

The emperor's lieutenant, the viceroy of Naples, showed there was still chivalry in warfare. He escorted the king to a monastery nearby so that his wounds could be dressed and he could avoid being taken into Pavia as a prisoner. As ill luck would have it, at the monastery François came face-to-face with his former Constable. The king ignored him, but Charles de Bourbon had triumphed.

WITH François in custody, there was nothing to prevent Charles de Bourbon conquering France and taking whatever he wanted. But the emperor would not risk Bourbon claiming such a prize and did not allow him to advance.

As soon as she received news of the defeat at Pavia and her son's capture, Louise de Savoie immediately set about organizing the internal defense of an incredulous country. The remnants of the court—women, old men, and children—were traumatized by the French defeat. There was not one among them who had not suffered a loss. With her son, her "Caesar" in captivity, and Queen Claude dead, it was up to Louise de Savoie to hold the country together and negotiate for the king's return. Her first thought was for François, and she sent him encouraging letters. She saw that Henry VIII had to be neutralized, and convinced the English king that to attack France would only help the emperor. Her task now was to negotiate with Charles V for her son's release. In order to be nearer Italy and news of François, the regent and her daughter Marguerite moved to Lyons. There can be no doubt that France lost the Battle of Pavia partly due to the treachery of the duc de Bourbon, and Louise de Savoie must have known she had contributed greatly to this. All her formidable intelligence and energy became engaged in saving what she could of the debacle.

11. Robert III de La Marck, seigneur de Fleurange (1491–1537), wrote the chronicle of his life while in Spanish captivity. It is an excellent source.

Fate was not kind to Marguerite's husband, the duc d'Alençon. Described as "a man of shallow understanding," he had the misfortune to survive the Battle of Pavia without injury. Left without orders, he did not join the king but, in his retreat, destroyed the bridges behind him and made his way to Lyons. There he met with a torrent of blame from the regent and from his wife. One month later, he died of pleurisy, although a number of historians incorrectly claim he died just after his arrival, unable to live with his shame and remorse.

Louis de Brézé was not at Pavia. As Grand Sénéchal, his role was to secure Normandy, which was vulnerable to an attack by the English. Shortly after the battle, Louise de Savoie appointed him governor of Normandy, a position of honor previously held by the duc d'Alençon, and usually reserved for a Prince of the Blood. It was, therefore, a mark of the great faith the regent had placed in him to hold Normandy against the English.

Diane was at Rouen when she heard the news of the French defeat and of the king's capture. At the request of the regent she returned to court and, in the absence of their father, comforted the royal children, who knew and loved her.

CHAPTER SIX

Imprisonment

$\mathcal{A}$S the prisoner-king of France was led on a mule through the battlefield, his eyes filled with tears when he recognized so many of his friends lying dead—Bonnivet, Bussy d'Amboise, François de Lorraine, the seventy-year-old veteran La Trémoille, the comte de Toulouse-Lautrec, René de Brosse, and René Batard de Savoie. In heavy rain, François I was escorted to the sinister fortress of Pizzighettone, near Cremona. There he remained in a tower for eighty days in isolation and discomfort. From there he wrote his first letter following the defeat to his mother: "Madame, all is lost save honor and my life." The king's words moved his mother so much that Marguerite replied to her brother: "Your letter has had such an effect on Madame, and on all those who love you, that it has been to us a Holy Ghost after the sorrow of the Passion. . . . Madame has felt her strength so greatly redoubled, that all day and evening not a minute is lost for your affairs, so that you need not have any pain or care about your realm and your children."

The king's fellow prisoners and friends, Montmorency and Philippe Chabot de Brion,[1] tried their best to distract him, but they were soon exchanged for imperial prisoners of equal importance. The *dead* French officers were also traded by the victorious imperialists, their corpses exchanged for gold. While François waited to hear the emperor's terms for a peace, and tried to forget the horror of the battle, he diverted himself with a little dog, two goldfinches, and a magpie. He wrote nostalgic poetry, and some melancholy verses to his mistress, Françoise de Foix. His routine was described by one of the officers on guard: "the king heard Mass daily and wore only black in mourning for his dead." Surprisingly, François was allowed to keep his dagger, with which he toyed constantly. The same guard described his hands as extraordinarily beautiful—strange for a large man who fought with a heavy two-handed sword.

François I felt sure that were he able to speak with Charles V they could quickly come to terms for a binding treaty, but that if this task was left to the courtiers, his incarceration would surely be long. More than anything, Charles V wanted Burgundy, which he believed should have been his by inheritance from his Burgundian ancestor, Marie the Rich, daughter of the last duke, Charles the Bold. Time after time, the king's negotiators explained to the emperor that he had no right to Burgundy under feudal law, because the inheritance he claimed came through the female line. Of course, the same could be said of the French claim to Milan.

The viceroy of Naples, Charles de Lannoy, was uncomfortable having to guard the French king in Italy where so many of the population had until recently owed their allegiance to him. François' cousin, Henri d'Albret of Navarre, had already escaped. Lannoy decided that the king must be moved to Spain. François welcomed this decision as he felt certain a treaty would only be made if he and Charles could meet. In May 1525, François was taken from Pizzighettone to Genoa, where he boarded a Spanish galleon. Escorted by a number of other ships, the king of France left ostensibly for Naples. The Spanish were taking no chances in case the great sea captain Andrea Doria, who was on the side of France, might rescue him; but no attempt was

1. Philip Chabot, seigneur de Brion, comte de Charny et de Buzançais, prince de Châtel-Aillon.

made.[2] In June, the king disembarked on the Costa Brava, where the convoy took to horse and headed for Barcelona.

The prisoner-king, a famously brave and handsome cavalier, made a triumphant entry into the capital of Catalonia and was treated as if on a state visit. At the cathedral he heard Mass seated on a throne, appearing more like visiting royalty. After two days of festivities during which François attended a bullfight, the king and his jailers continued on their journey, stopping at Tarragon and at Valencia, the ancient capital of the Moors. All the while, messengers passed back and forth between king and emperor, who continued to haggle over Burgundy. It may appear strange that the captured king of France was treated more like a conquering hero in Spain than a prisoner. Despite all the brutality of war, nostalgia for the Age of Chivalry still lingered among the mighty warriors of the day. As long as the king of France was in a position to grant the emperor's dearest wish—namely, to cede him Burgundy—François I could be received as a guest by the nobility of Spain.

Louise de Savoie sent a mission of bishops to Spain to negotiate, but they, too, found only deaf ears. She offered the emperor a fortune in return for the safe delivery of her son, but he did not want money. Charles V persisted in his claim to Burgundy, that beautiful part of France which had been the Holy Roman Emperor's reason for going to war.

Still en route to Madrid, the convoy stopped at Guadalajara, where the defeated king was welcomed even more like a conquering hero by the reigning duke.[3] Here François was greeted by triumphal arches, flower-strewn roads, music, and guards of honor firing salutes. The duke showed his guest—as he viewed the king—his palace studded with precious stones, and invited him to attend a banquet laid for hundreds of guests in his honor. On parting, the duke offered François extraordinary gifts for a man about to go to prison: exquisitely saddled horses, falcons, hunting dogs, golden bibelots. All that the prisoner-king had to give his host was a short sword, declaring that in France a man of such generosity could only be called a prince.

By mid-August, François had reached Madrid, where his triumphal

2. Montmorency's antagonism to Doria was such that eventually the captain changed sides and fought for the emperor.
3. The 4th duke of Infantado, Don Iñigo Hurtado de Mendoza.

progress ended rudely and abruptly. He was taken to the royal palace of Alcazar (now demolished), where he was housed in a cell no larger than five paces square. His window was heavily barred and an armed guard was stationed at his door. There could be no longer any doubt: the king of France was a prisoner.

Deprived of the physical exercise he had enjoyed every day of his life, François fell ill and developed an abscess in his nose. He would not eat and the Spanish doctors feared he might die as he was unable to speak, hear, or see. A dead hostage was of no use to the emperor, so Charles V came to Madrid, promising to release the king and treat him well. In his desperation, François had written begging his mother to come to him or he would surely die. Much as she loved her son, as regent, Louise de Savoie put her country first. If she came to Spain and was kidnapped by the emperor, what would become of France? Instead, she requested a safe-conduct for her daughter. The widowed Marguerite, with her tact, intelligence, beauty, and charm, would surely be able to negotiate for her brother and persuade the emperor to terms other than ceding Burgundy.

Marguerite de Valois, duchesse d'Alençon, was two years older than the king. She was tall, attractive, and devoted to her brother. She was also highly intelligent, charming, an intellectual, and had proven her worth to François during a number of delicate diplomatic exchanges. On her arrival at Madrid, Marguerite was cordially received by the members of the imperial court, but she soon realized that neither the emperor nor his courtiers were willing to meet any of her requests. Marguerite persisted, but despite her winning ways, the men of the court would avoid her on instructions from Charles V. Brantôme wrote of her discussions with the emperor:

> I have heard it said that during this time when she was in Spain, she spoke to the Emperor with such courage and nobility about his bad treatment of her brother the king that he was amazed. She reproached him for the hardness of his heart and for having so little care for such a great and good king; for such a noble, royal, and sovereign heart as that of her brother the king would not be won in dealing with him in this way. If he were to die as a result of this harsh treat-

ment, then his death would not go unpunished, for he had children who would one day be grown and would seek revenge.

She said these words with such force and courage that the emperor reconsidered his actions, visited the king, and promised him many good things which he then did not deliver right away.

If this queen spoke well to the emperor, then she spoke even better when given an audience with his council, where she triumphed with her good words and arguments, and her abundant good grace. Marguerite did not speak with anger or with hate but with pleasantness, and was also the young, beautiful widow of M. d'Alençon, in the flower of her youth.[4] All of this is what it takes to touch the hardest and cruellest people.

Meanwhile, the regent Louise de Savoie bribed everyone she could. Henry VIII received a fortune in gold to remain at peace with France. His cardinal, Thomas Wolsey, was also paid a large sum not to agitate for war. French claims and rights to Milan, together with the hand of one of the French princesses, were offered to the reigning Sforza duke there.

Even Pope Clement VII benefited from French largesse—France's enemies were being neutralized. Louise de Savoie looked beyond Europe for support. Then, on instructions from the king, she did the unthinkable. As regent of France, she sent an emissary to the Ottoman emperor, Suleiman the Magnificent. The Turk was an enemy of Christianity, and that also made him an enemy of the emperor. The first French courier was misunderstood and murdered, so the regent chose another, a Croatian, whose family was long established in France, with the exotic name of Frangipani.[5] He hid the royal message inside the heel of his boot, together with a golden signet ring to be given as a sign of François I's friendship. This initiative had little actual success because the Sultan did not offer money for the king's ransom—but it opened the door for a future alliance against the emperor. Even today, it seems

4. Marguerite was not yet queen of Navarre at this time.
5. Frangipani, or Ferdinand Frangepan de Veglia, belonged to one of the great families of Croatia. He was a great-grandson of Alfonso V, king of Naples, and is an ancestor of the current Prince of Wales.

an extraordinary initiative on behalf of The Most Christian King of France to take as an ally the infidel Sultan Suleiman to fight against the Holy Roman Emperor. From this time dates the remarkable relationship that France has enjoyed with the East.

The Sultan Suleiman the Magnificent, ruler of the Ottoman Empire.

Charles V remained immovable in his demands, and Louise's emissaries were in no position to sway him. The terms of the final treaty were so harsh that all of France united behind its defeated king, and countless citizens offered to share his imprisonment. (Conscious of the advantages to his family resulting indirectly from the treaty, Louis de Brézé was one of the first to offer.) According to the treaty, France was obliged to cede to the emperor the duchy of Burgundy, as well as Flanders and Artois. The king was to renounce his hereditary claims to the duchy of Milan and the Kingdom of Naples. Henry VIII was to be given all the former lands of the Plantagenets—Guyenne, Périgord, Aquitaine, Poitou, Anjou, and Normandy. Charles de Bourbon was to add Provence to his vast holdings in central France, a separate kingdom in all but name. As an added slight, the emperor gave the duchy of Milan to the traitorous Constable.

By the same treaty, the confiscated Bourbon lands in France were all returned to Charles de Bourbon, and the instigators of the plot against François I—including Jehan de Saint-Vallier—were pardoned and released from prison, their titles and properties restored. François wrote a letter in 1526 making it clear that, not only was Saint-Vallier's confiscated property returned to him, but he received more than he had held before. The king's decree stated: "Item: that the counties of

Valentinois[6] and Diois, belonging to Jehan de Poitiers through his rightful inheritance from Aymar de Poitiers his predecessor, should be returned to him along with their rights and privileges, and the fruits which have grown since these were confiscated, until the present day."

With France decimated through this treaty, there would be little left for the king to rule, and the country would certainly no longer be a formidable continental power. The Italian dream had dissolved. The emperor even demanded that France's mercenary army and ships be used to escort him to Rome so that the pope could finally place the crown of Charlemagne on his head.

To general surprise, Charles V did not invade France. His armies were spread throughout his empire and difficult to reassemble. His resources were greatly overstretched in Germany, with Lutheran preachers urging a break from the Catholic Church, and by peasant revolts in many areas due to poor harvests. Despite the enormous riches coming from Spain's territories in the New World—unlimited amounts, it seemed, of Inca gold, precious stones, and metals—not enough survived the exigencies of storms and pirates, and the Spanish coffers were empty. The mercenaries in the army had not been paid for some time and were deserting. The Holy Roman Empire was such a mixture of nationalities and cultures that the various populations had no common goal around which to unite.

The French nation, on the other hand, was uniting in solidarity against the terrible humiliation of its loss and anger at the crippling terms of the Treaty of Madrid. France was the motherland and she was worth defending. A national spirit rose up.

Because Charles V's forces were spread so wide and thin, he did not dare invade France without the participation of the English—and this was a risk Henry VIII was not prepared to undertake. The English king reasoned that if the emperor added part of France to his empire, Charles V would be so powerful that Henry might even find himself threatened. Instead, Henry VIII sent his ambassador, John Taylor, to visit the royal children at Amboise on the Loire, bringing them each a riding mare and two mastiffs. Taylor reported to Cardinal Wolsey that the two young

6. The county of Valentinois had been raised to a duchy by Louis XII, which might explain why Diane was referred to by that name before 1548, when she did indeed receive the title.

princes were most attractive, with charming manners, that they each shook him by the hand, asked politely about the English king's welfare, and thanked him with a mixture of dignity and delight at the gifts. "Verily, they be goodly children, Your Majesty's godson [Henri d'Orléans] is a quicker spirit and the bolder, as seemeth by his behaviour."

After three further months of discussion, François and Marguerite decided on a ruse to frighten the emperor into making concessions. They pretended that should François be kept in Spain indefinitely, the king would abdicate to secure the future of the French monarchy, that the dauphin would then be crowned in all haste and the emperor's prisoner would lose his value. The king wrote an act of abdication in favor of the dauphin which he gave to Anne de Montmorency, who had been exchanged for a high-ranking imperial prisoner of the French. This message was addressed to the regent and stated that should anything happen to Madame Louise, then the regency should pass to his "most dear and beloved only sister" during the minority of the heir to the throne. For this reason, François was anxious about the safety of Marguerite—he did not want the emperor to hold another hostage—and insisted that she leave Madrid at once. Traveling in easy stages in a comfortable litter, Marguerite received word from François not to risk being caught in Spain after December 25, the day her safe-conduct would expire. Marguerite immediately took to horse and galloped for the border where a French escort waited—arriving just one hour before the pass became void. Marguerite was safe and the king's letter of abdication was no longer required.

$\mathcal{F}$RANÇOIS I never had any intention of abiding by the Treaty of Madrid. Despite his promises sworn on the gospels, he reasoned with his courtiers that just as the emperor had broken his promise to release him as he lay seriously ill in his prison cell, so too could a king break his word to a treaty forced on him under duress. In fact, the thought of reneging on his sworn promise so distressed François that once again he fell ill with a raging fever. There would be a high price to pay if the king violated the signed agreement.

To guarantee that François I kept the peace once he returned home, the treaty stated that either his two eldest sons, or the dauphin and ten of François' most senior courtiers (including Louis de Brézé), were to be sent to Madrid for an indefinite period. To be a hostage for the king was indeed a dangerous honor as François I had already secretly declared to his staff in December, prior to the signing of the Treaty of Madrid on January 14, 1526, that he had no intention of adhering to it.

It was Louise de Savoie who chose to send the two little princes into exile rather than her son's ten most important courtiers. What use was the throne to him, she reasoned, if he had no advisers or senior nobles by his side? She desperately wanted her son back in France, and the idea of having to serve as regent until the dauphin came of age in five years was not practical—her health would not hold. Madame Louise insisted that François return and take charge of his kingdom. Finally, at the end of December 1525, the king agreed to the Treaty of Madrid, accepting the horrific sacrifice of sending his two eldest boys into captivity in place of himself. Louise knew her son well, and realized that the conclusion of such an ignominious treaty was certain to push him to war again.

There was only one more aspect of the treaty to complete before the exchange of hostages. François I was to meet his new queen. As was so often the case, there had to be a dynastic bond to cement an important agreement between two nations. The Treaty of Madrid stipulated that the king of France must marry the virtuous widow, Eleonore of Habsburg, queen-dowager of Portugal and sister of the emperor. (When he heard of this condition, François exclaimed he would happily marry the emperor's *mule* to be back in France again.) It would seem the libertine king was condemned to marry saints. Furthermore, Queen Eleonore's daughter, Maria of Portugal, was to be betrothed to the dauphin. This condition would at least bring the poor dowager-queen Eleonore some joy, as she had been forced to leave her son and daughter in Portugal when her husband died and return to Spain alone.

Marriage to Eleonore was the only part of the Treaty of Madrid that was palatable to François, since she was only twenty-seven and rather attractive. At the age of eighteen Eleonore had been obliged to marry the seventy-year-old king Emmanuel "the Fortunate" of Portugal, so the prospect of a union with the young, dashing, and handsome king of France had considerable appeal for Eleonore as well. Earlier, the emperor had offered his sister to Charles de Bourbon. Although we have no sure knowledge of Eleonore's feelings, faced with a choice between that somber traitor, who would have reduced her title to duchess, and the handsome, thirty-two-year-old Chevalier King, it seems obvious whom she would have chosen. It was Marguerite who urged the conclusion of this part of the treaty. She surmised, quite rightly, that an alliance by marriage between her brother and the emperor's sister would speed the king's release. In fact, the emperor was so fascinated by Marguerite's charm and ability that he sent a letter to Louise de Savoie proposing himself as *her* future husband.

Since the widowed Queen Eleonore resided at Illiesca, between Madrid and Cáceres, both king and emperor arrived there on February 17, 1526. The Spaniards were justifiably proud of Eleonore's brunette beauty—and her "pretty, full lips." The next morning, the bride and bridegroom met in a little house in the Calle Mayor where François had been billeted.[7] When Eleonore saw him and made to kiss his hands in greeting, the king declared himself charmed and gallantly countered that he would prefer to kiss her lips.[8] The betrothed couple spent the night there. In the morning, the emperor asked his sister to dance for the king, and it is said that François was truly enchanted with her.

Following this brief encounter at Illiesca, the future queen of France bid her husband-to-be and her brother farewell. Both king and emperor departed on their separate ways, the one to France, the other to his own wedding with the pretty Isabella of Portugal. Despite signing the Treaty of Madrid, François I was still not living as a free man; in fact, his guards were increased. At San Sebastian near the border, he wrote to the emperor asking whether Eleonore could join him soon, preferably before Holy Week. Eleonore must have pleased François as it was customary for Catholic couples to abstain from intercourse during Lent.

---

7. It is still there today.
8. To greet even a stranger with a kiss on the lips was normal practice in the sixteenth century.

CHAPTER SEVEN

The Hostages

HE time had come for the royal hostages to leave their beloved Amboise, their sisters Elizabeth and Madeleine, little Charles too young to appreciate their plight, the baby Marguerite, as well as the many young friends who lived with them there by the Loire. There is no record of how or when the two boys were told they were to take their father's place as hostages against his word, but as their aunt Marguerite was at Blois in early February, it was likely that she undertook this unenviable task. Their journey was most probably presented to them as an adventure as well as a duty; they would be ransomed very soon and treated according to their rank just as their father had been. The little princes began their journey toward the Pyrenees accompanied by their grandmother the regent, her court, and her ladies, among them Diane de Poitiers whom they knew so well, and their own staff, including their dwarf.

Louise de Savoie had aged noticeably during her son's imprisonment. She knew that her behavior toward the Constable had been responsible in part for all the misfortune that had befallen France and her efforts as regent had ruined her already fragile health. Madame Louise suffered badly from gout and many stops were necessary to ease the pain of the jolting litter. The cortège made slow progress.

As honored hostages, the two princes were able to take their personal suite of one hundred and eighty with them to Spain. However, the main escort of soldiers and all the court, who had come to welcome home their king, were not permitted to go further than Bayonne, which they reached the night of March 15. François' imminent arrival created a carnival atmosphere, and the cruel fate of the princes was almost forgotten. The dauphin, François, was eight years old; Henri was six. The dauphin was bright, like his father, and eager for adventure. The general air of celebration appealed to him; he was distracted by the glamour of the costumes and the large escort of soldiers who had arrived at Bayonne with them.

In the early morning of March 17, 1526, the princes made their heart-rending, tearful farewells to their grandmother and her ladies. On this cold gray day, the normally ebullient Henri reminded the courtiers of his sad mother Queen Claude—shy, timid, and in tears. How this day would have broken her heart. Diane de Poitiers, whose own two daughters were almost of the same age as the princes, saw the miserable little Henri with his head bowed, tiny shoulders hunched, and tears running down his cheeks. She ran out of the crowd of ladies and held the little boy in her arms, murmuring gentle, soothing words, and then kissed him.[1] The little prince was to remember her kindness and dream of her gentle beauty during the four loveless years he was incarcerated in a Spanish fortress. The comfort Diane gave the motherless Henri on that day eventually grew into a love that would only end with his death.

As dawn broke, two large rowing boats left opposite banks of the Bidassoa River, three miles upstream from the sea at San Sebastian. Both sides of the river had been cleared of people—farmers, shepherds, and soldiers evacuated as far as ten leagues away. Neither camp was taking any chances. The boat coming from the French side carried the princes, a French officer, and ten gentlemen armed with swords and

1. Biographers often describe this as Diane and Henri's first kiss, which is most unlikely as Diane de Poitiers had spent much of her time with the queen in the royal nursery, and had known all the children since their birth.

daggers. The boat from the Spanish bank carried the French king, a Spanish officer, and ten gentlemen similarly armed. Soon the barges, manned by the same number of oarsmen, reached a pontoon anchored in the middle of the river.

The king arrived first. It was twenty months since he had seen his sons, and as they landed, he embraced them together. François I loved his children and was at a loss for words as he held them. He had used them as pawns in this great diplomatic maneuver and yet was disarmed by their youth and misery. Moreover, he knew full well that their condition in prison would depend on his adherence to the Treaty of Madrid, a treaty he had no intention of keeping. Nevertheless, François reasoned that the fate of France must take precedence over that of his family. Tears welled and fell from the king's eyes as he lamely promised they would be well treated and soon be ransomed. He then gave his sons a father's blessing, and without looking back, was rowed to France.

From the French bank, the king stood and watched his sons disembark in Spain, but his joy at being back in France soon eased the pain of the parting. Mounting his horse, a fast Arabian, he left with all speed for Saint-Jean-de-Luz, exclaiming loudly: "God be praised—I am still the king!"

*A*T Bayonne François found his mother waiting. To welcome her "beau César" back to France, the regent Louise had gathered together all the beauties of the court, including Diane de Poitiers. The king was surprised not to find his thirty-year-old mistress, Françoise de Foix, among them; Louise, who loathed her, had contrived to have her remain at home in Brittany. Instead, his mother presented to her son an eighteen-year-old, clever, blond beauty from Picardy, with the unfortunate name of Anne de Pisseleu,[2] who had been carefully schooled by Louise for this role. She was the daughter of the seigneur d'Heilly who, having been married three times, had thirty

2. Meaning "worse than a wolf."

children. The king was delighted with Anne.[3] For the next few months, both Françoise and Anne shared his favors, but as one can imagine, the atmosphere between the two women was arctic. Finally Anne won the king, and Françoise returned to her husband, while the king sent some cruel lines to his grieving mistress:

> . . . *Pour le temps qu'avec toi j'ai passé,*
> *Je puis bien dire: "Requiescat in pace."*

(As for the time I've spent with you,/I can only say: "Rest in peace.")

Anne, with her blond pallor and piercing blue eyes, was very different from her predecessor. Even though she had not been faithful to the king,[4] Françoise de Foix was a grand mistress, a distinguished beauty, and a true companion to him. Anne de Pisseleu was clearly only interested in what she had to gain from François—power, influence, and riches for herself and her large family.

The poet Clément Marot described her:

> *Dix et huit ans je vous donne*
> *Belle et bonne;*
> *Mais, à vôtre sens rassis,*
> *Trente-cinq ou trente-six*
> *J'en ordonne.*

(I give you eighteen years/But with your serene composure/You appear nearer thirty-five or six.)

Perhaps captivity had warped the king's sense of judgment, but Anne was, after all, the choice of Louise de Savoie, who felt that she had more control over the young girl than over the exquisite, more mature François de Foix. Louise had trained Anne de Pisseleu for three years as her lady-in-waiting, and at the regent's court, Anne had served her apprenticeship in how to flirt and seduce.

In order to restore himself in the people's esteem and affection, the

---

3. There was a rumor that François had met and flirted with Anne de Pisseleu some years earlier, when she had just turned fifteen.

4. Francoise de Foix had affairs with Admiral Bonnivet and the Constable Charles de Bourbon.

king of France decided to make a grand "progress" through his kingdom. By visiting his cities and larger towns he also hoped to raise
enough money to refill the exchequer emptied by the recent wars and
to pay the huge indemnity demanded by the emperor.

In 1528, the king was at Rouen, capital of Normandy, to make his
official entry into that city. He was the guest of his Grand Sénéchal,
Louis de Brézé, who handed him the keys to the city. Instead of the
usual rows of worthy gentlemen to greet him, Diane de Poitiers had
arranged for a large number of pretty little flower girls, dressed in light
Grecian shifts, to scatter rose petals before the royal procession.
François was so charmed by this innovation and the splendid reception
Rouen gave him that he decided to interrupt his progress, and invited
himself to Anet for a few days' hunting. Since the death of Queen
Claude, Diane no longer held an official position at court, but she was
with her husband at Saint-Germain-en-Laye where the court spent
most of January, February, and March of that year.

Until the king's visit in 1528, Diane had not been sure whether her
father's treachery, and the opprobrium of his guilt, would affect the
king's relationship with her and her husband. During his stay with
them at Anet, François showed how much he admired Diane, her intelligence and culture. He was impressed by her tall, supple, fit body.
She galloped with him on long rides through the forests, her blond
hair tied in a snood of blue velvet ribbons joined with pearls, a short
veil brushing the nape of her neck. As they rode in the forests, the king
and Diane would stop occasionally to rest and talk, and she was relieved to sense his approval once again. She had so feared that her
father's treason would color their relationship, but her charm worked
in her favor. The king remained longer than planned at Anet, and during his stay he invited Diane to take up another official position at
court as a *dame d'honneur* (matron of honor) to his mother, Louise de
Savoie.

It was during this stay at Anet that the king decided to form his
band of twenty-seven maids of honor, "*La Petite Bande.*" Chosen for
their looks and intelligence, these young beauties were to accompany
his court wherever it went, and he invited the glorious châtelaine of
Anet to be one of their number. In making his choices, François looked

to his sister, the incomparable Marguerite, as his ideal. The king would dominate the lives of these twenty-seven young ladies. He dressed them like dolls to his taste and paid for their clothes. A lady's size did not disqualify her from joining the *Bande* (the rotund Madame de Canaples required sixteen "ells" [lengths] of silk to make a court dress when the average was eleven), but all had to excel in the saddle.

Princes could not choose their wives, but at least they could choose their companions and mistresses. It is certain that the king "sampled" a number of the ladies of his *Petite Bande,* but he was always courteous and treated all women with respect.[5] François I embodied the dichotomy of the time; despite his exquisite manners, he could be very crude in his jokes—even in the presence of ladies. Nor was he at all discreet about his conquests—but few at court could resist the dashing king.

*T*HE little princes were put into the custody of two Spanish gentlemen: the Constable of Castile, Don Iñigo Hernandez de Valasco, and his son, the marquis de Berlanga, who saw to it that they lacked for nothing. The emperor's gentle sister Eleonore, soon to become their stepmother, also kept a maternal eye on them. Initially, they were held in the duc de Frias' fortress in Villalba, originally built for the Knights Hospitalers and big enough to accommodate some eight hundred men. The French suite, headed by René de Cossé-Brissac, consisted of seventy lords and officers and one hundred and fifty servants paid by the king to tend to his sons. The maître d'hôtel was Louis de Ronsard, seigneur de la Poissonnière, father of the famous French poet Pierre de Ronsard. Accompanying them was also Brissac's wife and the boys' tutor, Tagliacarno.

Although the captivity of the French princes began relatively agreeably, it soon became apparent to the French staff that François I

5. From the royal household accounts we know that some of the *Petite Bande* had other duties than entertaining the king and sharing his company. There is an entry from François to his treasurer: "We wish and order you to pay from our funds to Cécile de Viefville, lady of the *'filles de joie'* following our Court, the sum of 45 livres for services during the month of May just passed."

had absolutely no intention of ceding any territory to Spain. Moreover, the agreement to cede Burgundy was to have been kept secret until the king had a chance to inform his good people there. Unfortunately, this condition of the Treaty of Madrid had leaked to the Burgundians. The elders of Burgundy complained that they had not been consulted by the king, and simply refused to comply with the treaty. François I informed Charles V that he could not force them to join his empire. He pointed out that the emperor was not abiding by his agreements either—why had he not sent Eleonore to France?

The king called his first meeting of his senior councilors at Dax and asked their advice. He proposed that if they were unable or unwilling to raise a large amount of money to restore the princes to France, then he would willingly go back to Spain and take their place. It was not the first time the king had offered to abdicate—Louise de Savoie had refused to allow him to do so after Pavia.

Following France's defeat at Pavia, Pope Clement VII had switched his allegiance to Charles V. But the spread of Charles' empire, and its stranglehold on the various Italian states, frightened the pope and he reverted his allegiance to the French king, making every effort to form a coalition against the emperor. When envoys from Venice and the Vatican came to visit the king at the end of March to persuade him to join a holy league against the emperor, he seemed interested, and prepared to leave his sons in Spain for two or three years. François said the boys would come to no harm; they would learn the language and make useful contacts. Nothing could have been further from the truth.

On April 26, 1526, the Papal States, France, Venice, and England all joined to form the League of Cognac, with the aim of expelling the imperial forces from Italy and bringing the hostage French princes home. On June 21, the chancellor of France officially announced to the viceroy of Naples and the Spanish ambassador that the Treaty of Madrid was null and void. Also in June the imperial viceroy, Charles de Lannoy, tried to take Burgundy by force and was repulsed—not by the king's army, but by the Burgundians themselves.

In July, war began again between France and the empire, and inevitably, the little princes had to pay for their father's breach of trust. The duc de Frias had died and the two Sons of France were transferred to the hostile fortress of Villalpando near Zamora, where their situation worsened considerably. An alleged escape plot resulted in thirty-one of their suite being jailed, including René de Cossé-Brissac, his son, the comptroller, the chaplain, and their staff; a number of the serving men were sent to the galleys[6] and some even sold as slaves.

By the end of August, the princes' French staff had almost all been replaced by about twenty Spanish guards under a brutal captain named Péralta. These guards spoke only Spanish. Louise de Savoie wrote to the chancellor of England, Cardinal Thomas Wolsey, to complain of the inhumane treatment of her grandsons, who had been deprived of their French servants by Henry VIII's ally the emperor. The English ambassador, who saw the boys in October 1526, reported:

> They be goodly children and promising, as we might, for so short a time, judge. Tagliacarno could not enough praise the Duke of Orléans of wit, capacity, and great will to learn, and of a prudence and gravity passing this age, besides treatable gentleness and nobleness of mind, whereof daily he avoweth to see great sparks, as may be seen in this tender age. He much passeth his brother in learning, and in manner hath overcome the rudiments of his grammar. Tagliacarno said that one day, on their removal to the castle where we found them, "he called nothing of them for learning"; but the duke, seeing him sit alone, came running to him, and said "Ah, master, now that I have you, you shall not go from me ever that you teach me my lesson."

In case any of the guards should feel sympathy with the young princes, others were placed to spy on them. Even the French priest who had been charged to report to France on the princes' welfare was prevented from doing so. Henri was a naughty child, who teased his jailers and grew fat on a diet of greasy Spanish food and lack of sufficient exercise. Occasionally the princes were allowed to ride in the countryside, the dauphin on a mule and Henri on a little mare with two grooms holding his bridle on either side in case he might gallop off out of frustration. François seemed to adapt better to prison conditions

---

6. A dreadful punishment as few survived the backbreaking pulling of the oars.

and faced his situation with fortitude, but Henri became increasingly bitter and never lost his sense of injustice over their treatment. All his life he would blame the emperor and hate the Spanish.

When even these privations imposed on the princes appeared to have little effect on the king of France, and Burgundy was no nearer the emperor's grasp, Charles went further. In January 1527, the noose was tightened; all the princes' French attendants were removed except their tutor and the dwarf. According to Joachim du Bellay, Henri fell ill and "was in danger of his life"; but it may be that this report to the English court was intended to annoy the emperor. In June, the discovery and execution of a French spy caused the two princes to be transferred again, this time to the château-prison of Pedrazza de la Sierra, north of Madrid. There they lived in two small adjoining cells, each with one little barred window above their reach. The cells were icy in the winter and in summer suffocatingly hot. The princes were never left alone but were spied on night and day by four Spanish guards, and they were only rarely allowed outside into the fresh air. Their rations were meager portions of salty dried fish, and seldom any meat—a poor diet for growing boys.

When Queen Eleonore heard of the boys' latest situation, she was so distressed that she retired to a monastery. With minimal tutoring, no companions their own age, and only their Spanish jailers around them all the time, the dauphin and his brother learned a vulgar Spanish and strange manners. A letter exists from March 1528 to the king from Brissac asking for more money as the boys "were increasing in virtue and size" and what clothes they had brought with them were worn out. In 1529, the spy Clermont reported to Anne de Montmorency:

Pedrazza was a cold and isolated place where the princes' already Spartan existence became even harsher. . . . In July 1529 a French spy saw the boys twice, once while they were going to Mass, and the other time going out to play. On the way to church a Spanish aristocrat and eighty soldiers accompanied them; when out to play, fifty horsemen. The spy commented on how big Henri had become and on his defiance of the Spanish: the townspeople had told him that the prince constantly hurled verbal abuse at the Spanish.

Although aware of his children's plight, the French king still would not relent; his country's welfare must come first. Help for the boys came from an unlikely quarter. Isabella of Portugal, the emperor's enchanting young wife, was so moved by the story of the two young princes that she sent the prison governor a large sum of money from her personal account to provide them with some clothes and ease their misery. Her letter explained that they were said to be in such a wretched condition that she wished to help them, but that she was anxious not to draw anyone's attention to an improvement in their circumstances.

A little later, in 1529, a gentleman-usher from the household of Louise de Savoie, Jean Baudin, gained access to the princes. He realized that the emperor hoped he would return with such a negative report that the French king would be persuaded to agree to the demands of the Treaty of Madrid. His description of their gloomy quarters and the state they were in was pitiable. He wrote that they were kept under heavy guard in "a dark chamber with neither carpet nor hangings or decoration save a straw mattress in which chamber my lords were seated on small stone stools beneath a window, furnished both inside and out with solid iron bars and so high that only with difficulty could they enjoy air or light." The walls were about eight or ten feet high, and the quarters would have been better suited to major criminals than two blameless children. Their clothes were so poor and worn, and their life so dull and restricted, that tears came to Baudin's eyes.

The prison governor showed him the drawings the dauphin had made all over the walls; seeing their explicit vulgarity, the courtier realized that their jailers were trying to break the boy's spirit so that he would never be suited to kingship. To Baudin's astonishment, when he addressed the princes, they replied in Spanish, asking if he could use that language, as they had had no one with whom they could speak French for some time and had forgotten much. With the governor's permission, Baudin followed them into a second room even smaller than the first and they rushed to the window to get some air. He saw them pick up a little dog to play with. Baudin had the impression that even the soldiers who watched them thought it a shame for such high-born princes to have to spend their time in this way.

The next day, not without difficulty, Baudin was permitted to return with gifts for the princes: caps of embroidered golden velvet, each with a white feather, which Baudin kissed reverently. He was about to give the caps to the boys when the guards snatched them away, showed them to the princes, and said they would keep them safe. The boys longed to have their first pretty objects since their imprisonment, but the superstitious Spaniards thought Baudin was a magician and that the hats might enable them to fly out of the prison and back to France. When Baudin asked to take the boys' measurements as they had grown so much, the guards refused. Baudin wrote that he found it hard to believe that such primitive men could be the guardians of the dauphin of France and his brother. As he left, the two little boys reverted to their strange mix of Spanish and French.

In fact, the princes had only been without their own attendants for eighteen months, and it is unlikely that they would have forgotten their French at this age. On the other hand, Baudin had no reason to lie, and the princes pretending they had forgotten their own language could be explained by their anger at having been abandoned for so long. According to the French spy, the princes did have outdoor exercise; indeed, when they returned to France they were not stunted physically in any way. Still, their imprisonment was to have a deep and lasting effect. The ebullient, cheerful dauphin lapsed into periodic lethargy and ill health, and a deep, black depression left Henri sullen and silent for many years.

*W*HILE the princes were languishing in prison in Spain, their fate appeared to be of little concern to the French court, which celebrated three marriages in 1527 at the Palace of Saint-Germain-en-Laye. As the king's sister, Marguerite, had not been happy in her first union with the duc d'Alençon, her brother tried hard to find her a suitable spouse. He negotiated a marriage with the king of Navarre, Henri d'Albret, comte de Béarn, a brave nobleman who had been captured at Pavia. He had escaped from prison two months later by letting himself

Veüe du Chateau de St. Germain en Laye.
dessiné et Gravé par Israel Siluestre 1648.

The château de Saint-Germain-en-Laye, near Paris, was the principal residence of the king and his court.

down from his cell window on a rope. Charles V had not honored a treaty with Henri d'Albret promising to restore his kingdom of Navarre, which lay between France and Spain, so he had lived for some time at the French court.

Eleven years younger than his bride, Henri d'Albret was a handsome man, a fearless soldier, an intellect, and a king to boot. As Marguerite had known him for many years and approved of the match, it is probable that she really wanted to marry him. Many criticized the king's decision to allow Marguerite, a pearl of the Renaissance, to marry Henri d'Albret, because he had only a tiny, rather miserable kingdom that was very far away. But there are many examples of a sincere love between Henri and Marguerite—a rare occurrence in marriages arranged for convenience and advantage. An inscription in Latin at the bottom of a miniature of Henri d'Albret means: "I have found a pearl [*margarita*] and have taken it to my heart."

François permitted one of his friends who shared his imprisonment, Philippe Chabot de Brion, to marry his niece, Françoise de Longvy, and elevated him to the rank of admiral. Anne de Montmorency, newly cre-

This portrait of Henri d'Albret, king of Navarre, shows him presenting a "Marguerite" to Marguerite, sister of François I.

ated Grand Master, married Madeleine de Savoie, niece of the king's mother. (Madame Louise wished him well, called him "my nephew," and gave him the additional charge of governing the Languedoc.)

The king of France was playing a political game of great risk by pretending not to care about the fate of his two eldest sons; he would rather have given them up for dead than part with a foot of his sovereign territory. In fact, François had renounced ever seeing his two eldest boys again, and had begun grooming his youngest son, Charles d'Angoulême, for the throne.

*F*OLLOWING the French king's breach of the Treaty of Madrid and the formation of the League of Cognac, Charles V sent the imperial army back into Italy. In early 1527 the renegade Charles de Bourbon captured Milan, but was left in Italy with his army and no further orders. The former Constable was now unrecognizable as the delicate, handsome young man painted by François Clouet just a few years previously. His treason and guilt, as well as the strain of constant fighting, had affected him badly. In Spain, he had tried to approach his captive former king, but he had been absolutely rebuffed. With his desperate look, hollow eyes and cheeks, he had become half warlord, half outlaw; yet he was adored by his *Landsknechte,* the wild German mercenaries from Franche-Comté.

Bourbon must have lost his senses when, after taking Milan, he promised untold riches to his untamed German troops, who had not been paid for months and were on the edge of murderous mutiny. The emperor was not aware of Bourbon's promise or his plan to get the promised booty by pillaging Rome. The *Landsknechte* were Lutheran and welcomed the opportunity to sack the seat of Catholicism. These Germans had suffered constant privations resulting in a total breakdown of discipline, and when they reached the Eternal City in April 1527, their generals were powerless to restrain them. Shouting: "Blood, blood, kill, kill, Bourbon, Bourbon," the men looted and burned, broke into convents and priories, raped nuns and tortured clergy. They desecrated altars and holy relics, and stabled their horses in Saint Peter's. The Medici pope Clement VII fled from the Vatican by an underground passage to the Castel Sant' Angelo and watched horrified as the city was laid to waste and plundered for several weeks. Not since the invasion of Alaric and his Visigoths in A.D. 410 had Rome suffered such a terrible fate. The frightful sack of the Eternal City was carried out with such senseless brutality that it is still remembered as one of the most abominable acts of war in history.

On July 6, 1527, as the German soldiers tried to storm Sant' Angelo and capture the pope, perhaps to hold him for ransom, Charles de Bourbon was struck by a bullet and killed.[7] He was buried by his

---

7. Benvenuto Cellini claimed to have been the marksman.

soldiers in Saint Peter's, but his body was later exhumed and exhibited in Gaeta as a curiosity until the eighteenth century, when it disappeared.

Pope Clement VII was forced to surrender and was imprisoned for six months. His release cost the Vatican a huge indemnity as well as several of the most important Italian cities belonging to the Papal States. The pope could not bear to live in the ruined city and moved first to Orvieto, then to Viterbo.

*T*HE struggle between the Holy Roman Emperor and the king of France had reached a complete impasse. It was too much for the fifty-three-year-old Louise de Savoie. Her grandsons' fate moved her even if it did not affect her son, and she decided to act. With the support of her daughter, Marguerite, now queen of Navarre, she boldly approached the emperor's forty-five-year-old aunt, Margaret of Austria, governor of the Netherlands, a lady as formidable as herself. She also contacted the emperor's sister, Eleonore of Portugal, who was still waiting in Spain to come to France and marry the king. As the men were too stubborn to see any form of reason, these four ladies agreed to put their redoubtable intelligence, subtlety, and good sense to the task of negotiating a solution.

On July 5, 1529, the four met at Cambrai, in northern France, with the aim of establishing a lasting peace. The French ladies settled into the imposing mansion of Saint-Pol, and the Spanish were housed in an abbey opposite. To facilitate their meetings, a temporary covered wooden footbridge was built to link the two buildings. Hung with tapestries, it kept the ladies protected from the stares of the passersby and their hems free from the dirt on the road.

After two weeks of hard bargaining, there came a moment when Louise felt it politic to pretend she was abandoning the clogged negotiations and returning home. The ruse worked. By the beginning of August, just one month after they arrived, all four negotiators were satisfied. The treaty was recognized as so sensible and fair that neither Eleonore's brother in Spain nor Louise's son in France could find a reason to reject it. Although it was officially called the Treaty of Cambrai, it became known as "*La Paix des Dames*"—"The Peace of the Ladies."

France would renounce any rights to Milan and Naples and abandon its Italian allies. Florence was kept out of the Treaty of Cambrai—Pope Clement VII had his own plans for his native city. François I's Italian dream had finally come to an end. France would cede its sovereignty over Artois, Flanders, Tournai, and Hesdin in the Pas-de-Calais. Once Charles V realized François I would not release Burgundy to him, he set an enormous ransom for the return of the princes: four tons of gold;[8] the emperor was very short of money. In return, Charles V would renounce his rights to Burgundy, Auxerre, Mâcon, and Auxonne, and the other claimed territories. The treaty was tough but fair.

What François I had wanted more than anything was to preserve the conquests of Louis XI. The treaty fulfilled this condition. The princes would be able to come home, and François would finally marry Eleonore of Portugal. Her dowry would be deducted from the amount due to Spain for the princes' return. Furthermore, the French king was to renounce his allegiance to the Sultan, who was currently threatening Vienna, the Habsburg capital of Austria. A clever realist, Louise de Savoie understood that in order to secure a safe future, Christianity—represented in this treaty by France, the Italian states, and the emperor—must unite against the Ottoman. For François to abandon an infidel ally was one thing; but to allow the Italian states to whom he had promised his protection to fall under the Habsburg yoke constituted betrayal. Still, the king of France did not hesitate.

To celebrate the successful outcome of their negotiations, the king's mother and sister mounted two white mares and galloped through the streets of Cambrai, scattering handfuls of gold and silver coins among the townspeople.

*F*RENCH officials signed the Treaty of Cambrai on August 3, 1529, relinquishing all rights to territory beyond the Alps. Pope

---

8. The equivalent of 4,500 ingots each weighing almost two pounds.

Clement VII and the emperor could now make it their common cause to act against schism in the empire and move against the Turks at the gates of Vienna. Further, with the help of the emperor, the pope could implement his plan to retake Florence, which had ousted the Medici in 1527.

While the Medici pope was being besieged in Castel Sant' Angelo in Rome in 1527, a hostile faction led by the Capponi family had seized power in Florence. Eight-year-old Catherine was brought to Florence and placed, for her safety, in a Dominican convent. When plague erupted in their quarters, the French ambassador moved Catherine to the Convent of the Santissima Annunziata delle Murate. There the good Benedictine sisters welcomed her with affection born out of admiration for her family name.

In the Convent of the Murate, Catherine received an excellent education in Greek and Latin and was able to absorb the sisters' sweetness, seriousness, and good manners. Although the young girl was completely reclusive, the nuns treated her as a pet and would do anything for her. Despite the austerity due to the siege, the nuns somehow managed to make Catherine little cakes and even baked patisseries in the shape of the Medici arms so that she could pick off the sugared pills.

One of the nuns, Sister Justine Niccolini, kept a diary from which we learn that Catherine was a likable child, whom they all loved. She was naturally caring, and sent parcels of food to the poor and those in prison in the city. Catherine learned charm and how to use it. According to the nun's diary, it was in the convent that Catherine perfected her most valuable attribute: the art of dissimulation.

With Florence in rebellion against the Medici, the incompetent Cardinal Passerini of Cortona, whom Clement VII had left to rule Florence once he was elected to the Holy See, fled the city to safety with Catherine's two cousins, Alessandro and Ippolito de' Medici. Catherine remained shut in the Convent of the Murate for the next three years, until she was eleven years old. There she was protected from though not unaware of the struggle for power among the many factions tearing Florence apart through vandalism, plunder, rape, and pillage. A few of the little patisseries in the shape of Catherine's arms found their way into the city and the nuns were accused of being part of a Medici plot against Florence. The flight of the cardinal with the two Medici boys infuriated the more extreme groups to such an extent that they threatened to hold Catherine hostage, or throw her into a brothel to ruin her potential as a political pawn, or even chain her naked to the city walls for use as target practice. Bernardo Castiglione (who should have known better, coming from that great family) suggested she be raped by all the soldiery. Happily, good sense prevailed. Catherine de' Medici was too valuable to waste.

The pope was convinced that only Charles V could restore the Medici to power in Florence; in return for his support, he promised to crown Charles Holy Roman Emperor at last. By June 29, 1529, Clement VII made peace with the emperor whose army under Bourbon had savaged Rome, and signed a treaty restoring the Medici as rulers of Florence. Of course, the treaty was cemented by a marriage: the pope's illegitimate son Alessandro de' Medici married the emperor's natural daughter, Margaret of Austria. Their wedding gift was to be Florence, which had been excluded from the 1529 Treaty of Cambrai. The emperor gave Clement VII an army with which to lay siege to his own city, the same force of wild German *Landsknechte* who had so brutally attacked and sacked Rome.

To prevent the pope or François I from attempting to rescue their valuable little Medici hostage, the Florentine city fathers decided to move her to the secure cloister of Santa Lucia. All reports state that, when the city commissioners came to take her away, despite the hysteria of the Benedictine sisters who loved her, eleven-year-old Catherine kept her nerve. She shaved her head, donned the habit of a novice nun, and announced to the commissioners that she had joined the order and that they could not remove her. Nonetheless, one month later, on July 20, 1529, Catherine was taken to Santa Lucia.

The following month, Charles V sent his vassal, Philibert de Châlon, the Prince of Orange, to punish Florence. Châlon arrived from Rome in mid-August with the army that had taken part in the sacking two years earlier. Having attacked Perugia, which surrendered, he approached Florence, while Charles V, en route to his coronation in Bologna, landed with his army at Genoa. The Florentine representatives who came to Genoa hoping to negotiate were summarily dismissed. Florence had failed to surrender unconditionally, and had to prepare for the consequences.

Civil war was the theme of Catherine de' Medici's most formative years, and she would never forget its horror. By September 12, less than three weeks later, the City of the Red Lily had surrendered due to hunger and plague and was in imperial hands. On February 24, 1530, Charles V was finally crowned in Bologna, and with this seal of alliance between the church and the emperor, a Holy League of States was formed. On April 27, 1532, the Medici were written into the constitution of Florence and Alessandro de' Medici was installed as duke.

THE ransom demanded for the French princes, four tons of gold, entailed a huge burden on the country, but the French people united and made an enormous effort to assemble the payment. Once it was gathered the Spanish claimed the gold was not pure and procrastinated by insisting on having each piece assayed in case of swindle. On June 10, 1530, one year after the Treaty of Cambrai, the Spanish ambassador at last announced himself satisfied. It took hundreds of loaded mules and four hundred cavalry to escort the gold over the Pyrenees and to bring back to France the two princes and the new queen.

The scene of the exchange was the same spot on the Bidassoa, and it was performed with rigid Spanish protocol. At eight o'clock in the evening of July 1, 1530, the princes and the Constable of Castile embarked from the Spanish side on a barge manned by twelve rowers and a helmsman, with eleven Spanish gentlemen in attendance. At the same moment, Anne de Montmorency and Don Alvaro de Lurgo, together with the gold, left the French bank in a barge with the same number of rowers, eleven French gentlemen, and two pages the same height as the dauphin and Henri. The princes and pages wore daggers, and the gentlemen were armed with swords and daggers.

The two boats headed toward a pontoon in the middle of the river, which was manned by one French and one Spanish gentleman. As the boats docked, one gentleman called out to the Grand Master, the other to the Constable of Castile, and they mounted the pontoon together. The Constable of Castile turned toward the boys, bowed, and made a sincere speech to the effect that he had done his best to treat them according to their station, and regretted any errors he might have made. The dauphin replied just as generously that the Constable had indeed done all that he could have been expected to do in his position and under the circumstances. But Henri was not feeling remotely gracious, and when the Spaniard turned to speak to him, he broke wind loudly and repeatedly.[9] Some sources say he blew a series of raspberries, but whatever he did, the message was clear.

The Constable of Castile then stepped into the barge that carried the gold and the Spanish rowers, and Anne de Montmorency joined the princes with the French rowers. As the gold left for Spain, Montmorency took charge of the real "treasure of France." While the exchange took place, the new queen of France, accompanied by her suite of one hundred, her ladies, and the cardinal de Tournon, was rowed across the river. The entire party, including the new queen in a litter, then left by torchlight for Saint-Jean-de-Luz.

As soon as the princes stepped on shore, a courier galloped off to Bordeaux to inform the king that his sons were safely in France. The messenger reached his goal one day later. Upon hearing the news, the king fell to his knees in front of a crucifix and wept tears of joy and gratitude. Couriers were sent galloping throughout the kingdom to spread the news of the princes' return. All the church bells of Paris started to ring, led by the great bells of Nôtre-Dame. Everyone who had a musical instrument came out into the streets, and blew or banged or otherwise made a noise to show their heartfelt relief that their princes were safe.

It was midnight when the dauphin and Henri, asleep on Montmorency's shoulder, rode into Saint-Jean-de-Luz preceding the new queen in her litter. The streets of Saint-Jean were lined with curious, cheering crowds, gathered to welcome these Sons of France they had

---

9. Brantôme describes the shock experienced by the Constable of Castile, Louis de Praedt, when Henri replied to his apologies thus: "il luis fit une pétarde."

all helped to ransom. There was rather less interest in Eleonore of Portugal, the new queen.

In spite of their miserable diet, both boys had grown, though Henri was the more compact of the two. It seems no one could understand much of what they said because they spoke to one another in a mix of the French they remembered and the Spanish they had learned from their rough jailers. Their language may also have been a secret code which they used deliberately and which bound them together through their mutual ordeal. For some time, they chose to dress in the Spanish fashion.

As the cortège with the new queen of France and the princes progressed homeward, they learned that their grandmother, Louise de Savoie, who had instigated their release, was again suffering from gout and could not come further than Bordeaux to meet them and embrace her new daughter-in-law. The boys' aunt Marguerite de Navarre was expecting a child and had remained at Blois, so Louise had sent her ladies of the court to represent her. As one of the three ladies chosen to attend Queen Eleonore on her triumphal entry into France, Diane de Poitiers rode at their head to welcome home the princes and the new queen.

Late on the evening of July 6, the caravan with the princes and Queen Eleonore reached the Abbey of the Poor Clares of Beyries, not far from Mont-de-Marsan, south of Bordeaux, where they would join the king and the whole court. The boys had collapsed from emotion and exhaustion and were in bed, but when their father arrived shortly afterward, he could not stop himself rushing to their room and kissing them awake, tears streaming from his eyes. Then he went to welcome Eleonore. She was at her dressing table, still wearing her formal Spanish court dress, with her reddish-blond hair undone and hanging loose about her shoulders and down to her ankles. François was quite enchanted.

Hours later, at one in the morning on July 7, 1530, the marriage was ratified. The service was conducted by the same Bishop of Lisieux who had heard the confession of the two Norman knights who exposed Bourbon's treason. Eleonore entered, glittering with jewels, accompanied by the two sleepy princes. Her headdress was made of golden filigree butterflies on a crimson velvet bonnet sewn with precious stones, and she wore white flowers on her ears. Her hair hung loose in curls all the way to her ankles and was threaded with ribbons. Her dress was of crimson velvet backed with white satin, and the sleeves were covered in gold and silver embroidery. Diane de Poitiers, as principal matron of honor, walked behind Eleonore, dazzling in her beauty, height, and her own magnificent gems. Witnesses to the marriage service were astonished that the king and queen chatted merrily throughout. They went to bed at 2 a.m. and did not emerge until 2 p.m. the next day. It seemed the king was quite taken with his new wife. For her part, as she had only known a husband in his seventies, poor Eleonore fell in love with her brother's greatest enemy. She would soon be disillusioned. Anne de Pisseleu was present at Bordeaux among the ladies of the court, and did not even leave the king on his honeymoon.

According to the court gossip Brantôme, it was François who was the more disillusioned; in her magnificent court robes and jewels, Eleonore had looked rather splendid. Undressed, her short legs and long torso made her look like a dwarf. He goes on to say: "it is true that this fault would be less apparent when the new queen was lying down." The king was a perfect gentleman, and if he was disappointed in any way, no one could tell; he always treated Eleonore with great respect and courtesy. There were no children of their marriage and it is not certain whether François had already contracted the syphilis that was the possible eventual cause of his death.

$\mathcal{A}$S the royal cavalcade continued on its leisurely way northward, the princes became accustomed to the unfamiliar faces around them and learned their language again. François noted that the boys looked physically well but that the dauphin, who was now twelve, was no longer the ebullient child who had left France. He spoke slowly and sparingly, was a serious lad, and refused to drink alcohol. He had absorbed Spanish etiquette and followed it carefully. The more sensitive Henri had become awkward, taciturn, morose, and unsociable—noth-

ing like the bright, intelligent child described by the English ambassador just prior to the princes' departure four years earlier. Clearly, the
two boys' extreme reserve was due to the lack of affection, sympathy,
and friendship they had endured; the boredom of their existence; and
the constant petty humiliations that had crushed their spirits.[10]

Henri's anger was immediately noted and censored, and he reacted
by disguising all emotion and becoming rigidly controlled. This gave
the impression that he was enduring a sullen, dark melancholy. Neither
the king nor his son reached out to the other, and Henri never really
forgave his father for causing the loss of his childhood. His lack of loving parents resulted in an unswerving attachment to the two people
who gave him affection prior to his departure. They were both there
for him immediately upon his return—Diane de Poitiers and Anne de
Montmorency.

Wherever they stopped, the princes were enthusiastically welcomed, as was the queen. Carried on a litter draped with cloth of gold,
Eleonore was a splendid spectacle. She held a huge fan to combat the
July heat and wore her magnificent Spanish dresses. One was "of double white taffeta, with huge bouffant sleeves covered with embroidery
in silver thread"; with it she wore a matching velvet cap covered in precious stones accentuated by a "white feather in the same style as worn
by the king on that day."

Everywhere in Bordeaux there were banners of welcome for the
princes bearing the message: "They left in tears, they have come back
in joy." Eleonore went to greet her new mother-in-law, Madame
Louise, who was residing just outside the city. Louise was in great pain,
but she joined the caravan the following day, requesting that her new
daughter-in-law dress in the French fashion. The court remained in
Angoulême for a month while the princes left for Amboise, where they
were reunited with their siblings, and in their favorite surroundings,
rediscovered their old haunts and toys.

What did the princes think or feel about their freedom; about seeing their dazzling father again; about getting to know their gentle stepmother Eleonore, who had been so instrumental in helping to free

10. Williams, *Henri II*, pp. 61–62.

them; and about watching their father's new mistress, Anne de Pisseleu, assuming the queen's place? We can only imagine. But the king
made plain his displeasure at the change in his sons, particularly Henri.
Some of François' annoyance might have been due to his guilt over his
role as the cause of their misery. The king was not a natural father.
More concerned with himself than his children, he did not give them
the reassurance, confidence, and affection they craved at this difficult
time. His court was devoted to the pursuit of pleasure. François felt it
was a courtier's duty to be always gay and lively, saying that "he did not
care for dreamy, sullen, sleepy children." He avoided the two older
boys and focused his attention on the youngest, Charles d'Angoulême,
now nine years old, who was so like him and had been his constant
companion for the past four years.

However, the king was not entirely unfeeling, and he was well
aware of his sons' miserable time abroad for almost four years—more
than half of Henri's lifetime. They had returned with no manners, no
idea of courtly behavior or how to conduct themselves within their
own circle. Not long after their return, the king decided to send the
princes to stay for some months with Louis de Brézé and his wife,
Diane, who loved them both and had known them since their birth.
Diane's feeling gesture in embracing Henri so warmly when the boys
left for Spain had not gone unnoticed. For the rest of the summer and
autumn of 1530, the boys stayed at Anet, having fun and hunting to
hounds with the two Brézé girls and their friends. In September,
the king joined them for a few days, inviting himself to hunt with his
hosts and his sons. Then the court decamped to Saint-Germain for the
winter.

CHAPTER EIGHT

The Young Knight

FRANÇOIS I was a king the Parisians appreciated. They liked his style and felt his paternal concern for their welfare. There was an ugly incident in the capital on June 1, 1529 when a much-loved statue of the Virgin, which stood at the corner of the rue des Deux-Siciles, was mutilated by Protestants. Heresy was gaining ground, and people were alarmed. The king offered to pay for a replacement and to punish the guilty. Two years later, he himself made reparation in public. Bareheaded, he knelt before the bishop of Paris in front of the empty niche where the statue had been. Holding a lit candle, François received the new statue from the hands of the bishop and placed it in its niche. This was the kind of gesture that showed the people how sensitive their king was to their religious feelings and won François I the love of his subjects.

The growth of Protestantism—or heresy, as it was called—troubled François. To "The Most Christian King," the Catholic religion was the basis of his "divine right to rule," his political policy, and the country's unity. To embrace another religion or to question Catholic teaching was akin to treason. On the other hand, François I was also

Marguerite de Navarre wrote the *Heptaméron,* a book of old French tales. Here, she presents it to Anne de Pisseleu, duchesse d'Etampes, François I's mistress.

the "Renaissance king" of France, the patron of the humanists. He had even gone so far as to invite Erasmus, the greatest of all humanist scholars, to head the classical college he had founded in Paris. (Erasmus did not accept.) The king was torn between his admiration for the "new learning" and his duty to defend the orthodox teaching of the Catholic church. His beloved and scholarly older sister, Marguerite, had a strong evangelical faith and protected and welcomed Protestants in her tiny kingdom of Navarre. She wrote the *Heptaméron,* the best known and most popular of all the classic French tales, which, although modeled on the *Decameron,* is also full of religious references to the cause of the Reformers. Some French critics have doubted whether the *Heptaméron* was the queen's own work. However, we have Brantôme's word that his grandmother, Marguerite's *dame d'honneur,* often took down the queen's dictation of these tales as Marguerite traveled about in her litter.

Queen Eleonore was staunchly orthodox in religious matters, as was Diane de Poitiers, but the king's mistress Anne de Pisseleu followed Marguerite de Navarre's inclination toward the "New Religion." The Protestant faction grew within the court, as discontent swelled against the established order in the outside world. Corruption in the church had spread in many areas throughout the Middle Ages, and the church in France was afflicted with problems very similar to those in the rest of Christendom. Decadence was rife among the religious leadership, prelates were openly living in luxury, the lower clergy were ignorant and impoverished. Drunken, violent, immoral friars and monks were a common sight. The dissatisfaction of people of all classes with their religious mentors led to the formidable spiritual and moral upheaval that would become the Reformation.

The teachings of the Reformation were spreading throughout Europe, and great scholars defected from the Church of Rome to join the Protestant cause. Copies of the reformers' works, already translated into the French vernacular, were rolling off German and Dutch printing presses in great quantity. These were changing times; printing presses were springing up all over Europe, and ideas were able to travel faster than ever before. By 1530, the Catholic Church in France was well aware that its unity and authority was being dangerously threatened.

François I tried to distance himself from religious quarrels as much as possible, and not until he felt his own authority threatened did he eventually react. The king detached himself more and more from church issues, entrusting the persecution and repression of the "New Religion" to the *Parlement,* which was backed by staunch allies within the established circle of the Sorbonne. In that enclave of academics, it was genuinely believed that humanist thought was responsible for heresy.

*O*N March 5, 1531, Queen Eleonore was crowned at Saint-Denis, and later made her official entry into the city of Paris. Diane de Poitiers, just over thirty years old, was one of Eleonore's three *dames d'honneur* officiating at the ceremony. As the queen rode into Paris, onlookers were dazzled. She wore a cloak of purple velvet lined with white satin and a tunic of ermine covered in precious stones; her long hair was entwined with ribbons, and her crown alone was said to be worth a fortune. Diane followed the queen's litter mounted on a white mare, her saddle draped with cloth of gold. Diane's train was held by two grooms in white satin who followed her on foot. Her son-in-law Claude d'Aumale walked alongside. Eleonore was the same age as Diane, but any other comparison was not to the queen's advantage. The critical French judged their new queen as being plain and re-marked on her long torso, short legs, and thick waist. Eleonore felt their rejection keenly. For the ceremony in Saint-Denis, she had arrived wearing a veil to hide her face, and the crowds surmised she must be old and wrinkled. But when they saw the size of the Brazilian dia-monds[1] adorning her veil, they cheered.

The new queen of France was determined to make an impressive entrance into her capital, and shine she did, covered in diamonds, sap-phires, emeralds, and rubies, and crowned with a circlet of rare feath-ers, all from Portugal's colony of Brazil. The Parisians loved the spectacle. People filled the streets, and those with balconies draped them in tapestries, leaned over, and scattered flower petals onto the procession passing below. At her moment of triumph, the queen looked up and saw her husband the king at a window, gazing down boldly and without shame, his arm around Anne de Pisseleu. This scene did not go unnoticed. Even the English ambassador was suffi-ciently scandalized to describe it to Henry VIII[2]—who had not yet shocked the world by divorcing Catherine of Aragon. Poor Eleonore had to continue throughout the day and the banquet in the evening, smiling despite her breaking heart.

To celebrate the Treaty of Cambrai, the king's wedding, the

1. A gift from her late husband, the king of Portugal.
2. *Calendar of Letters and Papers, Foreign and Domestic, of the Reign of Henry VIII*. Arranged and collated by J. S. Brewar and others. London: 1862–1932.

queen's coronation, and the return of the princes, Paris was *en fête* for one whole week. The festivities included masques, parades, and, of course, the traditional tournament in which the bold and the brave competed for honors. On the final day, the joust was dedicated to "Beauty"—officially that of the queen, but it was more likely that Anne de Pisseleu would be chosen as the most beautiful lady of the day by the votes of the onlookers. As always, the cobbles had been lifted from the wide, straight rue de Saint-Antoine next to the palace of Les Tournelles, and sand was pressed down to cushion the charges of the horses. The ladies sat in all their finery in a grandstand that had been erected in front of the houses.

It was to be the princes' first tournament, and they each wore a splendid new armor chased with their gold *fleur-de-lys*. Both were expert horsemen and entered the arena superbly mounted, surrounded by their pages carrying their standards. According to the traditions of chivalry, each contestant riding in single combat could choose a lady from the audience for whose honor he would fight. He would ask to wear her color or favor, dedicate his success to his lady, and be her knight for the day.

Since returning to court, the princes had been enveloped by its ladies, all vying to make them feel loved. The boys had inherited their father's magnificent physique; Henri looked more like a fifteen-year-old youth than a boy of twelve. During his incarceration in Spain, he had become romantically obsessed with the Spanish story of Amadis de Gaula which extolled the glory and chivalry of medieval times. It was a tale of courtly love, ostentatious beauty, and energetic outdoor activities: hunting to hounds, fencing, jousting. The court already called Henri "*Le Beau Ténébreux*" (the nickname of his hero Amadis) for his prowess at riding, jousting, and all sports, and Brantôme asserted that he was the finest runner and long jumper of all the young knights at court. Once he was freed, the young prince spent as much time as possible outdoors, but no one could say that they had seen Henri d'Orléans laugh.

*T*HE story of Amadis was very similar to Henri's own plight. The two elder sons of Périon, king of Wales, Galaor and Amadis, are abandoned and exiled to a strange country. Enslaved by a magician, they triumph over the many trials he imposes on them. Amadis, a precocious youth, seems three years older and stronger than his twelve years. He falls in love with Oriane, daughter of the king of Britain, and turns to the fairy, Urgande, to help him win his Lady. Urgande, gentle and reassuring as a mother, hands him an enchanted spear with which he is victorious in battle. Calling upon her magic powers, Urgande grants the lovers eternal youth. During those long, lonely years, the young prince yearned for a Lady to whom he could offer his protection and dedicate his heart, just as his hero Amadis had pledged himself to his "Lady," Oriane. These popular novels were written by a minor Spanish nobleman, Gracia de Rodriguez de Montalvo, as if for children, with many episodes of the saga appearing over the next fifteen years. The majority of the literature of the time concerned love, marriage, or adultery.

Henri's first tournament gave him the chance to play the role of his hero, Amadis. He watched as his brother, naturally courteous and diplomatic, stopped his horse in front of his father's new queen, Eleonore, and lowered his lance before her so that she could tie her colors—her scarf—to the tip. The dauphin raised the lance and the scarf slid down, as it should, to his arm, where it remained as his Lady's token. It was assumed by all in attendance that Henri d'Orléans would halt in front of Anne de Pisseleu, his father's acknowledged *maîtresse en titre*. Seated in the stands, however, was the lady who fitted the young prince's image of the perfect heroine: a magnificent huntress, the most beautiful, tender lady of his lonely dreams in prison. Diane, comtesse de Brézé, Grande Sénéchale of Normandy, sat according to her rank, her white translucent skin flattered by a light green dress[3] and holding a fan made of pheasant feathers. As always, her golden-red hair was dressed "*à l'escoffion*"—coiled in a snood of silk mesh dotted with pearls and precious stones, the edging band made of fur or jewel-encrusted silk. According to Brantôme, it was Diane de Poitiers and not Anne de Pisseleu who was really considered by the court to be "*la belle parmi les belles*"—"the beauty among the beauties."

---

3. Until her husband died, green and white were Diane's personal colors.

To the surprise and amusement of the onlookers—and not least of Diane—the younger prince halted his charger opposite the Grande Sénéchale. In a high thin voice, he offered to dedicate himself to her honor and protection if she would allow him to wear her colors of green and white. It was a charming gesture from a boy of twelve to a beautiful, grand lady of thirty. Diane took it as a sign of the boy's gratitude for her concern and comforting before and after his imprisonment, and it touched her. Her heart went out to this boy who had dared to be the champion of a lady old enough to be his mother. Diane asked the king if he would permit Henri d'Orléans to be her young knight, her *chevalier servant*, and he happily agreed. Naturally, the princes won the day—it seems likely that this had been prearranged.

As both Queen Eleonore and the comtesse de Brézé had already been honored by the princes, the rumor passed around the tourney ground that the king's mistress, Anne de Pisseleu, would be chosen as "the beauty among the beauties," the final prize of the day. Since the vote was cast in secret, no one was afraid of nominating someone other than the queen. Anne de Pisseleu had no doubt she would be chosen— after all, her sole rival, Diane, comtesse de Brézé, was ten years older. When the heralds advanced and stood in front of the stand, they announced that the votes had been cast equally for Anne de Pisseleu and the comtesse de Brézé. Diane remained silent, but a furious Anne burst into hysterical laughter and stormed off the stand. She would never forgive Diane de Poitiers for the slight she suffered on that day.

Diane had known Anne de Pisseleu for some years in the court of Louise de Savoie, and did not hold too high an opinion of her. Anne was a natural schemer, vicious in her jealousy of anyone who came within range of what she wanted. Her hold on the king would last for twenty-one years. Her malign influence might have been balanced by the restraining good sense of Marguerite de Navarre, but the latter had retired to join her husband at his seat at Béarn, all that was left of his kingdom.

Anne had many followers at court, among them an ambitious poet who was eager for preferment, Clément Marot. Marot had chosen, unwisely, to flirt in verse with the lovely Grande Sénéchale when Diane was about twenty-four. Marot's rather charming love poem mentioning her name was published without sanction and greatly offended her honor. She was a respectable married lady: insinuations about her virtue would surely enrage her husband and could endanger her position with the queen. In her anger, Diane de Poitiers denounced Marot to the authorities for eating bacon during Lent, a time of Catholic fasting when only fish was allowed. He was imprisoned on suspicion of heresy—with justification, it was later discovered; breaking the Lenten fast indicated Marot was a Protestant. But the poet was well connected and soon bailed out by a powerful friend and given a place at court. Diane's rage was to cost her dearly when Marot succeeded his father as *valet de chambre* to the king and became a devoted follower of Anne de Pisseleu.

*L*OUIS de Brézé had turned seventy and could not be expected to live much longer. Before his death in 1531, the Grand Sénéchal once again played host to his king at Anet. On this occasion, François did not come solely for the hunt; he wished to consult his friend on the vital political question of his sons' marriages, which was dividing his council. Brézé was considered the wisest of his courtiers, and his opinion, just as Montmorency's, was important to the king; it would help him decide whether to ratify or break the Treaty of Cambrai.

François I was still obsessed with Italy—if anything more so since his defeat at Pavia. He had long entertained the thought of continuing the tradition of marrying a member of his royal house to one of the ruling house of Medici, whose half-French heiress happened to be approaching the right age. However, like monarchs throughout history, François believed that kings must marry royal blood as only this distinguished them from their subjects. In spite of her wealth and connections, and even her descent from Louis IX, Catherine de' Medici was of bourgeois origin, and therefore a commoner. The Medici, no matter how rich and powerful, were considered by Europe's royal families to be no better than ennobled merchants.

Since François I's imprisonment in Spain and the recent treason and death of Charles de Bourbon, another strong man had begun to appear more in the king's immediate circle. Anne de Montmorency, appointed Grand Master by François I after Pavia, was also a protégé of Louis de Brézé. Now thirty years old, Montmorency had served his diplomatic apprenticeship under Brézé and was ready to take his place as a statesman. The Grand Sénéchal had imbued in him the same principles and political doctrine which he had instilled into his wife. Montmorency believed adamantly in the divine right and authority of anointed kings, and saw it as the duty of François I, as The Most Christian King, to defend the established Faith. But this powerful and influential Grand Master opposed the Medici marriage. He considered it a *mésalliance* and never really shared François' Italian ambitions. Rather, Montmorency promoted an imperial alliance with the Infanta Maria of Portugal, Queen Eleonore's daughter and Charles V's niece.

Louis de Brézé favored the Italian union, and strongly supported a Valois–Medici alliance, essentially for financial reasons. He would also have taken into account the fact that Catherine, through her mother, was his wife's second cousin. Who better than Diane to guide Catherine in the ways of the court and ease the Brézés nearer the throne? It is unlikely that the king of France would ever have considered a union of the dauphin with a Medici. But Louis de Brézé pointed out that the royal blood of France's future monarchs would not be diluted in the case of Henri d'Orléans—he was not the heir to the throne. Besides, François I was still "chasing the elusive phantom of Italy," and the promise of the duchy of Milan was irresistible to a king who had drunk the heady wine of the Renaissance there in his youth. His second son, Henri d'Orléans, must marry the Medici heiress.

The peace treaty with Spain had not solved France's problems. Henry VIII had not forgotten his meeting with François I on the Field of the Cloth of Gold in 1520 and had rejoiced in France's humiliation at the Battle of Pavia. Once again, there were rumblings from across the Channel as the king of England cast about for new allies in order to further humble François I and, at the same time, protect England from a possible threat from the Habsburg emperor. In the Vatican, Pope Clement VII knew that if he was to consolidate his influence among the Italian states, he needed the military strength of a strong Catholic ally, particularly in view of the growing Protestant threat. Whether his new

Catherine de' Medici was the orphaned heiress of that great Florentine family.

ally was to be the king of France or the Habsburg emperor was of little concern to him; but to win the support of either, he would have to provide attractive terms and seal the alliance with a dynastic marriage.

It is unlikely that a clever girl like Catherine de' Medici was unaware of her role in matrimonial politics and of the many offers for her hand being placed before her "uncle," the pope. In October 1530, Clement VII had Catherine brought to him in Rome. He had not seen her for five years. Nor had her cousin, the handsome Ippolito. Slightly older than Alessandro, Ippolito should have been the rightful ruler of Florence, but Clement removed Ippolito from the succession by making him a cardinal. Soon, even the pope could see that Catherine and Ippolito were in love. The Venetian ambassador Antonio Suriano described Ippolito's face as being "gentle and serious and having the melancholy expression one finds in those destined to a premature death." Ippolito was a poet, a musician, and a scholar; he played the lute, the flute, and the organ. He enjoyed hunting parties and tournaments and employed "barbarians" such as "Tartars skilled at drawing the bow, Ethiopians trained to battle Indians, daring divers, Turks to conduct his hunts. . . ." His ecclesiastical interests were known to be nonexistent—he was "ambitious and loved pomp, was passionate and restless."

Suriano reported home to Venice that Ippolito intended to renounce his cardinal's hat and marry Catherine. He had come to appreciate and admire her charm, her character, and her courage. According to comte Hector de la Ferrière, the editor of Catherine's collected letters, she had made Ippolito her heart's choice, even while the French marriage negotiations were in progress. With the *duchessina* of Florence as his wife, little would stand in Ippolito's way to rule Florence— except the pope.

Clement VII promptly sent Cardinal Ippolito to Hungary as a legate with rich benefices. It was thought at the time that Clement may even have planned for the brilliant Ippolito to become another Medici elected to the chair of Saint Peter, and he was not about to let the foolish love of the youngsters get in his way. Titian's portrait of Ippolito shows him on the eve of his departure, wearing a Hungarian Hussar's outfit, holding a baton and a sword. Ippolito died the following year, most probably poisoned by his cousin Alessandro, who feared his pretensions to rule Florence. Oddly, Catherine did not grieve when the news reached Fontainebleau. Alessandro was assassinated a few years later.

Ever since Clement VII had placed the crown of Charlemagne on the head of Charles V, he viewed the emperor as his ally, and yet the Italian states thought Charles V was as much a threat on the peninsula as the French king. François I would want to avenge himself on Charles V, that much was certain. The pope hesitated between the French marriage and the emperor's wish for Catherine to marry the Duke of Milan, Francesco Sforza. Such a union could force Clement to send arms to support Catherine in Milan. Were Catherine's husband allied to Spain and opposed to France, this would place Clement in a difficult position. The pope made his decision. The French union had more to offer.

This portrait by Titian of Ippolito de' Medici in Hungarian costume was painted just before Ippolito left for Hungary as Pope Clement VII's legate. The pope was anxious to quell Ippolito's ambitious designs to marry Catherine de' Medici and rule Florence.

In November 1530, François I sent John Stewart, Duke of Albany—Catherine de' Medici's Scottish uncle—as his envoy to the pope to ask for the hand of his "niece" for his second son. At Anet on April 24, in the presence of Louis de Brézé and his wife, Diane, François I signed the document dictating the terms of Henri d'Orléans' marriage contract to Catherine de' Medici. This important ceremony was the last great honor that the king would be able to bestow on his Grand Sénéchal of Normandy.

At the age of eleven, Catherine was still too young to consummate the marriage. According to the terms of the original contract, she was therefore to come to live at the French court and bring with her a sub-

stantial dowry. The pope was to create a new duchy for the young couple consisting of Pisa, Livorno, Modena, Parma, and, if they could be
taken from Charles V, Genoa and Milan. Ultimately, the pope decided
to keep Catherine in Florence until she was of an age to marry. This
move also made it possible for him to trim her dowry. With his eye
firmly fixed on the benefits to France in Italy of this marriage, François
was very eager to have her at his court, so much so that he was willing
to give up on some of the "dowry" towns in exchange for money. The
final outcome would certainly be to the satisfaction of both king and
pope. Only Charles V would be discomforted by these arrangements.
But the emperor was so blinded by his own dynastic prejudice that he
never thought the Valois king would allow his son to marry into a family whose coat of arms bore the pills of the apothecary or the golden
balls of the moneylender.

By the time she was twelve, Catherine was exchanging letters with
the king of France, who was, after all, a distant cousin through her
mother. François responded by sending envoys to visit Catherine in
Rome; they commented favorably on her character and charitable ini-
tiatives. During the horrors of the uprising in Florence, Catherine had
learned the advantage of self-effacement and invisibility. However, her
low profile did not erase her importance; she would not forget that
while the rest of Europe was fighting for her hand in marriage, in Florence they had wanted to hang her naked from the battlements. With
the blood of the politically astute Medici in her veins, and Machiavelli's
The Prince as her guide, the little *duchessina* "breathed in the subtle
and corrupt air of politics." No one during her childhood intimated
that Catherine possessed much, if any, spiritual feeling, despite the
time she spent in convents or lodging with her cousin in the Vatican. If
she had no real love of God, and the love of Ippolito was denied her,
then politics would be her master and Machiavelli her teacher. With
her sharp intelligence and natural ability to analyze situations, Catherine would have appreciated her position exactly. She was the ace in the
pope's hand, and she knew it. But a marriage to a son of the king of
France had been a goal way beyond her expectations because she was
not of royal blood, traditionally an essential condition for such a union.
It was a thrilling prospect, yet also a daunting one. She had no doubt

the marriage would be seen as a *mésalliance* by the French, and sensed the struggle she would have to face for acceptance.

Bronzino's portrait shows us Catherine at fourteen. Sadly, she had inherited none of her lovely mother's features. Catherine's is undoubtedly an intelligent face, serious and secretive, with hard eyebrows, bulging eyes, a large nose, a thin upper lip, and a thick and protruding lower lip. At fourteen, she was also far too thin for the taste of the day. In a word, she was no beauty. But Suriano adds that she was "lively, shows an affable character and has distinguished manners. . . ." Her lack of beauty did not exclude charm, as Giorgio Vasari noted in his section on Sebastiano del Piombo in *Lives of Seventy of the Most Eminent Painters, Sculptors, and Architects.* "Her charm cannot be painted or I would have preserved its memory with my brushes." Strangely, Catherine is described by several eyewitnesses as being both dark and fair. In fact, she had dark hair—we know she sometimes added blond hair extensions, which showed from beneath her headdress. When she arrived in France she was still not fully grown, which explains why some described her as short and others say she was of medium height. Despite these discrepancies, not one witness claimed that she was pretty.

CHAPTER NINE

The Widow

AS her husband grew weaker, Diane shut herself away from the world and nursed him devotedly. Neither her efforts nor the skills of the doctors she called to Anet could prevent the death of Louis de Brézé on July 23, 1531 at the age of seventy-two. He was the last to carry the title of Grand Sénéchal of Normandy.[1] The king ordered that the funeral should be appropriate for a natural grandson of King Charles VII, the most senior of his courtiers, and a loyal servant of the crown through four reigns. On August 18, Louis de Brézé was laid to rest in his family tomb in the cathedral at Rouen, with the great pomp and formality appropriate to his high station. Funerals of members of the royal family and the court had a solemnity and procedure that made them almost an art form of the time.

The Grand Sénéchal's red, black, and yellow standard was carried aloft, followed by the company of the King's Own One Hundred Gentlemen, led by Saint-Vallier, Diane's father. Then followed the proces-

---

1. Diane was to keep the title until she was created a duchess. The dauphin, François de Valois, would be named governor of the province.

sion of Louis de Brézé's decorations and orders carried by stewards on cushions. A wax effigy of the deceased, opulently dressed in full regalia, was placed on the coffin. Diane commissioned a young sculptor, Jean Goujon, to make a monumental tomb within the cathedral that took almost ten years to complete. She asked Goujon to include her in the sculpture in the guise of the goddess Diana. On the sepulchre she had inscribed in gold letters:

> *O Louis de Brézé, this tomb has been raised to thee*
> *By Diane de Poitiers, stricken by the death of her husband.*
> *She was thy inseparable and most faithful wife*
> *In the marriage bed;*
> *So shall she be in the tomb.*

Diane de Poitiers had genuinely loved and revered her husband and mourned Brézé sincerely. It may seem strange that a beautiful, intelligent young woman like Diane could have been a faithful and loving wife to an old man like Louis de Brézé. But theirs had been a marriage of minds, of mutual interest, respect, and admiration. After seventeen years of friendship and companionship, Diane keenly felt the loss of Brézé's wisdom and experience, as well as the protection that he was able to give her. For the rest of her life, Diane wore only black, with touches of white. With her very white skin and reddish-golden hair, black and white suited her admirably and made her stand out in contrast to the brilliant kaleidoscope of colors worn at the time.

Diane added to her coat of arms the symbol of a widow, a torch turned upside down with the motto *"Qui me alit me extingit"*—"He who inflames me has the power to extinguish me," which was also the symbol of the Valentinois branch of her family. From the moment of Brézé's death, Diane was determined to be seen by her contemporaries and posterity as a widow in perpetual mourning for her husband. Indeed, she would make her widowhood her career. For the rest of her life, in everything she created and built as well as in her person, Diane remained officially the honorable widow.

One might ask why Diane chose to stay in eternal mourning. Was it just to keep her position as the widow of the most senior courtier in

France after the Princes of the Blood? At thirty-one, Diane de Poitiers was a woman who was sure of herself, and she knew the king held her in sufficient esteem to allow her to cope with her new situation. She had observed the court for half her life and knew where she stood. Widowhood gave her unusual freedom for a woman at this time. If a wellborn woman had sons and, better yet, was a widow, she could rise as high as any nobleman. According to Brantôme, widows at court "want friends and lovers, but no husband, out of love for the freedom that is so sweet. To be out from under the domination of a husband seems to them paradise, and no wonder. They have the use of their own money, the management of the estate . . . Everything passes through their hands. Instead of being servants as before, they are in command; they can pursue their pleasures and enjoy companions who will do as they wish. They remain widows in order to keep their grandeur, dignity and possessions, titles and good treatment." Diane de Poitiers was to avail herself of every advantage of her new position.

*T*HE autumn of 1531 brought with it famine and the plague. The king shut himself up in Fontainebleau, leaving in mid-September to go on a pilgrimage to Nôtre-Dame-de-Liesse to pray for the ease of his mother's suffering. Louise had so many causes for complaint that her death was only a question of time. Since the Treaty of Cambrai, she had not taken any further part in the government of the realm. Her guilt over the consequences of the Battle of Pavia, her efforts to repair the harm she had done to France, and her many duties during her regency all had worn her out. She had worked so hard that she ruined her already fragile health. In her last years, Louise de Savoie developed an abhorrence of death and a morbid fascination with illness and its cures. Brantôme writes of both Louise's and her daughter's horror and fear of death. The regent could not bear preachers to speak of death in their sermons and complained that when they had nothing else to say, "ignorant persons fall to talking of death." Both Louise and Marguerite experimented with medical ointments and lotions. Marguerite wrote to François: ". . . after dinner . . . instead of doing her usual good works, she sends for all those who have any malady, whether in the legs, arms or breasts, and with her own hands she dresses them, in order to try out an ointment, which is somewhat singular." A few days after Marguerite wrote this letter to her brother at Chantilly, where he was visiting Montmorency, Louise left Fontainebleau with her daughter for a change of air and to avoid the plague in the area. She stopped at Grèz-sur-Loing, a little village in the Gâtinais, where she died on September 23, without seeing her beloved son for whose glory she had struggled all her life.

When François heard that his mother had stopped at Grèz because she was feeling ill, he raced to be with her, but he could not reach her before she died. Louise de Savoie was fifty-five. Her son was inconsolable with grief, and fainted on seeing the corpse.

As *dame d'honneur* to Madame Louise, the Grande Sénéchale of Normandy, Diane de Poitiers, returned to the court to take part in the funeral ceremonies. Louise's effigy had been placed on top of the coffin, dressed in her court robes, wearing her crown and holding her scepter. All the houses in the streets of the funeral procession were draped in black. On October 17, the convoy escorting the coffin, accompanied by torchbearers, wound its mournful way to the Cathedral of Nôtre-Dame in Paris. The cortège was led by three cardinals, thirteen archbishops, and the Princes of the Blood. They were followed by Louise de Savoie's empty litter, encircled by her *dames d'honneur,* and behind them members of the court and the *Parlement.* Two days later, after the celebration of three High Masses, the convoy left in pouring rain for the interment at Saint-Denis in the vault of France's monarchs. There Louise de Savoie would remain for 250 years, until 1789, when revolutionaries dragged her remains out of the tomb and threw them into a communal ditch along with those of all the other kings and queens of France.

With the death of Louise de Savoie, the tragic sequence of events that had almost ruined France came to an end. Anne de Beaujeu, the Constable de Bourbon, and now Louise, were all gone. Diane de Poitiers had lost her husband. The Grande Sénéchale of Normandy

had reached a time in her life when she must take stock and plan her future. Diane's only future lay at court. But, as a very rich widow without
sons, she was particularly vulnerable to those who wished to exploit her
possessions and her daughters' inheritance. If she were to survive, she
would need to find a second husband or a powerful protector to guide
her through the minefield of intrigue at Fontainebleau.

*A*FTER the funeral ceremonies for her husband and for the regent, Diane de Poitiers returned to Anet. During this time of
retreat from the court, she began to care for her looks in earnest, since
at thirty-one she was approaching what was then regarded as middle
age. To maintain her famous complexion, Diane used only rainwater for
washing her face, and she avoided cosmetics which, at the time, were
most damaging to the skin. Blessed with energy and abounding good
health all her life, she had never ceased to train and exercise her mind
and her body. Now she concentrated on preserving that perfect face.

If the secret of Diane de Poitiers' beauty lay in her daily routine,
she deserved her astonishing youthfulness and robust health. Summer
and winter in all weathers, she would rise at dawn and bathe her whole
body in ice-cold rain or well water. She breakfasted with a cup of
homemade bouillon (later this was to be described as a magic potion—
even by Brantôme) before leaving at first light for a brisk three-hour
ride through the woods and countryside around Anet. On her return
she would rest, and around ten or eleven, she would eat a simple meal.
Only then did Diane de Poitiers begin her public duties as the widow
of the Grand Sénéchal, attending to the affairs of her vast inheritance
and greeting the growing number of her callers. She would dine at six
in the evening and retire to bed early.

Diane de Poitiers epitomized the image of her era's beauty: tall,
slender though not frail, she had a long neck, and strong arms and legs
from riding. She had beautiful hands with long fingers, and her al-
abaster skin was shown to advantage by a décolleté of black velvet or
satin. Around 1530, well-built rather than thin women were considered beautiful in their sensuality. Ladies were careful to keep the sun off

their skin[2] while maintaining a healthy outdoor appearance, a flattering décolleté, and a small waist. A lady would only expose her throat, neck, hands, and décolleté, so these were the areas studied and cherished. Her throat should be white and soft, and it was quite usual for her lover to caress her neck in public. Unlike the breasts, the throat was not considered an intimate part of the body. A lady would know how to move her hands elegantly in conversation, play with her gloves, or take part in card games, tric-trac, or check. Her smile would be remarked upon and a lady's beauty depended much on the whiteness (and retention) of her teeth.[3]

Brantôme wrote how well Diane's black and white mourning became her, and how her clothes were always designed to show her figure to the best advantage. He added that "her style expressed more worldliness than mourning and, above all, set off her beautiful neck." Her clothes were always made of pure silk. Two waves of reddish-golden hair showed from a snood of black silk mesh encrusted with pearls. Often she would hang ropes of large pearls from each shoulder, swinging them across the front of a wide black velvet bodice with a deep décolleté. Her sleeves were tight at the shoulders and on the upper arms, and burst into delicate full white muslin above the elbow, to be caught at the wrist. Around her narrow waist she wore a chain of precious stones, which joined and then hung down the front of her dress. If the whole effect was calculated, it was done in order to please. Wearing mourning placed her on a pedestal above her rivals, a rare creature rendered more desirable by her isolation. Her signature black and white became the fashion for aristocratic widows thereafter.[4]

AT the end of 1531, François I decided to make a "progress" through much of his kingdom to show his people their new

2. Diane's parasol, which would have been carried in front of her by a page, can still be seen at the château d'Anet.

3. In some cases, good teeth were taken from corpses and attached by a bridge using gold wire.

4. When Christian Dior visited Anet, he declared that Diane was the greatest fashion leader of her time and the woman with the most influence on style during her era.

The dauphin François was François I's first son and heir.

queen and their dauphin. The king was justly proud of his heir, who
was so like him in many ways. A handsome young man, the dauphin
had his father's *joie de vivre,* his energy, charm, and a natural affinity
with ordinary people. His kindness and the care the young François
demonstrated on this tour caused people to compare him to Louis XII.
Like him, the dauphin began to be called "father of his people."

As the queen's senior *dame d'honneur,* Diane de Poitiers' place at
court and on the progress through France was at Eleonore's side. The
pace was stately, and Anne de Mortmorency's organization of the various entries of the queen into her cities was faultless. The court moved
through Picardy and Normandy. At Dieppe, François and his sons saw
a *tableau vivant* representing the New World, featuring exotic birds,
monkeys, reptiles, and even real savages. These were all then given to
the king and his sons. The next stop was Rouen, capital of Normandy
and Brézé territory, where the royal party was fêted magnificently.

They moved on to the king's new town of Le Havre on the coast, still under construction.

During the many leisurely stops in the royal progress, it is probable that the king reviewed recent developments in Italy with Diane de Poitiers, and in particular, Prince Henri's forthcoming marriage, first discussed at Anet with Louis de Brézé. As emperor and suzerain of Milan, Charles V had installed his natural daughter, married to Pope Clement's natural son Alessandro de' Medici, to rule in Florence as Duke and Duchess of Urbino. The Medici pope was powerless to prevent this move. As the only *legitimate* heiress to the duchy of Florence, Catherine was being distanced from her inheritance by her forthcoming marriage to a royal prince of France, even though her claim would not be affected. The French king and the pope had common cause in wanting to diminish the power of the emperor in Italy. Meanwhile, Henry VIII saw an opportunity in the French king's proximity to the pope, and arranged a friendly meeting with François I in Boulogne. Henry VIII was still seeking the annulment of his marriage from Catherine of Aragon.

Diane de Poitiers was in attendance on the queen as she made glorious entries into Rheims in March, and Lyons in May. The governor of the Auvergne, John Stewart, Duke of Albany, uncle by marriage to Catherine de' Medici, and cousin to Diane through his La Tour d'Auvergne wife, met the royal party in Lyons.[5] As Catherine had inherited property in Auvergne through her mother, the tableau in Lyons proclaimed the Triumph of Juno, goddess of marriage, alluding to the queen, and to the forthcoming nuptials of Henri and Catherine. On July 18, as the royal caravanserai reached Puy in the Velay, Barbarossa—pirate chief of the Ottoman fleet and envoy of the Sultan—presented François I with a lion, a noble animal renowned for its courage and a symbol of the Sultan's friendship.[6] This was the beast

5. John Stewart, Duke of Albany, had been regent of Scotland from 1515 to 1524. Both he and his wife were first cousins of Diane's father, Jehan de Poitiers.

6. The alliance between François I and the Sultan survived the Treaty of Cambrai and continued to form the basis for French influence in the Middle East until the twentieth century. The text of the treaty, signed in 1536, has never been found. Such copies as exist do not seem genuine, since treaties with the Sultan always took the form of a gracious concession from him, not a compact between equals.

François would later pass on to Catherine's cousin, Ippolito de' Medici. Neither the heraldic nor the mythological symbolism of the gift was lost on the French king. Since the days of Charlemagne, France, oldest daughter of the church, had always enjoyed courteous relations with the Ottoman rulers.

With the addition of the permanently hungry lion, which was kept as far as possible from the monkeys, the reptiles, the exotic birds, and the savages, the royal cortège was taking on the appearance of a circus on the move. François also had a lynx that proved a bit of a handful on his travels and had to be left at an inn. A receipt exists of payment to the innkeeper's wife for bandages![7] Having passed through Avignon and Arles, the procession finally reached Marseilles on October 8, 1533. There, the king's entourage installed themselves in the castle of the counts of Toulouse to prepare for the wedding of Henri and Catherine.

---

7. I am grateful to Professor R. J. Knecht for sharing this information. He found the receipt in France during his researches into the Valois.

CHAPTER TEN

Catherine's New World

*W*HEN Catherine arrived in France, the population numbered 16 million, compared with England's 4 million. François I's court was hugely extravagant, and he needed a source of income to match his expenditure. His large, fertile kingdom was blessed by nature, and French farmers worked hard. Vast areas were covered with fields of grain, vineyards, and orchards; and cattle thrived on the rich pasture. Little towns girdled churches, and great manorhouses had begun to replace the feudal castles that dotted the land. Rivers teemed with fish and sailboats, and barges carried the crops and livestock to the cities—especially Paris. Religion was an integral part of life and religious feast days were plentiful. Industry flourished in workshops, mines, forges, and quarries; cloth was woven from wool and silk and was exported. France was rich, and rightly described by Henry VIII as a "fair and abundant kingdom."

At the time of Catherine's arrival life in France was truly blessed, but did either Pope Clement VII or King François I consider the happiness or comfort of the two young people they had just forced to marry? In the sixteenth century, happiness was not a part of the marriage equation. A successful marriage was one in which power, wealth, and property increased, and heirs were born to consolidate the greater family unit. The royal newlyweds were mere tools in this traditional power play. This particular contract may have seemed unequal to the court, but the king was satisfied. Through the union of his son, Henri d'Orléans, to the heiress Catherine de' Medici, Clement VII and François I had secretly agreed to join forces in eighteen months' time in order to reclaim the duchies of Milan and Urbino. At long last, François would realize his elusive dream of repossessing his lost conquests on the Italian peninsula. The pope was even more satisfied than the king. Through this marriage, the parvenu Medici had joined an elite permitted to marry into the oldest royal house in Europe; together, king and pope would then vanquish their mutual enemy, the emperor. The two monarchs, Charles V and François I, were playing on the chessboard of Europe, and Henri and Catherine were mere pawns in the great game.

Two weeks after the wedding, François I left Marseilles with the court, but the pope stayed on for a month due to bad weather. He also hoped Catherine might be pregnant. The little *duchessina,* as the French court contemptuously dubbed her, would not know this joy for another ten years. Henri had done his duty in consummating the marriage but was not prepared to do more, and he ignored his bride thereafter. Catherine may have arrived, but she did not *belong* to the brilliant, subtle, extravagant community that was the French court.

To distract Charles V from his designs on Italy, François I followed Montmorency's advice and agitated the emperor's enemies in Germany. The Lutheran Reformation was gathering converts who, through their Protestant princes, were beginning to challenge the Holy Roman Emperor's right to rule them. Following his renewed alliance with the Sultan, François urged Barbarossa to attack imperial ships. To put even more pressure on the emperor, the king of France made public his son's right, as Catherine de' Medici's husband, to the duchy of Urbino. To that end he gathered a mighty force to join with Clement and push Charles V out of Italy.

Within a year of the Medici–Orléans marriage in Marseilles, on November 25, 1534, Clement VII died, and the treaties made with the king of France went with him. All possible advantage, financial or political, that could have accrued from the marriage of Henri and Catherine disappeared. Only the stigma of a *mésalliance* remained. The new pope, an anti-Medici Farnese, repudiated the alliance with France. The French court's opinion that their royal prince had been "squandered on a grocer's daughter"[1] was confirmed. With nothing gained, the French king would be heard to exclaim: "*J'ai eu la fille toute nue*"— "She came to me naked as a newborn babe." There is no record that Catherine grieved for Clement VII; his death merely added to the delicacy of her situation at the French court.

The new pope, Paul III, belonged firmly in the imperial camp, and François I's chimera of Italy evaporated once again.

$\mathcal{T}$HE king withdrew into the *douceur de vivre*—the sweetness of life—at Fontainebleau. François had not forgotten Diane's great skill in the saddle and often invited her to accompany him hunting to hounds, marveling at her ability to call for a fresh horse when even he was ready to drop. He renewed his invitation for her to join his *Petite Bande,* and she accepted.

This tall, serene Artemis, who appeared transformed, mature, and confident in black and white, stood out dramatically among the courtiers and ladies in their gaily colored luxury. With her extraordinary allure and air of self-possession, her presence was even more arresting. She was a perfect product of Anne de Beaujeu's training, repeatedly described as reserved and reflective, who spoke little and kept her distance. Her beauty was majestic.

La Grande Sénéchale[2] believed in her role as the perfect widow, but her black and white "uniform" was also full of allure. How else could she hope to find a protector or husband at the court? Despite the assertions of some biographers, it is doubtful that she looked to thirteen-year-old Henri to fill that role.

The Palace of Fontainebleau had been under construction for the

1. A reference to the early merchant Medicis' links with the spice trade.
2. Diane did not give up her husband's title or privileges until 1548.

past eight years; work was to continue for another thirteen. François delighted in leading the Grande Sénéchale (or comtesse de Saint-Vallier, as she now styled herself) through the endless stuccoed galleries emblazoned with his salamander symbol. He enjoyed her opinions, her reactions, and her knowledge. A true Renaissance man, he welcomed and admired this Renaissance woman.

The palace was still comparatively small and focused on the Galerie François I, the central section added to the old ruined keep. The gallery, a triumph of the French Renaissance, still exists but has doubled in size. It had a wing on either side. The main entrance was the fabled *Porte Dorée* (Golden Gate), which opened onto a straight wide passage leading into the château. Eventually, one came out into an avenue that led to the forest—Fontainebleau was, after all, a *château de chasse*. The king's apartment consisted of only four rooms.

The craftsmen imported for the stuccowork and the frescoes were mostly Italian, a good number of them pupils of Giulio Romano, who had just completed the Palazzo del Te in Mantua for Federigo Gonzaga. In the famous *Camera degli Sposi* (Bridal Suite), sixty-four little salamander lizards were depicted on the ceiling and in the frescoes lining the upper walls. The salamander was a symbol of a reputation that these two hot-blooded *patrones,* Federigo Gonzaga and François I, proudly shared.

The king had planned Fontainebleau as his homage to Italy within France, a palace made and filled with all things beautiful, dedicated to the pursuit of pleasure. Rare woods and marbles came from Italy; stucco reliefs surrounded the wall murals and the window embrasures; the wooden ceilings were all painted, and gold leaf glowed, highlighting everything. François loved this palace, with its gardens and shady walks, its Venetian crystal, and its elaborate system of mirrors reflecting the light and the water. His walls bore the works of Leonardo, Titian, Bronzino, Andrea del Sarto; and the magnificent classical statue known as the *Apollo Belvedere* stood gazing down the long gallery. Fontainebleau was François I's idea of heaven, and to be there gave him peace.

Fontainebleau also was the closest Catherine came to having a home in the early years of her marriage. Clement VII's death had placed her in a difficult position. She was well aware of the sniggers and the stigma of *mésalliance,* whispered in her presence behind cupped hands. Catherine's letters reveal that at times not even she could believe the honor of her elevation into the French royal house. The Venetian ambassador Giustiniani reported that the marriage had displeased the entire nation. Catherine, he wrote, kept her head down and was *"molto obediente."* It would be natural to assume that two young people, having both endured unhappy childhoods, outcasts in their respective ways, would have found comfort in one another's company. But Henri's imagination had been captured by Diane de Poitiers and Catherine was the outsider among François' band of dazzling young enchantresses. How they mocked the *duchessina.* As a young woman facing difficult circumstances, Louise de Savoie had made her motto: "Humility and Patience." It had worked for Louise (that great dissembler), and Catherine, in her cunning, chose the same maxim.

Since Henri was a younger son with an unmarried elder brother, the couple was not given an establishment of their own. Catherine moved into Henri's "bachelor" apartments, which he shared with his two brothers. Catherine's ladies and personal staff also attended to her sisters-in-law, Madeleine and Marguerite. The three princes moved about with the court, giving Henri and Catherine little privacy as they journeyed between Fontainebleau, Blois, Amboise, or to the seat of some great nobleman where the king wished to hunt. The arrangement did not seem to bother them at all.

Although the marriage had been consummated, there were a number at court who thought Catherine's health was still too delicate for the young couple to take part in marital relations. Henri was very aware that the court considered this marriage a gross *mésalliance*—something his stay in protocol-obsessed Spain had taught him was unacceptable in a royal house. As a result, he wanted nothing to do with his wife.

In order for her to learn the ways of the French court, Catherine had been placed in the care of her kinswoman, Diane. It didn't take the bride long to become aware of Henri's devotion to this serene lady. Catherine understood that her husband's love for Diane was of a chivalrous kind, and that ever since the tournament in Paris Henri had been Diane's *chevalier servant*. Catherine knew instinctively that she could not hope to compete for her husband's devotion to this beautiful older woman, secure in her high birth and experience. No amount of intelligence and education would ever be a match for Diane's power of enchantment over Henri. But she would try.

Catherine de' Medici was determined to succeed where Diane excelled. She began with riding lessons. Catherine had a short, awkward frame and little natural talent or ability, but she compensated with courage, and persevered until she became quite a proficient horsewoman. Catherine begged the king to let her join the *Petite Bande*. They all rode magnificently and shared the full confidence of the king, often to a greater extent than his Privy Council. To be one of their number was the greatest wish of the little *duchessina*, even though they mocked her accent and her origins.

Despite one horrific fall recorded by the Venetian ambassador Lorenzo Contarini, Catherine continued to try to emulate her rival on the hunting field. A born strategist and survivor, she was very vain about her pretty hands and legs, and cleverly devised a method of attaching her skirts to her saddle to expose her slender calves, which were much admired. For this reason she is sometimes credited with inventing the sidesaddle. In fact, ladies in Italy had long ridden with one leg— the right—crossed over to the left side supported in a crook, and Catherine simply encouraged this fashion in France. Ladies who were not skilled horsewomen rode sitting in a padded chair or *planchette* on the back of an ambling mare, a quiet hack trained to a smooth movement. Catherine is also credited with introducing the

Catherine de' Medici was credited with introducing into France the Italian fashion for ladies to ride sidesaddle. The custom enabled her to show her pretty legs.

divided skirt, or *culotte,* for riding. The *culotte* was then adopted by chaste ladies who did not wish any dissolute young blade to take the liberty of slipping his hand under their dresses while they were dismounting—quite a common practice at the time. It was essential, too, for ladies who rode astride, like Diane or members of the *Petite Bande,* to wear men's hose under their skirts or *culottes.* The king's sister, Marguerite de Navarre, was often described as looking magnificent in men's clothes at court. Cross-dressing is a custom as old as chivalry.

Catherine knew she would never be considered pretty, but by watching carefully she learned the strengths and weaknesses of the courtiers and ingratiated herself with all their various factions. She amused her father-in-law with new games, dances, and a variety of distractions. Catherine always tried desperately hard to please the king. She was wittier and better educated than most of the court ladies, and François genuinely enjoyed his daughter-in-law's company. He called her "*ma fille*" and spoke to her wistfully in Italian of his travels in her country and his love of Italian art. Her efforts to divert the king from his increasing ennui were so successful that finally he allowed her to join the charmed circle of *La Petite Bande* and to benefit from all its privileges. (Many years later, when Catherine ruled France, she remembered the *Petite Bande* and organized a similar troupe of young ladies, beautiful and noble, who were known as her "*Escadron Volant,*" or "Flying Squadron." These she forced to spy on foreign diplomats and even prostitute themselves for information during her baccanalian festivals at Chenonceau.)

Realizing that preferential treatment from the king would only arouse jealousy and further dislike from the courtiers, Catherine humbled herself before everyone. At every opportunity, clever little Catherine deferred to Diane. She went to great lengths to gain the affection of the king's sister, Queen Marguerite of Navarre. The *duchessina* also succeeded in winning over Anne de Pisseleu. Catherine recognized Anne's greed and wooed her with flattery and gifts, though she did not dare join her faction against Diane. In fact, Catherine made herself so agreeable and bland that she became almost invisible. Eventually, no one had anything to say against her—or even about her. Almost everyone was taken in; except perhaps Diane, and Anne de Montmorency, that shrewd judge of character. Not until Henri's death many years later would the true face behind Catherine de' Medici's mask emerge.

IT was considered more appropriate for a royal mistress to be married in the event she had children. Therefore, in 1534, the king arranged Anne de Pisseleu's wedding to Jean de Brosse, the intelligent, impoverished, and acquiescent comte de Penthièvre. He needed to be all three so that he would accept the arrangement, profit by it, and give Anne a pedigree. Thus she became a countess.

François allowed the newlyweds a honeymoon, and then, leaving Anne at court, the count returned to Brittany with money to renovate his ruined estates. Two years later, François made him duc d'Etampes

Anne de Pisseleu, duchesse d'Etampes, mistress of François I, and deadly enemy of Diane de Poitiers.

so that Anne could become a duchess. In the letters patent granting his dukedom, the king asserted that the title was in "recognition of the exceptional consideration and pleasant services rendered to him daily by 'my cousin' Anne." The new duke was dispatched as governor of a succession of distant provinces, until finally he was granted the prestigious post of governor of Brittany.

Displaying a wicked sense of irony, the king made Anne one of the queen's ladies. Poor Eleonore, who fancied herself in love with François, had to tolerate the daily presence of his mistress at her court. To make the situation worse for the queen, Anne d'Etampes was not subtle about her relationship with the king and used her power indiscriminately. Nor did the new duchess forget her enormous family. She saw to it that they received handsome appointments and pensions: several brothers became bishops and archbishops—one even a cardinal—and her unmarried sisters were made abbesses. But the ducal title alone was not enough for Anne. She was much in need of money, and so she stole her husband's ducal income and trafficked in his ducal prerogatives. The king gave his mistress a large house in Paris next to the Palais des Tournelles (which had a connecting tunnel) and two châteaux—Etampes and Limours—as well as numerous estates. Although her taste in dress and jewelry was wildly extravagant, François denied her nothing. It is sometimes said that Anne d'Etampes had a powerful influence on affairs of state; but the king was an absolute monarch, who had proclaimed at his accession: "I will not allow there to be more than one king in France."

Although he granted his ministers much power, François I would never permit a pretty woman to interfere in politics. Perhaps as compensation, the king indulged Anne in every other way and allowed her to recommend her favorites for some offices. As she was easily flattered, inevitably the wrong candidates were promoted.[3]

Anne d'Etampes befriended the extrovert dauphin, François, who was no friend of his brother Henri. Through Anne's influence, the dauphin shared her antipathy toward Diane. The king openly favored

3. According to the memoirs of the king's marshal, Blaise de Montluc, during the reign of François I women meddled far too much in the governing of France; he should have "shut the mouths of those who interfered as they were responsible for all the slanders."

his eldest son, who resembled him so much when he had been dauphin; whereas Henri, though tall and athletic like his father, brought back memories of the shy, sad queen François had so mistreated.

*G*ONTAINEBLEAU was built as a pleasure palace, full of allegorical paintings hinting at forbidden and secret delights. But as the king insisted on courtly behavior, no one dared to break his code of good manners. In fact, this courtly behavior concealed a snakepit of intrigues and political maneuvering, where the stakes were so high that a courtier could lose his fortune or even his life if the tide turned the wrong way. As an absolute monarch, the king was the source of all power, privileges, and benefits. To be in his favor was essential.

François made no secret of the pleasure he took in Diane's company by day, which increased the envy of his young companion of the night, the duchesse d'Etampes. Anne was ambitious, greedy, and fond of intrigues. She had certainly heard the gossip about the king and that Diane's favors had been the price of Saint-Vallier's release. It did not take long for Anne's jealousy of her lover's undisguised fascination with the chaste and beautiful widow to turn to hatred. Anne encouraged a group of sycophantic courtiers and intellectuals to write and circulate slanderous ditties and poems about Diane de Poitiers and to humiliate her whenever possible. When Diane was in her prime, but before Primaticcio and Clouet painted their famous portraits of her, some extraordinary pamphlets appeared, describing her wrinkled skin and double chins. Others claimed that her looks had faded, her hair had turned white, her teeth had fallen out, and so on.

The famous poet from Champagne, Jean Voulté, published three scathing epigrams against "Poitiers, old Woman of the Court" and dubbed her "the old gray mare." Though written in Latin, translations were not slow in appearing: "You may buy the superfine of that which constitutes woman, but you will not even then obtain the desire of your lover, for one must be alive and you are dead." Another of his published jibes warned: *"In Pictariam anum anulicam"*—"Painted bait catches no game." Diane merely smiled and ignored the insults. But she stored them all away in her implacable memory to avenge one day. Until that time came, Diane de Poitiers could rely on Henri's adoration to heal her wounded pride.

Many people wrote in praise of Diane de Poitiers—among them, Joachim du Bellay and the poet and charmer Clément Marot. While Marot was under Diane's spell, he had dedicated some beautiful verses in her honor:

> Dont le nom gracieux
> N'est ja besoin d'escrire;
> Il est escript aux cieulx
> Et de nuict se peult lire.

> A noble name
> Has no need of script
> It is written in the heavens
> And can be read each night.

When the passion he nurtured for Diane remained unrequited, and she subsequently had him prosecuted as a Protestant, Marot joined the clique around the duchesse d'Etampes. Then, his verses sang a different tune:

> Que voulez-vous Diane bonne
> Que vous donne
> Vous n'eûtes comme j'étends
> Jamais tant d'heure au printemps
> Qu'en automne.

(Diane is accused of trying to live in springtime when in fact she has reached the autumn of her life.)

For the benefit of her entourage, one day Anne d'Etampes greeted her rival with the claim: "Why, I was born on the very day Madame la Grande Sénéchale was married." Diane merely smiled and reminded her that she was Anne's senior by no more than nine years. Anne had Diane dubbed "the Wrinkled One," which led to endless vulgar permutations of the cruel jibe both within her circle and below stairs. But Diane could afford her silent smile. She was confident in her beauty. Later, the paintings and drawings of Primaticcio and Clouet, the modeling of Cellini and Goujon, and the writings of Brantôme, among others, would all proclaim her magnificence for posterity. Their testimony would, in the end, be her revenge.

However, Diane's beauty remains an enigma, as some of her portraits show her as less than remarkable. Beauty is in the eye of the beholder—and of the artist. Flatterers by profession, some saw her as lovelier than others, though none denied the magnificence of her body. She exuded health, and her expression and animation has been credited for much of her illusion of perfection.

Despite their open enmity, Anne and Diane upheld the king's rules of courtesy and behaved with impeccable *politesse* toward one another in company. But Anne was the antithesis of Diane in almost every way. The contemporary published criticism of Diane is voluminous since both she and the duchesse d'Etampes drew enormous support from the intellectuals of the day. As the king's official mistress, the duchesse was inevitably in the company of those who hoped to profit from her royal liaison. By comparison, those who came to the support of the widowed Grande Sénéchale did so primarily out of genuine appreciation of her. Apart from her wealth, Diane had neither power nor influence at this time. And yet Diane de Poitiers was still highly regarded by the king or there would not be so many instances of the court staying at Anet and Mauny after the death of Louis de Brézé.

Diane had good friends at court; but without a father, husband, or sons, she was essentially a woman alone. Stoically, she chose to ignore Anne d'Etampes' persistent and vicious attacks, hold her head high, and remain aloof. In verbal confrontation, the more experienced Madame de Brézé invariably triumphed. But when Anne and her coterie spread rumors that the lovely widow retained her looks by practicing witchcraft, Diane finally appreciated the very real danger of her unprotected position. Witches were burned at the stake, often without the benefit of a trial. If such a story were to spread beyond the court and gain credence, Diane's situation might well become extremely dangerous. The legendary huntress was becoming the hunted, and this she could not tolerate.

To the surprise of the entire court, it was the shy young Prince Henri who stepped forward to defend Diane de Poitiers from this new calumny. Henri had grown tall, and his prowess at the martial arts was already well known. As Diane was his mentor and he her young knight, he saw her regularly, but generally kept a low profile. This new insult he heard circulating at court alarmed him, however, and he would not tolerate it. He repeated his pledge of devotion and protection of La Grande Sénéchale before the assembled court, and defied his father's mistress to continue with her slanders against his "Lady." The protection of the king's younger son, no matter how disliked by his father, was a power to be reckoned with, and Diane's enemies took note. Despite Henri's clear adoration of Diane de Poitiers, it is hard to believe that her attachment to the fourteen-year-old prince could have contained any serious romantic ambition at this time.

*T*HE growing threat of heresy within his kingdom was a problem for François I. Increasing the church's influence had been a goal of Pope Clement, but even after his death, the French king was intent on curbing the growth of heresy. Yet how could François, a committed humanist, stamp out heresy without stifling the intellectual climate and movement he himself had pioneered? In France, the humanists studied the classics, poetry, and philosophy as a prelude to the Christian doctrines. Humanism was not just an intellectual movement with a spiritual element aimed at reviving religion through a mystical approach to the Scriptures. If François was personally ambivalent or inconsistent in his attitude toward heresy, he knew that, as God's anointed, the king should not tolerate heresy, and he repeatedly urged the appropriate authorities to stamp it out. Heretics were burned in public, their tongues cut out and hands cut off; the more fortunate were banished, their property confiscated.

Slowly, the zeal for religious reform permeated the French court, with the dauphin and Anne d'Etampes siding with the new order, and Henri d'Orléans and Diane de Poitiers standing firmly behind the teachings of the Catholic Church. The king was uncertain which way to turn and his allegiance fluctuated. Ultimately, however, no one had more influence over him than his sister, Marguerite de Navarre, who begged François to remain tolerant toward the reformers. The king began to see the wisdom of this policy with regard to the Protestant princes of Germany. François needed the help of the emperor's enemies there to keep Charles V occupied while he tried to recapture his lost territories in Italy.

Catherine de' Medici had been brought up in Florence, the cradle of humanism, in an atmosphere of tolerance for different faiths, which led the growing numbers of Protestants in France to pin some of their hopes on her. Catherine had observed firsthand the workings of papal diplomacy during her time with her cousin Clement VII, and had noted how flexible the Vatican could be. Uncertain how to proceed, she adopted the king's attitude and his policy of tolerance.

Diane de Poitiers was of the opposite conviction and adamantly opposed to the reformers. She was determined to protect orthodoxy from the threat of heresy, and influenced Henri in this conviction. In 1534, Ignatius of Loyola had begun his Counter-Reformation movement by enrolling his first recruits into the Society of Jesus, better known as Jesuits, and Pope Paul III (Alessandro Farnese) looked to them to help reconquer territory lost to the Protestants.

Everyone talked of religion, and the end of 1534 was marked by the "affair of the placards." While François was showing signs of forbearance and trying to heal the religious schism in Germany where many French Protestants had fled, a group of excessively zealous reformers printed broadsheets condemning the Catholic Mass as an "idolatrous rite." They described the church's hierarchy from the pope on down as "vermin, false prophets, damnable deceivers, apostates, wolves, false shepherds, seducers, liars and execrable blasphemers, murderers of souls, denouncers of Jesus Christ, of his death and passion, false witnesses, traitors, thieves, and robbers of the honor of God and more detestable than devils." These broadsheets went on to suggest that members of the church should burn themselves rather than burn the reformers. Statues of saints were vandalized and rumors spread that these acts were intended to intimidate the king.

During the night of October 17–18, the first broadsheets were nailed on some walls and doors in Paris. Panic followed as wild rumors spread that the faithful would be massacred. The hysteria increased when it was discovered that these broadsheets had also been found in five provincial towns—Orléans, Blois, Tours, Rouen, and Amboise. The king was in residence at Amboise when a placard was even found attached to the door of his bedroom.

The bold, widespread appearance of placards implied that a plot existed against the authority of the king. The *Parlement* ordered the arrest of two hundred people and the king himself took part in a penitent procession. He publicly admonished the culprits but advised the authorities to be prudent. Nevertheless, on the same day, several pyres were built and prepared, and on November 7, 1534, seven of the accused were condemned. The pope urged mediation and elevated the moderate Archbishop Jean du Bellay to the cardinal's hat. But under the guidance of Jean Calvin, the Protestants were unyielding.

The public executions began on November 13, and continued until the end of the year, when six heretics were burned at the stake on New Year's Day 1535 in the presence of the royal family. Others had their tongues slashed down the center or their hands cut off. At the banquet in the bishop's palace prior to the New Year executions, The Most Christian King made a speech urging everyone to fight heresy. Two hundred Parisians were banished that day and their property confiscated. More would have been punished but for the intervention of powerful patrons of learning, who prevented the closure of all the printing presses. Writers and publishers were henceforth subject to scrutiny. François quoted the emperor Maximilian to the Venetian ambassador: "The emperor is king of kings; the Catholic king is king of men; the king of France is king of beasts, because, whatever he commands, he is instantly obeyed, like men by beasts." Despite his genuine humanism, the king had committed himself to the repression of the foreign menace of the "New Religion." To the satisfaction of Anne de Montmorency and Diane de Poitiers, the divorce between the Renaissance and the Reformation was complete. The king's sister was of the opposite persuasion and was denounced by the Sorbonne's theological faculty for helping the heretics. A furious François blamed Montmorency for allowing such insolence against a member of his family.

Just three weeks later, more than seventy people suspected of heresy and, by implication, treason, were arrested. Among them was Clément Marot, whose insinuating verses had so offended the Grande Sénéchale. He managed to escape to Ferrara and the court of Princess Renée, sister of the late Queen Claude. It was believed that Marot had been helped by Marguerite de Navarre and the king's mistress, Anne d'Etampes.

*T*O escape from the horrors of the persecutions, in March 1535 the court, including Anne d'Etampes and Marguerite de Navarre, embarked on a grand tour through the kingdom. François proceeded to try to convince the Protestant princes of Germany that his persecutions in France were more against treason than religion. As Europe was beginning to divide in this great religious convulsion, the Turks under Suleiman the Magnificent had conquered the Balkan peninsula, controlled Egypt, and were terrorizing the Mediterranean with their powerful navy under Barbarossa, Bey of Algiers and Tunis and lieutenant of Suleiman. Mosques were replacing churches in Hungary. Slave traders were descending on Naples, Sicily, Sardinia, and Corsica, capturing entire families. The Christian world was outraged. Even François was so ashamed of his prospective ally that he was not averse to the emperor's call for a crusade.

Charles V saw himself as the standard-bearer for Christianity against Protestantism and the infidels; the French king agreed with him on the religious issue, but the struggle between the house of Habsburg and the house of Valois continued to dominate Europe's politics. If François I were to join forces with the emperor against the threat from the Turks, France would find herself dominated by her hated enemy Charles V. To the French king, the choice was clear. Within three years of Cambrai, all the treaties between the emperor Charles and François I collapsed. To the horror of Christianity, the king of France allied himself to the infidel Sultan Suleiman. One wonders if François could have been unaware of the mortal danger such an alliance would present to Europe. Suleiman had already declared himself the "only, true Emperor of the West, the Caliph of Rome."

It was a bold decision. Accompanied by his three sons, the dauphin, Henri d'Orléans, and Charles d'Angoulême, The Most Christian King was ready to ride to war as an ally of the Ottoman Turk against the Holy Roman Emperor. On the other hand, Diane de Poitiers and Montmorency were certain that the only way to move forward in Italy, and for Henri d'Orléans to receive his sovereign state, was to make peace with the emperor, not war. The pleas of Queen Eleonore were ignored. All three (Diane, Montmorency, and Eleonore) tried in vain to persuade the king to break his alliances with the Protestant German princes and with the Sultan Suleiman, against whom Charles V was mobilizing. War was again on the horizon.

CHAPTER ELEVEN

The Dauphin Is
Dead—Long Live the Dauphin

*I*N July 1536, Charles V decided to invade Provence. At the same time, he would attack France from the north and thereby divide François I's forces. The king instructed Montmorency not to engage the emperor but to harass him continually and force him to waste time while drawing him deeper into France toward Aix-en-Provence and Marseilles. However, Montmorency soon realized that Aix could not garrison his own force of six thousand troops and that it would take him too long to reinforce the city's defenses. Montmorency's new plan was to follow the Roman policy of "scorched earth" and *not* engage the enemy. Aix was evacuated and what could not be taken away by the population was destroyed. Nothing was spared—lower Provence was laid waste. The peasantry were forced to burn their farms, their mills, their crops, their stores, and their wood; in view of the greater danger, few refused. They let loose their animals, poisoned their wells or blocked them with grain, and fled. Fruit trees and vines were spared because in August the fruit was not yet ripe and would cause dysentery. The French had fortified all the towns guarding the Rhône, and the king waited at Valence. Some months earlier, he had ordered that the fortifications of Marseilles be reinforced; a French fleet sat in the harbor there; near Avignon, Montmorency's superbly organized camp was on full alert. All waited for the emperor and his massive army.

Charles V advanced steadily, capturing Aix on August 13. Soon he became aware that his progress was blocked in two directions by the French army, and that in the south his supply wagons were being plundered. The ships that tried to supply him from the coast were attacked. All around, the countryside had been laid waste, and his soldiers began to succumb to dysentery and starvation. There was no water, and whenever the soldiers went foraging, they were set upon and killed by the peasants. By September 13, just one month after capturing Aix, Charles V had lost twenty thousand men. He withdrew, defeated.

The court had remained in Lyons throughout the summer while the king waited with his army at the junction of the Rhône and the Durance rivers. At the beginning of August, before leaving Lyons to join his father and brothers with the army on the Rhône, the dauphin decided to play a game of tennis in a meadow by Ainay. It was a stifling hot day and thundery, but still the young prince insisted on playing a bristling game, as always, to win at any price. The price was too high. Dripping wet from his exertion, he "bade a page of his chamber go and

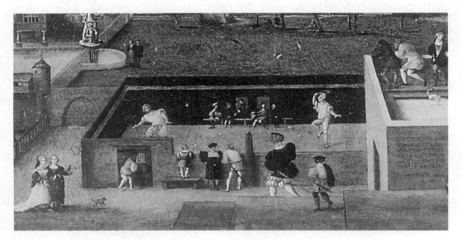

A game of *jeu de paume,* or "real tennis," in the sixteenth century.

bring him cold water in the little vase"[1] brought from Spain and given to him by one of Queen Eleonore's ladies. The little pitcher was small, made of earthenware "so subtle and fine that it has the virtue that whatever cold water you put into it you see it boil and make little bubbles as though it were on fire, nevertheless, it does not lose its coldness. . . ."

His Italian cupbearer, Count Sebastiano de Montecucculli, brought the dauphin an iced glass full of water from the pitcher, which he emptied. Shortly afterward, he felt unwell. Despite a burning fever, he managed to embark on a sailing trip down the valley of the Rhône toward his father's camp. After three days, the prince's condition had so deteriorated that he was brought ashore at Tournon. During the very early morning of August 10, 1536, eight days after falling ill, the dauphin of France fell into a coma and died. Overnight and without warning, Henri d'Orléans, the disliked second son of François I, had become the dauphin, and the Medici had one of their own as the future queen of France.

The king's grief was terrible. He had held such high hopes for his eldest son, whom he described as "my son so full of promise." François was proud that his heir, unlike Henri, had put the horror of his imprisonment in Spain behind him and had rejoiced in his freedom on his return. Everyone at court had a high opinion of him. The dauphin had the common touch, behaving with the same courtesy and kindness to princes and paupers, so that he was universally loved. The court plunged into deepest mourning for this remarkable and favorite prince. But the king knew he must think of the future of France and sent for his second son, Henri d'Orléans, to share his grief.

François advised Henri to try to imitate his brother's virtues and surpass his promise so that the French would never regret having lost their first dauphin. In haste, Henri was installed as Duke of Brittany, his mother's inheritance, which had passed to his elder brother. Then he was declared dauphin, the official heir to the throne.

With their return to France, the brothers' relationship had become strained. The dauphin was clearly preferred by their father and he had

---

1. Brantôme was writing after the event and may well have been influenced by the usual accusations of poison in the case of a royal death.

also sided with Anne d'Etampes against Diane. Nevertheless, Henri always deferred to his older brother, who would, after all, inherit the throne, and his sadness at losing François was profound. Henri had a soft and sentimental side to his character, and his older brother's leadership and protection during those dreadful, formative years in Spain colored his feelings for the dauphin his whole life.

As the new dauphin, Henri's duty lay with the army. With some relief, he left his grieving father and the court and joined Montmorency on the Rhône. Henri wrote to Jean d'Humières: "My cousin, the Grand Master has received me in this camp with all possible honor." This was the beginning of a lifelong, devoted friendship between the gruff older soldier and the melancholic youth destined to be king. François sent his commander-in-chief Montmorency instructions to make the dauphin Henri his apprentice and teach him the art of warfare by surrounding him with his best captains. He urged the brusque Montmorency to be subtle with his son and to continue in the same vein he had begun so well with his older brother.

Once the king was certain that Charles V had left for Spain by sea, François I was free to avenge the loss of his beloved eldest son. The autopsy was performed by seven doctors and showed that the dauphin had died of natural causes—his lungs had never really recovered from the years spent in the dank prison in Spain. Still, someone had to pay for his death. The king returned to the court at Lyons, where the wretched Montecucculli was brought to him in chains. Sebastiano de Montecucculli was a young gentleman who had come to France in the suite of Catherine de' Medici, had moved to the service of the princes, and had their complete confidence. Nevertheless, he was accused of poisoning the heir to the throne and of being in the pay of Charles V.

Montecucculli was totally devoted to the dauphin and surely innocent, but he had previously been employed by the emperor. A treatise on poisons, as well as an imperial safe-conduct, were found among his possessions, which was sufficient evidence to incriminate him. He was tortured horribly as the king's men filled him with enough water to burst his stomach. Not surprisingly, he confessed to pouring arsenic into the dauphin's water under instructions from the emperor Charles V, and his patron Federigo Gonzaga, and the imperial general who had taken

A common death for capital crimes in the sixteenth century was execution by quartering, shown here in the Place de Grève in Paris.

François prisoner at Pavia—and anyone else he could think of. He confessed that they were all working together and planned to kill one after another of the king's heirs and then the king himself. Although the wretched man later recanted, he was found guilty and condemned to death. At the Place de la Grenette in Lyons, Montecucculli was sentenced to be torn apart by four horses and "the four parts of his body to be hung at the four gates of the town of Lyons and his head put on the end of a lance." Before this sentence could be carried out, the people fell upon his corpse and tore away small pieces of flesh. They cut off his nose, tore out his eyes, smashed his teeth with stones, and children tore at his beard until not a hair remained. By the end the body was so disfigured as to be unrecognizable.

Not satisfied with the death of Montecucculli, the French accused the emperor and the Duke of Milan of murder, which they vigorously denied. The imperialists retaliated against the French by printing a pamphlet saying that the only ones to gain from the death of the dauphin were his brother Henri and Catherine de' Medici, and they must be guilty. The king paid no attention to this slander.

During the time of his military apprenticeship, the shy, silent new dauphin and the tough and taciturn Montmorency cemented their friendship. As a renowned champion of both church and monarch, Anne was the confirmed enemy of non-conformists, and would not tolerate any signs of disobedience to the pope or the sovereign. (Strangely enough, the emperor fulfilled Montmorency's ideal more than did François I.) Montmorency's influence on Henri was profound. The young prince kept no secrets from him, any more than he did from Diane.

Henri always deferred to Montmorency and gave him filial obedience. There is only one recorded occasion when the dauphin asserted his authority over his mentor. There was a young man at the camp from Provence called Brusquet, who said he was a doctor and convinced a number of soldiers of this fact with his smooth tongue and fluent patter. Unfortunately, the medicines Brusquet prescribed killed his patients when their illnesses would not have done, so Montmorency ordered his arrest and planned to hang him. Henri was greatly entertained by Brusquet during the trial, and, realizing he was just a foolish quack, ordered Brusquet's release and attached him to his household as a jester.

With his physical prowess, the seventeen-year-old dauphin loved the life of campaigning and felt much more comfortable living with soldiers than within the court. Henri was certainly not comfortable living with his wife. He and Catherine were awkward and self-conscious with one another, and married life had little appeal for either. This was an age when fourteen-year-olds married and produced children, but in the case of these two there did not seem to be any signs of that happening.

To make matters more complicated, the court doctors observed that Henri was born with hypospadias, which was thought to be affecting Catherine's chances of conceiving.[2] Other sources claimed she had not reached puberty. It is unlikely that Henri's condition had escaped observation in the nursery. The most famous surgeon of the seven-

2. Hypospadias, or hypospadies, usually a mild deformity, is characterized by an abnormal positioning of the urethra, along the underside of the male member. Hypospadias is usually but not always associated with chordee—a downward curve of the penis, in particular when erect. Several diplomatic dispatches allude to Henri having this condition, which does not necessarily preclude fathering children and often exists in several generations of a family.

teenth century, Pierre Dionis, alleged that the contemporary French physician and astronomer Jean-François Fernel had noted Henri's malformation and recommended acrobatic positions to aid conception. In this climate of marital uncertainty, Henri was more than happy to return to Montmorency and the army.

*I*T was hard for the king to mourn in public. Distraction was the only cure for François I's unhappiness over the loss of his eldest son, and he found it in the young king of Scotland, James V. François hoped James would ask for permission to marry his pretty daughter Madeleine, and so he let James into a little secret, the famous *Grotte des Pins* (Grotto of Pines) at Fontainebleau. The grotto was a favorite bathing spot for some of the ladies of the court; being alone, they would wear very little. Brantôme tells us that François knew about this grotto and had tiny holes pierced in the walls so he could spy on the unsuspecting ladies. Hoping that James would ask for Madeleine's hand, he took him to the grotto and allowed him to witness her charms. James was instantly smitten. On New Year's Day 1537, he married François' daughter in the Cathedral of Nôtre-Dame.

Seated behind the king, the queen and her ladies, including Diane de Poitiers, the new dauphin and dauphine were much in evidence. During the fifteen-day festivities that followed, Henri once again dedicated his lance to Diane at the tourney ground, distinguishing himself by his courage and skill, and showing a dignity appropriate to his new status.

On January 1, 1537, the day of Madeleine's wedding, the king canceled the treaties of Madrid and Cambrai, declaring that he had signed them both under duress. A few days later, Alessandro de' Medici, who had been created Duke of Urbino by his father, Clement VII, and appointed ruler of Florence by his father-in-law, the emperor Charles V, was murdered. As the only rightful heir to the duchy, Catherine de' Medici placed her hopes in the forces of the Florentine exiles, led by her uncle, Filippo Strozzi. She, and all the Valois, hoped Strozzi would prevent the emperor from installing another puppet ruler in Florence. As the French king's forces were occupied elsewhere and unable to come to his aid, Strozzi's army had no reserves to support him against the imperial forces. His defeat destroyed Henri and Catherine's chances of regaining control of Florence.

Too delicate for the hard life of Scotland, Madeleine died just six months after her wedding, and François mourned another of his children. Following his sister Madeleine's death, Henri rejoined Montmorency's advance force in Piedmont. Although the new dauphin was named nominal commander of the army, the decisions were still Montmorency's, by now a trusted and sincere friend to the eighteen-year-old prince. The French advance into Savoy and Piedmont was so successful that these conquered territories could make a fair exchange for the duchy of Milan. Henri might get his duchy after all.

While his companions amused themselves taking liberties with the town beauties, the dauphin accepted an invitation from a local squire, Gian Antonio Duci, to dine at his house. Duci introduced the dauphin to his sister Filippa, and a captivated Henri spent the night in her arms. Early the following morning, as so often happens in wartime, the young lover left with his troops.

As a result of the French victory in Savoy and Piedmont, a truce was signed between Charles V and François I. The king gave to his youngest son, Charles, duc d'Angoulême, Henri's title of Orléans, and promised him the duchy of Milan. This was a harsh blow to Henri as Milan had always been promised to him. Once again, his father appeared to be favoring another of his brothers.

Charles was everything Henri was not: bright, amusing, charming, and flirtatious. He also took over the role of his late brother as the constant opponent of Henri and Diane, and joined Anne d'Etampes in her efforts to lessen Diane's influence on the court.

While waiting for the pope's signature to seal the treaty with the emperor, the king wished to make a memorable event of showing his gratitude to Montmorency, and to remunerate him for his military expenses. On February 10, 1538, François I summoned the entire court to Moulins, former seat of the traitor Charles de Bourbon. François pronounced Anne de Montmorency Constable of France, and presented him with his sword of office. Further, the new Constable was appointed the king's lieutenant within and without France. This simple man was henceforth head of the armed forces and minister for affairs of state. No man in the kingdom held more power or was more trusted by the king. Thereafter, in the order of court precedence, Montmorency would rank directly behind the Princes of the Blood. Henri, eighteen years old, rejoiced at his friend's triumph as if it were his own. The two had become inseparable. The forty-five-year-old Anne de Montmorency had taken the place of a father in Henri's life, and, together with Diane de Poitiers, Montmorency was seen as the dauphin's closest friend.

After his night of passion with Filippa Duci, Henri took Montmorency into his confidence. Montmorency promptly sent the new marshal, his trusted friend René de Montjehan, back to Piedmont to discover what result, if any, there was of the tryst. The news flew around the court—Filippa Duci was expecting Henri's child. The dauphin was so proud to know he was able to be a father that he constantly demanded news of the mother's progress. With his military success and his paternal ability no longer in doubt, Henri was treated as a hero by the court ladies. Diane was chief among his admirers and arranged festivities, dances, and concerts for him. She teased out of him the tales of his military exploits and his conquests—even that of Filippa Duci. With Montmorency away from court at the peace negotiations with Charles V, Diane took complete charge of her young cavalier and involved him in her brilliant society.

While the court rejoiced, there were no glad tidings for Catherine de' Medici since the news of her husband's child put the onus of sterility squarely on her shoulders. Now that Henri was dauphin, it was his duty to give France an heir, and if Catherine could not provide one, another princess could be found to replace her. Brantôme writes that a number of forceful voices at court urged both the king and the dauphin to repudiate Catherine and send her home to Florence.

Some months later, it became known that Diane de Poitiers had in her care at Anet a baby girl, who was to be called Diane de France.

Filippa Duci had given birth to Henri's daughter in a convent, and she would remain there for the rest of her life.[3]

Henri brought his daughter home to France, giving her the name of his beloved friend and trusting that she would be brought up by his "Lady" with the same care as she devoted to her own daughters. Diane de France grew up to be attractive and intelligent, rivaling her foster mother in her skill with horses. Henri so wanted the world to think she was the child of Diane de Poitiers that when he became king, he decreed Diane de France legitimate. Thereafter she signed herself *"Diane Legitimée de France."* At fourteen she married Orazio (Horace) Farnese, Duke of Castro, but he died young in battle. She returned home and remained under Diane de Poitiers' protection until she married François de Montmorency, son of the Constable.[4]

The dauphin promised to care for the child who would have the rank of a princess, and gave the mother a generous dowry. Henri decided that Diane was to be the baby's godmother and bring up the little girl as her own. Thus, a scandal was avoided. By accepting the baby, Diane de Poitiers demonstrated her sense of responsibility for anything to do with Henri. It was a sign of how things would be in the future with all his children. Later writers who claimed Filippa Duci was just the baby's wet nurse, and Diane the real mother, have not taken her character into consideration, nor have they studied the accounts of Montmorency's surveillance of the mother's progress in Piedmont. That inveterate gossip and court chronicler, Brantôme, believed the child was Diane and Henri's, but it is not so.

*H*ENRI was now eighteen; Diane de Poitiers, thirty-seven. The shy young man with the dark, hooded eyes, and the splendid athlete's body under the careless clothes, developed a new confidence and a bearing appropriate to his status. His appearance improved

3. Some sources claim that Henri actually raped Filippa Duci, and that it was through remorse that he brought the child home. This is unlikely.

4. This young man had actually married secretly, without his parents' consent, and that marriage was forcibly annulled. A union with a daughter of the king was considered much more appropriate for a son of the Constable of France.

along with his manners, and he freely expounded his views on world affairs. He began to exhibit his slow, careful decision-making process and
the same loyal obstinacy with which he would stand by his friends, and
Diane, all his life.

Had Henri been born heir to the throne, he would have been a
more natural leader from the beginning. However, he had grown up
knowing that his elder brother, more talented and charming, was also
the more loved by his one parent. Henri had learned many lessons during his childhood imprisonment, not least among them to stifle his
emotions. Now he was learning that his thoughts and feelings were
very important. There was no doubt who was responsible for the dramatic change in the new dauphin of France.

Diane was ideally suited for her future role by Henri's side. Her
consciousness of her distinguished ancestry, and her sound education
in the house of a king's daughter and former regent, formed the
bedrock of her self-image. Marriage to the wise Louis de Brézé, Grand
Sénéchal of Normandy, had taught her much and had made her a
woman and a mother. The most recent years as a widow at court had
polished and perfected this ideal of a French Renaissance woman.
Well-bred, cultured, educated, and dazzlingly beautiful, she understood the world of men: politics, power, and money. Diane had been
taught by her father from her earliest years to consolidate the holdings
of her house and position and, if possible, to improve on them. She
knew how to use her intelligence and charm to please those she loved,
and she knew how to achieve her ambitions. This was neither more nor
less than what was expected of a lady in the sixteenth century with her
breeding and background.

Henri was still a quiet romantic, living in a lost world of gallantry.
The chivalric concept of *"amour de loin"*—"love from afar," was one
he understood and revered, and Diane would have shared his respect
for that tradition.

Henri's adoration of Diane de Poitiers had always been plain for all
to see, and at first she had responded by gently mothering him and giving him the attention and affection he craved. She encouraged his self-
confidence and guided his interrupted education. Henri was a quiet
intellectual, and their love grew out of a meeting of minds.

It is not certain when the relationship between the gauche, highly sensitive, lonely youth and the beautiful widow developed into physical love. Diane and Henri went to great lengths all their lives to observe decorum in public and to keep their *affaire* away from prying eyes. Most historians who have written about the couple are men, who cannot believe that a woman such as Diane might have genuinely fallen in love with her young *chevalier*. Yet what could be more attractive to a beautiful lady of her age than the constant homage of a handsome, virile young prince? Most historians estimate that they became lovers during the last months of 1536 or early 1537, when Henri was seventeen or eighteen.

Diane de Poitiers' capitulation to Henri probably took place at the Constable Anne de Montmorency's favorite seat, the château Ecouen.[5] This marvel of the Renaissance, built for Anne, is located about twenty kilometers north of Paris. A treasure trove of exquisite furniture and *objects d'art*, it was famous even in those days for its collection of erotic artifacts, said to have made even Rabelais blush. Members of the court often stayed there as guests, and Montmorency—one of Diane's oldest friends through her late husband—had included his young friend, Prince Henri, in their circle. There is a charming little poem Diane wrote and sent to Henri following their first morning of love[6] in a room where the light flooded in through windows painted with scenes from Eros and Psyche.

> *Voici vraiment qu'Amour, un beau matin,*
> *S'en vint m'offrir fleurettes très gentilles . . .*
> *Car, voyez-vous, fleurettes si gentilles*
> *Etaient garçon, frais, dispos et jeunet.*
>
> *Ainsi tremblotante et détournant les yeux,*
> *"Nenni," disais-je. "Ah! Ne soyez déçue!"*
> *Reprit l'Amour et soudain à ma vue*
> *Va présentant un laurl merveilleux.*

5. According to the contemporary Italian ambassadors Giulio Alvarotti and Girolamo Corregiani.

6. In the saga of *Amadís de Gaula*, "Amour" visited the lovers "one fine morning." Thereafter, romantic writers often referred to the morning as the time for lovers.

"Mieux vaut," lui dis-je, "être sage que reine."
Ainsi me sentis frémir et trembler,
Diane faillit et comprenez sans peine
Duquel matin je prétends reparler . . .

This is truly how Love, one fine morning,
Came to offer me sweet flowers . . .
For, you see, these sweet flowers
Were a boy, fresh, ready, and young.

Thus trembling and turning away my eyes,
"Nay," I say (to myself). "Ah! Do not be deceived!"
Love replies, and suddenly before my eyes
Lays a wondrous laurel.

"It is better," I told him, "to be wise than a queen."
And so I felt myself quivering and trembling,
Diane failed, and you well know
The morning to which I refer again . . .

Thus began one of the most enduring and unexpected royal liaisons in French history. The precociousness of the young prince was not unusual for the period. However, until this time, all Henri had known of love were the clumsy efforts with his wife, for whom he felt nothing, and fleeting adventures on his military campaigns. Henri had been worshipping this goddess from afar all his young life; now, holding Diane in his arms, already her slave, his joy overwhelmed him. Through her beauty and refinement, her intelligence and romance, Diane offered Henri infinite seduction. The morose and taciturn young man disappeared. With Diane constantly by him, he began to radiate happiness and joy. The change was remarkable.

Until Diane became Henri's lover, she had only known the touch of a man forty years her senior. Although Brézé was old enough to be her grandfather, she had experienced a complete marriage with him, bearing him two children. But their relationship had centered on the intellectual interests they shared and on the strong family ties so valued in the social structure of the day. With Henri, Diane discovered the pleasure of an inexperienced yet ardent adolescent lover. As his mistress, her womanly role was reversed; now she would be the teacher and pass on to this shy youth all the knowledge gleaned from her long apprenticeship with the clever, worldly Louis de Brézé. The sensuality of Diane's intelligence and her wisdom were part of the magic with which she enthralled the romantic young prince, just as his physical beauty, strength, and healthy youth were all part of his attraction for her.

For an independent woman like Diane to become the mistress of a much younger man placed her in a hazardous situation, not only with regard to her image but also to her own sensibilities. For years Henri had worshipped Diane as a goddess—serene, distant, pure—and was content to love her from afar. Diane was a Poitiers, too noble and proud to be a concubine. By stepping down from her pedestal and assuming human frailties, a woman old enough to be her lover's mother risked ridicule. She could also be forced to stand aside if her lover turned to a younger woman should Catherine be repudiated. That she accepted these risks indicates Diane's confidence in herself and her thorough knowledge of Henri's character. It also shows that she was in love. In giving herself to Henri, she made him feel she was bestowing on him the greatest possible honor.

Diane did not engineer her good fortune; it came of itself. She did not seek Henri's love; he gave it freely and without encouragement. But once it was offered to her, Diane did everything to keep that love aglow. As Henri grew in stature and maturity, Diane held him with the power of her imaginative mind, winding him ever tighter within the magic web of her intelligence. Henri now lost all interest in Catherine and virtually stopped seeing her altogether.

Some historians are of the opinion that the haughty, ambitious Grande Sénéchale would never have considered becoming Henri's lover if he had not become the dauphin. This is a man's way of thinking. To a lady who has never experienced a handsome, virile young lover whose lifelong devotion was so obvious, Henri was a wondrous gift. Perhaps Diane had so adored this child all his life that once he made her aware of his desire for her, she could deny him nothing. François I was only forty-two, and to all appearances would be healthy for many more years. If Diane was expecting the dauphin to inherit soon, she was taking a huge risk. She was also taking on Catherine without any guarantees, and the king's young mistress was her avowed enemy. No, Diane's capitulation to Henri was not a political move. Instead, what could be more natural than this beautiful widow falling in love with a young man of great physical beauty who was ready to die for her? Their story was the stuff of the romantic novels so popular at the time, and both succumbed to their emotions.

CHAPTER TWELVE

Emperor of Deceit

I N the spring of 1538, Henri, Diane, and Catherine went with
the court to Nice, where Pope Paul III was to mediate between
Charles V and François I. As both the emperor and the king had
ravaged his city, the duc de Savoie refused to open the gates. As a result, the king stayed in a château nearby and the emperor remained on
his galleon near Villefranche. From May 15 to June 20, the pope shut-
tled between the two camps. Finally, a ten-year truce was agreed between the two eternal opponents.

The emperor and the king met at Aigues-Mortes to confirm the
pope's treaty. Eight years had passed since Henri had left Spain, and not
one day had diminished his hatred for his erstwhile captor. Henri watched
as the monster of his childhood nightmares was rowed ashore from his
galley. Charles V, a little man with a sharp profile and a heavily jutting jaw,
stood awkwardly facing the tall, strikingly handsome king and his family.
Queen Eleonore broke the ice by coming forward and embracing her
brother. François smiled and embraced him, too. Then, treating the emperor as his honored guest, the king presented the dauphin and
dauphine, his sister the queen of Navarre, and his son Charles d'Orléans.

Suddenly and most unexpectedly, the emperor fell to his knees. Opening his arms wide before the king's family, he called out: "It is a tragedy for us and for our subjects that we did not meet sooner or the war would not have lasted so long." It was a remarkable approach; he spoke to the king and his son as if they had never been his prisoners. A witness wrote that the scene was so unreal it could have been out of a dream. Neither François nor Henri was taken in. They had suffered too much at the hands of this gentle, smiling enemy. Nonetheless, the meeting ended with an appearance of peace. France could expect the duchy of Milan to go to Charles d'Orléans, who would marry the emperor's niece, while Marguerite de France (Margot), youngest daughter of François, would be united with the emperor's son, Philip of Spain. As the threat of war receded, the court returned to the valley of the Loire.

While the king was preparing to go on a gentle "progress" throughout his kingdom, Diane was able to bring to fruition a project she had long desired. In January 1539, her eldest daughter, Françoise, comtesse de Maulévrier, was married to the powerful Robert IV de La Marck, prince de Sedan and son of the king's childhood friend of the same name. This dynastic marriage to a foreign prince, who would be nominated a marshal of France, could only have taken place with the king's approval, and was another sign of Diane's high position at court. The wedding was celebrated with great pomp in the chapel of the Louvre Palace in the presence of the king and queen.

It was a season of marriages within the court, and a number took place at Fontainebleau with the king attending. Notably absent from the various festivities was Henri, who had accompanied Diane de Poitiers to Anet following the marriage of her daughter. The papal nuncio thought this of sufficient importance to alert Cardinal Farnese.

The scandal of the season was the disgrace of the admiral Philippe Chabot de Brion, a friend of the king's youth. François had married him to a royal cousin, and the admiral was a great admirer of the duchesse d'Etampes. But for some years Chabot had been under the cloud of financial irregularities involving the royal coffers. Chabot opposed Montmorency's war strategies and Montmorency succeeded in convincing the king of Chabot's disloyal policies. A criminal trial was announced. Chabot was found guilty of taking bribes and misappropriating money intended for the wars. In addition to losing his property and incurring a great fine, Admiral Chabot de Brion was banished.

Montmorency was in favor of peace with the emperor. He was delighted to hear that Charles V had requested permission to cross France to reach his territory of the Netherlands, where his subjects in Ghent were rebelling. The urgency of the crisis required the emperor's presence as soon as possible; to sail from Spain would be difficult in winter and to travel around France would take too long. In October, at Montmorency's urging, François I sent an invitation to Charles V to traverse his kingdom as his guest. As the king was ill with an abscess in his groin, on November 27, 1539 the dauphin Henri and Charles d'Orléans, accompanied by the Constable of France, met Charles V at that unhappy crossing point on the Bidassoa River.

*T*HE dauphin and his brother accompanied the emperor across France, until they met with the king on December 10 at his castle of Loches on the river Indre. The royal caravanserai continued as François showed his kingdom and châteaux to the emperor. There is a legend that Anne d'Etampes was part of a plot to kidnap Charles V while he was in France. When Anne handed the emperor a towel to dry his hands before dinner one night, he dropped a large diamond ring into her lap. As she made to return it, Charles V is supposed to have said: "No, Madame, it is now in hands too beautiful for me ever to consider removing it."[1] In fact, Anne d'Etampes loathed the deeply religious emperor for his icy disapproval of her role as the king's mistress.

The royal party visited Amboise, Blois, Chambord, and Orléans, and spent Christmas 1539 at Fontainebleau. Splendid celebrations were planned in Charles V's honor—parades, illuminations, theatricals, and the obligatory fountain spouting wine. François proudly showed his brother-in-law his fabled gallery, which Il Rosso had decorated to the glory of France.

1. It is probable that this story was an invention of the seventeenth-century author Scipion Dupleix.

Charles V was not a healthy man. He had arrived in France with a bad chill, which had not left him, and he suffered terribly from hemorrhoids. His protruding lower jaw made elegant eating difficult. The emperor was by nature a glutton who wolfed down his food, and others dining with him were repelled by his table manners. He failed to chew his food and would hold his plate under his long chin, a napkin tucked into his neck, and literally shovel the food into his mouth by hand. At each meal he downed a full bottle of wine. With such a diet, it is not surprising that he suffered dreadfully from gout and indigestion all his life.

At some point on the journey, an exuberant Prince Charles had jumped onto the back of the emperor's horse and, holding him tight in his arms from behind, shouted: "Sire! You are a prisoner!" The sick emperor was seen to blanch and tremble. Henri is recorded as having been secretly delighted that his young brother was able to humiliate his former jailer.

The emperor made his grand entry into Paris on New Year's Day, 1540, with the customary splendid parades. He continued on as far as Valenciennes, where the princes bade him farewell. In gratitude for their services, Charles V presented them with some superb diamonds, and Montmorency was given a valuable emerald.

The emperor promised to sort out the question of Milan as soon as he had control of his rebellious subjects in the Netherlands. But by April—having regained his own territory again—Charles V changed his mind. Milan was no longer a bargaining chip in the peace treaty and he still claimed Burgundy. François was also required to withdraw from his conquered territory of Savoy and Piedmont.

The king was enraged, refused to withdraw, and blamed his Constable, Montmorency, who had always advocated peace, for Charles V's volte-face. The emperor's new proposition was to offer the hand of his daughter the Infanta Maria to Charles d'Orléans, together with the Netherlands, Burgundy, and Charolais. The wily emperor hoped that once Henri succeeded to the throne, he would surely go to war with his brother Charles over the disputed French territory. François I had been duped by Charles V, but as the king could not be at fault, Montmorency was demoted. Two camps formed at court: those for the Constable and those for his successor, the reinstated Admiral Chabot de Brion. Naturally, Diane was on the side of the Constable and Anne d'Etampes supported Chabot de Brion. Charles V's enemies rejoiced at the news that the peace between France and the empire was over.

Although François I had once again begun repressive measures against the reformers in France, he now signed a treaty with the Protestant German princes against the emperor. The treaty was formalized at Anet in front of the entire court and in the presence of Diane. Her son-in-law, Robert de La Marck, was a distant relation of the Duke of Cleves, leader of the German princes. According to the treaty, the duke would produce men-at-arms, and the king would consent to the duke's marriage with his niece, Jeanne d'Albret, daughter of his sister Marguerite and Henri d'Albret, king of Navarre. The king and queen of Navarre resisted this move, as they had hoped their daughter would marry Philip of Spain, the emperor's heir. But Diane was delighted by the king's arrangement because it would bring her family closer to the French throne. After all, the sister of the Duke of Cleves, Anne, had just married Henry VIII of England.

François I had recently left Anet to inspect his constructions at Le Havre, when an extreme heat wave hit northern France for the whole month of August. An epidemic of dysentery broke out, which even affected the king. The dauphin Henri seemed to be the worst sufferer. He fell seriously ill, and Diane's devotion in nursing him humiliated Catherine.

CHAPTER THIRTEEN

Three in a Marriage

THE court continued in the established pattern of moving from one of the king's châteaux to another: Blois, Chambord, Amboise, Chenonceau in the Loire Valley, then on toward Paris and Saint-Germain, La Muette, the Louvre, Les Tournelles, Fontaine-bleau. All the while, Diane continued Henri's education. Initially, he had shown no interest in the arts, but gently she opened his eyes to beauty and culture, just as she opened them to love.

At twenty-four, the dauphin was a man of whom Diane de Poitiers could be proud. Tall and fit, he was known for his courage at arms, the splendor as well as the moderation of his house, and the seriousness with which he handled his business. The Venetian ambassador Matteo Dandolo wrote home that the dauphin was probably the best cavalier in France. He had a mania for exercise and sport. He hunted with Diane, played tennis daily, and fenced with untipped foils. His cheeks glowed with health and he grew a small neat beard as black as his hair. Dandolo described him as "melancholy, taciturn and saturnine. He is convivial with his friends but few at court have seen him laugh. He is very generous to his brother, whom he seems to like a lot, as he is always short of money."

In 1540, the first French translations of Henri's childhood favorite, *Amadís de Gaula,* appeared and gripped the popular imagination. The translation from the original Spanish was very free, and it had been deliberately adapted by its translator so as to curry favor with members of the French court, in particular, the duchesse d'Etampes. Dedicated to the glamorous, frivolous, and impetuous Charles, duc d'Orléans, the translation was intended to please the king, his mistress, and the favorite prince. But the court already saw Henri as *Le Beau Ténébreux,* the embodiment of the novel's hero—the truly chivalrous lover—serious, passionate, and faithful. This was not lost on Diane. As the book was followed by eleven more in the series over the next seventeen years, she wove so much of the brave Amadis and his devotion to the proud Oriane into the mind of her lover that truth soon blended with fiction. All his life, Henri would be enslaved by this myth and remain the willing suitor of his Lady. By constantly underlining the chivalrous side of his nature and extolling the traditional virtues, Diane molded him into a man unable to look beyond her love without losing confidence in himself. In case there was any doubt in readers' minds about the identity of *Le Beau Ténébreux,* or of his heroine Oriane, the last two volumes, produced once Henri became king, were dedicated to Diane. Authors did well to remember the source of their patronage.

ONCE Henri had become dauphin, the need for an heir to continue the Valois dynasty became greater than ever. His only child was the little girl from Piedmont, who had grown to resemble him closely. Her very existence made it obvious that Henri was not the cause of his wife's childlessness. No matter how much the king cared for his Medici daughter-in-law, nor how many friends or allies Catherine had made at court, being childless placed her in a dangerous position. In desperation, she sent to Rome for quacks, doctors, and endless supplies of revolting aphrodisiacs, none of which worked. The whispered demands to replace "the Florentine" grew louder.

Catherine was rightly afraid for her future: the king was fond of her, but there was sound argument, and many a precedent, for sending her home. Following the death of the king's eldest son, Catherine's elevation to dauphine had so vexed the majority of the French, who despised her lack of royal blood, that many unjustly attributed the death of the dauphin to her agents. She was also aware of the Constable de Montmorency's power and influence at court, his antagonism toward Italians in general and suspicion of Catherine in particular. In addition, Catherine's fabulous dowry had turned out to be a mirage. She remembered her uncle the pope's words just after her wedding night— that a woman of spirit never lacked progeny. His meaning was clear. She would be wise to become pregnant—even with someone other than her husband. But this she could not bring herself to do and relied instead on talismans and potions.

Catherine was described at this time in some detail by Matteo Dandolo:

> The most serene dauphine is of a fine disposition, except for her ability to become a mother. Not only has she not yet had any children, but I doubt that she will ever have them, although she swallows all possible medicines that might aid conception. From this I would deduce she is more at risk of increasing her difficulty than finding the solution. She is, *as far as we can see* [italics in the original], loved and cherished by the dauphin her husband. His Majesty is also fond of her, as are the court and the people, and I don't think there is anyone who would not give their blood for her to have a son.

As discussion about Catherine's future consumed the court, Diane de Poitiers found herself in a delicate position. Should another wife be procured for Henri, that new dauphine might prove less malleable and far more attractive than the little Medici who was, after all, her kin. Already the Guise family was promoting one of their own for Henri's second wife. Ever since Marie de Guise had become queen-regent of Scotland, this powerful and talented clan of Lorrainers had been infiltrating the highest positions in France through promotion in the army, the church, and the court. The fall and disgrace of the Constable de Bourbon reduced the other princes of his family with him and enabled the Guises to take their places.

The ducal house of Lorraine was headed by Duke Antoine II. His younger brother Claude became the first duc de Guise, head of a cadet branch of the ruling house of Lorraine. Claude, born in 1496, received the French fiefs of his father, René II, duc de Lorraine et Bar. Connected by marriage to the French royal family, Claude fought in the Italian wars for François I, was wounded at Marignano, and was made a French duke and peer. Claude's ambition soared when his daughter Marie married the young James V of Scotland.[1]

Diane became alarmed when this emerging family of Guise promoted as Henri's next wife a candidate who was beautiful, a princess, and the younger sister of Marie de Guise. The ambition of the Guise family was such that, should one of their number become queen of France, the Bourbons and Diane de Poitiers might find themselves totally marginalized. Moreover, Diane had discovered passion with Henri. She had reached the age of thirty-seven before she knew the wonder of physical love. It would be unthinkable for her to risk losing Henri by encouraging him to repudiate Catherine and marry another princess who might be beautiful, with a powerful family who could destroy Diane. Having waited until now to know passion, how could Diane let Henri go? She made her decision: Catherine must stay and be helped to produce an heir for the dauphin. Diane went to Catherine with a plan. She suggested that the dauphine do everything she could to hold on to the king's favor. As for the dauphin, Diane would see to him.

Catherine was a quick learner, and her instinct for survival—some said Medici cunning—inspired her to throw herself upon the mercy of her father-in-law, weeping copiously with her head on his knee. She told the king that she was willing to withdraw into a convent, or even to become lady-in-waiting to the new dauphine. All she would keep and treasure was her pride in having once been a member of the royal

---

1. They became the parents of Mary, Queen of Scots.

house of France. Such declarations both moved and deeply embarrassed the king. He reassured her that, since God had decided she should be his daughter-in-law and wife of the dauphin, he did not want it otherwise. Perhaps God would still grant her most ardent wish, and also his.

Le Roi Chevalier was very fond of his cultured daughter-in-law, who spent hours discussing with him in Italian the art and artists of her native Florence. He appreciated her conversation and her knowledge of history, geography, science, and astrology. Ronsard wrote a poem eulogizing Catherine's gifts:

> *Quel dame à la practique*
> *De tant de mathématique?*
> *Quelle princesse entend mieux*
> *Du grand monde la peinture*
> *Les chemins de la nature*
> *Et la musique des cieux?*

(Is there another lady who possesses such knowledge of mathematics? Is there in the whole world a princess who better understands painting, the ways of nature, and the music of the heavens?)

Catherine faithfully followed the king out hunting, and was never angered by Anne d'Etampes, who managed to annoy everyone else. The papal nuncio Girolamo Dandino reported that Catherine was loved by the king, her husband, and all the court. Her deviousness in being charming to everyone was a sign of her duplicitous character, which she would only dare show later in her life. Catherine went to enormous trouble to surprise the king with *objets d'art* and rare manuscripts from Italy. She would sit endlessly watching him play tennis, and even tried the game herself. No, François I would not repudiate this child of his beloved Florence and send her back in disgrace to Italy.

Diane may have prepared the successful strategy for Catherine, but she, too, had some work to do. She convinced Henri that Catherine could and would bear children and therefore should stay. Faced with the dauphin's silence on the subject of rejecting his wife, the duc de Guise had to withdraw the offer of his daughter, Louise. Diane's plan had saved the dauphine. In return, Catherine was obliged to spy for Diane, to recount the latest machinations of her enemies at court, to report the words of the king and, more important, those of the courtiers. For Catherine, no price was too high to pay to remain in France. But Diane's promise that she would "deal with Henri" had confirmed to the dauphine that the relationship had evolved beyond the maternal.

What was Catherine's reaction to the new situation she faced in her marriage? Like all the Medici, she was intensely proud and would have been humiliated by Henri's preference for the older woman. His infidelity must have wounded Catherine; but, like Diane, she understood that her survival at the French court depended on their generous understanding of one another. Henri's lack of interest in her made it clear that only the women's mutual dependence would keep the dauphin near to them both. Diane was always discreet and went out of her way to make Catherine feel that her place was secure as Henri's wife. The Florentine in turn had learned the art of dissimulation to perfection in her childhood, and she remained courteous to Diane, showing no signs of the jealousy and hatred buried deep inside her. It was court gossip that her secret motto now became *"Odiate et Aspetate"*—"Hate and Wait." In later years she was to say, "Caress only your enemies."

Despite the comforting words of the king, the Medici dauphine was not prepared to leave her future in God's hands alone. In her desperate need to conceive Henri's child, this enlightened daughter of the Renaissance returned to the beliefs and practices of medieval times, and subjected herself to the most repellent magic potions, even at the risk of making herself ill. Catherine studied the works of all the current magicians and sorcerers. She relied mostly on the advice of Cosmo Ruggieri, whose family had served the Medici for generations and who had accompanied Catherine from Florence. Every day she secretly swallowed the urine of pregnant animals; the ashes of frogs; the powdered sexual organs of wild boar, stags, and domestic cats. She ate huge quantities of herbs crushed and mixed with her food and wine.

According to the Venetian ambassador Dandolo, Catherine drank a potion of crushed unicorn horn and ivory in water. Another recipe gleaned from ancient alchemists was a mixture of mare's milk, rabbit's blood, and sheep's urine. Others maintained that the blood of a hare and the left hind paw of a weasel mixed with vinegar would work wonders. Under her clothes Catherine wore a girdle of goat's hair, made by a witch and soaked in the milk of a she-donkey. Hanging from it were amulets that "guaranteed" success, such as the middle finger of a fetus born two months before its time. Around her neck she wore an amulet containing the ashes of a large frog to encourage the birth of a male child.

A well-known test for fecundity called for a garlic clove to be inserted into the vagina for twelve hours. If, after that time, the smell was on the patient's breath, she was fertile. If the breath had no garlic smell, then the womb had four possible faults: an excess of heat, cold, dryness, or moisture. The cures for all four conditions were equally hideous: "A purge of bilious or sanguine humour with cassia, rhubarb, or similar together with moderate bleeding from arm and foot . . . The woman should drink the juice of sour fruit and bathe in fresh tepid water after which it will be useful to anoint her parts liberally with a paste made of goose, duck and rooster fat mixed together and liquefied."[2] There were other purges made from syrup of absinthe, oregano, hyssop, citronella, and valerian. It is astonishing that Catherine had both the courage and the stomach for all these potions.

Other advice came from Jean de Lorraine, who recommended to Henri that he read the erotic poems of Horace for inspiration, but it seems Henri was not at all interested in "*les beaux poètes du diable.*" If Henri had been to blame for the couple's childlessness, there were a number of horrific methods for lengthening, shortening, or enlarging "the virile member" to choose from. These included the application of unguents compounded of castor oil, spikehead seeds, earthworms, and fermented goat's milk. Another popular cure for those that are "soft or flaccid" was "to apply leeches to the buttocks and groin; to anoint the *os sacrum,* the hips, kidneys, groin, lower belly and genital member with an oil of chervil to which has been added a powder reduced from the procreative parts of a bull or stag, as well as fine grains of onions

2. Chrestien, Guillaume. *Livre de la nature et etilite des moys des femmes et de la curation des maladies qui en surviennent.* Paris, 1559.

and dandelions."[3] As Henri had fathered a child with Fillipa Duci, happily he was not subjected to any of these absurd remedies.

Diane de Poitiers had no difficulty in prompting the confidences of the miserably barren Catherine. While Diane was sympathetic to her cousin's plight, it could not have been easy for her to help Catherine and encourage the man she loved to go to his wife's bed. On balance, however, it was the lesser of two unpleasant choices. Thanks to her early training by Anne de Beaujeu, Diane's decisions were always carefully considered. When the wretched dauphine revealed the horrors to which she had been subjecting herself, Diane immediately put an end to all Catherine's disgusting spells, magical and religious alike. Then, taking her aside and talking to her gently, like a daughter, Diane was able to give Catherine a little practical advice, including some alternative positions for intercourse that would compensate for her retroverted uterus and Henri's hypospadias. Diane suggested to the dauphine that she make love "*à levrette*."[4] It was also Diane who persuaded Catherine to allow the famous doctor Jean Fernel to examine her in her bed.

The next step was much more difficult for all three of them. On designated evenings when Catherine's conception was thought possible, Henri would retire as usual with his mistress, but after a while in her arms Diane would send him upstairs to Catherine's room directly above her own. Shortly afterward, his duty done, he would return to his beloved Diane and remain with her throughout the rest of the night.

As Henri's devotion to his mistress grew, so, too, did Catherine's resentment and jealousy. Neither she nor Henri had chosen the other as partner, and both had been educated to accept the political or dynastic choice imposed on them. It was Catherine's tragedy that she fell in love with Henri. Passionate, and constantly forced to suppress her feelings, she could not contain her curiosity about her husband's fascination with Diane. Like every deceived woman, she longed to know what he found so irresistible in her much older rival. According to Brantôme, Catherine summoned an Italian carpenter to the Palace of Saint-Germain and ordered him to make two small holes in the floor of

3. Calanius, P. *Traité excellent de l'entretenement de la sante.*
4. A *levrette* is a small greyhound bitch.

her bedroom, directly above that of Diane de Poitiers. There, with her friend the duchesse de Montpensier beside her, the dauphine of France would lie on the floor and watch her husband making love to Diane in the room below. She saw her rival's long, slim white body kept young and firm by daily exercise. A knife must have pierced fat little Catherine's heart as she saw how "a beautiful, fair woman, fresh and half undressed, was caressing her lover in a hundred ways, who was doing the same to her."

Brantôme recounts that she watched the lovers below on the huge bed, their playful caresses, their bodies lit by the glow of the great log fire until the heat of their passion was such that they rolled naked onto the floor and continued their caresses on a deep velvet rug. When Catherine saw for herself the passion and tenderness between them, she told her companion, sobbing, that her husband had "never used her so well." Inevitably, Catherine's lady told the court.

No matter how much the sight hurt her, the dauphine would not have her spy holes closed. With a fascination bordering on the perverse, she would watch the lovers until Diane chose the moment to send Henri upstairs to his wife and his duty—a duty in which he took no pleasure and certainly gave none. Making love *à levrette,* Catherine experienced the added shame of never seeing her husband's face during intercourse—which no doubt made his duty easier.

*T*HE dauphine was desperately unhappy. Her misery over her failure to conceive and her despair at her husband's love for Diane took a toll on her already plain features. Her eyes bulged even more as her cheeks became drawn, and her podgy mouth dominated her face. But Catherine could "Hate and Wait." The day would come when this unholy trinity of a marriage would make her queen of France. The key to her character was fear—which she had known all her life: fear as an orphaned child pushed around as a bargaining tool; fear as civil war raged outside her convent; fear as her family's opponents wanted to hand her to the enemy or string her up on the walls of Florence; fear of the hostile French and unfriendly court; and fear of being disowned

and banished. When the dauphin François died and his Italian cupbearer, who had come with Catherine to France, was accused of poisoning him, she was certainly afraid for her safety. All her life,
Catherine feared for her future. It is even possible that she thought
Henri might reject her in favor of Diane once he became king. Perhaps
it is not surprising that Catherine turned to astrologers for reassurance.
Years later she would admit in a letter to her daughter Elisabeth, queen
of Spain, that she had always been afraid of Henri.

The dauphin was fêted by the court and was regarded as a victorious general and father. His mentor and friend, Anne de Montmorency,
was Constable of France and all-powerful; his trust and affection gave
Henri courage and he grew bolder. As well as always dressing in
Diane's black and white, which he adopted as his own colors, Henri
took on Diane's symbol of the crescent moon for his personal cipher,
either alone or under his crowned "H." More often, he displayed her
three crescents intertwined, a secret symbol of their *ménage à trois*.
The intertwined crescents appeared on his arms, his clothing, the livery
of his servants; even his horses sported the crescent on their saddlecloths. To the uprights of his monogram letter "H" he added a crescent on the inside of both, making them read "HD." This could also
be interpreted to read "HC"—ambiguous again, even though the
crescent was Diane's symbol. His motto under the crescent moon became "*Cum plena est, emula solis*"—"When full, she equals the sun."
Others interpreted the motto as Henri's wish to fill the whole world
with his glory.

The king had given Catherine a rainbow as her personal device,
with the motto: "She brings light and serenity." The rainbow represented Iris, messenger of the gods, in constant communication between earth and the firmament. Catherine was indeed a messenger,
constantly moving among the courtiers, flattering them with charm
and smiles, eking out information to pass on to Diane. There is no evidence that Catherine felt her spying for Diane was too great a price to
pay for securing her place at court for the present, and to gain her illustrious future. To this end, the dauphine of France allowed her
husband's mistress to manage him and her household, and she reported her news to Diane each evening. Catherine even allowed Diane

to shine at all the court *fêtes* as if *she* were the dauphine of France. It made Diane's enemy, Anne d'Etampes, choke with rage to be out-shone, time and again, by the dauphin's lady.

In revenge, Anne charmed Henri's brother, the delightful Charles d'Orléans. Brantôme describes Charles at nineteen or twenty as being

> of medium height, rather thin, and if he lives he will fill out and be-come handsome. His hair is red to blond and he has the colouring of a redhead. He has a bright and extrovert personality and much ap-preciates the manners and pleasures of his father whom he follows everywhere, more than his brother. This greatly pleases the king who loves him dearly but he worries that he goes out at night fully armed. [Charles] is loved by everyone and, according to the Queen of Navarre, she knows no one with more courage and temperament and he will become even more outstanding with time. He makes much of Italians whom he likes to have around him, and receives them cour-teously even if they are unknown to him.

ALTHOUGH Montmorency remained as commander in chief of the army, slowly, one by one, his civilian offices were taken from him. The marginalized Constable withdrew to his château of Chantilly, a magnificent Renaissance building on an artificial island near Paris. Montmorency's departure seriously vexed Henri, who no longer had an insight into what political moves were being made at court. Anne d'Etampes did all she could to alienate Henri from his father, and the antagonism between Anne d'Etampes and Diane de Poitiers divided the court.

In March 1541, François began to consolidate his alliances. He re-newed all his treaties with the Sultan Suleiman, explaining to the Sul-tan that he had been under duress when he had allowed their joint enemy Charles V to traverse his kingdom. Then, to cement his alliance with the most important of the emperor's German enemies, François decided to proceed with the marriage of his niece Jeanne d'Albret and the Duke of Cleves. Jeanne was just thirteen and the duke twenty-four.

The king's sister, Marguerite, and her husband, Henri d'Albret, vainly refused to accept the marriage, but the king insisted. Jeanne was brought to Amboise, where she was to meet her fiancé.

Face-to-face with the king, however, little Jeanne d'Albret refused pointblank to marry the Duke of Cleves and swore she would rather throw herself down a well. In response, the king slapped her and had her taken to Châtellerault, where the wedding was to be held. As the château was still being renovated, a huge circular pavilion was constructed in the park with galleries and seats in the stands. On June 9, a splendid series of entertainments began, including parades and fencing competitions.

Men and horses were dressed in cloth of gold, silver, or velvet, and plumes bobbed on their helmets. The entire court, including the Constable Montmorency, watched as the king made his entrance with the royal family to the accompaniment of trumpets and tambourines. Diane was in rapture at the triumphal entrance of the Duke of Cleves, reflecting the glory of his house to which Diane's family was now allied through the marriage of her daughter, Françoise. On June 13, the king took the bride and groom by the hand and presented them to the cardinal de Tournon, who betrothed them.

The marriage was to be celebrated the next day at eleven in the morning in the pavilion, which had been turned into a chapel. The king and the Duke of Cleves approached the altar, but little Jeanne stood at the entrance, immobilized by her unwillingness and the weight of her dress of cloth of gold and silver, layered in precious stones. Faced with this impasse, the king ordered Montmorency, the Constable of France, third most important person in the realm, to pick up and carry his stubborn little niece to the altar as if he were a mere lackey. In full view of the entire court, Montmorency did as he was bidden. The next day, the Constable left the court of François I forever.[5]

Henri and Diane were distressed at the shame and departure of their friend, but they could not refuse to remain for the rest of the celebrations as Henri had arranged a tournament where he was to

5. This marriage was never consummated since the bride was too young. It was annulled in 1545 and the wedding gifts returned. In 1548, Jeanne d'Albret married Antoine de Bourbon, duc de Vendôme, and was extremely happy. Their son was the future king Henri IV of France.

publicly honor his "Lady" and wear her colors. Four champions com-
peted in this game of valor: the dauphin, his brother, the duc de
Nevers; and the comte d'Aumale. Henri excelled at the tournament as
Diane's champion, while dukes and grandees were deposited in the
dust. Diane sat serenely in the stand, secure in the knowledge that the
Constable's absence gave her complete control of the future king of
France.

After the marriage of the Duke of Cleves and his niece, the king felt
he could count on the allegiance of the German princes to the north.
In order to confirm France's treaty with the Sultan Suleiman, François
sent two trusted agents to Venice to make an alliance with the Serene
Republic, en route to Constantinople. They never reached Venice. The
emperor's governor of Milan had them assassinated at Pavia. Once
again the king felt misled by Montmorency's advice and he named
Chabot de Brion to replace the Constable as commander-in-chief. On
the advice of Diane, the dauphin agreed, reluctantly, to serve under
Chabot. Another war was on the horizon, and no one doubted that
this one would be long and drawn out. The king raised money and
melted gold and silver from his vaults. Once he received the confirmation that the Sultan had come onto his side, François I declared war on
the emperor. That same year, Chabot had a heart attack; he died soon
afterward.

THE year 1543 began with rumblings from across the Channel
as Henry VIII broke his treaty with the French and allied himself
with Charles V. His real objective was Boulogne, but among his official
complaints against François I was the French king's hasty recognition
of the eight-day-old Mary as queen of Scotland upon the death of her
father, James V, on December 14, 1542. The duc de Vendôme was successful against Henry VIII near Calais. Charles d'Orléans regained
Luxembourg, but the Duke of Cleves, France's ally, was defeated by
the emperor. Meanwhile, the Turkish fleet under Barbarossa, together
with the French fleet, terrorized the populations on the Mediterranean

François I, patron of the French Renaissance, receiving a painting of the Holy Family by Raphael.

The Battle of Marignano was fought on September 14, 1515. It was a mighty victory by which France regained all the lost territory of northern Italy. François I can be seen in the center with his signature white plumes on his helmet. An eighteenth century depiction by Fragonard.

Emperor Charles V, by Titian. The emperor was rather short, and the famous Habsburg elongated jaw made tidy eating difficult. He was recognized as the greatest military leader of his time.

François I, by Titian. Titian did not meet the king and worked from a medal. Nevertheless, his portrait is considered the best of them all, capturing the strength and charm of the French king.

The Battle of Pavia near Milan was fought between Charles V's imperialist army and that of François I, king of France. The French lost badly, and the king, who fought to the last, was captured.

The Renaissance château of Fontainebleu was built by François I and was the place he was happiest in France.

The solemn entrance of François I with Charles V into Paris in 1540. The Emperor Charles requested and received permission to cross France in order to more speedily reach his rebelling subjects in the Netherlands. Detail of fresco from the Sala dei Fasti Farnese, by Taddeo Zuccari.

An imaginary depiction by Ingres of the death of Leonardo da Vinci in the arms of François I. François was hunting elsewhere when Leonardo died.

Henri as a child painted c. 1523, two years before
his departure from France to be a hostage for his
father in Spain.

Henri on horseback. Note the HD monogram
worn on his horse's regalia.

The marriage of Henri and Catherine de' Medici with Diane de Poitiers at the wedding breakfast table, by Leonard Limosin. An apocryphal depiction showing the intimacy of Diane de Poitiers with Henri, who is wearing her colors of black and white in his hat.

left: Fountain sculpture of Diane de Poitiers as Diana the Huntress with stag and hounds. Made by Goujon for the courtyard of Anet, the sculpture stood there until its recent removal to the Louvre. Note the frieze of interlaced HD's.

below: Catherine de' Medici by Leonard Limosin.

Catherine de' Medici in her youth,
by French school.

Catherine de' Medici in her widowhood,
by François Clouet

The cortège of drummers and soldiers at the royal entry of Henri II into Rouen with Diane and Catherine on the stand.

Detail of one of a set of tapestries made for the château d'Anet, called *The Drowning of Britomaris*. It now hangs in the Metropolitan Museum in New York. It is said to be the most true likeness of Diane that exists. See detail of the hem of her dress showing HD cipher.

The Dauphin Henri as he would have appeared at his first tournament in the rue de Tournelles at which he asked to become Diane de Poitiers' young knight.

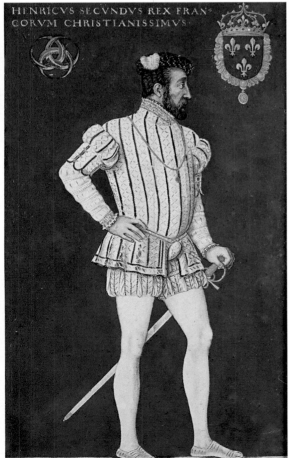

Henri II of France painted not long after his accession.

A court portrait of Catherine de' Medici in all her finery. Catherine was famous for the luxury of her court, but dresses such as this, which is covered in pearls, were more for parade than for everyday wearing.

Henri II, by a follower of François Clouet. His contemporaries considered Henri a most handsome man.

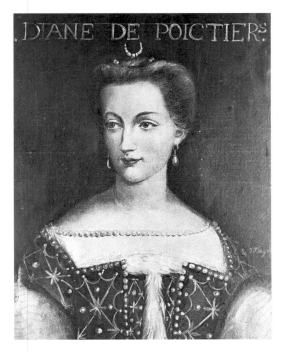

Diane de Poitiers, French school. No doubt an idealized depiction of her, but evidence again of her legendary beauty.

Pope Leo X and the future Pope Clement VII, painted by Raphael. Both Medicis, these two popes restored the power and might of their famous family.

Queen Eleonore of France, sister of Emperor Charles V, widow of the king of Portugal, and second wife of François I. Eleonore was a gentle soul and a few years older than François I. She bore him no children and following the king's death, returned to Spain.

Anne de Montmorency, Constable of France, by François Clouet. Montmorency was the highest ranking noble in France who, as Constable, was the most senior officer in the army after the king. He also had the charge of the royal household.

Diane de Poitiers as Diana being surprised by Acteon. The figure in the upper left is Henri as Acteon the hunter prince, wearing Diane's colors of black and white. The goddess turns the hunter into a stag for spying on her in her bath, and he is then hunted down and torn to pieces by his own hounds at lower right. The message was not lost on Diane de Poitiers' enemies.

Diane de Poitiers painted by Salviati. Previously attributed to Primaticcio, this portrait hangs at Anet.

Diane de Poitiers, by School of Fontainebleu. This painting hangs at Althorp in England.

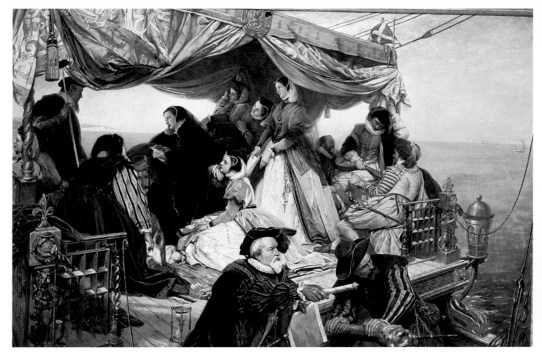

Mary Stuart's Farewell to France, by Henry Nelson O'Neil. She cried, *"Adieu, France! Adieu, France! Adieu donc, ma chère France. . . . Je pense ne vous revoir jamais plus."* A nineteenth century depiction of Mary's tragic departure.

Château de Chenonceau, by P. J. Ouvrie. The most beautiful of all the châteaux of the valley of the Loire. Appropriated by François I, coveted by Catherine de' Medici, it was given to Diane de Poitiers as Henri II's coronation gift to his mistress.

coast. The wild Turkish fighters were given permission to winter in Toulon, which had been vacated by its careful burghers. Once François rewarded them generously, the Turks finally left in May 1544.

Having been cashiered from the army, Henri returned to court to the joy of his wife and mistress. They had not been idle in his absence, but had been to see every doctor, quack, magician, astrologer, and alchemist—anyone who might be able to help the dauphine conceive. At the time, there were two eminent physicians at the French court, Louis de Bourges and, above all, Jean Fernel. After thorough examinations, Fernel surmised that Catherine's inverted womb would not be an obstacle to conception with any man other than Henri, about whose congenital malformation nothing could be done. All he could advise was what Diane had already told Catherine—try alternative positions, and take his pills made of myrrh. Diane spared herself nothing to have Catherine conceive and resumed the routine of regularly sending Henri upstairs to his wife.[6] Diane de Poitiers had fallen completely in love with her dashing young *chevalier* and one can imagine her agony at having to make this decision. But the alternative was so much worse, and he always came back to her for the rest of the night.

Finally, the miracle happened. Whether it was due to Fernel's pills, Diane's advice, or simply nature, a son was born at Fontainebleau on January 19, 1544, ten years after Catherine's marriage. She was twenty-four. Even the most intimate moments in the life of a future queen had a public significance and dozens of people had direct access to her during the labor and birth. Her cousin Cosimo de' Medici was informed by his ambassador that according to custom, when the time came for the baby's birth, several Princes of the Blood were present at the scene separated from Catherine by a flimsy curtain.

As soon as the child was born, according to custom, the astrologers were called to cast the boy's horoscope. Their verdict was that the positions of the stars were favorable. The papal nuncio entered the room so promptly after the baby's arrival to offer his congratulations that Catherine was still lying on the floor where she had given birth.

6. According to Brantôme and the Italian ambassador Contarini.

It was assumed that the baby's fragility was due to the many exotic remedies the mother had taken before and during her pregnancy. The doctor who delivered the baby, Jean Fernel, recommended no bleeding and no purges.[7] Catherine was to avoid spicy or salted food, and she was not to resume marital relations. The baby was named François in honor of his grandfather, who also assisted at the birth, as did Diane.[8] Like a soothsayer, the king did not hesitate to examine the afterbirth, and then he pronounced that his grandson would be a healthy lad and that there would be many more births to come—at least six! Everyone was delighted. Marguerite de Navarre wrote her brother a charming letter on the joys of being a grandparent.

The papal nuncio visited the royal mother and child several times, and the cardinal de Bourbon officiated at the baptism. The godfathers were the baby's grandfather the king, and his uncle, Charles d'Orléans. His godmother was Henri's sister Marguerite de France, Catherine's friend. After a stay at Anet, François allowed Henri back into his council. The rifts between the king and his heir appear to have been healed to some degree by the birth of an heir. To the joy of both wife and mistress, François I rewarded the dauphin by appointing him commander-in-chief of the army for the spring campaign against Henry VIII and Charles V.

*F*OR the next ten years, the dauphine had a child almost every year. The marriage of Henri II and Catherine de' Medici was one of the most prolific royal unions in history. Other women who married in their early teens and had multiple pregnancies often wore their young bodies out with the strain, like poor little Queen Claude, who began her seven pregnancies at age fourteen. Catherine was already twenty-four at the first birth and physically completely mature. When it

---

7. Following the birth of Henri's heir, Jean Fernel was officially given the credit and a pension for life.

8. Diane de Poitiers would assist at the births of all the future royal children, just as she assisted at the birth of their father.

was safe for her to conceive again, Henri did his duty; but once she was pregnant, he did not go to his wife's bed but remained with Diane. It was said that thereafter the dauphine concealed her pregnancies for as long as possible.

Henri's gratitude was expressed by the gift of a sum of money to Diane, described in the accounts as being in recognition of her assistance to the dauphine. Once again, Diane had made herself useful. Having had two children, she knew what she was doing. Diane de Poitiers was unusual in that she took on the active role of both parents in the life of her daughters following the death of Louis de Brézé. There was far less family feeling about children in those days because of the frequency of early death in childhood. Parents deliberately distanced themselves, and babies were given to wet nurses, nannies, and tutors to bring up. Fathers made the decisions concerning their sons after the age of seven. Diane, however, was very close to her two daughters, remaining in constant touch with them and deeply involved in establishing them in good marriages. Her duties as a mother did not end there; she spent much time with her grandchildren and planned their marriages as carefully as those of her two girls. A woman of her time, she lived by the philosophy she had learned from Anne de Beaujeu—to consolidate her holdings and those of her children, and to secure their succession.

In seventeen years, between 1546 and 1563, the queen wrote less than twenty letters concerning the welfare of her children. Henri, on the other hand, was a doting father, probably a reaction to the lack of affection he received during his own miserable period of childhood in the Spanish prisons. He concerned himself with every detail of the progress and health of his children. Later he would quiz them on their studies, especially their knowledge of Latin and Italian.

If Catherine's position in France was now no longer threatened, the same could be said for Diane. The arrival of a son and heir made no difference to Henri's feelings for Diane—if anything, they were stronger. He knew how she had worked to see that he had an heir. More and more often, Henri would escape to Anet to spend time with his "Lady" within her magic circle of entertainments, culture, and pleasure; hers was a chivalrous court along the lines of *Amadís*. There he could forget his difficult relations with his father and brother, forget his wife, and above all, forget the insidious maneuverings of Anne d'Etampes.

A great favorite of the king's and Henri's, François de Bourbon, comte d'Enghien, asked permission to invade Milan, and scored an important victory on April 14, 1544 at Ceresole Alba. Though longing to join his friends Saint-André, Dampierre, Brissac, and La Châtaigneraie fighting the emperor in Italy, Henri had to stay in France on his father's orders. News of the senseless cruelty of Charles V's army in burning the captured city of Vitry-en-Perthois in northern France traumatized the population. Ill in bed again with another abscess in his groin, the king finally gave Henri the command as lieutenant general of the army. Vitry was to be avenged.

Just when the imperialists were about to abandon the siege of nearby Saint-Dizier, the king's personal seal fell into their hands. With this incredible stroke of luck, they sent a forged order to the commander of the French garrison, the comte de Sancerre, instructing him to capitulate in the name of the king. He did so, to widespread French disbelief. Scandal hit the court; it was rumored that Anne d'Etampes, in her hatred of Diane and fear of the dauphin's victorious return from the war, had passed the king's seal to the emperor and state secrets to Henry VIII.[9] Henri's friends Enghien, Saint-André, and Brissac rushed back from Italy to join his army to defend the capital as the imperialists drew nearer to Paris. Perhaps recalling what happened to Rome when the imperial army arrived in 1527, the inhabitants panicked, packing their goods and fleeing the capital. Among the first to save their gold treasures and abandon the capital were the monks and nuns—not a good example.

François I, who had installed himself in Paris to give confidence to the population, knew his army was fit and intact. Henri waited with his force of forty thousand outside the capital, but to everyone's astonish-

---

9. There is no historical proof of her guilt.

ment, the imperialists did not give battle. Many of the emperor's mercenary army had not been paid for some time and when reinforcements did not come from Henry VIII in Normandy, they deserted. Having fortified his position in the north of France, Henry VIII had no intention of coming to the rescue of the emperor and watching him extend his territories. Meanwhile, the dauphin had forced the Spanish to retreat and, at the same time, managed to keep his army together. If the war continued, Henri would surely be covered in even more glory. To avoid such a triumph for the dauphin, Anne d'Etampes urged François to make peace. In fact, Charles V was quite willing to negotiate—his credit had run out and he had no funds to continue the war.

By September 16, 1544, peace was declared, and on the 18th, the Treaty of Crespy (Crépy) was signed with terms that did not really benefit either side. Charles d'Orléans was to marry the emperor's daughter the Infanta Maria, this time with the Netherlands or Franche-Comté as her dowry. Alternatively, he could marry the emperor's niece, the Princess Anne, and she would bring with her the duchy of Milan. From his father, Charles would receive four French duchies as his domain.

Again, the emperor hoped that by ruling over this sizable territory, Charles d'Orléans would one day be inspired to challenge Henri for the throne of France. For his part, the king renounced all claims to Savoy and Piedmont, and the emperor abandoned his claim to Burgundy. The two monarchs formed a secret "holy alliance" against the reformers, with the aim of bringing the Protestant princes of Germany back into the Catholic fold. The French agreed to lend support to (Charles V's brother) Ferdinand of Austria, and to the duc de Savoie against his erstwhile allies the Swiss. Neither nationalism nor loyalty was a factor in sixteenth-century warfare. François I was to renege once again on his alliance with Suleiman—a treaty considered against nature by all Christianity—and join with the emperor to fight the Turks. When he heard this, the enraged Sultan almost impaled the French ambassador, Gabriel d'Aramon.

François I and his family left for Brussels to celebrate the peace with the emperor and his other sister, Queen Maria of Hungary, regent of the Netherlands. The peace was not universally praised in France, but Queen Eleonore was delighted that her husband and brother were no longer in conflict. To the surprise of all and the embarrassment of most, during Queen Eleonore's official entry into the city, Anne d'Etampes was seated next to the queen on her gold-draped litter. The dauphin was outraged at this show of *lèse-majesté*, and many of the king's advisers refuted the treaty. The *Parlement* only agreed to ratify it following a second order from François, and he in turn blamed the dauphin's negative reaction for the attitude of his *Parlement*.

There was more trouble to come. In council, Henri suggested replacing the timorous Admiral d'Annebaut, his father's appointee. The admiral had singularly failed to take advantage of his opportunities while sharing command with Henri at Perpignan, resulting in French retreat and shame. Although called admiral, he had no experience of the sea and failed abysmally to command the French navy. When Henri suggested that an officer with more experience might be useful, Anne d'Etampes was furious at this interference with her favorite. She convinced François that Diane de Poitiers was behind the dauphin's suggestion and wanted to install one of her own protégés—no doubt, the disgraced Constable de Montmorency.

François was not deaf to the rumors at court concerning Anne d'Etampes, but he could not face her constant recriminations and volatile temper tantrums, invariably aimed against Diane. The king's mistress and the dauphin's mistress were implacable enemies; François must have regretted his description of Diane de Poitiers in his gallery of beauties as "*honnête à hanter*." After all, it was the king who had asked her to concern herself with the young Henri on his return from prison. Now, he wished it were otherwise. In the absence of the dauphin, who was with the army, François banished Diane de Poitiers from the court.

With both Diane and Henri gone, Catherine was in her element and rediscovered her own temperament. She went back to studying Latin and Greek, took singing lessons, learned to play the guitar, and entertained. Catherine introduced to the French court an Italian custom of singing rounds for up to eight voices with accompaniment. Clément Marot's translations into French of the first thirty psalms of David were set to the music of the composer Clément Janequin, and became very popular. Members of the court, including the dauphin, chose their personal psalms and sang them, or had them sung accompanied by lutes, viols, spinets, and flutes. Once psalm singing became popular with the early Protestants, the court decided to abandon this rather attractive custom. Instead, they chose to set the erotic odes of Horace to music.

Catherine had always been fascinated by child care and hygiene, and in Diane's absence she took charge of the royal nursery. During the winter of 1544, Catherine held her court, receiving Italians, even those who had fought against the French, with guitar playing and Neapolitan songs. Returning from the rigors of campaigning, Henri was shocked by the festive air in her apartments, but even more so to hear of the unwarranted disgrace and banishment of Diane. Failing in his efforts to have her recalled, Henri joined Diane at Anet.

While there, the dauphin resolved to contest the recently signed Treaty of Crespy, which robbed him of his chance to avenge his humiliation at Perpignan as well as of Milan, which he considered his birthright, and four French duchies. Joining in the plot with him and Diane was the duc de Guise and his son the comte d'Aumale, along with the duc de Vendôme and the comte d'Enghien. On December 2 at Fontainebleau, in the presence of two notaries, Henri affirmed his wish for the crown lands to be indivisible and remain intact. His formal protest to the *Parlement* was signed on December 12, 1544, and witnessed by Vendôme and Enghien. The Guises decided not to sign. The protest was a serious act, which surprised and annoyed his father and destroyed the brothers' friendship. For Henri to dare to challenge his father and the emperor through the legal system took courage. Tensions between the king, Henri, and Charles stretched close to the breaking point.

On New Year's Day 1545, the traditional day for an exchange of gifts, the dauphine received a beautiful diamond and a most valuable ruby, as well as a large sum of money from the king. His elder son's legal attack eventually sobered François, who realized that he could have been too harsh with his heir. François' health was declining— perhaps the time had come to make amends. In February, the king felt sufficiently recovered to set off in a litter to hunt in the valley of the Loire, and declared himself well again "except in respect of the ladies." Diane was recalled and regained her former position at court by

Henri's side, where she took overall charge of the education and nutri-
tion of, now, two royal children.

While François I continued to behave as if there was nothing
wrong with him, members of the court noticed he was growing
weaker. Since 1540, the king had been a sick man. On the eve of the
emperor's visit to France in 1539, François had fallen ill with an abscess
in his lower stomach. Now six years later, in July 1545, the imperial
ambassador, Jean de Saint-Mauris, wrote home predicting that the
king would die from a burst vein in his prostate and the development
of an abscess in that area. The doctors tried everything, even a course
of "Chinese wood," or gayac, a tropical wood now known as lignum
vitae, imported by the Portuguese from their colony of Goa, and used
for the treatment of syphilis. The Sultan Suleiman had Barbarossa send
the king his own pills, which contained untreated mercury, a famous
cure for syphilis, with notorious side effects. François I, this lover of
women, was heard to lament: "God punishes me there where I have
sinned."

*W*ITH spring, the war began again. This time the enemy was
Henry VIII, and France launched a three-pronged attack against
England. Armed with the blind courage of youth, the two princes and
their friends—Brissac, Aumale, Enghien, Nevers, Laval, and Louis La
Trémoille—competed fiercely for the laurels of a Lancelot. During one
skirmish, François d'Aumale was pierced by a lance just below the eye.
The blow came with such force that the lance broke off in his head to a
depth of six inches. Aumale was taken at once to the rear guard, and
operated on by the king's famous surgeon, Ambroise Paré, who had
nothing better than a pair of blacksmith's pincers to extricate the piece
of lance from Aumale's face. In the presence of his officers, the brave
count said he resigned himself to the inevitable torture, and did not
flinch or move or cry out. Only once did he make a sound—at the most
dreadful moment of the operation. He exclaimed, "O my God!" as the
surgeon pressed his foot against Aumale's face to give himself the lever-
age to pull out the shaft. For four days and nights it was not certain he

would survive, but he did. Henri was overwhelmed by the man's courage and announced that he would trust this hero to lead him anywhere, even blindfolded.

Campaigning and sharing hardship succeeded in bringing the two princely brothers closer together. The court case that Henri brought against the terms of the Treaty of Crespy was not directed against his brother Charles, but against the manner of its implementation; and, rightly, he blamed the influence of the duchesse d'Etampes.

In the early autumn of 1545, the dauphin, Charles d'Orléans, and their friends were en route to Boulogne to join the French

François d'Aumale, duc de Guise, was known as "*Le Balafré*," or "Scarface," due to a horrific battle wound he received when a lance pierced his cheek.

army, which was besieging the English there. They were all young and full of energy, and the constant danger of war made them foolhardy. Near their lodgings at Faremoutiers, they found several houses that had been abandoned due to an epidemic. Ignoring the signs of plague, they broke in and began a grand pillow fight, scattering feathers on one another, and shredding mattresses with their swords. Announcing that "No son of the king of France ever died of the plague," Charles lay down on a used bed, and, for a wager, rolled in the sheets.

Later that evening, after dining with his father and brother in an abbey not far from Boulogne, Charles began to run a fever and vomit, his arms and legs shaking violently. The doctors opened a vein and bled him. Fearing contagion, they refused admittance to the king, and Henri had to be forcibly restrained from going to his brother's side. The prince rallied for a while, but then succumbed. The twenty-three-year-old Charles d'Orleáns, a young man so full of promise, was dead.

When he heard the news, the king fainted. At first, poison was suspected, but then all agreed he had died of the plague.[10]

François I's greatest source of pride was his sons: now another had been taken from him. With Charles d'Orléans died François' dream of joining the Habsburg and the Valois dynasties. Nothing had come of the king's last effort—an attempt to marry his youngest daughter, Marguerite (Margot), to Philip of Spain as Charles V wanted a French *prince,* not a princess, to join his family. The king of France descended into a deep depression, and abandoned his plans to invade England. On June 7, 1546, François I and Henry VIII signed the Treaty of Ardres, guaranteeing England's neutrality in the next war between France and the empire.

That same year, the Venetian ambassador Marino Cavalli wrote a detailed description of François I:

> The king is now fifty-four years old; his aspect is entirely regal, so that merely to look at him, without any previous sight of his face or portrait, one would say at once "He is the king." His movements are so noble and majestic that no prince is capable of equaling them. . . . He is of very sound judgment, of very wide erudition; listening to him one recognizes that there is scarcely a subject, study or art upon which he is unable to discourse as pertinently as those who have devoted themselves to it. . . . Truly, when one reflects that despite these skills, so many exploits have escaped him, one is disposed to conclude that his wisdom is rather on the lips than in his spirit. . . . What one might wish from him is a little more attention and patience, and not quite so much brilliance and knowledge. . . . He affects a certain elegance in his costume, which is laced and braided, rich in jewels and ornaments of price; even his doublets are beautifully worked and woven with gold.

François had succeeded in bringing the Renaissance to France, but no amount of beauty and pleasure could keep the restless king in any of his splendid châteaux for longer than a week or two, except in winter. If anything, he moved around the country more than before, desperate

---

10. Many epidemics were described as "plague" at the time.

to visit every place he loved. With the death of his son Charles, François had transferred his affection to another gallant youth to remind him of his own early manhood. His choice fell on a young friend of Henri's, the comte d'Enghien, a brave soldier and a positive influence on the dauphin, balancing that of the Guise family.

With the passing of each year, the king searched more feverishly for distraction: distraction from his failures; distraction from sorrow; distraction from the horrors of the Protestant persecutions and his confusion as he ordered burned for heresy great humanist scholars he had encouraged and promoted; distraction from his painful venereal disease and from his growing impotence. Anne d'Etampes took a lover, Etienne Dolet, to compensate for the king's inadequacies, and scandals shocked even this lax court. At the wondrous château of Chambord, described by Charles V in admiration as "the essence of what human industry can achieve," François wrote two lines with a diamond tip on a windowpane:

> *Women often change*
> *Woe to him who trusts them.*

The king built more houses, created more gardens, collected more paintings, and continued the frantic, endless hunting of game with the whole court of twelve thousand following him from one château to the next. It was as if he had to chase the stag until the last moment of his life in order to forget the gnawing pain in his body.

There was a story that François I caught his venereal disease from a Spanish lady with whom he had dallied during his captivity in Madrid. Her husband had objected strongly to his wife's behavior, and as he was forbidden from fighting a duel with the hostage king, he devised a hideous vengeance. Visiting a brothel, he deliberately had himself infected, then passed the painful keepsake to his wife. According to other sources, François had already contracted venereal disease at the age of seventeen—it was virtually endemic in Europe—and a surviving early letter from his mother, Louise de Savoie, mentions it. But the king's constitution was so robust that he not only survived the ravages of the disease (and the efforts of his doctors) for many years, he was reported by a reliable witness to appear in excellent health as late as 1540.

Diane could already see ahead to the inevitable palace revolution that would follow the king's death. She knew that Henri would oust many of his father's favorites, and especially those of Anne d'Etampes; but Anne and her allies would be vicious and dangerous in defending whatever power they could salvage. In her eagerness to help Henri, Diane turned to the ambitious Guises. Their fortune was immense, and in their talented family they numbered several victorious captains and eminent churchmen. The most attractive of the younger generation was the twenty-year-old archbishop of Rheims, Charles de Lorraine, brother of the heroic *Balafré*. He was tall, handsome, well built, spiritual, and extremely eloquent. Most important, he had great charm, personality, and a beautiful voice, with which he masked his overwhelming ambition and pride.

Five of the Guise brothers, together with their father, the duc Claude, were received at Fontainebleau by the king.[11] François appraised them correctly and was well aware of the family's ruthless ambition, fueled by their matriarch, Antoinette de Bourbon, duchesse de Guise. Antoinette felt the king's distrust and pushed her family's fortune toward the future: the dauphin and Diane de Poitiers. It is interesting that the extremely pious Antoinette did not look at all harshly on Diane's relationship with Henri—rather the contrary. To Diane's delight, Antoinette de Guise suggested a marriage between her third son Claude, marquis de Mayenne, and Diane's younger and favorite daughter, Louise. A union of such important families required the approval of the king: he readily gave it. The marriage took place at Fontainebleau at the end of July 1546.[12] After suffering one miscarriage, Louise was expecting a child toward the end of the following year.

This clan of Lorrainers were counting on the next reign to raise

11. Claude de Lorraine and Antoinette de Bourbon had eight sons and four daughters. A pair of twins died in infancy and one son was still too young to attend the court. Their son Claude de Mayenne would become duc d'Aumale.

12. Most writers incorrectly put the marriage date during the reign of Henri II, based on the writings of Peer Ensile, published at the start of the eighteenth century. See Patricia Z. Thompson, "*De nouveanx aperçus sur la vie de Diane de Poitiers*" in *Le Mythe de Diane en France au XVIe Siècle, actes du colloque* (E.N.S. Bd Jourdan [Paris], 29–31 mai 2001) edited by Jean-Raymond Fanio and Marie-Dominique Legrand; ouvrage publié avec le concours du Centre National du Livre Niort (Paris: Association des Amis d'Agrippa d'Aubigné, distributed by Librairie Honoré Champion, 2002).

them still higher at court and make their fortunes even greater. They would succeed in casting their malevolent shadow over the throne of France for the next fifty years. Even the group around Anne d'Etampes was indignant when one of the eight Guise sons was made cardinal-archbishop of Rouen—at the age of nine.

AT Fontainebleau, the careful minuet of court life had altered dramatically following the death of Charles d'Orléans. While she felt her sun setting with the king's fading life, a desperate Anne d'Etampes had promoted Charles' marriage to the Habsburg princess in the hope that he might unite with his father-in-law the emperor and France's enemy. She shared the emperor's wish that Charles would eventually wage war against his brother Henri and take the throne from him—and from Diane. Now this last chance for her survival at court after the death of the king was gone. Catherine, too, realized that without the king, she would be forced to rely completely on the good-will of Diane de Poitiers who, as Henri's mistress, would occupy the most influential position in the greatest nation of Europe.

The atmosphere at court was tense as each faction engaged in an undeclared duel of dissimulation, with no one quite sure where they stood, and quarrels among the young gallants frequent. Among those forcibly idle due to the peace, tempers heated easily. Camps formed among Henri's friends—one behind the comte d'Enghien, dazzling victor of Ceresole, and the other behind his first cousin and rival, François d'Aumale, *Balafré* hero of Boulogne. Both were twenty-six. The point of contention was the Treaty of Crespy. Enghien supported the dauphin's stand, whereas Aumale threw his weight behind the other side, and his defection was harmful to Henri. Seeing an opening, the Guise brothers offered to act as mediators.

The young men surrounding the dauphin—Vieilleville, La Châtaigneraie, Tavannes, Saint-André, Damville, Brissac—were a wild bunch. They liked to make their horses jump chasms from rock to rock, and they themselves jumped from one roof to another across narrow streets. Bored with the enforced lull in the hostilities due to the winter season, the young men acted out battles with snowballs as weapons. During one such fight in the winter of 1546, the dauphin, Aumale, and their team were on the offensive, and Enghien led the defense. Not surprisingly, the mock battle got a little out of hand and blows were exchanged. Eventually, the exhausted Enghien sat down against a wall to catch his breath. Above him a window opened, and unseen hands dropped a heavy chest onto his head. It broke his neck. François de Bourbon, comte d'Enghien, Prince of the Blood, heroic soldier and charmer, remained in a coma for five days. He died on February 23, not yet twenty-seven. Suspicion fell on a young Italian friend of Henri's who was known to have had a quarrel with Enghien, and Aumale was also a suspect. Both protested their innocence. Fearing that Henri might be implicated, the king would hear no more and treated the incident as a dreadful accident.

Many historians have suggested foul play, but it is more likely that this tragedy was the result of the usual rough horseplay common among high-spirited young cavaliers used to the horrors of war. Throwing furniture at one another, or food, for that matter, was acceptable behavior in a court dedicated to unrestricted pleasure. Enghien's death was a typical example of the strange mixture of civilization and the lack of it so prevalent during the French Renaissance, when courtly manners and elaborate codes of behavior were interchangeable with primitive habits and brutal actions.

Tensions at court continued to distance the king from Henri. The dauphin, in jest, spread the slander that a young nobleman called Guy Chabot, later baron de Jarnac, who had no known source of wealth yet dressed exquisitely, must be the gigolo of his young stepmother. The effete Jarnac was outraged, but as he was not permitted to challenge the dauphin to a duel, another of Henri's friends offered to stand and fight in his stead. The king had to step in and forbid a duel of honor among the young gallants at court. Jarnac was the nephew of Anne d'Etampes, who had been involved in the dispute, and it is therefore likely that Henri only made the allusion to discredit his father's mistress. François I realized the whole issue was one of rivalry between the two royal mistresses; although both parties begged to be allowed to defend their good names, the king refused to respond.

However, François *did* react to the next ill-fated incident involving Henri. There had never been much love lost between father and son, and now Henri resented his father even more for his recent humiliation of Diane. The dauphin was champing at the bit to be put in charge of the realm. Late one evening, in company with a group of his close friends, Henri speculated about his future reign and whom he would put in which position at court. They discussed who would escort the king on his funeral bier to Saint-Denis, and who would accompany the dauphin to his coronation at Rheims. Henri began to ponder aloud about his appointments, the first of which would be to recall his friend, Anne de Montmorency. He then made other allocations to all his friends, as if the king were already dead.

No one noticed the king's fool, the dwarf Briandas, in a corner, who slipped out and ran to François. In that strange, overfamiliar manner that fools traditionally used with their patrons, the dwarf warned the king to take care, as he no longer ruled—indeed, he was dead. He related to François and his companions that they had been deposed and had all lost their positions in the reshuffle. Worse, he maintained that the Constable was back and they should flee.

As confused as his courtiers, the king demanded an explanation for this nonsense. When she heard the story, Anne d'Etampes had a fit of terrified hysterics and François was furious to have been treated with such *lèse-majesté*. He ordered the fool to give him the names of all those who had been present at Henri's table. The two sons that the king had preferred were dead, as were many of the artists and writers he had promoted, and the dashing young companion of his last years, the comte d'Enghien, had been killed in a silly prank at court. Could his dead sons have been poisoned? Strange scenarios filled his head and his temper was roused to fever pitch. François called for his Scottish guard [13] and, escorted by thirty of the best, marched to his son's quarters. When the king and his guards arrived, only the dauphin's valets were left in his apartments. In his anger, François thrashed the staff and destroyed the furniture.

---

13. The king's Scottish guards protected the person of the monarch. They were mounted and were the oldest military unit in the French army.

In sixteenth-century France, jesters or "fools" had a most privileged position at court and were permitted incredible familiarity with the monarch.

Henri prudently left the court and remained for a month at Anet with Diane, until his allies mediated with his father for his return. Diane reasoned with Henri that with his father's health declining so rapidly, he would not dare remain alienated from his heir for long. She knew how to calm Henri and reassured him he would soon be recalled. She was right. But one of the conditions of his return was that his friends, among them Saint-André, Brissac, and Dampierre, who had dared to mock the monarchy, remain in exile.

With the French king now visibly ailing, the various ambassadors wrote home to characterize the king-in-waiting. The Venetian ambassador, Marino Cavalli, describes Henri at this time:

> The fortune which seemed to be shared between the other two [dead] brothers is whole again with this one who is now the dauphin. His personal qualities promise France the best king she has seen for a hundred years. This hope is also a great comfort for the people, who console themselves for the present unhappiness with the promise of what is to come. This prince is twenty-eight, in good health, robust and has a good constitution. His character is perhaps a little melancholy, he is well versed in arms, he is not full of clever retorts, but he is very clear and firm in his opinions—once he has said something he sticks to it *rigidly*. His intelligence isn't the quickest possible, but it is often these kinds of men who succeed the most, like autumn fruits which are the last to ripen, but which are stronger than those from

the summer or the spring. He intends to keep a foot in Italy, and has never thought of giving up Piedmont, which annoys those Italians who are unhappy with affairs in their state. He spends his money both wisely and honourably. He does not abandon himself to women—he is happy with his own, and for conversation he turns to Madame la Sénéchale de Normandie, who is forty-eight. He has a real tenderness for her, but opinion is that it is nothing more, and that this affection is as if between mother and son, for this lady had taught, corrected and advised monsieur le dauphin, and directs him to actions which are worthy of him.[14]

However, another contemporary, Giovanni Capello, wrote that "all his amusements are honest, excepting his illicit pleasures which he well knows how to hide." Whether or not the ambassadors were being blind or diplomatic, they all agreed that Diane de Poitiers, in one capacity or another, had greatly changed Henri for the better.

*I*T would seem that the only joyful news in the spring of 1546 was the birth of a daughter to Catherine de' Medici at Fontainebleau in April. The birth coincided with the reconciliation between François I and Henry VIII, and also between the king and his son. The baby was called Elisabeth, and in view of the new treaty, Henry VIII agreed to be godfather. The christening was a splendid affair, celebrated with great rejoicing in the new atmosphere of peace. The English ambassador stood proxy for his king, held the baby over the font, and presented generous gifts from Henry VIII. The customary tournament accompanied the festivities, with the proud father and his team jousting in baptismal white, their shields adorned with interlaced crescent moons in honor of the new birth—and Diane.

The tiny princess joined her brother at Blois in the care of Monsieur and Madame Jean II d'Humières,[15] the children's governor and his wife, an excellent couple chosen by Diane de Poitiers and answer-

14. Baschet, Armand. *La Diplomatie venitienne: Les Princes de l'Europe au XVIe siècle.*
15. Jean II d'Humières was a distant cousin of Diane de Poitiers.

able to her. Diane would refer to them as "my allies," and she was always in contact concerning the Children of France. D'Humières and his wife already had charge of the dauphin's little daughter, Diane de France. Once again Catherine renounced her right as a mother and allowed Diane to take over, but she must have thought her cousin a little too zealous in her care of her children.

CHAPTER FOURTEEN

The Death of the Renaissance King

*I*N June 1546, the Treaty of Ardres was signed between France and England. François purchased Boulogne from Henry VIII for a considerable sum, to be paid over eight years.

The king spent the rest of the season traveling on horseback inspecting the perimeter of his frontiers. This must have caused him the most terrible pain; the abscess on his prostate was said to have grown very large and to have five heads, all suppurating. To ease their patient's discomfort, the doctors resorted to the traditional remedy of bleeding him. This did little to help, so they decided to open four of the heads on the abscess, release the poison, and cauterize the openings. The pain was no doubt intense, but afterward François at least felt some relief. By Christmas 1546, the abscess had closed and the doctors had to operate again. This time the improvement was so marked that François took Anne d'Etampes to bed. Under the circumstances, one has to wonder whether she was driven by passion or ambition to have consented.

The king returned to his peripatetic lifestyle. After visiting his palace at Compiègne in the north, he stopped at Villers-Cotterêts in

Alsace-Lorraine at the beginning of February, and there he heard the news of the death of Henry VIII on January 27, 1547. The English king had died of complications due to blood poisoning from an abscess on the leg. In his last weeks he could not walk and had become so obese he had to be carried·about in a large basket made of iron, winched up by chains when he wanted to move from one floor of his palace to another. His open ulcers smelled horrible and he suffered great pain.

The English king died just as these two great monarchs had become allies. Although François was said to have rejoiced with the court that France's enemy was dead, Martin du Bellay, who was at the king's bedside, writes in his memoirs: "[It] occasioned the king much sorrow . . . because they were almost of an age, and of the same constitution; and he feared that he must soon follow him. . . . Those, moreover, who were about his person perceived that from that time he became more pensive than before."

Shortly after François received the news of Henry VIII's death, a royal messenger arrived from London with a letter Henry had written just before he died saying that "they" too were mortal and would die like any other men. The French king was profoundly moved by this message, and developed a fever.

On February 17, François was on the move again, passing by Saint-Germain, and headed toward the duchesse d'Etampes' château at Limours, where her brother was the bishop of Condom. Three days later, he was well enough to join in a hunt. On March 1, he arrived at Rambouillet, but was unable to move on as he wished. However, the king still had business on his mind and gave instructions for the fortification of Provence in case the emperor returned to reconquer Piedmont.

By March 20, François was bedridden. The doctors hoped that if the abscess was opened again, he would improve. The operation revealed so much infection that it was impossible to do anything. François developed septicemia and, like Henry VIII, began to succumb to blood poisoning. Henri was at Anet, his sanctuary, but on the insistence of Diane and the Guise brothers, he left to be at his father's bedside at Rambouillet.

Two days before the end, Anne d'Etampes came to say her farewell. She knew her time had come and that with the king's death her reign would be over. Still young, blond, and beautiful, her future could only be exile. She knew how badly Françoise de Foix, her predecessor, had suffered at the hands of her husband, who had shut her up and mistreated her until she died. There was so much doubt about the circumstances of her death that the king had sent Montmorency to investigate. He announced that she died of natural causes, but the fact that Françoise's husband made Montmorency his only heir cast some doubt on his conclusion.

Anne d'Etampes made a dramatic scene at the king's deathbed, throwing herself on the floor and loudly begging the earth to swallow her. For once, the king could not accommodate her demands; he requested she leave the court and retire to Limours. Only then could he receive the Last Sacraments.

In his parting words to his dauphin, François assured Henri he had been a good son and he was satisfied with him. The king gave Henri his blessing and asked his son to remember him. François declared, ingenuously, that he was dying without any remorse concerning the justice of his reign, as he had never treated anyone unfairly, but he admitted that on some occasions he had made war on slight pretexts. He also regretted that he was not kinder to his poor neglected queen, Eleonore. Henri's mother, Claude, had been long forgotten. François urged his son to "preserve the purity of the Catholic doctrine," and not to recall the Constable Anne de Montmorency.[1] In the sole, oblique reference to Diane, he warned his heir against placing his will too much in the hands of others as he himself had done. His final request was that the duchesse d'Etampes be treated with courtesy, as "she was a lady."

The dauphin was so moved that he agreed to everything, and begged his father for his blessing again. This he was given on three occasions in the king's last days. During the night of March 30, Henri fainted on his father's bed, and the king, half embracing him, would

1. A number of sources claim that François warned Henri against the ambitions of the Guise family, but as there is no mention of them in the transcript of his last words, it is more likely that this warning was added to contemporary accounts of the king's death in later years after the disgrace of the Guises.

not let him go. François asked his priest for a particular homily to be read and still had enough presence of mind to know he was hearing the wrong one. Among his last requests was that Henri should find a fitting husband for his sister, Marguerite (Margot), defend the Faith, and not overtax his subjects.

At two in the afternoon of March 31, 1547, having defied the predictions of his doctors for years, the Salamander King, François I, patron of the French Renaissance, died at Rambouillet. He was fifty-two years, six months old, and in the thirty-third year of his reign. His last words were: "Into your hands I commend my spirit . . . Jesus Christ" (spoken in Latin). The only members of his family missing from the king's deathbed were his wife, Queen Eleonore, and his sister, Marguerite de Navarre. Eleonore had simply been overlooked, and it took two days for her to learn of her husband's death. Marguerite was in retreat in a convent in Navarre. After she heard the news, she remained there for some months. With the passing of his father, Henri collapsed at the end of the bed sobbing, his head in his hands. It was his twenty-eighth birthday. He rose only when twelve large white candles were brought into the room. The king was dead—Long live the king!

Henri crossed to the antechamber where Catherine was weeping and consoled her. With François' death, she was queen of France, something neither her cousin Pope Clement VII nor her illustrious Medici ancestors could ever have believed possible. But her friend and protector was dead, and her husband was more devoted to and dependent on his mistress than ever. Henri himself also needed consolation and comfort. He sent messengers to Diane and Montmorency to meet with him at Saint-Germain-en-Laye, and left Rambouillet to join them there.

It is not certain that François I died of venereal disease, but he certainly had it. Doctors have argued for centuries about his symptoms. The autopsy showed he had blood poisoning from an infection of the urinary tract. He also had a diseased lung and a huge abscess in his stomach. His kidneys were wasted, his intestines decayed, and his throat cankered. It is more likely that he had gonorrhea, and also quite possibly cancer.

*T*HE achievements of the man described by one historian as a "brilliant spoiled child"—and by his mother, Louise de Savoie, as "my Caesar"—were formidable. He was a man who had genuinely loved honor, despised treachery, and adhered to his belief in chivalry and humanist ideals. He had helped France take its place as a modern power; his alliances with the Sultan Suleiman and the Lutheran princes of Germany were bold and intelligent moves for France at the time; and to have been consistently outmaneuvered by the emperor Charles V, generally acknowledged the cleverest politician in Europe, was not such a disgrace. The king's Italian wars cost his country a great deal, but they also brought France in contact with the Renaissance.

François I was a splendid patron of the arts and father of letters. He not only imported the great Italian masters—Leonardo, Cellini, Primaticcio, and many more, but also acquired their works. The artistic circle that made up the School of Fontainebleau, which dictated the taste and style of his era, was a remarkable assembly. Critics decry his high spending, but without the patronage of the king and his court, the wonder of the French Renaissance would never have existed.

François I was responsible for great buildings, including the marvelous châteaux of Fontainebleau, Rambouillet, and Chambord. He embellished Blois, Amboise, and the Louvre. With the help of Girolamo Della Robbia, he built the delicious little château de Madrid in Paris, a monument to his release from captivity and to the Treaty of Madrid. A model for Fontainebleau, tragically, it was destroyed during the French Revolution. The king inspired the building boom of the early sixteenth century, when classical, open, comfortable houses replaced existing fortified, inward-looking buildings.

As a humanist, François I set up lectureships from which the Collège de France derives its origin. The king's library formed the nucleus of the future Bibliothèque Nationale. His edict making French, not Latin, the language of all legality transformed the ponderous machine of the law in France. The king subsidized the voyages of Jacques Cartier and delighted in his discoveries in the New World, particularly the great river he called the St. Lawrence. As a result of all the expeditions to the New World, François I gave his country a navy.

The whole of François I's reign was a struggle to control the balance of power in Europe. The French king has been criticized for his never-ending wars against the emperor Charles V, but he feared that France would be encircled by the empire and cut off from the rest of Europe. To keep his exit to Italy open, the king did all he could to stir up trouble within the German part of the Holy Roman Empire. Because they shared the same vulnerable borders, France was as much of a danger to the empire as the empire was to France. It was essential for François I to woo England as an ally in order to tip the balance between France and the empire.

The Renaissance king is also criticized for his treatment of heretics. He was accused of being "Catholic at home, Protestant abroad" because he protected and used the Protestants when he needed them. At his coronation, François I swore to uphold the Catholic Faith. The 1520s, the early days of his reign, were a period of religious anarchy. As a committed patron of humanism, the king tried to ignore the issue by handling it over to the Sorbonne and the *Parlement*, but he never condoned heresy. The "affair of the placards" in 1534 was a turning point in the king's attitude. He felt his royal authority had been challenged and regarded his persecution of the reformers as a way of honoring his solemn coronation vow. By the end of the reign, the church, state, Sorbonne, and the *Parlement* had all united against heresy. On his deathbed, the Most Christian King told his heir he felt "no remorse" because he genuinely believed he had lived according to his principles and reaffirmed the authority of the monarchy.

THE day François I died, the new king gave instructions for the simultaneous burial of his father and his two brothers. The late dauphin's body had remained at Tournon where he had died, and Charles d'Orléans' body was still at Beauvais. According to an ancient French belief dating from the time of the Roman emperors, the soul of the departed ruler did not leave his body for some weeks. To show evidence of the king's earthly presence, an effigy had to be made. On the evening of his death, the king's official portraitist, François Clouet, was summoned to make a funeral mask and take measurements to build the most lifelike effigy possible. This took two weeks to complete. Overnight, Mendicant friars stood vigil and prayed by the body, and in the morning the autopsy was carried out. The king's heart and entrails were placed in separate caskets while his body was embalmed and placed in a coffin.

The next day, the coffin was put on a chariot drawn by six horses caparisoned in black and carried very slowly to the royal priory at Haute-Bruyère, about six miles north of Rambouillet. For the following two days, prayers and masses were held there while the church bells rang continuously. On April 6, the two caskets with the heart and the entrails were buried in the priory church. On April 11, the cortège with the rest of François' mortal remains proceeded to the Palace of Saint-Cloud, home of the bishop of Paris.

On April 24, just over three weeks after François' death, the doors to the great hall at Saint-Cloud opened. Inside, the walls and ceiling were lined in blue velvet, covered in *fleur-de-lys* and golden salamanders. The effigy of the late king lay on the bier, draped in cloth of gold and edged with ermine. A large silver *torchère,* its candles lit, stood at each corner of the catafalque. There was no other light in the hall, which was permeated with the smell of burning incense. The wood-and-plaster effigy was dressed in the late king's robes of state; a shirt of crimson satin, the collar of the Order of Saint-Michel, a tunic of blue satin covered in golden *fleur-de-lys,* the great coronation cloak of purple velvet also stitched with *fleur-de-lys* and edged with ermine, and a velvet cap on the head under the coronation crown. The hands were clasped on the chest in prayer. A red velvet cushion with François' scepter lay on one side of the bier, and on the other, the hand of justice. The bier was covered by a canopy of cloth of gold. A crucifix lay at the effigy's feet. Two heralds kept watch day and night while the nobles and clergy sat on benches along the walls.

Twice a day for the next eleven days, at the time the late king would normally take his meals, his effigy was placed in front of the royal dining table. Those who had usually been present at the king's meals would attend the effigy-king. The guests bowed before the "king" and sat down at the table. The place settings, plates, glasses, and cutlery were blessed for each meal by the cardinal, and the king's napkin was presented to the senior guest by the maître d'hôtel. Serving dishes for three courses, and the appropriate wines, were brought in by the gentlemen ushers, preceded by the steward. The cardinal would say Grace and add the *De Profundis,* appropriate for a funeral. The food was tasted by the steward, served, and left untouched. At the end of the meal, the effigy was laid back on the gold-draped catafalque and the food distributed to the poor. Throughout this bizarre repast, the public continued to file past in a silence broken only by sobbing.

The macabre ceremony was enacted twice a day until May 4, when the effigy was removed. Overnight, the blue and gold hangings were changed and the *"salle d'honneur"* became the *"salle funèbre,"* the walls and ceilings completely draped in black. The king's coffin was brought into the center of the room where the effigy had lain. The crown, the scepter, and the hand of justice were placed on the coffin.

On May 18, Henri, dressed in the dark purple velvet of deep royal mourning,[2] his cloak held by his cousins the Princes of the Blood, bowed for the last time before the coffin. For this ceremony, the effigy was not on view. This was Henri's only part in the traditional funeral ceremonies, since the living king could not be seen while the late king was still alive in the form of his effigy. It was not acceptable to have two French kings simultaneously present together. On May 21, François' coffin joined those of his two sons in Nôtre-Dame-des-Champs, all without their effigies. En route to Saint-Denis, the cortège passed through a Paris transformed: houses draped in purple velvet edged with silver thread, the flash of metal arms, black bobbing plumes, lanterns draped in black, a profusion of lit candles, the mourning costumes of all the many military and other groups, and expressions of sincere affection and admiration for the deceased king. Unable to join in the general mourning for reasons of protocol, Henri, accompanied by his friends Vielleville and Saint-André, watched the procession from a

2. Males of the French royal family generally wore black for mourning. The new king wore deep purple. Unlike other Christian queens who traditionally wore white, Catherine wore black, adding some flattering white trimmings in emulation of Diane de Poitiers.

window. It must have crossed Henri's mind in his sadness that no matter how tragic the scene, the deaths of his father and two brothers had made his own ascendancy possible.

After a requiem Mass the next day, the church was closed and the three effigies were placed on litters. The king's now had a different pair of hands—one holding the scepter, the other the hand of justice. The doors were opened to admit the members of the *Parlement* who had come in solemn procession from Paris. Once they had paid their respects, the elaborate funeral cortège comprising the country's great and good set out for Nôtre-Dame-de-Paris. The three effigies on litters preceded the three coffins. More ceremonies followed; the last rites were once again administered and the effigies removed. Finally, François and his sons were laid to rest in the vault of the Abbey of Saint-Denis. Some months earlier, Henri had joked with his friends about this day and speculated how it would be. To his own surprise, he was deeply moved. As the new king, Henri II was not permitted to follow the coffin to Saint-Denis, but because he wanted to watch the procession, he again placed himself discreetly at a window overlooking the funeral route. His eyes were so full of tears he could not tell which was his father's coffin and which were those of his brothers.

CHAPTER FIFTEEN

King Henri II

*F*RANÇOIS' death freed Henri from a cloud that had hung over him since the time of his return from Spain. The new king had not been close to his father, nor had he felt appreciated by him. He had never forgiven his father for sending him to Spain as a hostage, for cheating him of his childhood. Now, at last, for the first time, he was his own master. The countenance and carriage of the twenty-eight-year-old king changed markedly and he looked as if a great weight had been lifted from his shoulders. He smiled; he *laughed,* and radiated a new confidence, a joyfulness unseen in him before. Henri's time had come.

The many early reports of his silent, sullen, taciturn, and melancholy nature described a confused and troubled prince returning from a harsh imprisonment imposed on him unjustly by a father and grandmother whom he had loved and respected. On Henri's arrival home, his grandmother died, and his father and king, the person whose love and understanding he wanted more than any other, was too preoccupied to ease him gently back to normality. The king asked Diane de Poitiers to help his troubled son while he made no secret of his preference for his other two boys. By the time of Henri's accession, everyone from that sad and sorry era had died—except for his enemy Charles V, and the two people whose support and devotion he had never been given reason to doubt: Diane de Poitiers and Anne de Montmorency. Now the new king could show them how highly he valued them. His enemy he would deal with later.

The inevitable, predicted palace revolution began. In defiance of his father's last wishes, the new king's first decision was to recall his mentor and friend, Anne de Montmorency. They met at Saint-Germain on April 2. For the past six years, the Constable had been living on his estates in self-imposed exile, but he had always kept in touch with Henri. Their friendship was based on trust and admiration, a true father-to-son devotion, and they shared the same opinions on politics and religion. Montmorency was a tried and seasoned warrior, zealous, sincere, and utterly devoted to his young king. He was a good choice.

Henri knew he still had a great deal to learn and immediately installed Montmorency as president of his newly appointed Privy Council, which consisted of old friends or cousins he cherished, including three members of the Guise family.[1] The fifty-four-year-old warrior saw himself as the power behind the throne. To stay there, he knew that he must watch the emergence of the powerful Guise family, and also the Princes of the Blood—the Bourbon brothers, natural rivals to the Lorrainers. Unfortunately, Montmorency had never been popular. His brusque manner and rudeness, not to mention his brutality, made him feared and loathed. He was reasonably intelligent politically and quite a good military strategist; but his greatest qualities were undoubtedly his physical courage and his endurance. This was a time of heroes, and the Constable de Montmorency was acknowledged as a giant among them.

Montmorency was confirmed as Grand Master of the household and took the oath as Henri's Constable of France, with all his former

---

1. The new appointees to the Privy Council were Henri d'Albret, king of Navarre, uncle to the king through his marriage to Marguerite; the duc de Vendôme; Charles de Lorraine, archbishop of Rheims, soon to be cardinal; his brother; the comte Claude d'Aumale, son of the duc de Guise; the comte d'Harcourt; Jacques d'Albon de Saint-André; Robert IV de la Marck, duc de Bouillon and son-in-law of Diane; and Jean II d'Humières, governor of the royal children (and a cousin of Diane's).

prerogatives and incomes restored. Four years later, the king created him a duke and a peer, placing this mere baron on a par with the highest in the land. Inevitably, there were those who felt Henri was taking a chance relying on a man twice his age. Some thought the king was substituting the authority of one father for another. But Henri knew that for his confidence to take root, he needed the experience and advice of Anne de Montmorency. The king had good reason to be grateful to his friend. As Grand Master and Constable of France, he and his family held the colonelcy of the French Infantry, the admiralcy of France, and the four great governorships of Provence, Languedoc, Picardy, and the Ile-de-France. Gray-haired and solid, Anne de Montmorency was a man to whom no treachery came as a surprise, but who gave his friendship and love to this young man. He had known his new king since he was in his cradle, and would serve and advise him loyally, as he had his father.

Factions had always existed at court and Henri aligned himself with the two most powerful of them: the Constable in conjunction with the three feckless Bourbon brothers, Princes of the Blood; and, to counterbalance the power of Montmorency, the Guise brothers, cold, brilliant, fanatically Catholic—and supported by Diane. For the time being, all was harmony between them. Catherine was not yet consulted, but she knew Diane wanted what she did—glory and success for Henri II, the new king of France.

Catherine's resentment and private humiliation went deep, but she and Diane had no cause to be enemies in public. Although she was now the queen, nothing really changed for her. Diane and Montmorency made all the decisions, just as Louise de Savoie, and not Queen Claude, had done for the young King François I on his accession. Hate and Wait.

On the evening of April 2, the late king's favorites, and in particular those promoted by the duchesse d'Etampes, were thanked and relieved of their duties. Some were even imprisoned. The king gave the *Parlement* his new appointments and they were approved. Among those to benefit was Diane's son-in-law Robert de La Marck, duc de Bouillon and prince of Sedan, who was made a marshal of France. At the end of May, Henri's official mourning ceased. He rewarded his close friends and relations by according them the insignia of the Order of Saint-Michel, the highest of the royal orders.

*A*T last Henri could take his revenge on Anne d'Etampes for all the many years of her malevolence toward him and Diane, and especially for her involvement in the Treaty of Crespy. Her ruin was just and immediate. Two days after François I's death, she arrived at Saint-Germain, thinking to move back into her apartments, and was told that their gift was in the hands of the dowager-queen, Eleonore. Anne was forced to retire, knowing her lovely home of twenty years would be given to the Constable. More retribution would follow.

It was not solely revenge. Anne d'Etampes had long been suspected of passing on military information she had overheard during her time with the late king. Her suspected treason presented Henri with an opportunity to punish his father's mistress for all the years of insults and slanders against his "Lady." The imperial ambassador in France, Jean de Saint-Mauris, wrote that Anne had made so many enemies, if she appeared in public she would have been stoned.[2] Her nominal husband, the duc d'Etampes (who had been created duc de Chevreuse in 1545), was appointed to Henri's Privy Council. To punish Anne for stealing his income for the past fifteen years, her husband, who was also the governor of Brittany, locked her in one of his châteaux there. She was accused of selling secrets to the enemy, so Henri confiscated the duchy of Etampes and returned it to the crown.[3]

The jewels François I had given Anne d'Etampes from the royal

2. R. J. Knecht in *Franics I* cites A. Castan, *La Mort de François Ier,* "Memoires de la Société d'Emulations du Doubs." Fifth series, iii (1878), page 446 and *Calendar of State Papers, Spanish,* edited by G. Bergenroth, P. de Gayangos, and M. A. S. Hume (London, 1863–1895), volume ix, pages 73–77.

3. In 1553, the duchy and title of Etampes was given to Diane de Poitiers. Catherine's son Charles IX gave both title and estate back to Anne and her husband in 1565. When he died the same year, Etampes reverted to the crown.

treasury were reclaimed, as were those of Queen Eleonore, but in the latter's case, without any recrimination.[4] It was to his mistress, Diane de Poitiers, and not Catherine, his queen, that Henri gave these jewels, including an extraordinarily large and beautiful diamond seized from Anne.[5] Henri also took Anne's town house in the rue Saint-Aubine next to the Palace of Les Tournelles and gave it to Diane.

The king himself appeared as a witness at Anne's trial by the *Parlement*. Most of her household, staff, and servants were imprisoned. Anne herself remained a prisoner in Brittany until her husband died eighteen years later. By then, fat and friendless, she spent the rest of her days in pathetic efforts to help the Protestants. Anne d'Etampes survived until 1580, outliving everyone in this story by many years. In her prime as François I's mistress, she had been described as "*La plus savante des belles et la plus belle des savantes*"—"The most erudite of the beautiful and the most beautiful of the erudite."

Many accused the new king's mistress of being as greedy as her predecessor. It is true that Diane enjoyed the honors she received as well as the king's many gifts, although it could be said that Anne d'Etampes' avarice was for her pleasure, whereas Diane's was for her glory. Finding herself as powerful as her erstwhile teacher Anne de Beaujeu, Diane never lost her head or forgot her teachings, especially: "Show restraint in everything," and "Always carry yourself with dignity, be cool of manner and confident, look modest, speak softly, be reliable and strong, and never flinch from doing the right thing at the right time." Nor would Diane forget all that she had been taught by her husband, who had served through four reigns. Rather than play the power game as he could so easily have done, Louis de Brézé had taught his young wife to follow his example and adhere to the values of the day— namely, to consolidate her house, build her fortune, and bring up her children to do the same. Nonetheless, Diane de Poitiers, true to her era and her breeding, must be acknowledged as acquisitive if not rapacious. She would also prove implacable in her vengeance.

---

4. Queen Eleonore had always been kind to Henri and he invited her to remain in France, but the dowager-queen left for Flanders. In 1556, she moved to Spain to be near her brother. She died in February 1558 in Talavera, aged sixty.

5. Henri gave Diane the key to his strong room—she could take her pick of its treasures at will.

The demands of life at court required enormous financial resources. Diane's only income came from her estates; to entertain the court of some twelve thousand people, including their servants, she counted on the king's generosity. Equally "greedy" were others who were close to Henri and obliged to entertain as lavishly as Diane—the Guise family, Montmorency, and, in particular, Henri's close friend Jacques d'Albon de Saint-André. All benefited handsomely from the king's largesse. The secret of Saint-André's success was his ability to juggle the various factions at court and somehow remain on good terms with them all—the Guises, Montmorency, the Princes of the Blood. But most important, he was close to Diane. His sister was a *dame d'honneur* to Catherine, his son one of the *garçons d'honneur* to the dauphin. Brantôme writes that Saint-André lived in extraordinary style: Philibert de l'Orme himself renovated his château, where he entertained the whole court in enviable splendor.

*T*HE new regime was summed up by one of the few of François I's favorites to keep his place. Claude de L'Aubespine wrote that there were two great stars in the sky, the Sun and the Moon: Anne de Montmorency and Diane de Poitiers. They held all the power in the realm—the one ruling over the crown, the other over the person. Another marshal of France, Gaspard de Saulx-Tavannes, wrote that "the Constable is the captain and navigator of the ship of state, but Diane de Poitiers holds the tiller."

There were many at court who were still not entirely sure of Diane's position in relation to the king. Henri II seemed to be content with his wife and did not flirt with others, so these courtiers hardly imagined that such a dashing young man of twenty-eight would have a mistress of forty-six. It was therefore naturally assumed by most that the relationship must be platonic. But Henri was madly in love. Gentle since birth, attached to Diane by habit, he lived out his childhood fantasy and was proud to have made a conquest he never imagined possible.

Diane de Poitiers did not assume the role of an official royal mistress. She saw herself as the king's partner—someone he could trust, love, and in whom he could confide. At court and in public, Henri always referred to Diane as "*Ma Dame*"—"My Lady," which signifies the true relationship between them. His subjects called her "*Madame*" just as they would a sister or daughter of the sovereign. She was his fair Lady in the true chivalric sense. She was the Lady for whom he would slay the dragon. He would be willing to die for her. To the outside world it was the perfect platonic love, but for Henri and Diane, it was much more.

Henri II began his reign by distributing the possessions and revenues confiscated from the incumbents of the previous regime. The Guise family gained far more than Henri bestowed upon his other friends, who all received high posts and incomes—in particular, his childhood friend Jacques de Saint-André. The new queen, Catherine, had to make do with crumbs from her husband's table. She was allowed to keep the income from her own dowry, and she received a sum of money and some posts for her Strozzi cousins.

At Diane's request, Henri allowed her to pass on property that had no known heirs, to those she wished to reward. She had a fascination with the treasury and wanted to understand the financial workings of the kingdom. Diane installed her own candidate as treasurer, and through him learned about the movement of funds, whether due to business transactions or wills or lawsuits. She was especially interested in those dealing with confiscation of property, and anything else from which she might derive a benefit. But this was just the beginning.

From early June, the king, queen, and court resided at Anet, where Henri drew up documents giving Diane de Poitiers the revenues of her husband's estates for the duration of the court case settling their ownership.[6] Following the death of Louis de Brézé, Diane had been forced into a prolonged battle in the law courts to hold on to her inheritance. The case dragged on for almost fifteen years, and she had lived in fear of losing even Anet to the machinations of Anne d'Etampes. At last Henri was able to reward her for the many years she had spent as his mentor, guide, and lover. In return for all she had done for him, and as

6. The case was only finally resolved in Diane's favor in July 1553.

further proof of his love, the king presented Diane with the most beautiful of his father's châteaux in the Loire, perhaps the loveliest Renaissance castle in all of France: Chenonceau in the Touraine, roughly a
two-hour gallop from Bois or Amboise.

François I had always coveted the little château of Chenonceau in
its charming setting on the banks of the Cher river. In 1535, the king
had engineered a bad debt against the castle's owner and claimed his
house in lieu of payment. Thus Chenonceau became royal domain, and
as such, inalienable. It took Diane three years to complete the complicated legal process to ensure it would not revert to the crown with
Henri's death. Officially, the king made the gift to the Grand Sénéchal
of Normandy, Louis de Brézé, for "services he had rendered the
crown." Legally, therefore, ownership passed to his widow, Diane. Before Henri could accomplish this transfer, an act was passed to say that
François I had claimed the property unfairly, and it was reinstated as
belonging to the original owner's heirs. However, this ruling also stipulated that the heirs must immediately sell Chenonceau to Diane de
Poitiers. Naturally, Henri gave her the necessary funds.

Diane received a number of benefices of property confiscated from
Protestants and Jews, and several valuable tax revenues. Among others,
she received a part of a tax imposed on every church bell in France,
which prompted the poet Rabelais to remark that the king had hung
the bells of his kingdom around the neck of his riding mare. The tax
was so rewarding that it enabled Diane to pay for much of the construction work and decoration at Chenonceau.

Diane de Poitiers was not alone in appreciating this château.
Catherine de' Medici yearned to own it; indeed, she claimed furiously
that François I, who surprisingly was not so taken with Chenonceau
once he had acquired it, had promised it to her. On July 3, Diane was
installed as the new châtelaine and received the homage of the citizens
of her town. She had always admired the whitestone turreted castle
perched on the edge of the river, with its idle swans and green banks,
and she longed to hunt in its deep forests. Diane saw Chenonceau as
the perfect romantic setting for herself and Henri, an enchanted place
to further enthrall her lover. No matter how grateful and how devoted
Henri might be, she knew that to hold the love of a handsome, virile

young man who was also the king of France, she would need all the magic powers she had been accused of possessing, and more.

Throughout her life, Diane's aims never changed: acquire, consolidate, secure. She spent fortunes extending and improving Chenonceau with the help of the great French Renaissance architect Philibert de l'Orme, who designed the elegant arched bridge over the river, planned by the original owner. The work began even though the estate was not legally hers until 1553. The king donated fifty trees "to our very dear and well beloved cousin, Diane de Poitiers, to build and construct a bridge she intends to make at her house at Chenonceau on the River Cher." To pay Philibert de l'Orme for his work, Diane gave him three abbeys. She purchased some nearby land to double not only the size of the estate but also its value and income. Chenonceau was not just a magnificent château and home; the number of farms that made up the *seigneurie* was a valuable source of income.

Large sums were spent on the gardens at Chenonceau. A century later, the great French landscape gardener Lenôtre was to study Chenonceau and work there as a prelude to his creations for Vaux-le-Vicomte and Versailles. Diane de Poitiers commissioned Benoît Guy, sieur des Carroys, to create a parterre on the right bank of the Cher, at the northeast corner of the estate. The parterre was in the Italian style and covered over two acres with a combination of flowers, vegetables, and an orchard. It still bears her name today. Benoît Guy installed a wide, sandy avenue lined with one hundred and fifty elms leading to the château, and shady trellised walks with cool meeting places surrounding fountains.

In all, the gardens comprised four acres, surrounded either by moats or by stone walls with terraces above. In the midst of the terraces stood a fountain with a water jet. The grounds also boasted an orangery and an aviary, and yielded a sumptuous feast of peaches, apricots, strawberries, gooseberries, artichokes, cucumbers, and melons, as well as the usual French vegetables. Gifts of plants and trees were sent by the hopeful and grateful. The archbishop of Tours sent musk roses, lily bulbs, rare melons, and artichokes. Hazelnut trees arrived to be planted as leafy hedges; apple, peach, and other fruit trees were meant for the shady maze and to supply the house. Admirers sent rare plants and vegetables, including thirteen thousand aubergine plants, many varieties of currants, nine thousand strawberry plants, and carpets of violets.

Diane planted one hundred and fifty white mulberry trees. Since she wore no other fabric but silk, she established her own silkworm industry, and soon all the black and white silken cloth for her clothes came from Chenonceau.[7]

The original owner of Chenonceau had imported grapevines from all over France, and the new châtelaine tended these carefully for her own cellar. The wine from the Cher was much in demand: Diane sent hers from Chenonceau by barge to Anet. The châtelaine also received live game for the hunt. From Navarre, Antoine de Bourbon, husband of Jeanne d'Albret, sent her a Pyrenean chamois. For exercise, there was a *paille-maille* yard,[8] also used for tennis and tilting.

Diane oversaw the work of gardeners, horticulturists, designers, and architects, whose efforts combined to create the perfect union between the castle and nature. Chenonceau—with its slender stone arches spanning the Cher, seemingly neither completely on land nor on water[9]— came in time to symbolize its enigmatic châtelaine, who appeared to be part woman, part goddess. Chenonceau developed into one of the court's main residences, with Diane its undisputed sovereign.

ONE of Henri's first acts on his accession was to legitimize his natural daughter, Diane de France, and grant her the prerogatives of a royal princess, making over to her the duchy of Angoulême.[10] Diane de France inherited her father's skill on horseback as well as his

7. Louis XI had brought the silk industry to France from Italy in 1470. The Lyons silk factory was established and by the end of the century was a major producer. The demand for silk in England was so heavy that James I ordered his Lords Lieutenant to import over 1 million trees. Unfortunately, they ordered the wrong kind. As a result there is almost no seventeenth-century house in England without one or more fruit producing mulberry trees (including the author's own three old trees in Gloucestershire). Diane introduced Henri and Catherine to the first silk stockings made in France, which all three wore thereafter.

8. *Paille-maille,* or Pall-mall, was a sort of croquet played on a pitch, from which several straight roads in London derive their name.

9. Although the bridge was begun under Diane's ownership, it was far from complete by 1559. The gallery was built twenty years later.

10. Thereafter she signed herself "*Diane, Legitimée de France.*"

grace on the dance floor. On June 30, 1547, a marriage contract[11] was signed between the relevant official parties guaranteeing that Henri's daughter Diane would marry Orazio Farnese, grandson of the reigning pope, Paul III. The pope had sent Orazio to the French court as a child to be educated there with the intention that he would marry Henri's firstborn. As Orazio was twelve years older than the nine-year-old Diane, it was decided that the generous marriage contract would only be paid once the union was consummated. The pope bestowed large incomes on his grandson, as well as

Diane de France was the natural daughter of Henri II. Her mother was Filippa Duci, a young lady with whom Henri spent one night while on campaign in Italy.

the duchy and patrimony of the boy's family, creating him Duke of Castro. Pope Paul III gave Catherine a golden rose he had blessed, and to Henri's mistress, the real power behind the throne, he sent a string of perfect Oriental pearls. This union between *Diane, Legitimée de France* and Orazio Farnese was seen as the living symbol of France's pledge to renew hostilities against the imperialists' stronghold in Italy.

To further unite France with Italy, the pope elevated Diane's charming favorite, the Guise archbishop of Rheims, Charles de Lorraine, to the cardinal's hat on the day of Henri's coronation, July 26. The new cardinal wrote to Diane: "I cannot refrain from thanking you again for the special favor you have shown me, and for the great happiness it has given me. I will use every effort to serve you more and more, and I hope from these efforts to reap good fruits for you as well as for myself, since my interests henceforth cannot be separated from yours." How Diane would learn to regret those words. It is also highly likely that the cardinal encouraged his niece, Mary, Queen of Scots, to be subservient to Diane.

11. The marriage was not formally celebrated until February 1552.

One month later, Orazio Farnese's father was assassinated on the orders of the emperor, a gesture calculated to show his displeasure at the pope's alliance with France. Henri II installed his future son-in-law into the Order of Saint-Michel, and the young bridegroom left for Italy to take up his inheritance.

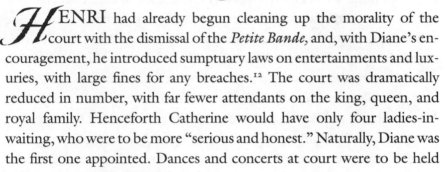

*H*ENRI had already begun cleaning up the morality of the court with the dismissal of the *Petite Bande,* and, with Diane's encouragement, he introduced sumptuary laws on entertainments and luxuries, with large fines for any breaches.[12] The court was dramatically reduced in number, with far fewer attendants on the king, queen, and royal family. Henceforth Catherine would have only four ladies-in-waiting, who were to be more "serious and honest." Naturally, Diane was the first one appointed. Dances and concerts at court were to be held only once a week. Henri loved to dance, but it is unlikely that Diane, a widow, would take part except in the more solemn, slow, parading dances. Henri stopped some of the more louche practices—for example, gentlemen of the court were no longer permitted to be present when the *filles d'honneur* rose in the morning or went to bed at night. The new chancellor proclaimed severe penalties for blasphemers, murderers, and ambushers.

Henri also brought in new social measures. Each district in Paris was to pool its wealth for the needs of the poor, and on certain days convents would hand out food and

Cardinal Charles de Lorraine, a brother of the great *Balafré,* was duc de Guise, and a protégé of Diane de Poitiers.

12. Sumptuary laws were originally designed to limit personal extravagant expenditure, especially in food and dress.

money. The more robust beggars were put to work repairing the city's roads and walls, while those who were ill or crippled were moved into hospitals. Even the *Parlement* was to reform and to accept only members over thirty years old whose morals and way of life were above reproach.

An incident from Henri's past resurfaced to stain the somber moral character of his court. The aborted duel between Guy Chabot, later baron de Jarnac, and Henri's representative, La Châtaigneraie, had left both men unsatisfied, and the recent disgrace of Jarnac's aunt, Anne d'Etampes, exacerbated the situation. With the advent of the new reign, the calumny against Jarnac, namely that he was the gigolo of his young stepmother, was again repeated by La Châtaigneraie. Would the new king allow the duel his father had refused? Henri discussed it with Montmorency at Ecouen and later with Diane at Anet. The king liked the concept of chivalric duels and finally agreed to let the contest take place. It does seem strange that a man of such noted kindness and consideration would agree to a duel to be fought to the death. The imperial ambassador Saint-Mauris wrote that, having seen Charles V, he knew what it means to be a real sovereign and found Henri II immature: ". . . It is his youth which can cause him to do some very trivial things."

La Châtaigneraie would boast that he could throw a bull by holding his horns and was risking nothing insulting this young man. Having originally challenged La Châtaigneraie as Henri's representative under the previous reign, and perhaps suspecting that Henri II *would* allow the duel to take place, Jarnac begged Diane to cancel it. But Diane hoped that the memory of Anne d'Etampes would be further disgraced by the defeat of her nephew in a duel of honor, and she refused to oblige. If Jarnac lost and was dishonored, the late king's mistress and her regime would be, too. Diane's enthusiasm for the duel was a rare example of her thirst for vengeance, albeit against a woman who had grievously wronged her. She saw herself as the pure influence on Henri, who would transform his court from the decadence of the past reign.

In the context of the new propriety, the duel between Jarnac and

La Châtaigneraie rapidly became a contest of the new morality versus the immorality of the past regime. Diane felt confident that La Châtaigneraie's inevitable victory over Jarnac would represent the triumph of her virtue over the vice of Anne d'Etampes. The Guises suggested that François d'Aumale, the brave *Balafré,* should be La Châtaigneraie's second. As Montmorency was forced to be the judge of the contest, he chose an excellent knight and Master of the Horse, the sieur de Boisy, to act as Jarnac's second. Henri was delighted with the chivalric content of the contest, especially the point of view that the winner would be "God's choice." More than anything, he liked the fact that Diane would wreak her revenge on Anne d'Etampes.

The contestants began to train. The handsome but delicate Jarnac was clearly at a disadvantage against the massive bulk and strength of his adversary, who boasted having taken on several swordsmen at once and winning. Jarnac was as good as dead, and prepared himself for the inevitable outcome. However, on the advice of a friend (and some say Catherine was behind this), he agreed to take some fencing lessons with an Italian master named Caize. His opponent's superior strength was obvious, but La Châtaigneraie was also slow and stupid, and he had an old wound that could weaken his right arm. Jarnac was advised to use his wits and his nimbleness. The date for the duel was fixed: July 10, 1547.

At dawn, a huge crowd began to travel from Paris and the surrounding countryside to the tournament site on the edge of a forest, next to Saint-Germain-en-Laye. Not since the reign of Saint Louis had a king of France authorized a duel to the death to attest to "God's judgment." By six in the morning, the area was already crowded. At midmorning, the court and the royal family took their places in the stand, with Henri sitting between Catherine and Diane. Catherine glittered in diamonds and pearls, in brilliant contrast to Henri and Diane, who looked confident and sober in their usual black and white. The spectacle began with a parade led by La Châtaigneraie, his second, the duc d'Aumale, the trumpeters, and behind them, three hundred young men dressed in white satin. After a circuit of the arena, the champion withdrew to his luxurious tent hung with tapestries, where he had arranged a grand victory feast to celebrate with the court after the contest. La Châtaigneraie had even borrowed gold and silver plates from the local nobility to embellish the long center table.

When Jarnac appeared and paraded before the crowd with a small retinue all dressed in somber black, with little finery, the people murmured their disappointment. Boisy, his second, presented Jarnac to the king. As the offended party, Jarnac exercised his right to choose the weapons. To the great surprise of the crowd and the court, Boisy announced that the weapons would be huge swords, weapons not used since the fifteenth century, and that each man would carry a heavy shield. Suddenly, the contest looked a little more even: brute strength against nimbleness and wit. The heavy weapon could quickly weaken the mighty champion's damaged arm. Aumale protested on behalf of La Châtaigneraie, and Anne de Montmorency, who presided over the tournament's jury, took the whole day to deliberate the problem in great detail. Once the jury had referred to each aspect of the armaments, the verdict was decided in favor of Jarnac, and the competition was judged fair. By now it was six in the evening and the crowd had grown restless with the waiting.

At the given signal, La Châtaigneraie charged at once, hoping to annihilate his opponent before the weight of the sword could slow his movements. Jarnac easily dodged the manic approach, then dived toward his adversary. The crowd was stupefied. What was Jarnac trying to achieve by rushing at La Châtaigneraie? The young man's Italian fencing master had taught him a new move unknown to swordsmen in France. It needed courage, and Jarnac had that. It had to work or he was a dead man. To the amazement of everyone, as La Châtaigneraie rushed past, Jarnac plunged his sword into his opponent, whose blood spurted onto the sand from a deep cut to the back of his knee. The wounded man hesitated and was struck again by Jarnac with a second deep cut in the same place. La Châtaigneraie collapsed.[13]

Seeing his man crumple, Henri turned white with rage, Diane red with embarrassment. They had set the scene as if they were paragons of

13. To this day, a *coup de Jarnac* in French means a lucky or devious blow by the underdog.

virtue and now their champion lay in the dust. Did Catherine dare a slight smile?

With measured steps, Jarnac approached the king to ask if he might be spared having to give his adversary the death blow, which was legal but unnecessary. His honor had been vindicated and he did not wish to strike a fallen man. Henri was still in shock at the outcome and did not, or could not, in his fury and shame, reply. Jarnac approached his victim and ordered him to give him back his honor. La Châtaigneraie pulled himself up on one knee and lashed out wildly at Jarnac with his sword before collapsing once again. When asked by the victor for the third time if he could forgo the death blow, the king managed to pull himself together and announce that Jarnac had done what he had set out to do and had indeed been vindicated. Instead of letting the victor take the traditional lap of honor, his second spirited Jarnac away to avoid the wrath of the many losing punters.

In the chaos that followed, a section of the crowd surged toward La Châtaigneraie's celebration tent and looted everything they could find—the gold and silver dishes as well as the food—until the king's guards dispersed them. All this while, the wounded man lay on the ground in the arena, spilling his blood. Montmorency noticed and called for help, but the doctors could do nothing more. In his shame, La Châtaigneraie pulled off their dressings and allowed himself to bleed to death. In the eyes of the cavaliers of the time, death was far better than dishonor. Cowardice was unforgivable.

The result of this foolish and tragic event was a great rush by the gallants of France to the fencing schools to learn the latest Italian techniques, and dueling became quite the fashion, to the detriment of the court. It also made Diane and Henri take stock of their power and how easily they could abuse it. This failure to demonstrate their virtue over the regime of vice headed by Anne d'Etampes in the last reign must have taught the lovers a lesson. The Jarnac incident remained on their conscience for some time.

ON July 24, 1547, following the traditional ninety days of royal mourning, Henri II made his solemn entrance into the city of Rheims, in a wondrous procession on horseback. He passed under three triumphal arches each emblazoned with his arms, the queen's, and the dauphin's, bordered by *fleur-de-lys* and crescents. On the pediment in the center of each arch was Henri and Diane's motto: "*Donec totum impleat orbem*"—"Until it fills the whole world." At the first archway, the king stopped to receive the keys of the town and to watch a curious fight between satyrs and savages. At the second gate, he was met by twelve magistrates who carried a canopy over his head decorated with the crescent moon. Once he had passed down a narrow street and through the third *arc de triomphe,* he saw thirteen effigies representing all the virtues, the first letters of their

Diane's symbols as Diana the Huntress with motto.

names in French spelling out HENRI DE VALOIS. Cannons boomed, church bells rang, trumpets and sundry musical instruments were banged or blown, and fireworks were let off everywhere.

Catherine was seated at a window overlooking the processional route; at a window nearby the other *dames d'honneur* surrounded Diane. The king's wife and mistress were no doubt equally proud to see the man they loved in his glory, acclaimed by his people. Henri had grown into a fine figure of a man, always at his best on horseback, an accomplished athlete. A likable person, with beautiful manners, gentle, tender, and refined, he had no difficulty in winning the love of his subjects. He also had great charm. Henri reined in his horse and saluted his wife, then he halted beneath Diane's window and saluted her. Everywhere the crescent moon shone silver, symbol of the dawn of a new reign—and of the goddess with whom Diane shared a name.

It was customary for a new monarch to give a splendid gift to the cathedral—Henri brought with him a fifteenth-century silver-gilt reliquary in the shape of a pyramid, inscribed: "King Henri II brought me here in 1547, the day of his coronation."[14] It housed a stone from the Holy Sepulcher, and depicted the tomb of the risen Christ. It was not large, but it was exquisite. Henri's monogram had been added to either side, the "H" with the two crescents forming the "D," one side in black, the other in white; three interlaced crescents were also added, two in white and one in black in the center of a circle representing the full moon. The same decoration was embroidered in pearls on Henri's tunic. Having left his gift on the high altar, Henri retired to rest and hold a vigil on the night before his coronation.

It is during the king's entry into Rheims that several sources mention he "sleeps in the same bed with Montmorency"—and not for the first time. A number of the ambassadors, including Jean de Saint-Mauris, allude to this, as does the usually reliable Ivan Cloulas, but most biographers omit it completely. In fact, Henri is mentioned as sharing a bed with others of his senior officers on various occasions. It seems it was quite normal in the sixteenth century—and until comparatively recent times—for men to share beds, particularly among the military, without suggestive overtones. It was taken as a sign of friendship, respect, and of trust. The greatest mark of esteem a victorious general could offer his vanquished opponent was to share his bed with a man who could easily kill him during the night.[15]

Two days later, on July 26, Diane was seated among the *dames d'honneur* beneath the queen's dais in Nôtre-Dame. Everything in the cathedral glittered gold—the vessels, the candelabra, the sovereigns' and archbishops' thrones, altar cloths, and vestments. Catherine was heavy with her third child and needed to sit comfortably during the long ceremony. Preceded by the Constable, the king entered the cathedral in procession with the bishops. He wore a fine white shirt and a blue satin tunic, lined in scarlet taffeta and scattered with embroidered

14. Out of all the gifts given by French kings, only those of Henri II and his son Henri III survived pillage and destruction during the Revolution. They are now in the Louvre.

15. I am grateful to Professor R. J. Knecht for this explanation.

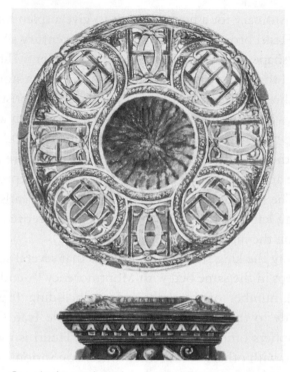

Ceramic plates and vessels were issued frequently during the reign of Henri II, featuring the joint monogram of Henri and Diane de Poitiers.

golden *fleur-de-lys*. It was slit down the front at his chest and in the back between his shoulders to enable him to be anointed with the Holy Oil, which symbolized the Most Christian King's bond with God.

Henri II had ordered new robes for his coronation. To the astonishment of all the assembled dignitaries, his robes were embroidered in tiny pearls with Diane's symbols—her quiver, bows, and arrows, her interlaced crescents and the double "D" attached within the letter "H." The same symbols were embroidered on his black velvet doublet, which prompted one ambassador to exclaim that these represented "the two spirits of two lovers." From now on, these would be the symbols of his reign. Many recognized the crescent as Diane's symbol, but others thought it was adopted by the new king as the opposite of the emperor's symbol of the sun. It was the defiant gesture of a man in love who was able at last to reveal to the world, with pride, how his life was entwined with that of Diane de Poitiers, and had been for at least the past ten years.

Nowhere was there a sign to be seen of the queen's crowned letter "C," although Henri's monogram could be read ambiguously as a crescent "C" but the queen knew it was Diane's symbol and not hers. She suffered, but her shame remained private. The serpent would Hate and Wait. Her time would come. Seated on his golden throne, the king received the symbols of his office: the magnificent ring with which he married the kingdom, the scepter, the orb, and the hand of justice. Later, according to the Venetian ambassador Matteo Dandolo, Henri confided to Diane he had prayed that if his reign was good and worthy of his people, God should make it last a long time. If not, He should cut it short.

The moment that the closed, heavy gold crown of Charlemagne was placed on the head of the twenty-eight-year-old king, the heralds shouted, "*Vivat rex in aeternum*." The congregation responded with a loud "*Vive le roi! Vive le roi!*" The cry was taken up by the crowds outside the church and resonated through the streets. *Vive le roi! Vive le roi!* Two dozen silver trumpets played an *intrada* within the cathedral, and from the upper galleries a shower of a thousand gold and silver coronation coins rained down on the congregation. Henri turned and smiled at his queen, but even in that most sacred of moments, he did not forget Diane and shared his smile with her. The *sacre* was followed by a sung High Mass, and afterward there was a great banquet in the archbishop's palace at which each of the thirty courses was announced by a fanfare of trumpets.

At the archbishop's palace, the king exchanged the heavy gold crown for a new, lighter one he had commissioned using precious stones out of his treasury, and he put on more comfortable clothes. As his father had done before him, Henri then left for a nine-day retreat in the Abbey of Corbény. There in the chapel, in accordance with tradition, he laid his hands on some poor souls with scrofula who dutifully claimed they had been healed.

Diane took part in the solemn ritual as the principal lady in attendance on Catherine de' Medici. It is recorded that while the new queen's robes of crimson velvet and white satin were festooned in gold and jewels, Diane was no less bejeweled and drew as many eyes. Her habitual deep, wide décolleté, draped with pearls from one shoulder to the other, was of black velvet, setting off to perfection her white skin and fair coloring. Her long black velvet skirt opened in front to reveal a white satin panel covered in gold and silver embroidery. She wore great pear-drop pearls in her ears and her hair was as always *à l'escoffion,* in a snood of trellised black velvet ribbon studded with pearls. On the top of her forehead, she wore a diamond crescent as her crown. Many people continued to believe (as did the chronicler Ronsard, who described her as a "good, wise, kind lady . . . the perfect friend") that Diane de Poitiers was a cherished older friend of the king's. And yet the Italian ambassador wrote that after the banquet, Henri withdrew into his quarters, but that instead of sleeping, he "went to find the Sénéchale."

CHAPTER SIXTEEN

The King's Mistress

*T*HE family obsession with Italy had not faded with François I's death. Like his father before him, Henri needed to make an ally of the pope and demonstrate the strength of the Faith by stamping out heresy. He also inherited his father's dilemma of having to choose between his genuine desire to nourish and foster the intellectual climate of the time and his conviction that the new heresy of the reformed church had to be eradicated. But, even more than François I, Henri II believed in the perniciousness of heresy and that it was allied to treason. At his coronation, the king had been urged by the newly created cardinal, Charles de Lorraine, to rid France of heresy and become the saviour of the Catholic Church. Diane also encouraged Henri in this mission.

A few months after Henri's coronation, the *Parlement* established a special court solely for the trial of heretics. It quickly became known as the "*Chambre ardente*" because of the number of people sent from there to the flames. In the first two months, five hundred heretics were sentenced to death. Of all those condemned for crimes against the state, heretics were given the worst punishment—to be burned at the stake *au petit feu*—very slowly. If too many faggots were lit at once, the smoke would usually kill their victims and spare them from the horror of the flames. A small fire would ensure they suffered a slow and painful death. Within the Holy Roman Empire, heretics fared even worse as they were often tied to a seesaw dipped in and out of the flames to prolong their agony. Although Diane was accused of being responsible for the increase in the persecutions, the Guise brothers and the Constable were the instigators of the infamous "*Chambre ardente.*"

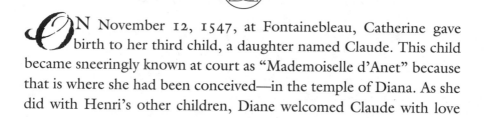

ON November 12, 1547, at Fontainebleau, Catherine gave birth to her third child, a daughter named Claude. This child became sneeringly known at court as "Mademoiselle d'Anet" because that is where she had been conceived—in the temple of Diana. As she did with Henri's other children, Diane welcomed Claude with love

Heretics (Protestants) were burned at the stake during the reigns of François I and Henri II.

and tenderness. Diane continued to be in charge of the royal children's lives and upbringing, and Henri dubbed her the "Titular Genius of the Royal Nursery." It was Diane, not Catherine, who advised when the royal nursery should be moved to another château if an epidemic was rumored to be approaching. Diane, not Catherine, chose the wet nurses and made sure they were clean and healthy, and some of them were first trained by Diane at Anet. When she heard that the baby Charles was rejecting his nurse's milk, Diane made her drink cider or beer to "refresh" it. It was Diane who decided when to wean the babies and what to feed them. The chief physician, Jean Fernel, wrote that Diane chose the "wise and prudent governesses; while she caused them [the children] to be instructed by good and learned preceptors, as much in virtue and wise precepts, as in love and fear of God." Diane was sanguine about childhood illnesses and remained cool and calm when they developed coughs and colds. She preferred to trust her own judgment rather than that of the doctors—except for Jean Fernel. The wife of the children's governor, Madame d'Humières, had given birth to eighteen children, and Diane trusted in her experience to help her make decisions.

In the royal nursery, as everywhere else, Diane's word, not the queen's, held sway. As the careful guardian of France's children, Diane de Poitiers' influence would reach beyond her own time. The king and queen agreed to abide totally by her decisions. The children's routine consisted of Fontainebleau during winter; Blois, Amboise, and Tours in the Loire Valley during the spring; La Muette or Saint-Germain-en-Laye for the summer; and Compiègne for the autumn months. No matter where they were based, all orders for the children's welfare were made by Diane. She organized the doctors, and arranged for the medications to be made under her supervision. As the king and queen were often traveling in the kingdom, Diane arranged for portraits of the children to be sent to them. Sadly, all of the children, except the last, Margot, had serious physical defects, large jowls, and the "Medici snout." None would bring the queen any joy or esteem.

Were Catherine a typical mother, it might have been difficult for her to renounce the care of her children, especially to her husband's mistress. But if Catherine ever had any maternal feelings, she must have weaned herself of them rapidly because she only showed an interest in her children when they were much older. The queen almost died giving birth to her sixth child, and during that time she briefly forgot her animosity and relied on Diane's expertise and experience. "Without your wisdom, diligence and goodness of heart," wrote the king's physician afterward, "the queen would have been without hope in her last illness." While Catherine pretended to tolerate the royal *ménage à trois,* just as Louise de Savoie had tolerated her husband's mistresses, privately she seethed with hatred at the woman who occupied *her* rightful place by her husband's side and in his heart.

*H*ENRI the king was very unlike Henri the prince. The change was remarkable. He became more affable, more open and friendly to all comers; he smiled often and laughed. His coronation had a mystical effect on him as well, and he carried himself with a new dignity and pride. Naturally affectionate, he was sentimental, honest in word and deed, and faithful to his friends. He was a contemplative man, who loved to read; he was steady, moderate, profound, and rather silent, yet the members of the court recognized his goodness of heart. Henri was a romantic knight from the days of chivalry, quietly going about his business and focusing on his goal with a steadfastness akin to obsession. That obsession was Diane and her glory, just as hers was his.

Henri wished to demonstrate his love for his mistress in every possible way. Soon their cipher was to be carved in stone on all his palaces, and her arms were to share his motto. His first commission to his architects was to rebuild and extend his favorite palace, Saint-Germain-en-Laye, by adding two semicircular wings at either end of the long straight building, forming the shape of a "D." The vast palace lay in the midst of a forest teeming with game. A real tennis court had been installed in the hollow of a dry moat. At one end of the court, a little gallery was built with a cloth cover fixed to the walls. Here Diane and the ladies of the court could watch the game protected from the afternoon sun.

In Paris, with the help of his architect Pierre Lescot, Henri tore

Henri II's monogram consisted of a crowned "H" resting on a crescent moon, the symbol of Diane de Poitiers.

down and replaced two wings of the ancient Louvre Palace, carving the "HD" cipher large in the stone of the pediments above his own crowned "H." This is still clearly visible today. Inside, the goddess Diana was depicted everywhere, in the plaster walls and on the ceilings in low relief. Perhaps it was to escape from all these "Dianas" that Catherine later on built the Palace of the Tuileries opposite the Louvre on the other side of the city wall.

Diane's symbols came from mythology: the crescent moon, the triangular *delta* (the Greek letter for D), the bows and arrows of the huntress, and the new king emblazoned his reign with them. Diane de Poitiers' crescent rose like that of the moon. With the accession of Henri II, Venus, goddess of love and symbol of François I's devotion to Italian art, ceased to be the dominant female deity of the French Renaissance and was replaced by Diana, goddess of the moon and the chase. The worship of Diana led quite nat-

Diane's symbols: the crescent, delta, and hunter's bow and arrows.

urally into the cult of Diane, mistress of Henri II, and she and the goddess merged inexorably in the people's imagination.

A year after his coronation, when Diane was forty-eight, Henri begged her to accept and wear a ring "for love of me. May it always remind you of one who has never loved and never will love another but thee."

In all that he wrote to his mistress, his love was touchingly full of humility:

> *Hélas, mon Dieu, combien je regrette*
> *Le temps que j'ai perdu en ma jeunesse;*
> *Combien de fois je me suis souhaité*
> *Avoir Diane pour ma seule maîtresse;*
> *Mais je craignais qu'elle qui est déesse*
> *Ne se voulût abaisser jusque-là*
> *De faire cas de moi, qui, sans cela,*
> *N'avais plaisir, joie ni contentement*
> *Jusques à l'heure que se délibéra*
> *Que j'obéisse à son commandement.*
>
> *A nouveau prince (ô ma seule princesse!)*
> *Que mon amour qui vous sera sans cesse*
> *Contre le temps et la mort assurée*
> *De fosse creuse ou de tour bien murée*
> *N'a pas besoin de ma foi la fortresse,*
> *Dont je vous fis dame, reine et maîtresse*
> *Parce qu'elle est d'éternelle durée!*

Alas, my Lord, how much I rue
The time I lost in my youth;
How often have I wished
To have Diane as my only love;
But I feared that such a goddess
Would not deign to stoop so low
To take notice of one, who
When denied her love,
Had no pleasure, joy, or happiness

Until the day she granted him leave
To obey her commands.

Once more a prince (oh, my only princess!)
My love for you will never cease
Resisting time and death
My faith has no need of a fortress,
A deep moat or fortified tower,
For you are my lady, queen and mistress
For whom my love will be eternal!

Theirs was a great love—the perfect meeting of minds and bodies. Henri adored Diane without reservation: "I [beg] you to remember him who has known but one God and one friend, and rest assured you will never be ashamed of having allowed me to be your servant, and as such I implore you to keep me forever." All his letters and notes are signed with the interlaced initials "HD."

A number of historians like to claim that Diane's relationship with Henri was motivated entirely by self-interest. But her interest lay always with Henri and his with her. Why should she not be the most fortunate woman in his realm? She had cared for him since his childhood, mothered him, counseled him, and finally, she had fallen in love with this handsome, athletic young man who blatantly worshipped her. He freely gave what he had to give both as king and lover, and she repaid him with her total devotion, love, and wise counsel.

Diane de Poitiers was the choice of the king's heart. If he could have married her, he would gladly have done so. One can understand that he felt her place should be beside him for the world to see. When one considers the extent of the hold Diane had on Henri, she could have asked for so much more. It is a sign of her breeding, her sensitivity and basic good manners that so few people were aware of her true relationship with the king. Diane was discreet not only because she wished to be seen as the pure widow eternally in mourning for her husband, but also out of respect for the institution of the monarchy. These were the values and the behavior she had been taught by the inimitable Anne de Beaujeu.

*W*ITH the death of James V of Scotland in November 1542, his tiny daughter Mary Stuart had inherited the throne. To the annoyance of Henry VIII, who sought to incorporate Scotland into his kingdom, Mary was instantly recognized as sovereign Queen of Scots by the king of France. In September 1547, the English scored a great victory over the Scots at the bloody Battle of Pinkie Cleugh, near Edinburgh, and it became clear to Scotland's dowager-queen, Marie de Guise, and the Scottish nobles that an alliance with France was in their best interests. Although stunned at first by the enormous implications of such a union, in January 1548, the regent, James Hamilton, second Earl of Arran, signed a contract with Henri II that the queen of Scotland would marry the dauphin of France. Arran was Mary's cousin and the heir apparent, and he had hoped that the little queen would marry his own son instead of Henri's heir; but because of the menace of England, his country needed a strong ally.

In June 1548, the French fleet of over one hundred vessels landed their men at Leith near Edinburgh to join the fifty captains who had arrived the previous December. Their number included German and Italian mercenaries and totaled six thousand. This force marched to besiege the important market town of Haddington in East Lothian, occupied by the English. In a nunnery there, the French and Scots signed a treaty which decreed that, because of the pending marriage of the dauphin of France to the queen of Scotland, France would defend Scotland. Scotland would need protection because, once the English realized that Mary Stuart would no longer be the bride of their own child-king Edward VI,

The dauphin François, first son of Henri II.

and would instead join her kingdom to France, retribution would surely follow, and there was a real threat that Mary would be kidnapped and forced to marry Edward. Even before the Scottish Parliament had consented to the marriage, in view of the danger to their little queen's life, and to the great sadness of Marie de Guise, preparations began for her daughter to leave for France as soon as possible. The dowager-queen had lost her two sons with James V[1]; her only other son (by her first husband, a French duke) lived in France; and now she was losing her enchanting daughter. But despite the urgings of her Guise relations to return to France, Marie de Guise would stay behind to protect her daughter's inheritance.

Meanwhile, the French took extraordinary precautions to avoid the possibility of the English intercepting and capturing Mary Stuart. On June 24, the galleys intended to escort Mary slipped out of the Firth of Forth heading for the west coast. Mary was seen in Dumbarton and the English must have had a good idea that she would try to leave from there for France, taking the long western route. In July, the Scottish Parliament consented to the marriage on condition that they could count on the French to defend them as they would their own country, while respecting Scotland's independence. Mary embarked on July 28, but the ships stayed in the Firth of Forth until August 7, when a long-awaited east wind sprang up. Following a wide northern route, the galleys reached the west coast of Ireland, successfully evading the English ships lying in wait off St. Abb's Head. On August 20, Mary landed safely in France in the tiny port of Roscoff near Brest, where a small chapel still stands to mark the spot.

While his soldiers were demonstrating French might and guile to the English by spiriting away Mary, Queen of Scots, Henri II, encouraged by Montmorency, decided to go on tour to Turin, capital of his conquered territory of Piedmont, situated between France and the north of Italy. In April 1548, accompanied by only a small entourage, he made his first progress through this domain as its king. The bulk of the court remained near Lyons, the first city to stage a royal "entry" for Henri other than Paris. Diane's brother Guillaume died at this time, so

1. Arthur Duke of Albany, one year younger than James V, died the same year.

she was unable to join the king on his stately progress through Piedmont. Judging from the letters that passed between the king and his mistress, he missed her dreadfully.

Henri II made a leisurely, triumphal progress through the country and was lavishly received. During September, the king and Montmorency left the court's gentle caravan in order to quell the wholesale rebellion of La Rochelle and the people of the salt marshes. Henri had tried to increase the *gabelle,* or salt tax. Montmorency put down the rebellion very harshly while the king rejoined the queen, Diane, and their suite at Ainay, then journeyed to the Rhône to sail in the royal galleys toward Lyons. The new king was jubilant. The earlier morose young man had disappeared, and he rejoiced in his good fortune.

After Paris, Lyons, ancient capital of the Gauls, was the second richest city in France, predominantly due to its trade in gold and silver. Lyons was also the second most progressive, cultured city in France, and its citizens wanted to stage a spectacular state entry for their new king. Sixteenth-century France was in the grip of the cult of antiquity and the provinces followed the lead of Paris. To honor Henri II, the city chose to stage a Roman triumph.

The celebrations began on September 23, 1548. The guard of honor, consisting of 338 infantry, wore new black and white uniforms, and the hundreds of representatives of the various guilds that paraded in front of the king also wore only black and white. The façades of the houses and balconies along the processional route were covered with tapestries. Although there was no mention of Diane de Poitiers in the official address, it was to her that the dignitaries turned after greeting the king, her fingers they kissed. Everywhere Henri looked, he saw his cipher joined to that of the woman he loved: on the canopy above him, on the fluttering pennants, on the carpet beneath his feet, on the saddlecloths of the horses.

The pageant was staged in an artificial forest complete with live deer, set up in the main square. A group of beautiful nymphs was central: they played Amazons stalking elegantly through the undergrowth, their tunics cut to expose one breast, their hair caught up in ropes of pearls and precious stones. Brantôme describes their leader, a strikingly beautiful girl who represented the goddess Diana, wearing a brief black tunic covered with silver stars, black knee-high stockings, crimson stocking-sleeves edged and laced in gold, and short red satin boots covered with pearls and embroidery. A silver crescent set with diamonds glittered on her forehead; her Turkish bow hung from her shoulder, and she carried a golden arrow in her hand.

Several of the nymphs led *levrettes* and various small hunting hounds on silken cords of black and white. Others accompanied running dogs and carried little gilded daggers, spears, and golden hunting horns, all hung with ribbons or tassels in black and white silk. The cornet players and trumpeters wore gold and silver sashes with more black and white ribbons.

Suddenly, out of the undergrowth, a mechanical lion appeared at the feet of the goddess Diana, who slipped a silver and black leash about his neck.[2] He was the trophy of their hunt and the symbol of the city of Lyons. The goddess presented the lion to the king while reciting a poem from the city written in his honor. As Diane and the queen watched the spectacle, the meaning of this gesture was not lost on either of them, or on the audience: the goddess Diana presents the city of Lyons to the king, just as Diane gives him her devotion, a lion/city tamed by love. He was her Actaeon; she, Diana, goddess of the hunter's moon. It was a charming conceit and tableau, which delighted those watching. History does not relate the feelings of the two rivals, but one can imagine Diane's glow of triumph to be accepted by this great city as the king's lover, just as one can sense the humiliation of the queen.

More entertainment followed: a staged combat between twelve Roman gladiators, six in red against six wearing white; and a staged naval battle, with one set of participants wearing black and white against another in red and green, the queen's colors. Needless to say, the black and white team won.

---

2. Such a mechanical lion was kept (and even modified) from one royal entry to the next. It had certainly been used for the entry of François I into Lyons some years earlier. The beast would bare his chest, revealing the arms of the monarch. It is possible that Lyons' mechanical lion was designed by Leonardo da Vinci. Leonardo was employed by the French governor of Milan, Charles de Chaumont, in 1506, and Louis XII asked the artist to meet him there the following year. Leonardo was known to have worked on pageants for Louis XII's entry into Milan, and his *Virgin of the Rocks* was already in the king's collection.

The famous courtesan Louise Labé, muse and mistress of French and Italian poets, and herself an outstanding poet in both languages, held a literary salon in the city.

In honor of the state entry, Louise Labé planted the interlaced "HD" initials and moon symbols in her garden and posed there, dressed as a *chevalier* in velvet doublet and hose, and sporting a plumed velvet beret. Her lover, the poet Olivier de Magny, included this poem[3] dedicated to Diane in his *Odes:*

> *Par un eclipse elle perd ses clartés,*
> *Mais vous jamais ne perdez vos béautes:*
> *Car le soleil dont, Princesse benigne,*
> *Vous recevez ceste clarté divine,*
> *Et bien plus grand que celluy dont Phébé*
> *Prend la lueur de son front recourbé.*

> With an eclipse she [the Moon] loses her light,
> But you will never lose your beauty:
> For, good Princess, the sun from which you
> Receive your divine radiance
> Is far greater than the one
> Which sets alight Phoebe's [the Moon's] domed brow.

Throughout all of these festivities, it was perfectly clear whom the city had chosen to honor. For the rest of her life, Catherine de' Medici never forgot the humiliation she had suffered in Lyons. Matteo Dandolo described the unhappy Catherine: "She has the big eyes and thick lips of the Medici. Many say she strikingly resembles her great-uncle, Pope Leo. But, nevertheless, she loves the king above everything, so much so that the object of all her thoughts seems to be nothing else but how to please him and to be with him. For this reason, without bothering about the effort or the fatigue, she follows him wherever she can." Today, Henri's treatment of Catherine may seem callous, yet it

---

3. Love letters and poems were a popular literary form of the time. The ability to compose a good poem was akin to having good manners or being well dressed; it was required of young courtiers of either sex. By the rules of Courtly Love, a gallant knight always destroyed any love letters he received.

should be remembered that he neither chose her nor wanted her as his partner for life. Henri was devoted to another, and blind to Catherine's love. The serpent lay still.

The next day, it was the queen's turn to make her official entry and receive the city's homage. The same pageant was performed for Catherine, but this time the nymphs and Amazons wore satin in Catherine's green. All the ladies of the court were present, including Marguerite de Navarre and Jeanne d'Albret. Diane, striking in the stark simplicity of her black and white, rode on a dancing black stallion behind the queen's litter, and drew the crowd's cheers. Although they disliked many of her policies, in particular, her intolerance of Protestants, few of them could resist the magnetism of her dramatic, silent presence. The Spanish ambassador was there and wrote home describing Catherine's entry: "It is indeed true that little could be seen when the queen made her entry, because night came on . . . and the people say that, as she is not good-looking, the king gave orders that her pageant should be kept back until a late hour, so that Her Majesty should pass unnoticed." This seems hard to believe of the courteous Henri. Brantôme tells us that although the queen's entry was indeed at night, the town was so well lit that "one could see it as light as day: which went very well, for the lovely fireworks accompanied those in the eyes of the beautiful ladies, which worked together to make fire and light everywhere."

It was during the court's stay at Lyons that Henri created Diane "duchesse de Valentinois," restoring to her the titles, taxes, and dues of the duchy which her family had forfeited in 1419, and which had passed to Cesare Borgia. Once France and Italy had resumed hostilities, however, the estates were reclaimed and returned to the crown. Diane had been known as the comtesse de Brézé or La Grande Sénéchale, but from this day, she became the duchesse de Valentinois, the highest dignity for a lady not born a princess. In France, the dukedom had always been reserved for the blood royal or foreigners like the Guises, and until then, Anne d'Etampes had been the only other exception. French royal though illegitimate sons had also been created dukes in the past. This placed the new duchess on a par with the Princes of the Blood.

As if all this were not enough, the king had a gold medal struck with Diane's head on it—something never done before by a French sovereign to honor a mistress. Under her profile are the words: *"Diana dux Valentinorum clarissima"*—"Diane, illustrious duchesse de Valentinois," and on the other side, she is shown as the goddess Diana, bow in hand and Cupid at her feet. Beneath is the inscription: *"Omnium Victorem Vici"*—"I conquered him who conquered all." An alternative translation could be "I conquered the King, Love, and Time." A companion gold coin depicts Henri II in profile. On the reverse is a large crescent interlaced with bows and arrows, one arrow crowned with laurels and Diane's monogram. Beneath, the famous motto: "Until it fill the whole world."

Sometimes Henri used three intertwined crescent moons as his symbol, with the motto, seen here on a floor at Anet.

*H*IS father had never cared for him, nor admitted him to his Privy Council until he became dauphin. Thus, Henri had not been trained to rule. As the task was really above him, he left most of the government in the hands of Montmorency and the Guises, and retreated into his dreamworld and that of his hero, Amadis. What little he did know of state affairs he learned from Montmorency; but the Constable had been absent from the court in the last six years.

Surrounded by intrigues and rivalries all his life, Henri had only ever relied on one person, and it was to her that he now turned for advice. Diane was always there to help, but she could only teach him what she had gleaned from conversations at court. In a number of state matters, the new king placed so much trust in his mistress that many of his official letters were written in her hand and jointly signed with one name: "HenriDiane." The lovers would amuse themselves by writing to

Montmorency half in one hand, half in the other, then ending with their joint signature.

Wisely, Diane encouraged Henri to appoint ministers who were not only loyal to him but also true patriots. Diane became a member of his Privy Council and largely controlled the others. In every appointment, no matter how small, observers could see her sure hand guiding the young king. Those who had openly opposed Diane in the past were amazed that, instead of taking her revenge, she gave them appointments if she felt that they could be of use to the kingdom. Without the help of brilliant men in the key positions of his government, Henri's reign would not have been described by the Italian ambassadors as one of the most remarkable in French history for the wisdom of its policies. The Italian ambassadors wrote home with nothing but praise for

Diane de Poitiers and Henri II often wrote letters together and even signed documents with their joint signature.

Diane's wise counsel, and declared that, as a result, the king filled his time "only with things useful and honorable." Contarini claimed in his dispatches to the Vatican that Henri "was as weak in private as he was strong in public," and that Diane took advantage of this. The ambassador added that Henri showed a "real tenderness" for Diane, "but it is not thought that there is anything lascivious about it, but that this affection is like that between a mother and son." He wrote this in 1547 around the time of the coronation, when Diane had been Henri's mistress for at least ten years, which shows the lengths to which the lovers went to keep the true nature of their relationship private.

*L*IKE his father, François I, Henri ruled a court that was the most sophisticated in Europe. Henri's love of courtly manners and values formed the perfect frame for the art, architecture, music, and literature of his time. Yet remnants of a previous, darker age could still be seen in some aspects of court life, particularly in the pranks and games of the young men. Henri's brother Charles and his friend Enghien had died as a result of the rather brutish behavior that was acceptable at the time. Just three months after his father's death, Henri staged his first water tournament at Anet. The imperial ambassador Saint-Mauris noted that Henri delighted in pushing people into the river and succeeded in almost drowning a page. A few months later, in 1548, Henri loosened the bridle on Montmorency's horse during a hunt so that the horse bolted off into the forest and Montmorency had no way of controlling it.

One of the many strange customs couched in a religious framework took place every December 28, the Feast of the Innocents, held in remembrance of the biblical slaughter by Herod of firstborn sons. Henri would actively take part in breaking into strangers' houses to try to catch young people still in bed early on the morning of the saints' day. The idea was to "admonish" those still sleeping for the sin of sloth by smacking them liberally on their naked bottoms. This was termed "to innocent" them and the phrase often appears in licentious and comic texts. Naturally, this old custom was turned into a ribald event. Many a young gallant took to the role with more vigor than perhaps necessary.

It seems Henri derived particular pleasure in this task. No doubt anyone wishing to avoid such delicious punishment would rise early.

Henri's jester Brusquet was constantly involved in complicated pranks at court. Jesters were an institution inherited from the Middle Ages and the king and queen regarded them as an integral part of their court. The fool or jester was in a class of his own. He could be as familiar with the king and queen as if he were one of their children; he could come and go into their private apartments as he pleased, pop into council meetings uninvited, or beg favors of the king for courtiers. Despite his highly privileged position, the fool wore green and yellow, the colors of shame. Brusquet, whom Henri II had saved from the gallows while he was still dauphin, had been an accomplished con artist and was intelligent enough to make himself a fortune in the service of the king. He was such a success that he rose to become *valet de garde-robe,* then *valet de chambre.* He ended up as head of the postal services[4] and had over one hundred horses in his stable. One of the funniest of his tricks was the occasion when he introduced his wife to Catherine de' Medici after confiding to each of them that the other was deaf. The resulting chaotic scene of the two women miming and gesticulating was, by all accounts, hysterical. Like so many of the court, Brusquet was suspected of Protestant sympathies, but as long as Henri lived, he was safe. After Henri's death, Diane protected him at Anet, where he died in 1563.

Diane was always a party to this colorful group of people, and her court rivaled that of the queen. She had dwarves, musicians, and entertainers, just as Catherine did. All the important members of the court had their own violin and guitar players and often played the lute themselves. The queen had been at the papal courts of her relatives, Popes Leo and Clement in Rome, and those of her Medici family in Florence, and she tried to imitate or outdo them in splendor.

Catherine spent lavishly and generously on her attendants, her jesters, her "tame madwoman," called La Sardinière, and another female jester, called Cathelot, as well as a whole stable of dwarves, freaks,

4. Mail was carried by relays of mounted couriers for the king, the royal family and their staff, and also for foreign dignitaries. As the mail horses were under Brusquet's command, this enabled the king to know everyone's itineraries. Brusquet developed the idea of renting out his horses to carry mail for specific clients, French as well as foreign.

and parrots. Included in this gathering were the queen's *dames d'hon-neur,* among them some close friends in whom she could confide. Although Diane and Catherine needed one another, and were outwardly friendly, the queen remained consumed by jealousy.

ON May 15, 1549, two years after the coronation in Rheims, the king made his official entry into Paris. This delay was unusual—due, it was said, to a number of political and religious reasons. However, Henri had already made entries into thirty of his cities in the previous two years, so one must assume he could have made one into his capital sooner had he wished.

Entering Paris in state gave him the opportunity at last to honor and acknowledge Diane in the capital. From a balcony erected especially for her, she watched the king's official entry. The day's festivities began with the arrival of a huge procession of two thousand pages dressed in black and white, walking in front of the king. They were followed by the representatives of the *Parlement,* the city and guilds, the university, and every trade. Even the printers turned out, 3,500 of them, all dressed in black and white—and armed.

The new fashion for the antique overcame the organizers in Paris, and the capital was filled with model pyramids,[5] obelisks, and *arcs de triomphe* covered with Greek and Roman verses, all mixed among the new Renaissance buildings.

The Parisians conceived a novel way of honoring the "royal trinity": they placed a large face of the sun in gold and the moon in silver on the bridge of Nôtre-Dame (for Henri and Diane) and with them Iris, the messenger of Juno, represented by the rainbow (the symbol of the queen). The city's renowned humanist, Jean Martin, devised this scenario, which was carried out by a team of artists, including the sculptor Jean Goujon and the painter Jean Cousin, who both worked at Anet for Diane. Her architect, Philibert de l'Orme, whom Henri had nominated as his Superintendent of Buildings, was responsible for

5. Made of wood and covered in painted oilcloth.

The Fountain of the Innocents is the only monument still remaining from Henri II's formal entry into Paris.

creating the triumphal arches. A beautiful monument dating from Henri II's entry still exists—the Fontaine des Innocents, although altered and in a new setting.[6] Henri commissioned the fountain in 1547 from Pierre Lescot and it was completed in time for his official entry in 1549.

For this great day, the king sported a suit of polished white armor chased in gold filigree; over it, he wore a tunic of cloth of silver embroidered with his devices, and a silver belt chased in gold decoration. His sword scabbard, covered with precious stones, glinted in the sunlight; a white satin beret perched with panache on his head, a plume of

6. The Fountain of the Innocents was built by Pierre Lescot and Jean Goujon. It was originally an open loggia with three sides, the fourth backing onto one of the church buildings on the corner of the rue Saint-Denis and the rue-aux-Fers. Since 1786, it has stood on the site of the former Church of the Innocents, in the middle of the Place des Innocents in Les Halles, the old quarter of Paris.

white feathers affixed to the side by a
brooch with a large diamond and three
huge drop pearls. He rode on a young
white stallion, caparisoned in cloth of
silver to match his ensemble, which
pranced and shied and showed off his
master's skill in the saddle.

Behind the king rode the kaleidoscope of the court. As its members
passed beneath the open windows and
balconies, they marveled at the ladies
there, with "faces like angels," wearing
splendid jewels and ravishing dresses,
and they exclaimed that Paris was more
like "Paradise than an earthly city."
One commentator wrote that the

Henri II and Diane de Poitiers
shared a monogram "HD," seen
here with the Greek D, or *delta*,
symbolizing the royal *ménage à trois*.

courtiers were so inspired by the beauties they saw about them that
they encouraged their mounts to pirouette and prance, showing off all
along the processional route.

When Henri passed under a triumphal arch surmounted by a huge
crowned "HD" and stopped beneath her balcony, Diane could see
their joint cipher on his tunic embroidered in pearls as he saluted her.
His personal guard wore her colors of black and white, a large silver
crescent moon on the front and back of their liveries, as well as the
"HD"—and all his household staff had the same. If he could not make
Diane his queen and the mother of his legitimate children, Henri
would at least proclaim his love for her to the whole of France. Catherine de' Medici watched the parade wearing a heavy, elaborate gold
dress embroidered with pearls. She was nearing the end of her pregnancy with her fourth child and made herself ill from a combination of
chagrin and too much of a new vegetable imported from Rome called
the artichoke.

As a consequence of the ancient Salic Law, no woman could rule in
France or be more than a consort to her husband. For this reason,
Catherine could not share Henri's coronation at Rheims. A French

queen's coronation was often delayed, probably for financial reasons. The king's coronation was so costly that his queen often had to wait some time until the coffers could be replenished. Three weeks after Henri's entry into his capital, on June 10, and two years after his coronation, Catherine was crowned at Saint-Denis. She dazzled in red velvet adorned with large pearls, diamonds, rubies, and emeralds. Her cloak, edged with ermine, was made of "Persian" velvet, which means it was threaded with gold and changed reflection as she moved. It was covered with embroidered gold *fleur-de-lys* that must have added considerably to its weight. And all these velvets and furs were worn in June! It was noted that the dresses of the Italian ladies were more striking than the French with their abundant, luxurious fabrics. The Protestants were easily spotted in their somber and austere clothing.

To observe this ceremony, Diane was placed near the queen in a seat normally reserved for royalty. She wore a dress similar to Catherine's, in the classical antique style, with an "over-coat" of ermine. To further underline Diane's elevated status, Catherine's chief lady-in-waiting was Françoise de Bouillon, Diane's daughter. There was a moment in the ceremony when the heavy golden crown was removed from the queen's head and replaced with a lighter one. This was accomplished by Diane's other daughter, Louise, who positioned the heavy crown on a cushion at her mother's feet.

One week later, on June 18, Catherine made her own solemn entry into Paris, carried on a litter draped in cloth of gold, and preceded by the members of the diplomatic corps, each accompanied by a bishop in red robes. Once again, all Henri's officials rode in the parade, wearing the black and white he shared with his "Lady." Among Catherine's mounted entourage were the Guise brothers, the Constable de Montmorency—and Diane, riding a prancing white steed. Even on her day of triumph, Catherine could not forget that there were always three people in her marriage.

Diane's elder daughter, Françoise, as chief *dame d'honneur* to the queen, led a group of ten high-ranking ladies in the parade. According to her rank as a duchess, Diane was seated just behind the royal princesses, but she had the added satisfaction of having her two daughters placed by her. Henri's first child, Diane de France, the other living symbol of her husband's infidelity, was also seated in a prominent position, adding to the queen's discomfort.

As a special gesture to his queen on this day, Henri confirmed the right and privilege given to Catherine by his father—that of appointing a master in every guild throughout France, a considerable authority at the time. The Parisians had erected a grandstand for the tournament that followed her entry. To spare the queen any embarrassment, the grandstand was decorated with Henri's "H" and a double "K" for the queen.[7] But over the gateway through which the gallant knights had to ride to the lists, emblazoned high, was a gigantic "H" with crescent moons, and other letters "H" with the double "D" added.

*A*LTHOUGH Henri's court celebrated intellectual enlightenment and humanism through the coronations and royal entries, the grotesque persecutions and burnings of those with different faiths continued. In the various cities through which he passed, the king had made a habit of granting the most unfortunate of his subjects an audience, and just three weeks after the glorious celebrations and processions to honor him and his queen in Paris, he chose to hear the pleas of one of the imprisoned heretics. The cardinal de Lorraine was asked to choose such a man, and brought before the king a simple tailor, whom he assumed would be ill-educated and overawed by the royal presence. But when the wretched man stood in his tattered clothes in the middle of the glory of the court of France, to the combined astonishment of the king, cardinal, and the assembly, he answered the questions put to him as deftly as any theologian. When Diane, who had suffered much abuse at the hands of the Protestants, turned to ask him some riddles to test his faith, he raised a hand to silence her, and said: "Madame, be satisfied with having corrupted France, and do not intrude your filth upon a thing so sacred as the truth of God."

---

7. As Latin inscriptions were used on triumphal archways, a "C" represented the numeral 100, so a "K" was used instead for the queen's name.

The charge of "filth" against his beloved Diane was too much for Henri, "who loved nothing in the world so much as this lady." The Protestant's words so greatly enraged him that he declared he wished to see the tailor burned alive in the rue Saint-Antoine. Four other heretics joined the tailor at the stake, and Henri watched as the flames rose. The tailor's eyes found the king's and while the others screamed in agony, the tailor remained silent, staring steadfastly at the king until it was over. Henri maintained afterward that he felt those eyes on him night and day and swore he would attend no more burnings. He kept his word; but the burnings continued.

The incident of the tailor hardened Diane in her attitude toward the "reformers," particularly as the delicacy of her position had been so openly exposed. In order that the Catholic Church would not condemn Diane de Poitiers for the king's adultery as the tailor had done, she had to be recognized as the church's staunchest ally against heresy, and a committed champion of the Catholic religion. Although it is true that a royal mistress was somehow considered above the normal laws of the church, it was possible that Diane could be accused of being the cause of the king's adultery and Henri be forced to banish her. As Brantôme writes, "Sleeping with the king is not sinful." Diane de Poitiers believed in her religion and was not one to defy the teachings of the church; she went to enormous lengths to show respect for its traditions. Her piety was both expected and typical of the time, neither false nor exaggerated. Her detestation of heresy was genuine; but she also used her influential position in the fight against heresy to protect her status by Henri's side.

Protestantism was so widespread that in 1551, the king ordained that even more "Burning Chambers" be established throughout the country. People were encouraged to denounce one another with the lure of gaining half of the property confiscated from condemned heretics. Although these persecutions appear appalling to us today, at the time, Henri believed he was doing God's work, and his reputation was enhanced, not diminished. Horrifying as such a thought might be, a burning in sixteenth-century France had the same spectator appeal that a good sports event has in the twenty-first century.

Both François I and Henri II are generally considered by historians to have been less cruel than contemporary monarchs such as Henry VIII and his daughter, Bloody Mary of England, or the Holy Roman Emperor Charles V. In view of Henri's need for the support of the Protestant German princes in his fight against Charles V, his early days on the throne showed a tolerance he did not avow.[8] However, the persecution begun by the French *Parlement* in the reign of François I, which (with the encouragement of the duchesse de Valentinois) continued under Henri II, is the one great blemish on an otherwise glorious reign.

While Henri's subjects sent their neighbors to the Burning Chambers for the slightest religious transgression, humanism was embraced by many at his court. Renaissance philosophy encouraged cultured women to study the humanists and some women adopted the "new learning" with energy and enthusiasm. The new emphasis on piety among such learned upper-class women, in addition to the constant absence of men at war during the first half of the sixteenth century, produced a new phenomenon: the feminine humanist-reformer, personified by the king's aunt, Marguerite de Navarre. These women, and their male counterparts, walked a fine and dangerous line.

Like most courtiers, the queen's opinions were dependent upon circumstances and how they favored her. She owned a French Bible, and yet her closest friends during her early days at the French court were Henri's aunt, Marguerite de Navarre, and Marguerite de France, sister of Henri, both sympathetic to the reformers. Her five dearest friends at court all became Protestants; and the feeling among their group was that Catherine would not support them, but she would not be hostile, either. These noblewomen, benefiting from a humanist education and attached to the court or the entourage of a lady of the *haute noblesse*, were, after all, in a position to become influential and powerful, and thereby useful to Catherine.

8. It was the danger of a treaty between Henri II and the Protestant princes opposed to him that prompted Charles V to agree to the Treaty of Passau, resulting in the 1555 Settlement of Augsburg. This treaty gave rulers the right to determine the religious denomination of their subjects. A Catholic ruler had Catholic subjects, a Lutheran ruler had Lutheran subjects, and should they not agree, emigration was the alternative offered. It also led to savage repression by some rulers.

Diane believed unswervingly that the so-called reformed religion was a heresy against God, His church, and His divinely appointed king. She shared the view of most of her class that to preserve the Catholic Church and the monarchy, this heresy had to be eradicated. Although she was a highly educated lady who read Erasmus, Thomas More, Guillaume Postel, Tommaso Campanella, and who qualified as a humanist, she dreaded and detested the new ideas, and had no sympathy for anyone who stepped outside the existing religious hierarchy. Diane embraced the High Renaissance, and shared the vision and dream of François I to create an intellectual, artistic climate in France that could rival the great courts and seats of learning in Italy; but she was also a woman of her time, deeply embedded in the social fabric of French public life. Diane de Poitiers could not be perceived to be anything other than a most pious Catholic.

As the mistress of Henri II, Diane's position vis-à-vis the church was difficult. By the standards of the previous reign, Diane and Henri led very sober lives, and their attitudes and behavior were instrumental in effecting a dramatic change in the morals of the day. Because of her vehement support of her faith, Diane was still regarded as the "pure one," and neither she nor Henri allowed any reference, indelicate or otherwise, to be made about their relationship. She had been born in the land of the troubadours and brought up on their tradition of Courtly Love, where only pure love was permitted to transcend the bonds of marriage. Therefore, Catherine was expected to silently acquiesce to her husband's enduring love for Diane. It is proof of her fear, and her love of Henri, that she did so.

As the unfortunate tailor's remarks indicated, not everyone was impressed by Diane's behavior. One person who wished Diane ill was France's great enemy, the emperor Charles V. Diane was a royal favorite he knew he could not buy. The emperor, who had expected little opposition from the weak successor to the formidable François I, saw Diane as the source of Henri's strength, and he was right. His ambassador had reported that Henri II was the "slave" of the duchesse Diane; that he discussed everything with her and was more than ever under her spell.

After dinner he visits "Silvius" [Diane][9] and when he has reported to her details of all the matters he has discussed in the morning meetings, he sits on her lap and plays the guitar to her, frequently asking [the duc de Montmorency] whether she had not preserved her beauty, occasionally caressing her breasts and looking at her face, like a man dominated by his infatuation. . . . The king has many good qualities, and I would hope much more of him if he were not so foolish as to allow himself to be led as he is . . . none may dare to remonstrate with the king in case he offends "Silvius," fearing that the king will tell her, since he loves her so much.

As Charles V's ambassador reported, the king was physically infatuated with Diane. She wore a lightly peppered scent especially made for her, and it acted on Henri as a potent aphrodisiac. One evening, in the presence of Montmorency and the duc d'Aumale, the king leapt on Diane and almost dragged her to the bed while the other two looked aside. The bed could not withstand this onslaught of passion and collapsed under them, Diane rolling on the floor with laughter. This was not a unique occasion. In a letter home dated October 1549, the Venetian ambassador Alvarotti recounts how on one occasion, Diane went to bed with the king, who began to caress her with such passion that again the bed collapsed and Diane exclaimed, "Sire, do not jump on my bed so violently or you will break it."

It was not unusual for serving women to remain in the room at all times, even during intimacy. These claimed that *"Madame"* never

9. "Silvius" was the code name for Diane used by the imperial ambassadors. There are three possible explanations for this. First, Jacques Silvius was a famous gynecologist whose works were translated from Latin into French by Guillaume Chrétien. He dedicated the part of his book referring to women's nature to Diane for her help with the royal conceptions. It was rare that medical books were translated from Latin into the vernacular and therefore available to everyone. Apart from midwives, women were excluded from all medical knowledge. According to the sixteenth-century writer Christine de Pisan, women were allowed to know the "secrets of nature" but not to "name them," nor were they allowed to know of anything considered "indecent" or embarrassing. Guillaume Chrétien's translation of Jacques Silvius made it possible for women to learn about the most intimate, feminine details of their bodies.

The second possibility is that Diane's avid interest in medicine was well known, and that she was seen as a natural instructor who wanted to help other women. Diane was intelligent, capable, and overwhelmingly practical, in sharp contrast to the frivolous court. A third is that *silvius*, the Latin for a wood or forest, refers to Diana as the goddess of the moon, the forests, the chase, and childbearing.

showed herself naked or undressed, and so "one never saw her with hanging breasts as she was always wearing a bustier." Maids and valets slept on the floor or in corners of their master's or mistress' bedrooms, the rooms leading one into the other. Privacy was almost nonexistent, and it was never long before information from the servants reached the courtiers.

Of course, Catherine was aware of such incidents. Her marriage forced her to endure constant humiliation, private and sometimes public. The queen had grown grotesquely fat from constant childbearing and the rich Italian food she preferred, and the sight of Diane's ageless beauty and slender grace made her hate her husband's mistress the more. Henri's gift of Chenonceau to Diane had caused quite a stir in Paris, especially among the queen's entourage. For once, Catherine dared express her fury over losing the château she had come to regard as hers by right. Her rage was so violent that Diane took notice and asked her powerful friend the cardinal de Lorraine to calm the queen. But for the most part her shame, anger, and pain were private and silent. After all, Catherine had time on her side. She was much younger than Diane and could afford to hate and wait.

The Medici queen began to turn again to her quacks, magicians, alchemists, and apothecaries, this time to help her in her struggle with her rival. Diane's friends warned her to watch out for poison in her food and drink. Although Catherine did not buy the château of Chaumont-sur-Loire (with her own money) until 1560, she used the house for some time before her purchase and installed her sorcerers there. At this time, the queen's main soothsayer was the famous mystic and healer "Albert le Grand," although the Italian, Cosmo Ruggieri, played an important part. Ruggieri's family had been soothsayers to the Medici for generations and he had come to France with Catherine from Italy. Then there was the great Nostradamus, who lived in Provence and would be summoned by Catherine to court. According to one source, "the real pope of Catherine's strange religion was Ruggieri, not the occupant of the Vatican." [10]

The nineteenth-century writer Balzac, who admired Catherine de'

10. Jean Orieux, *Bussy-Rabutin: Le Libertin galant homme.*

Catherine de' Medici used the château de Chaumont while Henri was alive. Once widowed, she bought the château and forcibly exchanged Chaumont for Diane de Poitiers' château de Chenonceau.

Medici, claimed the queen kept a private room at Chaumont, barely lit, with green glass in the only window.[11] It was empty save for shelves holding rows of jars containing ingredients for the "great work." The "alchemical Athana, the philosopher's egg, the crucibles and the alembic" were kept under the giant chimneyhood. Beside the altar was the purification fountain, "with its pentacles and avocatory spells." A book, inkstand, pen, knife, and a piece of virgin parchment were left on the altar, ready for "supernatural pacts." There was also a death's-head and an incense burner to drive away spirits. Hebrew inscriptions covered the left-hand wall and circles were drawn on the floor here and there. On the right-hand wall hung the famous magic mirror: an astrolabe, a divining wand, an hourglass, balance, pentachord, and a sphere were all placed on a table.

The queen had good cause to hate Diane de Poitiers, but all she could do was plot in secret, while publicly continuing to smile politely

11. This room is situated between the chapel and the west wing of the château. It can still be visited today.

at her rival. Catherine made almost no references to Diane in her correspondence until almost twenty years after Diane's death, in a letter written in her own hand to Secretary of State Bellièvre, the contents of which were to be passed to her daughter Margot, queen of Navarre. In it Catherine wrote that she was polite to Diane, as it was her husband's wish, but that she always let him know how unhappy his relationship made her as "no wife who loves her husband can also love his harlot; as one cannot call her anything but that no matter how vulgar the word"—a revealing comment from this pupil of Machiavelli! By today's standards, we may sympathize with Catherine; but by the rules of the time she had only one purpose for her dynastic partner—to provide heirs to the throne. Her love for Henri, and her obsession for his love in return, was regarded as her personal affliction, almost a curse, rather than an injustice done to her.

Catherine was very conscious of her power as queen, but dared not make a move against Diane for fear of Henri's wrath (or that of Diane's friend, the Constable). The Medici queen was not a fool. She knew she would always be a foreigner in a hostile court, and forced herself to hide her burning hatred of the favorite. As long as the king felt as he did toward "*Madame,*" Catherine never lost sight of the very real possibility of her exile and disgrace. Quietly, and only among her own circle, would she dare to vent her spleen. But when the duc de Nemours offered to cut off Diane's nose, and another, Gaspard de Saulx-Tavannes (who hated Diane), suggested throwing vitriol at her and scarring that lovely face for life, Catherine demurred, repeatedly assuring the courtiers that she felt nothing but goodwill toward the duchesse de Valentinois. Of one thing the queen could be confident—that her own time would come. She could wait until nature took its course and removed her much older rival. Given time, her husband would grow to appreciate his clever wife. Yes, she could hate and wait.

Whatever Catherine de' Medici lacked in real power, she made up for in magnificence. Brantôme describes the splendor of her court, the opulence of her banquets, the abundance of gold plate, rich carpets, tapestries, and *objets d'art*. The rooms were decorated in bright colors, with many gold touches and trims. Gilded leather painted with flowers and arabesques covered some of the walls. Oriental carpets imported from Venice were scattered on the parquet floors. Clothes were not just designed to adorn, they were also meant to indicate the wearer's social position, and could cost a fortune. Her courtiers wore the most ornate clothing in France, made from heavy cut velvets and rich silk brocades in bright colors, covered in gold and silver lace, all imported from Italy.

Ladies followed the fashion for paint on their faces, especially rouge, and the servants were clad in clothes half red, half yellow. As there were still no pockets in clothes, ladies carried a purse, which hung from their waists next to their rosary.

The gentlemen were as brightly dressed as the ladies, with much gold lace at their wrists. They wore tight silk hose with shining garters; their exaggerated codpieces were stuffed and padded like their doublets as they preened and strutted. In their midst sat Catherine on a low padded stool, with another, slightly higher but always empty, beside her. Catherine herself dripped pearls and was the acknowledged queen of this glorious assembly.

According to Brantôme, Catherine "took great pleasure in her shoes and in them being well dressed and tied, and I believe she had the prettiest hands I have ever seen. In addition, she dressed magnificently, and always with some new and clever fashion." The queen adored "dressing up" and adorning herself—she even wore extensions in her hair. He adds that she "loved noble exercise such as dancing, in which she showed much grace and majesty. . . . Nowhere in the world," claimed Brantôme, "was there anything to equal the sight." Diane's one real concession to Henri's wife was her tolerance of Catherine's personal extravagance. After all, "*Madame*" had the satis-

A window catch at Anet using three entwined crescents, one of Henri's symbols.

faction of seeing wherever she looked, on the ceilings, the chimney-pieces, furniture, tapestries, and silver—even on the window catches—that ambiguous symbol: three intertwined crescent moons. No matter how rich or powerful she was, Catherine could never rid her life of the one person she envied the most.

CHAPTER SEVENTEEN

Anet

A S energetic in war games and sport as he was in his in-
dulgence of the senses, Henri took his lead from his en-
thralling mistress. Diane had indeed enchanted the young
king—the courtiers could find no other explanation for his devotion to
her—and she was an expert at her art. Besides Diane, the king's two
great passions were war and the chase, and horses were an integral part
of each, an interest Henri and Diane shared.

In summer they would rise at dawn, and in winter an hour later
when the sun had warmed the air a little. Both looked splendid on
horseback and often chose their mounts to compliment the color of
their costumes. At Anet, Diane kept one of the best stables and packs of
hounds in France, and as she knew the countryside around her home
so well she was able to provide the most exciting day's hunting, with
picnics prepared in romantic rendezvous.

In the evening, her guests would be entertained with magnificent
banquets in rooms designed to set off her special beauty. Only princes
and grandees knew such luxury and comfort. The rooms were furnished with deep, soft seating; and chairs were covered in black velvet,

edged with silver brocades, fringes, and appliquéd with three interlaced crescents of silver satin. There was little organized seating and
young ladies would sit on squares of tapestry on the floor. Chests and
early wardrobes held clothes that would be folded and laid flat.

Diane often visited the horses in the three royal studs—Amiens,
Saint-Léger, and Oiron in Poitou—and a number of her letters are
dated from these places. The animals there were bred for Henri by
Claude Gouffier, seigneur de Boisy, *grand écuyer,* or Master of the
Horse of France, whose stable was so beautiful that the king's stud
groom told Henri he had nothing to equal it. At Oiron, the greatest of
the three studs, Diane had a gallery constructed for portraits of her
favorite mounts, and the monogram "HD" can still be seen today on
the walls.

Henri was a consummate equestrian, who treated his horses as if
they were his pets. They had the best of everything and their trappings
were extremely ornate. His harnesses were gilt leather, while the saddles
were stuffed in the Mantuan or Turkish fashion, very comfortable for
horse and rider. For state occasions, his horses always wore tall plumes
on their headbands. Among his favorites were Quadrant, whom he
trained to kneel before him; the renowned sire Gonzague, who came
from the famous Mantuan stud of Federigo Gonzaga; the high-
stepping Mireau, trained by Carnavalet, the greatest trainer in France;
the oddly named warhorse, Le Bay de la Paix, whom Henri rode at
Amiens; and the gentle, highly bred Hobère, perhaps the most beautiful of them all. Henri was so devoted to his horses that their names and
feats became as famous as those of his courtiers. Henri was known as the
best horseman in the kingdom, and it was said that none of his squires
could show off a horse's ability or its flaws as well as the king.

Henri turned Oiron into a cavalry school for one hundred and fifty
of his pages, scions of the grandest families of France. The two famous
riding masters, Carnavalet and Sipire, took charge of these young gentlemen and turned them into a crack regiment. War was considered
a sporting, moral occupation and a safety valve to tame wild young
spirits.

Henri II was naturally affectionate and loved animals. In addition
to horses, he had quite a collection of dogs—hunting hounds and

greyhounds, spaniels, and little white Maltese lapdogs which he fed himself. Mary, Queen of Scots, who came to France in 1548, became so attached to the Malteses that she owned as many as twenty-five, and years later took some of them back with her to Scotland. According to Brantôme, Henri kept a small zoo to include the many exotic animals given to the royal family.

The king's court was orderly, and, it was alleged, even more "gallant" than that of his father. Henri II was a man of discipline and habit. He rose early, heard Mass, then spent three hours at his desk, sat in council or held audiences. He ate moderately, and in winter when there were no military campaigns, rode or hunted on horseback with hounds to keep fit. In the afternoons he would attend to more deskwork and hold councils—invariably with Montmorency or Diane. The evening meal was always held in public with full ceremony, after which he might attend one of the queen's receptions. He never stayed late and spent much time alone with Diane.

Other sporting pastimes at court included *jeu de paume,* or tennis—Diane installed a court at Anet as early as 1548. According to the imperial ambassador Saint-Mauris, Henri always played tennis entirely dressed in white, "with white shoes also, and with a fine straw hat upon his head. He wore his doublet for playing. When one sees him thus at his game one would scarcely realize it is the king who is playing, for even his errors are openly discussed, and more than once I have heard him taken to task."[1] The king always played in the most dangerous and difficult second or third positions, and excelled in both. If he won, he gave the prize to his team; when he lost, he paid for everyone. It was the same with billiards and pall-mall. Skating was another of the king's favorite sports, and when the ice was thick enough to hold him, he would skate on the pond at Fontainebleau. If it snowed, he staged snowball fights with his gentlemen. Having lost his childhood, Henri was always searching to recover it.

Many sports, like jousting, were of a violent nature and during peacetimes they acted as a substitute for war. According to Tavannes,

1. Saint-Mauris. R. J. Knecht in *Francis I* cites A. Castan, *La Mort de François Ier,* "Memoires de la Société d'emulations du Doubs," Fifth series, iii, 1878; *Calendar of State Papers, Spanish,* 12 volumes, edited by G. Bergenroth, P. de Gayangos, and M. A. S. Hume (London, 1863–1895).

Henri could "break" as many as sixty lances a day, galloping on German chargers at his opponents. After energetic exercise, the king's companions had their limbs massaged with almond oil to help them sleep, whereas Henri would attend a ball and dance all night—another thing he did superbly.

At this time Ambassador Matteo Dandolo described the king to his superiors in Venice:

> He is ruddy in complexion and in excellent health. . . . In his person he is full of courage, very daring and enterprising. He is extremely fond of the game of tennis at which he never misses a day unless it rains, for he plays under the open sky, sometimes even after hunting a stag or two at full speed. . . . On the same day . . . he will indulge for two or three hours in military exercises. He is one of the most famous of swordsmen, and in jousting, always accompanied by danger, he carries himself most valorously. . . . The same day after he has done this he will then fence for two or three hours, and he is well known for his skill. During my previous time here I watched a number of his jousts, and I can say that sometimes they were not without danger. One day as they were running the lists, the father and son crashed into each other, and François gave him such an injury to the head that it really damaged the flesh.[2] It should also be said that he is as good a soldier and captain, for I find him to be a trustworthy person, and if he was in a dangerous situation he would not leave but would remain intrepid. . . . His Majesty is religious, he doesn't ride on Sunday or at least not in the morning. One might say that these great princes, surfeited with ordinary pleasures, like to court fatigue and perils for the fun of the thing.

Although young gentlemen were trained for the noble and honorable pursuit of war, the king worked hard with "*Madame*" to remain at peace with his neighbors. Henri was in love, and he would rather spend time with his beloved, reading or sharing their enjoyment of music, art, and philosophy, than at war. Wherever he was, Henri would summon

---

2. François had often challenged his sons to a joust.

his Italian lute player, Alberto de Ripa, to send him into a reverie with his gentle art. He would listen to the melodies of Palestrina, or the verses of the great French poet Pierre de Ronsard, set to music for four voices. (Ronsard was actually tone-deaf, but he loved music.)

Henri so wanted the world to know and remember the strength of his love for Diane that every stone façade built during his reign was carved with their combined initials and he summoned all the great artists of the day to immortalize his duchesse de Valentinois. In the early days of his reign, Henri commissioned a portrait of himself from the great enameler Léonard Limousin, painted as he wanted posterity to remember him: the mighty king astride his powerful horse, turning to look at Diane, seated almost naked behind him, his arm caressing her neck, his eyes gazing into hers. In another portrait of Diane, Limousin depicted her as Venus, again half clothed, this time protecting a winged cherub.[3] At Anet there is a bas-relief of Diane, again naked, with Juno's sacred peacock at her feet. The court painters and sculptors were able to portray the ladies of the court naked with impunity because they were meant to represent famous characters in classical mythology. No one was in the least shocked. Not only those with beautiful bodies were painted; even Catherine appears naked on horseback next to a clothed Henri in another enamel by Limousin. The classical tradition had taken over and the French gloried in the naked body.

Once the antique and the classic became Diane's passion, she set out to develop a French school, although this did not prevent her from patronizing Italian painters such as Primaticcio. The court painter François Clouet was commissioned for the portrait of *Diane de Poitiers at Her Bath,* in which she appears superbly naked, aristocratic and almost sculptural, and without a hint of shame. The Roman practice of bathing had become fashionable during the Renaissance, especially as a setting for conversation. Diane was proud of her perfect body and saw no reason that it should not be admired. It was this oddly formal painting which began the tradition in France for ladies and courtesans to be painted at their bath.

Diane often posed as the goddess Diana; for another Clouet por-

---

3. The Limousin enamels described here are now in the Louvre.

Diane de Poitiers at Her Bath by Clouet. Diane was responsible for reviving in France the classical tradition of ladies being depicted at their
bath. The wet nurse feeding the baby in the background was seen as a
symbol representing Diane's domination of the royal nursery.

trait, she appears in a natural setting by a woodland spring, bathing
with her nymphs. Wearing a doublet of black and white stripes, Henri
is depicted as Prince Actaeon, who has been separated from his companions while out hunting, and, catching sight of the goddess, falls in
love. The startled Diana is defenseless in her nakedness. For an instant,
captured in this painting, the huntress becomes the hunted. In the
conclusion of the myth, to punish this insolent voyeur, Diana splashes
Actaeon with water and transforms him into a stag to be chased by his
own hounds, which tear out his heart. The message of this painting was
not lost on Diane's enemies. When her boundaries are violated, Diana
is a cold and vengeful goddess. This allegory was one of the many by
which Diane created a deliberate confusion between the goddess and
the king's mistress, fusing the reality with the legend in her quest for

eternal life as her namesake. There is also a *Metamorphosis of Actaeon* at Anet, which is accompanied by the inscription "*No Lice a Ogniun Veder Diana Ignuda*"—"No one has the right to see Diana naked."

Diane commissioned French artists, particularly the French pupils of Primaticcio (who painted her twice), and many of their allegorical portraits cast her as the central character. When the great hunting painting for Chenonceau was completed, all the court saw Diane portrayed as the divine *chasseresse,* the huntress Diana, a goddess radiant in her naked beauty. Diane was fifty. We see her shoulders, her long limbs and firm torso, her high, powerful forehead, her well-modeled chin, and delicate tapering fingers. Her hair is still titian gold and her skin extraordinarily white—whiter even than the cavorting cherubs around her. The color of her eyes is ambiguous: contemporary records and paintings disagree whether they were blue or green. If, as seems likely, this portrait was true to life, then Diane de Poitiers was as worthy of her handsome and virile thirty-two-year-old king as he was of this stunning older beauty.

There has been much argument about the portraits of Diane de Poitiers and whether they were stylized rather than true likenesses. It must be assumed that some are stylized portraits because the early

Diane de Poitiers as Diana the Huntress, painted for Chenonceau when Diane was fifty years old.

drawings of her by Clouet are certainly lifelike. Some of the later portraits are even said to have been interchanged with portraits of the blond favorite of François I, Anne d'Etampes.[4] There are contemporary sources that claim Diane's beauty was only truly visible in animation, when her eyes sparkled with wit or intelligent conversation. Enough accounts claiming her to have been fascinating and beautiful exist for there to be some truth in the stories. In Henri's eyes, she certainly remained the striking young woman of his first tournament.

Stories of Diane de Poitiers' beauty secrets abound: that she bathed in crushed gold, or the milk of pregnant animals; used sorcery and magic potions—and many more. There is no evidence that Diane practiced sorcery (unlike Catherine) and no one is mentioned in contemporary writings as having worked for her in that capacity. Diane's only beauty aids were a powder made of musk and rosewater and a paste used against wrinkles that she mixed herself, from the juice of a melon, crushed young barley, and an egg yolk mixed with ambergris.[5] She applied the paste to her face like a mask. Whenever Diane was alone, she slept propped upright on deep pillows to avoid creasing her face.

Diane's beauty regime was entirely natural and makes good sense even today. We know that young ladies of the time were advised against cosmetics because they wrinkled the skin at thirty and turned the teeth black. Indeed, some young women were poisoned by cosmetics. According to a popular beauty manual of the time, brides who wished to seduce their husbands were advised to bathe daily and keep themselves clean and tidy. They were also advised to boil a variety of pleasant scents in their rooms if they did not wash so often, and to douse their hair and clothes, gloves, collars, and hats with delicious perfumes. Ideally, they brushed their teeth once a week with a mixture of a powder of crushed red coral, "dragon's blood," tartar of white wine, cuttlefish bones, peach stones, and cinnamon. A manual by the king's surgeon, Ambroise Paré, mentions teeth made from bone and ivory that he at-

4. Since Diane took the title of "duchesse d'Etampes" in 1552, it is possible that paintings of the two women became confused by biographers.

5. At the château d'Anet there is a small pestle and mortar marked with Diane's emblem used for crushing powders or delicious-smelling plants and herbs; ambergris is a waxy, grayish substance formed in the intestine of sperm whales and found floating in the sea or washed ashore. It is added to perfumes to slow down the rate of evaporation.

tached to the real ones alongside with gold thread. (The manual does not relate whether this technique actually works.) As for the hands, they were treated with a mixture of mustard, honey, and almonds, or lemon and sugar. Hair extensions were commonplace: poor women would often bring their children to have their hair cut off and sold to a grand lady.

*D*ESPITE all the legal precautions taken by the king, Henri knew that Diane's acquisition of Chenonceau might one day be questioned, but from 1548, Anet was truly her home in perpetuity. Anet lies approximately fifty miles west of Paris in a valley between the rivers Eure and Vesgre, near the towns of Evreux, Dreux, and Mantes. The easiest way to reach Anet from Paris was by boat on the Seine. The journey by road took two days and required a minimum of fourteen horses.

Less than two hours' gallop from Blois or Amboise, Anet is the perfect *château de chasse,* or hunting lodge. Originally called Ennet, an ab-

The existing façade at Anet.

breviation of the name of a tree
growing by the river, it later became Annet, and finally Anet. The
first château d'Anet, built in the
tenth century, was transformed
into a fortress by Charles II the
Bad, king of Navarre in the mid-
fourteenth century. A hundred
years later, Anet was given to Pierre
de Brézé, grandfather of Louis, for
his help in chasing the English out
of Normandy. The Brézé family
enlarged the fortress haphazardly
in every direction, without any regard to symmetry. Between 1545
and 1547, Diane acquired considerable land around Anet to enlarge

A casement window at Anet showing the joint "HD."

the estate. She drained marshes, replaced much of the soil, and built
the new château, which became known as one of the most perfect examples of French Renaissance architecture. Philibert de l'Orme began
work at Anet in 1543 and carried on for the next ten years. Throughout the reconstruction, despite the dust and noise, Diane and Henri
continued to stay at Anet. The bulk of the work was done from April to
November 1548, when Diane joined the king on a lengthy "progress"
of his kingdom. By the end of the year, the central block had a roof.

Although there were still finishing touches to complete, the
château was finished by 1553. For the enormous task of remodeling
Anet, Philibert de l'Orme was given a free hand by his illustrious patroness, provided he incorporated any alterations carried out by Louis
de Brézé during his lifetime. The whole edifice was originally meant to
be seen as a monument to Louis by his eternally grieving widow. This
plan placed too great a restriction on the design and was later abandoned, but in a niche at the bottom of the main grand, sweeping staircase, Diane placed an imposing statue of Louis de Brézé.

Much of the work was carried out in black and white French marble, and the chimneypieces and other decorations were to be made in

VÜE DE LA MAISON ROYALLE D'ANET.
Apartenant aujourd'huy à S.A.S. Madame la Duchesse du Maine.

The château of Anet as originally built by Philibert de l'Orme.

the shape of tombs. Diane was careful to use local materials as much as possible and not to shop abroad. Most of the stone and marble came from Rouen and Paris, sent to Anet by barge up the Seine and then on the Eure to the "port of Anet." Diane's passion was for interior decoration, and she supervised every detail. From Ferrara in Italy she commissioned antique statues, as well as fine leather—natural and dyed, some even embossed—to cover the walls. Countless contracts exist for the decorations and for marble, porphyry, pictures, and books.

Ultimately, Anet was a temple to the goddess Diana, a temple Diane erected to herself. It is said no man praises us unless we first praise ourselves. At Anet, Diane set out to glorify herself. She succeeded by blending the persona and virtues of the goddess Diana with her own. Henri paid for much of the work, and Anet was regarded as a royal residence. But there was never any doubt that it was the home of the duchesse de Valentinois. Just as Fontainebleau had been his father's masterpiece, Anet would be Henri and Diane's.

Although François I was responsible for bringing the Renaissance to his country, Diane must be given some of the credit for the development of the *French* Renaissance. She had long realized that Henri did

not have the same passionate interest in the arts as his father,
and would never become a
major patron. But François I's
School of Fontainebleau had
been an extraordinary achieve-
ment, which she felt Henri II
should continue. In his name,
she decided to found the School
of Anet, exclusively for young
French craftsmen and artists,
which the king could partly
fund through her. Students at
the school were encouraged to
develop their own ideas for
works of art with which to fill
the château. At the time of
Louis de Brézé's death, Diane
had found the seventeen-year-
old sculptor Jean Goujon work-

Throughout Anet are reminders of Diane's
widowhood. This marble chimneypiece is in
the shape of a tomb.

ing as a stonemason in Rouen.[6] His brilliant monument for the Grand
Sénéchal in the cathedral there had brought him fame, and he came to
teach at the school at Anet, where he created several superb portraits of
the châtelaine as the goddess of the chase.

Philibert de l'Orme, Diane's architect for Anet, had been an
eighteen-year-old prodigy in Rome, where he had three hundred men
working under his direction, and had gone on to build Fontainebleau
for François I. As all the great and renowned artists of the day taught or
worked at Anet—Pierre Lescot, François Clouet, Primaticcio, Pierre
Bontemps, Jean Goujon, Jean Cousin, the cabinetmaker François
Scibec de Carpi, among others—the talented young students had the
best possible masters. Nor were the lesser arts and crafts neglected.
Diane discovered that bookbinding, enameling, and pottery seemed to
appeal more to Henri's refined but less intellectual tastes.

6. Goujon's origins are obscure. The majority of his work was commissioned by Anne de
Montmorency.

Anet had featured strongly in Henri's life since his youth. It was there that he recuperated from his Spanish ordeal, and there that his marriage was negotiated. Military campaigns were planned at Anet, and it was to Anet that Henri ran when his father lay dying and he feared for the future. Anet was a sanctuary and a temple, and yet it was also a home. The royal children loved to be at Anet, and Henri broke with convention by rushing there immediately after the birth of his son Charles. There is a record of the dauphin and Mary Stuart being there with the other children for a long stay in November 1550, of which the boy writes: "was with my king and my cousin of Valentinois and have to say what pleasure we had staying at Ennet . . . the beautiful house, wonderful gardens, galleries, aviaries and many other glorious and good things. I have never slept better than in the big bed in the king's room."

In 1553, the English ambassador wrote: "I left for the court which was at Anet, admirable and sumptuous mansion belonging to Madame de Valentinois, three leagues from Poissy; after my audience with the king, Madame de Valentinois arranged for me to have a meal in one of the galleries and then I saw all the wonders of the house which were so grand and so princely that I have never seen anything like it."

Everywhere at Anet, the cult of Diane was perpetuated, until she became synonymous with the goddess. Her mythological presence is ubiquitous. In one of his poems, Joachim du Bellay dubbed the château "Dianet," and the villagers followed suit.

De vôtre Dianet (de vôtre nom j'appelle
Vôtre maison d'Anet) la belle architecture,
Les marbres animés, la vivante peinture,
Qui la font estimer des maisons la plus belle:

Les beaux lambris dorés, la luisante chapelle
Les superbes dongeons, la riche couverture,
Le jardin tâpissé d'eternelle verdure,
Et la vive fontaine à la source immortelle.

Après ceux-ci faut dire
Le Paradis d'Anet;

Mais, pour bien le décrire,
Nommez-le Dianet.

I'm calling your house of Anet by your name,

For its beautiful architecture,

Paintings and marble sculptures which seem alive,

Those things make it prized as the most beautiful of all houses:

The glowing gold paneling, the lustrous chapel

The splendid keeps and dazzling rooftops,

The garden carpeted with never-ending green,

And the fountain flowing from the eternal spring.

In view of all this, it should be called

The Paradise of Anet;

But, to describe it more accurately,

Let us call it Dianet.

Although Diane never allows us to forget that the house is a tribute to the memory of Louis de Brézé, the overall concept of the new Anet was that of a Temple of Love dedicated to Diane as goddess and lover of Henri. From the crests on the casement windows to her monograms within the marble floors, she is represented within the symmetry, serenity, and classical perfection of Philibert de l'Orme's architecture. In her room, her great carved bed still stands, adorned with her symbols. One motto she used was inscribed on the *boiserie,* or wood paneling— "*Sola vivit in illo*"—"live only through him." The "HD" cipher, the Greek *delta,* the crescent moon, and interlaced "D's" were all inlaid in black silex stone on the floors, and engraved in the window glass in *grisaille d'Anet*—a technique invented there by Jean Cousin. The effect was achieved by painting in a delicate, shadowy-gray design onto finely enameled glass sections of the windows. These windows were particu-

A ceiling design for the château at Anet, using some of Diane's symbols.

When alone at Anet, Diane slept in an elaborately carved bed,
propped up on pillows so as not to crease her face.

larly noted by Philibert de l'Orme in his description of the house. Sadly,
today just a very few remain.

Anet was also full of reminders of the glories of the hunt and of
its patron goddess. Over the castle's moated entrance, in the exquisite balustraded gateway, which could be called classical—almost
imperial—the king installed Cellini's magnificent bronze lunette of the
Nymph of Fontainebleau, originally commissioned for that palace. According to the symbolism of the time, the stag represented the king.
With the move to Anet, the nymph in the lunette became Diana the
huntress, a reclining, long-limbed beauty, her arm embracing a seated
stag surrounded by hounds; Diane protectively embracing her king-
lover. The dome above is covered in marble from Rome, and below the
lunette, on a slab of black marble, Henri had inscribed: "*Phoebo sacrata
est almae domus ampla Dianae, verum sapere adversis moneat, felicibus
uti*"—"Phoebe [the Moon] dedicates this magnificent dwelling to the
beneficent Diana, who brings him all that she received." The gateway
to Anet is almost a triumphal arch: at the very top stand sculptures of

François I commissioned Cellini to sculpt the *Nymph of Fontainebleau*. After the king's death, Henri II gave the lunette to Diane de Poitiers for the entrance portico of Anet, her *château de chasse*. The original has been moved to the Louvre.

Diane's hunting dogs and a stag, all in bronze. They were once part of a marvelous clock whose hounds opened their jaws on the quarter hour, while the stag stamped his foot the number of times needed to indicate the hour.

The same motif was used by Jean Goujon, the "French Phidias" of his time, for Anet's great fountain sculpture. He created Diane as the legendary huntress, young and fresh, rising out of the water, immortal. The proportions of the goddess are absurdly elongated but work wonderfully. The model for the sculpture was not Diane de Poitiers herself, but posterity is asked to believe that it was—her long legs, the small, proud head and firm, high breasts, her arm clasped about the neck of the great royal stag Henri, her hounds standing by. "At the palace of eternal youth, every moment of the day produced some marvel, and life was sweetened by the perfume of everlasting spring."[7] Anet was a

7. From Jules Michelet (1798–1874), *Bête royale*. Although considered one of France's greatest "national" historians—his *History of France* was published in seventeen volumes in 1833–1867—Michelet's work was influenced by his family's traditional leanings toward the Huguenots. His books are anticlerical and republican. He was also the first to use the term *renaissance* meaning "rebirth."

The pediment of the portico at Anet features bronze hounds, a stag, and the famous clock.

fitting setting for a goddess. Within her magical circle, how could Henri fail to be enchanted?

Built near water, Anet was surrounded by fountains and flowered walks. The Renaissance had brought an end to the feudal fortress and introduced the gentler art of the garden. In sixteenth-century France, Anet's gardens were considered one of the great wonders of the Renaissance. When he studied architecture in Italy, Philibert de l'Orme also absorbed the Italian style of gardens and adroitly adapted it to suit the French. One of the features of Anet's garden was a vast covered walk. Totally surrounding the formal parterre, the covered gallery shielded promenaders from cold, rain, and sun. A series of ornamental canals were filled with fish and dotted with little islands. The park contained a number of small woods where herds of assorted deer roamed freely. One wore a silver collar beguilingly inscribed "*Dianae Me Vovit Henricus*"—"Henri dedicated me to Diane." According to tradition, a wild animal identified by a silver collar had nothing to fear from hunters, and had the right to stray anywhere throughout the estate in complete safety.

There was more to the French concept of the royal Renaissance garden than just an appreciation of long bodies of water and avenues of trees; it was, rather, an affirmation of certain ideas of power. By controlling nature and imposing on it quite deliberate restrictions, the king used the landscape artist to affirm his larger political and intellectual control over the state. François I, Henri II, and later, Louis XIV and XV were all absolute monarchs, and their parklands and gardens were part of the intellectual symbolism they used to maintain absolute power.

Inside the château hung wonderful tapestries showing glorious incidents from the life of the goddess Diana, woven after cartoons drawn by Jean Cousin. The paintings were by Primaticcio, Cecchino Salviati, and Il Rosso, as well as by French artists, and there were superb gifts of silver, furniture, and *objets d'art* presented to Henri or to Diane by visiting potentates. To remain in her good graces, cardinal du Bellay sent Diane an exquisite antique head of Venus.

The period is famous for its filthy streets, and hygiene among the ordinary people was generally nonexistent—at the public baths one was more than likely to catch something pernicious. Water was a luxury, and the opulence of château life could be seen in Anet's sensuous fountains and baths. Rich grandees all built themselves baths in the Roman style, with different compartments, spacious and with large windows, and they adopted the Turkish habit of the *hammam,* or hot steambath. The baths were actually intended less for washing than for socializing. Personal bathtubs were made of wood (lined with a linen sheet before water was added) or of silver. Anne de Beaujeu recommended that her young charges take a bath once a week. In each bedroom there would be a basin for hand-washing, and in an alcove nearby, a *chaise-percée,* or commode, often covered with a lid of velvet or satin.

Diane was immensely proud of her famous library. Except for the very rare volumes, all her books were bound in red morocco leather with gold tooling, emblazoned with the joint monogram of the king and his Lady. One book she cherished above all the rest—Anne de Beaujeu's book of *Enseignements,* which she had read as a girl. This was a gift to Diane from François I, who knew how much she had loved and admired that remarkable lady. It remained her moral code for life, and was among her most precious possessions.

Diane's library contained one of the finest collections of the Renaissance: many valuable illuminated manuscripts on vellum, lavishly illus-
trated manuscripts, and countless folios of rare charts, contracts, laws,
receipts, and letters.[8] All were bound in calfskin or morocco leather.
Diane's choice of books is a good guide to her interests. French authors
mingled with translations—unlike François I's library, which was largely
devoted to Italian works. Among her collection were religious books,
histories (particularly of the kingdom), fictional tales, and scientific
works. Books on birds and nature featured strongly. Surprisingly, there
were few books of poetry, and not many works in Latin. Diane's choices
did not include any great works of scholarship or modern literature.

Henri loved music and was considered quite knowledgeable on the
subject. Diane commissioned Philibert de l'Orme to erect two small
pavilions by the river where they could relax and listen to his musicians—the flute and the spinet in particular. Dancing was another of
Henri's pleasures, and balls at Anet were frequent. There were many
fashionable dances at the time—the elegant and solemn *pavane;* the
galliard; the *tourdion,* with gentle, light movements; Oriental inspira-
tions in the *Canaries* and *Moresques;* the Provençal *volte;* the *branles,*
which could be lively or slow, performed with torches, or with couples
clapping each other's hand in time to the music. Some of these dances
were considered rather daring as the ladies were tossed upside down.
The only undergarments worn were shifts and young ladies exposed
their thighs without shame. Those of the "New Religion" were more
scandalized than others. Salon games were popular—games of chance,
dice, and card games that could last the whole night long and have excessively high stakes.

When the king was at Anet, the courtiers vied with one another in
their sense of fashion. There was quite a change in the clothes worn at
this time. The handkerchief had come into common use; for the first
time, ladies wore camisoles as undergarments. White under-linen,
often embroidered and edged in lace, absorbed perspiration and dirt,
and acted as a protective layer between the rich outer fabrics and the

---

8. Since poison—the easiest way of getting rid of someone—could be added to parchment,
clothes, gloves, even a bouquet of flowers, princes took the precaution of having someone else
read their letters to them. The fear of poison during this century reached endemic proportions.

body. Clothing also indicated the differences between the classes. Only ladies wore under-linen. The same applied to sleeping, which until that time had been mostly in the nude. To wear a nightdress became a mark of chastity (and most comforting in winter).

Court dress stipulated long bodices for women, pointed at the front below the waist; large, rigid skirts; high ruffs—as high as possible at the back in order to frame the face—and large hats with Austrian feathers. Men wore jerkins, breeches slashed with silk, with tight-fitting hose, short pelerine coats, and hats decorated with a feather. In general, gentlemen wore dark colors; and short, pointed beards were fashionable, in imitation of the king's. Henri was very interested in fashion and, as so often happens, created a new look of his own by chance. Due to an accident as a child, he had an ugly scar on his neck. To hide it, he took to wearing tight, high-ruffed collars, and this attractive fashion was adopted by his courtiers. The king felt there should be a distinction between the princely families and their suites, so he ordained that only high-ranking families could wear crimson. Young ladies were permitted to wear crimson petticoats and muffs. This rule was intended to underline the difference in social status but also to lower the cost of some of the expensive pigments by decreasing the demand.

The mid-sixteenth century was also the time when French gourmet food emerged. French cuisine began to achieve such a reputation that foreign princes sent to France for chefs and pastry cooks. The expression "*faire bon chère*" litters the correspondence of the time and was used to signify the quality of the guests' welcome and comfort as much as the excellence of the fare.

Cookbooks had been available since the advent of printing and the cult of cuisine was developing. Already some members of the court were known for their appreciation and knowledge of good food, among them Henri's friend Jacques de Saint-André, who wrote of the splendor of the food to be had at Anet and Chenonceau.

At her own table, Diane preferred to drink *vin clairet* or rosé. Her wines came from her vineyards at Chenonceau or from Beaune. Although dairy products were considered more suited for the use of the common people, Diane believed in healthy food and served butter and cheese from Normandy at her table. Traditionally, there were three courses for dinner or supper—boiled food, followed by the roasts, and then fruit—a departure from earlier in the century, when dishes were brought in one after the other with no heed for order. Fish, including whale and dolphin, came from Rouen and was often cooked in white wine. It was used especially on Fridays and on "days of obligation" (religious fast days). According to Erasmus, during Lent, the kitchen was busier than ever as the chefs were hard put to render delectable the meager rations permitted.

Diane's table was always laden with an abundance of food. Pork was butchered into ribs or chops, or was sometimes served as hams or sausages made from the trotters or the ears. Beef, lamb (the tongue was a delicacy), and poultry were in abundant supply. Vegetables—especially cabbage, spinach, leeks, and turnips—were cooked in lots of water (probably boiled tasteless) and often puréed to digest more easily. Cooked together with the meat, the vegetables ended up as a sort of stew, which was easy to eat with a spoon. There were still no forks. All this fare was accompanied by a variety of sauces, hashed meat, and pastries. Wine was drunk warm (blood temperature), but slowly the fashion for chilling white wine came from Italy. White wine was then drunk at cellar temperature or snow and ice added. The Italian sculptor Bernard Palissy designed a clay drinking fountain for keeping wine chilled in the summer months.

Presentation of food also became important—the look of it as well as the aroma and the taste. Even the table linen was impregnated with the scent of lavender, flowers, and herbs, and exquisite dinner services were used. Flowers covered the tables and cloth. Napkins were made of damask, toothpicks of gold and silver, and there were small silver dishes filled with sugared almonds. The napkins were scented and often tucked into necklines to save clothes from falling food and messy fingers. Each place was laid with a goblet, a knife, a spoon, and sometimes a smaller spoon like a teaspoon. The only utensil resembling a fork was a two-pronged spike used by servants for holding down the meat during carving. Elegant guests ate with just two fingers—their hands regularly washed in bowls brought to individuals at the table.

The art of conversation dates from this time, led by intelligent ladies blessed with polite manners. Not all had the fabled charm of Marguerite de Navarre, but the phrase "*tenir compagnie à la française*"—"to entertain in the French manner" came into usage at this time. According to du Bellay, the French court was the only school where one could learn the art of conversation. Catherine de' Medici was considered very cultivated and Mary, Queen of Scots, could hold charming conversations in Latin. No wonder that during the mid-sixteenth century, the French court was reputed to be the most civilized in Europe.

*A*NET was as close to Paradise as Diane could make it, and wherever he found himself, Henri wanted to return to its enchantment. For the king, Anet and Chenonceau were the settings of the chivalrous romances that had influenced those lonely years in Spain. The king so loved the peace of this beautiful château on the Eure that he hurried back there after any absence. Philibert de l'Orme wrote, "The King was more anxious to know what I had done there [Anet] than at his own houses. This was all he cared about." Henri was at Anet so often that he made it a virtual seat of government, holding audiences on a dais of black velvet surrounded by seven pillars topped with white plumes. Hundreds of his documents and royal edicts state that they were "Given at Anet."

Diane always tried to help the queen maintain her dignity, and at Anet she created a series of separate state rooms for her. Whenever Catherine accompanied the court for a sojourn there, she could stay in royal apartments decorated with her own crowned cipher just as if she were in residence at any of the king's châteaux. One can only imagine the queen's discomfort within this house, but both Diane and Catherine took great pains to avoid embarrassing the king, and the world assumed all was harmony between the two women. Catherine's château of Montceau-en-Brie was also a magnificent country property, and a huge amount of money was spent on making it luxurious; but Anet was considered a modern work of art and the talk of the foreign courts. Even if the creation of Anet cost the king a fortune, he knew it was also a symbol glorifying the art and culture of his reign.

For more than one hundred years Anet would remain untouched. Then, in the 1680's, the duc de Vendôme, who inherited the house, redecorated it in the taste of Versailles. The *Diana* tapestries, dedicated to the goddess, were removed at this time. Four were brought back later—*Diana Saving Iphigenia, Diana Slaying Orion, The Death of Meleager,* and *Jupiter Turning the Peasants into Frogs*—and one can imagine the immense pleasure the châtelaine must have gained from gazing at them.[9] There is one remarkable example of this set in the Metropolitan Museum in New York called *The Drowning of Brito-maris.* Scholars generally agree that the figure of Diana in the tapestry is as true a portrait of Diane de Poitiers as exists.

9. These tapestries can be seen at Anet today.

CHAPTER EIGHTEEN

A Delicate Domestic Balance

I N 1548, the year of Mary Stuart's arrival in France, Henri sent forces to help the Scots against the English. In return for this assistance, and at the urging of the Guises, the king of France asked for the hand of their niece, Mary, Queen of Scots, for the dauphin. The family of Guise was triumphant and deeply in the debt of the duchesse de Valentinois for this enormous boost to their family's elevation. The six-year-old Mary arrived in France on August 13, 1548. Her mother, the dowager-queen of Scotland, Marie de Guise, had lost her husband, James V, prematurely, and this continued bond with her homeland was her dearest wish. Rightly, she judged that it would be safer to keep Mary far away from the intrigues of the Scottish and the English courts, and she stipulated that Mary should be put in the care of Diane de Poitiers. The duchesse de Valentinois was only too willing to have charge of the eventual successor to Catherine as queen of France. Almost immediately, Mary's great-aunt Antoinette and her Guise uncles extended their influence and remonstrated with Mary's mother that "her train was not handsome and as little appropriate as could be."

Mary Stuart's first stop in France was at Carrières on the Seine, a little downstream from the Palace of Saint-Germain. The royal children were there while Saint-Germain was being renovated to receive the little Queen of Scots. The king had issued strict instructions that no workers coming from an area that had the plague were to be employed. At the time of Mary's arrival, there were four royal children in the nursery: the dauphin François, born in January 1544; Elisabeth, born in 1545; Claude, born in 1547; and Louis, born in 1549. Mary was one year older than the dauphin. Subsequently, six more children would be born: Charles in 1550, Henri in 1551, Margot in 1552, and Hercule in 1554. Twin girls appeared in 1556, but did not live long.

In his letters to Scotland, Henri II assured Mary's family that she was being treated as a sovereign queen. "She shall be received, treated, and honored in all our towns and other places through which she may pass [on her way from the coast to Saint-Germain] as if she were our dearly loved consort the queen in person, having power and right to grant pardons and to set prisoners free."

Among the many *enfants d'honneur* in the royal nursery when Mary Stuart arrived were her Guise cousins—Henri, son of the duc de Guise; and another Henri, son of the duc d'Aumale—whose fathers were away campaigning. Not long after the little queen was installed in her rooms, the royal children's governor, Jean d'Humières, received letters from the king and Madame de Valentinois concerning her care. Diane's letters are to the point, friendly but not really warm. It was not her way.

Mary's grandmother, the duchesse Antoinette de Guise, wrote to tell the king how well the little dauphin and Mary were getting on—as if they had known each other a long time. Both children were aware that they were engaged, and they danced together at the marriage of the duc d'Aumale soon after Mary's arrival. Diane wrote a number of letters to the children's governor to encourage him to promote the friendship between Mary and the dauphin and also between Mary and Elisabeth, saying the two girls were to share a room to aid their companionship. Mary's mother, Marie de Guise, wrote with advice and admonitions; it seems Mary did not wash her hair often enough and her mother insisted she should do this every month as her hair was always oily.

Although Diane could overrule him, Anne de Montmorency (Grand Master of the Household) was officially responsible for the royal nursery. As the caring father of eleven children of his own, he often selected the doctors for his royal charges. Among his many instructions to Humières was to ensure that the dauphin should not go out in cold weather and must always carry a pocket handkerchief for his nose (which was always running). The dauphin also had permanent colitis and the Grand Master recommended cures. Mary Stuart was the only really healthy child in the nursery, and she was deeply distressed when the dauphin fell seriously ill in the autumn after her arrival. It was said that the Children of France were tainted by the "Italian disease." Although syphilis was not hereditary, and Catherine was healthy enough, all her children except the youngest, Margot, were born undersized and sallow-faced. Later in life they would be tormented by ill health.

The enchanting little queen and her Scottish entourage were allocated rooms especially prepared in a wing of the Palace of Saint-Germain. Mary brought her own household with her and was indeed treated much more lavishly than the other royal children, owning three brass chests for her jewels and having sixteen dresses made in one year.

Catherine grew to dislike Mary. It has been suggested the reason was that Mary's aunt, the pretty princess Louise de Guise, had been put forward by her father the duke to replace Catherine when she was still childless. Catherine's education of Mary has been unjustly blamed for the Scottish queen's alleged "wickedness"; but in fact, Catherine avoided Mary as much as possible and had no part in her education. Mary wrote to her mother in Scotland that she was not in the good graces of the queen, who was the daughter of merchants. Unfortunately, little Mary repeated this comment within Catherine's hearing. The queen never forgot the slight, and the Scottish queen would regret the remark later in her life. Meanwhile, Catherine wrote to Marie de Guise in Scotland: "You are wonderfully fortunate in having such a daughter, and I am more fortunate still because God has so disposed matters as to grant her to me, for I think having her with me will be the strength of my old age."

Unlike the dauphin, Mary Stuart was a keen student, and she was

urged to encourage him. She wrote to François: "*Ama igitur literas,
princeps illustrissime*"—"Love learning, most illustrious prince." The
Venetian ambassador Giovanni Capello reported that the dauphin
"does not care much for letters, at which the king is displeased. Very
good teachers have been provided for him . . . yet their success is
small." Young François was more interested in soldiering.

Although the dauphin was named after his grandfather, he could
not have resembled him less. This François was physically weak and subject to every sort of childhood illness and disease, which left him looking pale and waxy, with none of the physical prowess of his father or
grandfather. Henri did all he could to make the child's life happy. There
is a letter written by the king to his governor when François was four
years old saying he no longer wants to be dressed as a girl "and I agree
with him. He should have breeches as he asks for them."

Giovanni Capello described the dauphin around this time to the
pope, his godfather: "Their Majesties have three girls and three boys.
The first son is his most serene dauphin whose name is that of his grandfather François I and is the godson of Your Serenity. This month he will
finish his eleventh year and for his age he is not well advanced. He is
aware that he is a prince, but he speaks little and is perhaps a little bilious. For his traits, he has more of the *physiognomies* of his mother than
his father."

The dauphin's dull eyes protruded from a bloated head, and he
had his mother's receding chin. His bulbous nose dripped constantly
in tandem with his open mouth, through which the unfortunate boy
had to breathe owing to problems with his adenoids. Sometimes his
ears ran as well. Charles, seven years his junior, had a narrow, ratlike little face, and a sly expression. Henri, younger still, appeared normal,
but the baby, Hercule,[1] had far too large a head and ugly features. The
eldest girl, Elisabeth, one year younger than the dauphin, was slight
and pretty, with the large dark eyes of her mother and her receding
chin. Claude, two years younger than Elisabeth, was as misshapen as
her namesake grandmother; and the youngest girl, Marguerite, or
Margot, was rumored to be barren from birth.

1. After his eldest brother's death in 1558, the puny Hercule was spared the humiliation of his
name and rechristened François.

"The dauphin is not without ability," continues the Venetian ambassador Capello,

> but he prefers playing games of swordsmanship, of the lance, of ball and of tennis, to studying letters. He does not seem very generous. He enjoys the company of the duc de Lorraine, his cousin, who is fourteen, and his court has lots of princes, little boys like him, including Louis de Gonzaga, the son of the Duke of Mantua, who seems to be growing into a valiant and handsome prince. Monseigneur the dauphin is treated with more grandeur than his father. He does not have fixed revenues, but the king gives in to everything. He likes very much Her Serenity, the young queen of Scotland, Mary Stuart, who is promised to him as his wife. She is a pretty girl of twelve or thirteen.

According to Brantôme, the cardinal de Lorraine supervised the children's Bible studies, and he sat and read with the dauphin himself. Like many of the Guise family, Mary was taught music, the cittern (a flat, pear-shaped instrument similar to a guitar), harp, and harpsichord, and loved to sing. All the royal children were taught to dance, and they learned languages—Italian, Spanish (French for Mary), and Latin. The girls were also taught needlework. Mary's Latin schoolwork shows her writing to her uncle, the cardinal de Lorraine: "Many people in these days, my uncle, fall into errors in the Holy Scriptures, because they do not read them with a pure and clean heart." This would indicate that she was being trained in the Catholic religion. Mary's moral and religious instruction was given her by Antoinette de Guise, her grandmother, renowned for her piety, charity, and monastic links. She was also an excellent wife and mother and ran her houses beautifully.

At this time, the queen asked Nostradamus, the better known of her two soothsayers, to cast the children's horoscopes. These were far from accurate. Prince Louis was supposed to live long and prosper, whereas in fact he died at less than two years old. Nostradamus said Charles IX would be a great and valiant ruler, whose glory would equal that of Charlemagne, but the exact opposite came to pass.

Two years after Mary's arrival, the children's governor, Jean d'Humières, died, and his wife, the mother of seven sons and eleven daughters, was retained to take care of the matrons and maids of honor. Diane wrote to her that she trusted Madame d'Humières' judgment over that of the doctors, "especially in view of the many children you have had." Henri II also assured Madame d'Humières that he found her services excellent and he wanted "no other person ever to look after the children." In all, thirty-seven children of noble families were brought up with the Children of France.

Marie de Guise, queen-dowager of Scotland, was the mother of Mary, Queen of Scots.

In 1550, Marie de Guise returned to France to visit her daughter Mary and her son, the duc de Longueville, whom she had left in France as a baby. This visit by the queen mother was intended to ensure the continuance of the Franco-Scottish alliance; but Marie de Guise only really succeeded in annoying everyone at the French court by persistently asking for money and support. The following year, 1551, she returned to Scotland in great distress with her French son. Four years later, Marie de Guise took over the regency from Mary's cousin, James Hamilton, Earl of Arran, who had been given the title duc de Châtellerault by François I.

By 1553, the dauphin had his own separate household under d'Humières' successor, Jacques I, seigneur d'Urfé,[2] but the queen decided to keep Elisabeth and Claude by her and not give them a separate establishment. This was possibly to prevent Diane from appointing her own favorites to care for the girls. A year later, in 1554 when Mary was twelve, she was, in fact, given charge of her own household and entertained her uncle the cardinal de Lorraine as her first guest.

Strangely enough, the children seemed to cling to their father rather than their mother, and thought nothing odd about spending so

---

2. Jacques d'Urfé became marquis on his father's death five years later. His wife was Renée de Savoie, a niece by marriage of the Constable. Urfé was related to the king through his grandmother, Louise de Savoie. The charge of the Children of France was a most important post and family ties counted.

much time with Diane at Anet. Little Mary Stuart was warmhearted and sincere. That warm heart ruled her head, and her love and support were instinctive rather than strategic. In this age of cynicism, Mary Stuart was somewhat unusual in her deep sincerity, especially toward her Catholicism, which could only lead to eventual disaster. Mary gave her love to "*Madame,*" and Diane returned her affection, taught her to ride, and gave her a falcon, remembering her own childhood passions for both. Mary wrote to her mother:

> I am bound to do what I can for Madame de Valentinois and her relatives, because of the affection which she shows me more and more. I could not render her a better service than by arranging for something which she wants, the marriage of my cousin Arran with her [grand-] daughter, Mademoiselle de Bouillon. It would not be difficult to manage this if you approved, for he is very devoted to her. The king would like it very much, for he has spoken to me affectionately about him, saying that he had promised to find him a wife, and he could not do so in a better family.[3]

The king, who was generally bored by women, delighted in children and, like all the court, fell under the spell of the little Scottish queen. He called her his *reinette,* treated her like one of his own, and became very attached to her. By the age of eleven, Mary had learned so much from Diane that she could entertain the king as well as any woman of twenty-five. Henri wrote that she was the most perfect child he had ever seen, and openly preferred her to his own children, insisting that she take precedence over them at court. Indeed, he had written to Humières when Mary first arrived: "I have to inform you that it is my desire that she should take the precedence of my daughters. For not only is the marriage between her and the dauphin settled and concluded, but she is a crowned queen, and as such it is my wish that she should be honored and served."

Aside from his father's love, François was blessed with the company and affection of his intended bride. Mary was everything the

---

3. *Letters of Mary Stuart.*

dauphin was not, but she returned his affection and allowed him to follow her everywhere like a little lamb. One Italian visitor at the court,
Giovanni Capello, wrote that the two were always "going off together
hand in hand to the corner of a room, where no one could overhear
their little secrets."

The royal children's household numbered over two hundred, with
a further fifty-seven in the kitchen. Huge quantities of food were listed
in the accounts for just a single day—276 loaves of bread, eighteen
sides of beef, eight sheep, four calves, twenty capons, one hundred and
twenty pigeons, three kids, six goslings, four hares, etc. To judge from
this, the Children of France did not owe their miserable physiques to
starvation.

Anet was the royal children's favorite palace and they often traveled
there from Saint-Germain by barge, the most convenient and safe form
of transport. Diane saw to their entertainment with her usual care and
attention. As well as the horses and falcons, there were big dogs to
romp with, including two muzzled mastiffs, and twenty-two little lapdogs to cuddle. In their rooms were small caged birds to amuse them.
Their father's friend, the marshal de Saint-André, sent the children a
gift of a bear, which ate a great deal and was responsible for considerable damage wherever it went with the royal nursery. Two lion cubs
were sent by the Duke of Tuscany to add to the children's little zoo,
which already included wolves, wild boar, and animals from Africa.
The dauphin also had a tame doe and several ponies. In addition to hir-
ing a dancing master, singers, and tambourine players, *"Madame"*
arranged for passing troupes of traveling actors and Italian acrobats to
entertain the nursery.

Perhaps herein lies the reason for the failure of Henri's brood. Because Henri and Catherine had both been neglected as children, they
overindulged and spoiled their own. Whereas deprivation had made
Henri a humble king, the mollycoddling of his children turned them
into disasters, despite Diane de Poitiers' efforts (her own two daughters were remarkable in every way). In 1550 the king and queen's son
Louis died at not quite two, and the twin girls died shortly after their
birth. Still remaining were three girls and four boys, three of whom
would become the worst kings in the history of France. Catherine

nearly died giving birth to the twins, Jeanne and Victoire. Jeanne died in the womb and the doctors had to break one of the baby's legs to get her out. Victoire died seven weeks later. The king was advised there should be no more children.

*L*ADY Fleming, governess to Mary, Queen of Scots, arrived at the court of France toward the end of 1548, and letters exist which state the king was very taken with her. Lady Fleming was a beautiful widow of thirty-five, with flaming red hair and the whitest skin. Born Lady Janet Stewart, the illegitimate daughter of James IV of Scotland and the Countess of Bothwell, she was proud of her royal blood, which made her an aunt of her charge. With this background, she considered herself qualified to follow in her mother's footsteps, and she deliberately planned a liaison with the king of France.

In 1550, when Diane was as old as the year, she broke her leg in a riding accident and was forced to retire from court for a while to the château of Romorantin, near Blois. In June of the same year, Catherine gave birth to the king's fifth child, Charles, at Saint-Germain. Henri remained with his wife far longer than usual on this visit, spending time particularly in the nursery, playing with his children. It was during Diane's absence and Catherine's convalescence that the king began a flirtation with Lady Fleming. If Henri was careful to conceal the exact nature of his relationship with Diane de Poitiers, he went to extraordinary lengths to hide this flirtation from his mistress. Brantôme relates that Henri posted his page outside the door to Lady Fleming's chamber with instructions to warn him if anyone approached.

Diane moved to Anet to continue her recuperation and the king joined her there for a while before returning alone to Saint-Germain. Naturally Montmorency, as Grand Master of the Household, had access to the royal nursery and was spending so much time there that the Guises thought *he* was conducting a flirtation with the dashing governess. They wrote this amusing gossip to Diane, who sent them a key to a door adjoining Lady Fleming's apartment so they could find out more. This was a key Diane used to enter the nursery and monitor the

care of the royal children. Thinking they were spying on Montmorency, the Guises were stunned to find the Constable leaving the
governess' apartment accompanied by the king. They immediately informed Diane that Henri and Montmorency were often in the private
company of Lady Fleming. Not long afterward, Lady Fleming let it be
known, in broad Scots-accented French, that she was carrying Henri's
child.

Diane de Poitiers was always aware of the activities and gossip of
the court, and kept herself fully informed of this flirtation. According
to Alvarotti's dispatch (dated September 1550) and also that of Contarini, Madame de Valentinois returned to court at once, and for the
first time that anyone had witnessed, lost her legendary composure.
Diane waited outside Lady Fleming's door. When Henri and Montmorency emerged, she made a tremendous scene, accusing the king of
every sort of perfidy, including appointing a whore to his future
daughter-in-law. However, the main thrust of her anger was aimed at
Montmorency, the friend she had supported and advanced for so many
years, the friend of her late husband: "And you, you are so wicked as to
have allowed, if not encouraged, the king to have done such a thing.
Are you not ashamed to have injured the Guise family to whom I have
always shown such favor just as I have to you and in His Majesty's presence?" Diane heaped insults upon Montmorency, forbidding him to
speak to her or to make any contact. Her instinct told her that without
the encouragement and connivance of Montmorency, Henri would
not have succeeded in his flirtation. It was clear to her that Montmorency had been trying to oust Diane from her powerful position by
the king's side and leave him in sole control of Henri.

Shyly, Henri tried to appease her, but she exclaimed that the Constable's wickedness had brought shame on the crown itself, and might
even endanger the dauphin's marriage if he refused to wed a young girl
brought up by a whore. Henri was terrified that he would lose the support of the Guises if they found out about his affair, and begged Diane
not to tell them. Reluctantly, she agreed, but of course the Guises knew
everything. Overwhelmed, Henri capitulated and meekly returned
with Diane to Anet.

This event was one of the most momentous of Diane's life. She had always been in command of herself; this was the only known time, facing potential disaster, that she let her emotions run out of control. Diane de Poitiers' beauty was fading and she was realist enough to know it. To be faced with an attractive rival at this vulnerable stage—one who could create a situation that would upset a long-established pattern—must have been devastating.

When Lady Fleming's son, Henri d'Angoulême, was born in September, the king recognized him. But the Scotswoman made the mistake of giving herself the airs and graces of a woman entitled to the post of official mistress. Since Catherine would give birth three months later to the future Henri III, she was deeply offended and made her feelings quite clear. Finding himself caught between his wife and his beloved Diane, Henri was left with no choice: Lady Fleming was sent home to Scotland.

The "Fleming affair" was the only occasion when Catherine and Diane joined forces—united not so much through their jealousy of the interloper as their horror of an open scandal. Although Diane was always by Henri's side, her public position was ambiguous and always dignified. Catherine's inner humiliation was total, but as Diane went to enormous lengths to adhere to Anne de Beaujeu's high standards of decorum, the queen's shame remained private. In flaunting her relationship in public, Lady Fleming behaved in a manner unacceptable to the established balance of power within the triangle. As soon as the lovely redhead was banished, the royal *ménage à trois* settled down again, and life continued as before.

When the duchesse de Valentinois had completely recovered her strength and returned to Saint-Germain, to the surprise of some and the relief of others, she and the king appeared more in love than ever. Diane de Poitiers was not only wise; she knew how and when to forgive. Although he may have had the odd dalliance, Henri was never unfaithful to her in his heart or in his mind, and Diane had made her point and won. But "*Madame*" knew that the Constable had been partly responsible for the Lady Fleming *affaire,* and she turned against him, throwing the weight of her power behind the rival Guise faction. Henri could not bear to be deprived of the company and guidance of Montmorency, and he begged Diane, for his sake, to forgive the Constable. There followed a semblance of civility between the two; but Diane neither forgot nor forgave Anne de Montmorency. Her violent reaction could even have been caused by a degree of jealousy of Henri's affection for him—an affection that this incident did nothing to alter.

*H*IS efforts at dislodging Diane de Poitiers from her position as Henri II's mistress cost the Constable dear. During the state visit to Normandy, the cardinal de Vendôme gave a banquet for the king. When the duc de Montmorency came to the table, there was no place prepared for him, the most senior of all Henri's household. Diane was at the pinnacle of her power and had succeeded in turning the entire court against Anne de Montmorency, everyone except the king. Henri arrived back late from the hunt, ignored the banquet, and joined the Constable for dinner in his room.

Alvarotti wrote at this time: "The Guises know everything because Madame de Valentinois tells them and the king keeps nothing from her, whereas he does keep some things from the Constable. Alone, she cannot really do much, but with the help of the Guises she is all-powerful and it is true that the king is afraid of her. The queen goes along with her [Diane] and wishes her well as she is the reason the king sleeps with her more often than he would otherwise."

But Diane did have a heart. When the toddler Prince Louis died, it was Diane who helped Catherine by taking on the difficult duty of sorting his household effects and staff. The royal couple even stayed with Diane's daughter Louise during this sad time, while Diane took care of the practical side. According to two receipts signed by her on January 31, 1551, the king was most generous to "*Madame*" in gratitude for her good services.

To the relief and delight of Henri, it was the royal children who brought Diane and Montmorency together again. Their duties concerning the Children of France overlapped constantly, so an accord had to be reached. Montmorency's return to good grace in the eyes of the duchesse de Valentinois was confirmed in 1554 by his being asked to be the godfather of Henri's eighth child, Hercule. The new godfather went to great lengths to show his affection and concern for the royal children and provided their ponies, litters, and tiny, shaky carriages. His wife concerned herself with the girls' clothes and called them her little dolls. Montmorency's letters, and Diane's from this time, show them both to be preoccupied with the welfare of the royal children. Diane saw to their practical needs and Montmorency to their fun. In this way, a measure of stability was reached between Diane de Poitiers and Anne de Montmorency through the well-being of the royal family.

Henri bestowed even more favors on his Constable to counterbalance the still-growing power of the Guise family. France's most brilliant military tactician—and clever politician—François d'Aumale, *Le Balafré*, became duc de Guise on the death of his father in 1550, and his brother Claude, Diane's son-in-law, became duc d'Aumale. The third brother, the handsome Charles, cardinal de Lorraine, was just twenty-three years old and was to become the richest prelate in Europe. The brothers had the wholehearted backing of Diane de Poitiers. Others in the family obtained military and naval promotions. Nor should one forget that their sister Marie was the queen-dowager of Scotland, and that her daughter, Mary, Queen of Scots, would become queen of France. This family had caught the tail of a meteor and none could stop its rise.

But the Guises were still not satisfied. They wanted the *Parlement* to declare them royal princes of France, on a par with the French Princes of the Blood—the Valois and the Bourbons; Montmorency managed to block this. The Constable was occupied with making pacific moves toward England, which needed appeasing. At stake was Calais and its surrounding territories. Grand orders on gold chains were bestowed on the English king, ambassadors were exchanged between the two countries, as well as royal brides. Since Mary, Queen of Scots, was promised to the dauphin of France, Henri offered the English ambassador the hand of his six-year-old daughter Elisabeth for their young king, Edward VI. Edward reciprocated the proposal with a promise to stand as godfather for Catherine's sixth child, the future King Henri III.

The truce with England did not last long as the young English king died two years later, in 1553. His Catholic sister, Mary Tudor,[4] daughter of Catherine of Aragon and Henry VIII, became queen of England and married Philip II of Spain in 1554. This marriage suited both parties as Philip II gained England as an ally in his struggle against France, and Mary Tudor was quite willing to see her country play such a role.

Diane's letters from this time are mostly concerned with her estates and business dealings, and the reader is hard put to find her personality in them. One letter shows that she meticulously observed her brother's will and paid the dowries of poor girls so that they could marry. In another touching letter, she writes to the mother of her son-in-law, Robert de La Marck, about the execution of seventeen-year-old Lady Jane Grey: "I have just heard the news of the poor young queen Jane, and I shed tears for the sweet and resigned words she spoke as her last, for I have never seen such a good and accomplished princess. And you see that it is this kind of woman who dies at the hands of criminals." Mary Tudor was not going to leave another queen alive in England, still less a Protestant one. Diane took note how the mighty have fallen and wrote that "*L'abîme est en haut*"—"Ruin [or punishment] comes from above [meaning God, or in the case of Lady Jane Grey, the queen]." Somehow she was always conscious of the precariousness of her position and aware of the sinner's eternal damnation. At a time when death could strike so unexpectedly through wars, sudden illnesses, and epidemics, there was always the fear of being unable to confess one sins and thus losing Paradise.

*W*HEN Henri II was in his thirty-third year, the Venetian ambassador Contarini wrote a detailed description of the king:

"[he is] tall, well-built, with black hair and lively eyes, an attractive head, large nose, normal mouth, and a beard as long as the width of two fingers, and altogether he has one of the most gracious figures

4. Known in history as "Bloody Mary"—not to be confused with Henry VIII's younger sister, also Mary Tudor, who married Louis XII.

and a real air of majesty. He has a very robust complexion, which is helped a lot by his physical exercises, such that every day, from two hours after lunch until evening he spends his time playing tennis or ball, or [in] archery. . . . He also enjoys hunting all animals as did his father, especially the deer, which he does two or three times a week at the risk of being at the least overtired, if not putting his life in danger. . . . He is extraordinarily good at swordsmanship and horsemanship, and he can maneuver a horse and every kind of weapon that his court possesses. He is an excellent fighter, and there is never a tournament (and there are plenty) where he does not appear in arms and put on his helmet alongside the other knights, and he can run [a tournament] as long as anyone. He is the same in all other combats on foot or on horseback, and he always succeeds in these games. His body is very healthy, it is only his teeth which sometimes cause him pain and he suffers from nothing except occasional migraines, for which he takes pills. He is very fit and muscular but if he does not take care and watch his food, he could easily gain weight. His appearance is a little melancholic by nature but also shows great majesty and kindness. His eating, drinking and sleeping habits are simple. He eats and drinks moderately. After his audience, he retires with a small group to Madame de Valentinois' bedroom where he stays for about an hour before leaving to play pall-mall, or tennis or other exercises. After dining in public, he visits the queen where he joins a large group of the court's ladies and gentlemen and chats to them for about an hour.

His natural goodness is so recognized that there is no other prince who could equal him in this matter, even from many years ago. He wants and works for good; he is welcoming and does not refuse anyone an audience. While he eats, there is always someone who tells him particular things to which he listens, and replies to everything in the most courteous fashion. He is never angry when something goes wrong, except sometimes when hunting, and he never uses violent words. It could be said that he is well-loved for his character. . . . He has a certain temperament, and when compared to his father the king, and certain others of his predecessors, he is very chaste in matters of the flesh, and he conducts his affairs in such a way that no one can discuss them very much, which was not the case with king François.

Contarini also described Diane de Poitiers in the same year:

But the person who without a doubt is most loved by the king is Madame de Valentinois. She is a lady of fifty-two, the widow of the Grand Sénéchal of Normandy and daughter of M. Saint-Vallier. . . . She came into the hands of this king while he was still dauphin. He has loved her a great deal and loves her still. She is his *mistress*, old as she is. It is true to say that, although she has never worn face paints, and perhaps because of the minute care that she takes, she is far from looking her age. She is a lady of intelligence who has always been the king's inspiration.

That year, Contarini wrote of Catherine:

Since the beginning of her reign, the queen cannot bear the love and favor the king shows to the duchess, but thanks to the insistent plead-ing of her husband [for her tolerance] she is resigned to it, and puts up with it patiently. The queen is even continually with the duchess, who for her part does her best possible service for the sake of the king, and it is often she who *persuades the king to sleep with the queen!* [italics in the original].

Catherine, he says, is treated like a "legal concubine," whereas Diane has the dignity of a queen.

Elsewhere, Contarini writes of Catherine:

She is not beautiful but possesses extraordinary wisdom and pru-dence—*there is no doubt that she would be capable of governing*. How-ever, she is not consulted or considered as she merits, for she is not of royal blood, but she is liked by everyone including the king for her character and her kindliness. In terms of ordinary things she is very well treated, for she has 200,000 *écus* at her disposal each year, and more would not be unfit with her natural *liberalissima*. She holds a good court of lords and ladies and even princesses, and she looks after them well. She spends lavishly on her food, stables and clothes. Her generosity on the marriages which she loves to arrange is such that the king is often forced to give her increased funds for these extraordinary gifts. [italics in the original].

The king, the queen, and Diane had established and grown accustomed to this gentle routine, in which all three knew their roles. Catherine was as much in love with Henri as on the day they married and buried deep her resentment and jealousy of Diane. Hate and Wait. *She is so much older, she must die sooner.* But it was obvious that Henri was as infatuated with Diane as ever, and did not see or care how time had surely affected the beauty of his beloved. Contarini continues that "it is clear the king still loves Diane, [but] he never shows his feelings in public. She is seen as wise and gives good advice. The king shares his secrets with her and grants favors more easily if approached through her, ecclesiastical privileges especially." He noted that the queen was in her rightful place, due to the intelligence of Diane, who played to perfection the role of the "perfect friend," sparing all three of them any embarrassment in the most delicate of situations.

CHAPTER NINETEEN

Henri II at War

*A*FTER the death of François I in 1547, Henri and Diane knew that it was only a matter of time before hostilities with the emperor erupted again. The king's hatred of Charles V was veiled but intense. He could never forget or cease to blame the emperor for his childhood imprisonment, which was, no doubt, the reason behind his demeaning invitation to Charles V to attend his coronation as his vassal count of Flanders. The emperor replied that he would gladly come—at the head of five thousand soldiers. Some contemporaries even claimed this enduring hatred was the reason why Henri refused to notify Queen Eleonore of his father's death. It also annoyed the young king of France that England still held the French port of Boulogne, another score to settle. To strengthen his forces for the inevitable confrontation, he reinstated France's alliances with Scotland, and the infidel—the Sultan Suleiman.

In François I, the emperor Charles had recognized a formidable adversary, but the reports Charles received on Henri described his former child-prisoner as a weakling. Time and again the young French king, intent on peace, ignored the emperor's baited jibes and focused on strengthening his army, demanding strict discipline from his soldiers, securing pensions for them, and establishing homes for the mutilated. His other great military interest was in enlarging his navy, and this he did with defense rather than aggression in mind. In his foreign policy, Henri II invariably agreed with Montmorency, who advocated peace at almost any price and believed firmly in "one King, one Faith, one Law." The Italian ambassador Alvarotti maintained that when Henri was in the presence of the Constable, the king behaved like a child before his master. Despite his own heroic nature, Henri II was himself a hero worshipper, whether that hero was Montmorency, or the Guises, or Diane de Poitiers. If he had to go to war, then it would be for the glory of France and of his beloved "Lady."

The emperor interpreted Henri II's tolerance to his persistent aggression as the weakness of a man dominated by an older woman. Certain that he would meet little or no resistance, a confident Charles V decided to annex the rich, independent town of Cambrai, ruled by its count-bishops, into the Spanish Netherlands, and annexed as well the independent towns of Metz, Toul, and Verdun in the duchy of Lorraine. These towns had been under French protection since 1551 with the agreement of the German princes opposing Charles V.

In 1552, on Diane's advice, the king took the precaution of signing a secret treaty with the delegates from the threatened towns, enabling France to fight a war of defense with their total support. The French armies would be ready, properly equipped and ably led by his wise Diane's nominees or relatives. To save the lives of the wounded and help ease their suffering, "*Madame*" had appointed a famous surgeon to set up field hospitals in readiness for war.[1] It is possible that the German princes intimated to Henri that they would like to elect him "king of the Romans" and therefore emperor. This vote included protecting those parts of the empire where French was spoken—Cambrai, Toul, Metz, and Verdun.

When the king left Paris for Metz at the head of his army, his flying banners emblazoned with the "HD" cipher and the crescent moon, the despondent queen, appointed regent for the second time, did not

---

1. Once Diane de Poitiers saw the appalling conditions in the hospitals in Paris, she completely altered the existing methods of hygiene and medical care in the capital.

share her husband's confidence about the outcome. To her dismay, Catherine learned that she was to share her regency with the chancellor and Keeper of the Seals, Jean Bertrand, an appointee of Diane's, and she became aware of other measures to diminish her authority. With Bertrand her ally, Diane de Poitiers was effectively sharing the regency with the queen, who complained bitterly that Louise de Savoie had had far more power as regent for François I. Montmorency warned Catherine not to overstep her authority; it was a battle she was sure to lose. Catherine and her ladies promptly donned the deepest black mourning and gave themselves over to prayer.

Henri had prepared well, and in the euphoria before his departure for Metz, he composed these charming lines to leave with his beloved Diane:

> *Elle, voyant s'appricher mon départ [pour la guerre],*
> *M'a dit: "Ami, pour m'ôter de langueur,*
> *Au départir, las! laisse-moi ton coeur*
> *Au lieu du mien où nul que toi n'a part!"*

> She, seeing me depart [for war],
> Said: "Dispel my languor—
> Leave me your heart in place of mine
> [A heart] that none but you can share!"

The lover-king was no distance from Paris before a breathless courier galloped up to him with a tender reply:

> *Adieu, délices de mon Coeur,*
> *Adieu, mon maître et mon seigneur,*
> *Adieu, vrai estoc de noblesse.*

> *Adieu, plusieurs royaux banquets,*
> *Adieu, épicurieux mets,*
> *Adieu, manifiques festins,*
> *Adieu, doux baisers colombins,*
> *Adieu, ce qu'en secret faisons*
> *Quand entre nous deux nous jouons,*

Adieu, adieu, qui mon Coeur aime,
Adieu, liesse souveraine.[2]

Farewell, my heart's prolonged delight,
Farewell, my master and liege knight,
Farewell, true scion of nobleness.

Farewell, so many a royal feast,
Farewell, oh dish of subtle taste,
Farewell, superb festivities,
Farewell, sweet kisses like a dove,
With lip and tongue; farewell again
The secret sports betwixt us twain,
Farewell, farewell, love of my heart,
Farewell, my joy, my sovereign.

One must wonder if we would have a gentler glimpse of Diane's character if Henri had *not* obeyed Diane's instructions to destroy her letters. Her remaining correspondence is devoted mostly, and coldly, to business matters. Gaillard Guiffrey, who so ably edited the letters, remarked that "her signature appeared at the end of a note like a magic word, radiant and with an irresistible strength." Strength certainly, but tenderness?

Joachim du Bellay wrote at the time:

Dieu vous a fait entre nous
Comme une miracle apparaître
Afin que de ce grand roi
Vous puissiez posséder l'âme.

God made you appear among us
As if by a miracle—
Until this great king
Granted you
Possession of his soul.

2. Quoted by Brantôme.

*B*Y April 1552, Montmorency had occupied Toul. Meanwhile, the king visited Nancy, capital of Lorraine where he was received by the nine-year-old ruling duke, Charles II,[3] with great ceremony. He effectively took possession of the boy's country. The next day, Henri declared that Charles II would be brought up at the French court and that his tutor would stay on and govern Lorraine. It is possible that Henri, who was always thinking of marrying off his children well, had already decided to marry the young duke to his daughter Claude. This union would certainly strengthen the political ties with Lorraine, which was a buffer against the empire. One thing is certain: the French king was resolved that Charles V would not absorb Lorraine into his empire.

True to the word he gave to the German princes, Henri stopped his advance at the Rhine, having "watered his horses" in the great river. On June 12, he entered Verdun. The French army had also moved into Metz and strengthened its fortifications. The "German voyage" had been a tremendous success, with three strategic towns secured on the French northeastern border, as well as a permanent foothold in Lorraine.

The emperor launched his campaign to recover Metz after signing the Treaty of Passau with Moritz of Saxony on August 2, 1552, although the siege of the city did not begin until the autumn. In November, Charles V brought up a huge army and laid siege to Metz, bombarding it for forty-five days. But the citizens would not yield, secure in the knowledge of the French king's concern for their well-being, and bolstered by the courageous leadership of François de Guise, accompanied by his brother Claude d'Aumale. A small force of just six thousand men and a few guns held their ground, despite the murderous barrage of the Spanish cannon. With Guise was the cream of France's army, including Orazio Farnese and Catherine's cousin, Piero Strozzi. Autumn became winter; digging into the surrounding

3. His grandfather was Duke Antoine II, head of the senior branch of the house of Lorraine, whose younger brother Claude founded the ducal house of Guise.

Diane de Poitiers' signature was strong and businesslike.

boggy flatlands, the imperial forces continued their siege. With half his army incapacitated by fever, Charles V also fell ill and had to command his forces from a litter.

The snow and ice had the same effect on the imperialists as the heat of the sun of Provence had achieved back in 1536. Ill with fever and troubled by the cold, the emperor had had enough, and on New Year's Day 1553, he gave the order to withdraw. *Le Balafré*, François de Guise, whose tiny force had trounced the huge imperial army, became an even greater hero. The most enduring memory of Metz was the generous way in which the victors treated the enemy, giving their wounded the same assistance as the French soldiers. Henri II was praised thereafter for the "regal chivalry of Metz."

The French king's careful preparations had been vindicated, and on Christmas Day 1552, the French won a resounding victory. The jubilation of the Italian states at this triumph was overwhelming, and Henri declared himself protector of Siena. To mark the event, on February 14, 1553, during the season of carnival and amid great rejoicing, he married his natural daughter Diane de France to Orazio Farnese.

Catherine's cousin Piero Strozzi was sent to Siena as the king's lieutenant, and Catherine asked and received permission from Henri to raise troops in her territory of the Auvergne to help Strozzi recapture her heritage in Tuscany. Tragically, Orazio Farnese was killed fighting alongside Strozzi at the Battle of Hesdin on July 18, 1553.

Diane was deeply affected by the death of Orazio Farnese. He had been married for just five months to her adored ward. Some years later, on May 3, 1557, Diane de France married François, duc de Montmorency, eldest son of the Constable Anne, at Villers-Cotterêts. Their only child, another male Anne, died before his father in 1579. Diane de France was a gentle, benign influence on the French court, who would later work for the alliance of Catherine's son Henri III with Henri de Navarre, the future Henri IV, exercising much good influence during his reign.

The pendulum swung back. In August 1554, the emperor took his revenge, defeating the French forces under Strozzi at Marciano. Siena was lost and Diane's son-in-law Claude d'Aumale was captured.

The following year at Hesdin, Robert de La Marck, Diane's other son-in-law, was taken prisoner by the imperialists and maltreated by the Spanish in Ghent. Charles V tried to seduce him into joining his forces and freed him "on his honor" to obtain the money to pay for his enormous ransom. It was said that Diane used money confiscated from disgraced Protestants to gain his release. However, there are records of her daughter, Françoise de La Marck, selling much of her Brézé inheritance to her sister Louise in order to pay her husband's ransom. On the way home to Sedan following his release, La Marck fell ill and died at Guise. Brantôme maintained that he was poisoned.

Charles V never recovered his health or his spirits after this disastrous campaign of 1552. Bit by bit, he gave up his responsibilities, first abdicating in the Netherlands, and then, in September 1556, handing over Spain to his son Philip. The Electors considered the empire too large and unwieldy for one ruler, and divided it. Thus Charles V's brother, Ferdinand, who had been in charge of the empire since 1556, became Holy Roman Emperor in 1558, following Charles' death.

*T*HE abdication of Charles V coincided with the election of a new pope, Paul IV, a dedicated enemy of Spain. With the nepotism expected from the Renaissance Vatican, the pope insisted that the new king of Spain, Philip II, should grant the See of Naples to his nephew, the newly appointed cardinal Carlo Carafa. When Philip refused, the pope excommunicated him.

With trouble now brewing again between Spain and the Vatican, Henri saw an opportunity to move the main theater of war away from France and into Italy, "in order to relieve our territories and subjects on this side [of the Alps]." In December 1555, the French king signed an alliance with the pope, who promised the Kingdom of Naples to one of Henri's sons and Milan to another. In return, the French were to capture for the pope the rebellious city of Siena. The Valois mirage of Italy was rising like a phoenix out of the ashes of past defeats.

During December 1555, the French and the Spanish negotiated for the release of their military hostages. In February 1556, seeing that his treasury was empty due to the endless wars with France, Philip II of Spain signed a five-year truce with Henri II, whose coffers were in a similar condition.

When Pope Paul IV excommunicated the Colonna, one of Italy's great families, and seized their property for supporting Spain, Philip II's viceroy in Naples, the Duke of Alba, attacked the Vatican's territories on his borders. The pope immediately appealed to the king of France for help in accordance with their new treaty. The Constable strongly advised Henri against going to the pope's aid, which would mean a war with Philip, who would have on his side Spain, the empire, and England, allied to Philip through his wife Mary Tudor. But the king saw an opportunity to gain Naples, and allowed himself to be persuaded by the strongly Catholic duc de Guise, his brother Charles, cardinal de Lorraine, and the tears of his wife, Catherine, who was desperate to regain her inheritance. On the pretext of helping the pope, Henri sent his great *Balafré*, François de Guise, as his lieutenant general to Italy.

By January 1557, France was again at war with the empire. That February, François de Guise joined his father-in-law, the Duke of Ferrara, with a small army. Perhaps the French "David," having vanquished the imperialist "Goliath" at Metz, thought he was invincible. Without support or supplies, *Balafré* marched his army directly toward the French goal: Naples.

This initiative into Spanish territory promptly annulled the year-old truce with Spain and began the three-front war Montmorency had predicted. At the end of spring, in support of her husband, Philip II, Queen Mary Tudor brought England into the conflict; by summer, Philip's imperialists attacked northern France.

Emmanuel Philibert, duc de Savoie, was as famous a young commander on the Spanish side as François, duc de Guise, was on the French. As his own lands had been confiscated by the Valois, Philibert de Savoie burned with revenge and ambition. But Guise's army was in southern Italy, and Savoie's route to do battle with him in the south was barred by the Constable of France, Anne de Montmorency. On August 10, 1557, the French army, commanded by Montmorency, met the duc de Savoie and the Spanish army at Saint-Quentin on the Somme. Due to a major tactical error of the Constable's, the French were completely surrounded. Montmorency declared: "Gentlemen, it is here that we must die." The battle was vicious and bloody, and a disaster for France, whose army was annihilated. Montmorency was injured and captured, along with Henri's friend Saint-André, the duc de Montpensier, and six thousand others. Three thousand lay dead and five thousand more were wounded.

The victorious duc de Savoie allowed his troops to rampage through the large town, and only three thousand women were spared. Once again, the road to Paris lay open to the enemy. It was a terrible blow for France, and the imperialists' brutality at Saint-Quentin would not be forgotten. Miraculously for France, the Spanish did not move on to conquer Paris despite the eagerness of Emmanuel Philibert de Savoie for more French blood; Philip II of Spain was not prepared to see his captain gain more glory.

At the time of Saint-Quentin, the king was at Compiègne, a little farther north. He wrote urgently to Catherine in Paris for her help in raising desperately needed cash to rebuild his forces. Just as his father had relied on his regent, Louise de Savoie, after the crushing defeat of Pavia, Henri now relied on Catherine de' Medici to represent him as regent before the Parisian authorities. Henri needed Catherine's intervention with the higher-ranking citizens in Paris, but it was Diane he sent for to be near him. She arranged for prayers for Montmorency's recovery, and the king's own surgeon, Mâitre Ambroise Paré, was dispatched behind enemy lines to attend to the Constable's wounds.

The queen's moment had finally come. She was thirty-eight years old and had waited for her husband's need of her for twenty-four years, all her married life. This was the first time she felt of real use and saw her chance to win favor with Henri, her life's obsession; she might not have another chance to show her true diplomatic worth. Once satisfied that the dauphin was safely at Blois and that the other royal children, including Mary, Queen of Scots, were sent there as well, she savored her triumph.

Yet Catherine's was not an easy task—Henri had asked for enough money to pay for ten thousand troops. Nor did she have the support of the court around her. Not one of Henri's entourage knew of Catherine's political gifts or how cool she could be in the most difficult circumstances. She was seen by everyone as a breeding mare, capable of giving the kingdom a prince or princess each year, and little else. For so many years Catherine had perfected her image as the silken-tongued, agreeable matronly queen that few knew her brilliant, steely qualities, or of the poison in her heart. Diane might be appealing to God for help, but Catherine knew that armies ran on money, not prayers, and she summoned the bankers.

While the Parisians were fleeing the capital and able men were joining the army, Catherine carefully prepared her next move. Accompanied by the king's sister Marguerite, and her own young daughter Elisabeth, the queen of France went to meet with the Parisian authorities. Draped entirely in black, as if in mourning for the fallen at Saint-Quentin, the queen and her ladies made their grand entrance into the Bureau de la Ville. She stood before these somber men with downcast eyes, then slowly raised them to look at each of the councilors full in the face. She was here, she said in all sincerity, to plead for her children's country, to defend the throne of her sons. The king, she avowed, knew his peasants were too poor to give any more for the war effort, so she had come in person, to beg the worthy citizens of Paris to be an example to his "good towns" and give generously to the war effort. Years of dissimulation had made Catherine a consummate actress, and, as her eyes filled with tears, her audience wept with her. When she finished her appeal, the queen was asked to withdraw so the notables could debate. It did not take them long. Without a murmur they agreed to raise the enormous sum the queen sought for the king—and the bankers in the other towns would double it.

The presence of the queen in their city gave the Parisians heart, and those considering fleeing decided to remain, while many returned to Paris. This day marked a turning point in Catherine de' Medici's life. From now on, she became a force to be reckoned with. The Parisians regarded her as their saviour and even the king had a new regard for his wife, who had finally won the hearts of his people. Recognizing

After her triumph in raising money from the French *Parlement*, Catherine hoped Henri would see her in a new light.

Catherine's worth, Henri accorded her a new respect after her states-manlike and successful appeal to the Parisian authorities for funds.

Meanwhile, Diane was at Compiègne at Henri's side, consoling him after the horror of Saint-Quentin and the capture of his treasured Montmorency. In the opinion of a number of historians, at the age of fifty-eight, Diane's role in Henri II's life was that of a wiser, older in-spiration, "a dowager goddess," and there was no longer any physical attachment between them. However, a letter of the king's exists dated August 10, 1558 in which he implores her never to forget the one who has always and will always love her. This passion was most certainly not platonic.

*S*HOCKED by the terrible defeat of Saint-Quentin and of Noyon, which was brutally pillaged and burned to the ground, Henri decided to chance his luck and revive an old plan of Mont-morency's. Against all advice, he instructed his lieutenant general François de Guise to make a surprise attack where it was least ex-pected—on the English lines at Calais. In the fourteenth century, much of France had belonged to the then king of England, another Henry II. Now, the strongly fortified city of Calais was all that was left of English France. The French had tried many times to reconquer Calais but failed. To attempt the impossible at this time was a bold ges-ture against all the odds. Henri would be condemned if it failed, but lauded as a genius if it succeeded.

With the capture of Anne de Montmorency, the greatest political opposition to the Guise brothers was removed. The Guises stepped into the Constable's empty shoes and took over the government of France. One of their first decisions was to conclude the marriage be-tween their niece Mary and the dauphin, so their family would have one of their own poised to take her place on the throne of France. Since the victor of Saint-Quentin, Philip II, was also the king of England, he might now turn his attentions north to Scotland. This union with France would signify the Scots' defense against the imperialists.

Diane was not at all delighted at the prospect as she realized how the ravishing new young dauphine would tip the balance of power firmly onto the side of the Guises. The duchesse de Valentinois rued the day she had promoted this family, who were becoming noticeably arrogant even to her, their patroness. The Constable, still in prison, was no less anxious and suggested Diane put forward an alternative candidate: the dauphin should marry instead Philip II's twenty-one-year-old widowed sister, Juana. Henri was persuaded and declared the dauphin's wedding postponed. The duc de Guise knew his king, did not insist, and set out to convince him through the glory of a great victory.

In June 1557, Lord Wentworth, the English governor of Calais, noticed ships of the French fleet in the vicinity but thought nothing of it. At the time, England was the chief maritime nation in the world, and that fact made Wentworth blind to the danger the French fleet represented. "Bloody Mary"—as Queen Mary Tudor was known for her persecution of the Protestants—paid no heed to the French fleet's presence, either. She, too, believed Calais was impregnable.

On New Year's Day 1558, Henri II's army, led by François de Guise, supported by his brother, Claude d'Aumale, moved their cannon over the frozen marshes right up to the two forts protecting Calais, while the French navy bombarded the city from the sea. It was only then that Wentworth appreciated his predicament. With the city surrounded, his sole source of reinforcement or escape was across the frozen marshes and dunes to the sea—where the French navy was firing at him. Five days later, Lord Wentworth capitulated. The last English stronghold in France was no more and the population of Calais was "invited to cross the Channel." The English had always avowed that Calais would only be taken when "iron and lead float like corks." It had taken just eight days to conquer Calais.

As Queen Mary Tudor lay on her sickbed, tormented with pain and anguish, she cried out that when she died, "*Calais*" would be written on her heart. Never again could the monarchs of England divide their arms with those of France. Saint-Quentin had been avenged. This glorious victory caused French national spirits to rise so high that the *Parlement* voted Henri a huge amount of money for the campaign to continue. The star of the Guises was on vertical ascent as France celebrated the "Scarface" duke's victories. Meanwhile, the hostilities on the Continent, and the endless negotiations and jockeying for position between the European powers, continued.

With this decisive victory behind them, in the spring of 1558, the Guises pushed for the wedding between the sixteen-year-old Mary, the Rose of Scotland, and the fifteen-year-old dauphin finally to take place. Despite the queen's pleas that the dauphin was too young and weak, as well as Diane's gentle persuasion, Henri still would not yield. The only success story in the endless war had been the heroic leadership of François, duc de Guise, and the king could refuse him nothing. Diane had no choice but to make the best of the decision and try to swing the balance of power away from the Guises. After the eleven years of underhand hostility between them, Diane once again joined forces with Anne de Montmorency. The king sorely missed his wise, imprisoned adviser and was daily more enraged by the arrogance of Charles, cardinal de Lorraine, who had moved himself into Montmorency's place.

Mary, Queen of Scots, came to the French court at the age of six already betrothed to the dauphin.

*B*ECAUSE Mary Stuart had lived at the French court since the age of six and grown up with the Valois children, the young Scottish queen welcomed the decision on her marriage, as did her country and her Guise relations—each for different reasons. In conquering Calais, the Guises had triumphed. Mary would control the weak dauphin and her uncles would rule her, France, and Scotland—perhaps even England. As most of Europe's Catholic countries considered Mary to be the rightful queen of England as well as Scotland, the heraldic devices displayed all over France for this dynastic union included not only those of France and Scotland but those of England as well.

Prior to the wedding, at the request of the Scottish commissioners, Mary had signed guarantees that Scotland would keep its ancient liberties, and that her Scottish heirs would inherit the kingdom should Mary die without issue. Nine commissioners were sent by the Scottish Parliament to show the country's approval of this union with France—on these conditions. Subsequently, in secret, the little queen signed three documents presented to her by her Guise uncles. In these she gaily promised the exact opposite: first, that she would give Scotland to the king of France if she died without heirs; second, that she would grant the French immediate possession of Scotland unless King Henri was repaid the 1 million *livres* of gold he had spent on Mary's upbringing in the last ten years—this represented Scotland's entire revenue; and finally that any promise she had made to the Estates of Scotland that could harm France would be invalid. It is likely that Mary was pressed by her Guise relations into authorizing these documents; nor could such an agreement, should the circumstances have arisen, ever have been made binding. The betrothal contract was signed in the Great Hall of the Louvre, in the presence of the king and queen, the papal legate, and the court. Antoinette de Bourbon, the duchesse de Guise and Mary's aunt, acted as guardian to the marriage. The ceremonies were arranged by her son, the hero François de Guise, with his brother the cardinal officiating.

The spectacular marriage ceremony took place on April 24, 1558 in the Cathedral of Nôtre-Dame in Paris. Carpenters had built an arched platform and gallery draped in vine leaves, with a canopy of blue velvet covered with gold *fleur-de-lys,* shading the entrance to the cathedral. In the center, prominently displayed, were the arms of the new king of Scotland and his queen. The crowds waited outside as the parade approached to the sound of cheering and music—drums, trumpeters, and finally the viols, guitars, zithers, and oboes played by the many dozens of musicians dressed half in red and half in yellow. The ladies of the royal household wore their most splendid robes; silks, satins, velvets, and jewels glowed in the sunlight, while the courtiers doffed their feathered hats pinned with glittering brooches. Princes of the church also paraded, all the clergy walking before the cardinals, who were dressed in red silk and wore their small four-cornered hats. The groom, the stunted dauphin, was the next to appear, walking alongside the taller, handsome young Henri of Navarre—a striking contrast.

Finally, the sixteen-year-old bride arrived on foot, walking between the king and her uncle, the duc de Guise, a great favorite with the crowds since his victory over the English at Calais. The dauphin had drawn little cheering, but when the king, François de Guise, and Mary appeared, the murmuring hum swelled to a roar. Brantôme wrote that the bride was radiant in a dress "white unto a lily, fashioned so richly and so beautifully that none could imagine it. The train thereof six ells in length, was borne by two maids. About her neck hung a circlet of untold value." The wedding dress was made of cloth of silver and was covered in precious stones, which shone white in the bright sun, blinding the onlookers. From Mary's shoulders hung a cape of purple velvet embroidered in gold, and a gold crown studded with pearls, diamonds, rubies, sapphires, and emeralds was fixed to her titian hair. Sighs and gasps and appreciative murmurs rose from the audience.

Brantôme described the bride as "a hundred times more beautiful than a goddess from the sky. . . . In the afternoon she danced, and in the evening she walked with modest steps and proud face to make her vow to Hymen and to consummate her union in such a manner that the conversation in the Court and the capital was that the Prince, who was being united to this Princess, was beyond all measure fortunate. If the Kingdom of Scotland were a thing of value, its queen surpassed it therein."

Although the country was crippled by debt, Henri II was determined that the wedding of the heir to the throne would be unforgettable. He had a footbridge erected across the main entrance to Nôtre-Dame, and to loud cries of "*Largesse, largesse,*" his heralds tossed countless handfuls of gold and silver coins into the crowd. The service was performed under the canopy in front of the cathedral door by the cardinal de Lorraine, using a ring from Henri's own finger. Then the bridal party entered Nôtre-Dame to hear Mass. By all accounts, it was the celebration of the century, and a unique occasion in which "a queen became a dauphine and a dauphin became a king."[4]

The following year on January 22, 1559, Henri and Catherine's eleven-year-old and rather unattractive daughter Claude married the young, dashing, sixteen-year-old duc Charles II de Lorraine, with great popular approval and celebrations. Charles de Lorraine was the head of the senior branch of the family.[5]

Few could deny that Charles de Lorraine was a much more attractive prospect than the dauphin. He was bright, charming, skilled, and graceful, and had been brought up at the French court. During a visit to his mother with the cardinal de Lorraine in May 1558, he was told he might choose to remain in France or return to Lorraine. Charles replied that he would not know how to live anywhere else than where he had been raised. He returned to France and was welcomed joyfully by Henri II, the queen, and by the new king-dauphin as an integral part of the French court. Once again the Guise family were in charge. They celebrated this marriage with splendid, hugely expensive fêtes, and the traditional jousting. During the festivities at the Hôtel de Guise and the Hôtel de Lorraine, it was noticed that Mary Stuart's arms were quartered with England's, drawing comments from the various ambassadors. When the English complained, they were reminded

---

4. Rene Guerdan, *Marie Stuart: reine de France et d' Ecosse.*

5. Since the Guise family was from the junior branch and he was totally Francophile, he was a good match for Claude.

that their own Queen Mary Tudor continued to quarter hers with the arms of France.

*D*IANE'S health had always been excellent and, although approaching sixty, she was still beautiful. Sometimes the endless movement of the court from one château to another tired her, so she would spend more time at Anet or Chenonceau, often with her grandchildren. At Chenonceau, the magnificent vaulted bridge over the river was still being constructed. From her bedroom, which opened onto the bridge, a small trapdoor in the floor led down steps inside the nearest arch, not visible to the shore, and into the water. She would slip secretly into the river and swim naked.[6]

During these later years, most of her creative energy was spent on the gardens of Chenonceau, importing new varieties of flowers from America. So many of today's herbaceous flowers were unknown at the time and her neighbors vied with one another to present the duchesse de Valentinois with interesting plants and trees. The garden inventory shows an extraordinary collection of plants, fruits, and vegetables from other countries in Europe, as well as from the Near East. To perfume the rooms, Diane would scatter her own mixture of dried roses and essence of lily of the valley. During this quieter time, Anet, that refuge where the lovers had spent their happiest days, was not forgotten. The château always retained its slightly medieval air despite the exquisite imposition of the Renaissance structure by Philibert de l'Orme. Lacking native flowers, the garden was largely green, interspersed with fountains and the gentle lap of water.

*I*T had taken time for Philip II of Spain and his father, Charles V, to realize that the sole victors of all the fighting between the two great Catholic princes were the Protestants. Henri II began to come to this

6. By taking a small rowing boat, the author discovered this little staircase under the first arch of the bridge.

realization as well. Inside his kingdom, religious dissent had grown alarmingly. The martyrdom of the tailor had serious repercussions; pamphlets and broadsheets appeared publicly denouncing the duchesse de Valentinois and condemning the king's adultery. The *Parlement* had continued to persecute heretics throughout the wars, but in a rather haphazard manner. Once Henri realized with horror the extent of the growth of the Protestant movement, he undertook the most drastic measure: the king of France invited the pope to send him the dreaded Inquisition in order to stamp out heresy. In 1557, at the time of Saint-Quentin, Henri II had issued the Edict of Compiègne, a virtual declaration of war upon heretics. The *Parlement* opposed it fiercely and the French defeat at Saint-Quentin distracted the king from putting it into effect.

Initially, the reformers appeared to be mostly from the working classes, but in recent times it had become clear that more and more conversions had occurred among the upper classes. Calvinist preachers dared to infiltrate France to make converts, and this greatly worried the king and the staunchly Catholic Guise family. Calvinist meetings became less secret and more frequent until a mass demonstration convinced the king that once he returned from war and peace had been declared, he would have to put a stop to these threats to his authority.

By the autumn of 1558, both sides, the imperialists and the French, wanted peace. Their treasuries were once again empty and the mounting threat of the new religion alarmed the Catholic monarchs more than their desire for territorial gains.

Charles V had retired to the Monastery of San Geronimo de Yuste in Estremadura in central Spain, where he lived in great luxury among some fifty of his courtiers. His gout did not improve with his gluttonous diet of rich and rare food. Oysters and fish were brought by mule, packed in nettles and ice; pâté, game, and pies were sent by his sister from the imperial Netherlands. Charles V had organized for himself the perfect place to retire, surrounded by his favorite *objects d'art*, his tapestries, pictures, and books, and his astonishing collection of clocks. Having left the worries of his empire behind, Charles V had never been so content. The emperor died peacefully in September 1558. He had renounced all his titles and honors, and many people speculated that his forswearing of so vast an empire was in part due to a genetic inheritance from his mother, Joanna the Mad. A month before he died, he ordered his own formal funeral to take place with all pomp and honor in the Monastery of Yuste. His catafalque was draped in black surrounded by candles, and his household attended in deepest mourning, also carrying candles. The emperor himself joined in as one of the mourners and prayed to God for his soul, "to which the Lord had granted so much Grace during life and prayed that now He show pity. . . ."

Following the death of his father, Philip II hurried back to Spain. A truce between France, England, Spain, and Savoy was signed on October 17, 1558. Negotiations over what form that peace should take were moved from Cambrai to nearby Câteau-Cambrésis, but the two sides maintained their intransigence. With the death of Mary Tudor on November 17, the issue of Calais no longer presented any difficulty to her husband, Philip II, who, as king of England, had been duty-bound to defend the city. When he heard the news of the death of his wife, Philip II immediately proposed that he seal the treaty by marrying the fourteen-year-old daughter of Henri II, Elisabeth de Valois. Mary Tudor's death also prompted the French to assert the rights of Mary, Queen of Scots, to the throne of England.

Henri II trusted Montmorency more than anyone else to negotiate the peace, so he secured his release with a down payment on his exorbitant ransom. To the Constable's shame, he learned that two of his nephews had converted to Protestantism, news which delighted his enemies, the staunchly Catholic Guises. For five months, Montmorency and the Guises argued over what France's position should be. The pope was anxious about the rapid spread of heresy, and he decided to intervene by appealing not to the French queen but to Diane de Poitiers. He wrote her that it was her Christian duty to join him in prayer to convince the king that peace was the right way, God's way, to bring an end to the religious conflicts tearing the Christian world apart. As a partner to the king's adultery, Diane must have been impressed to receive an appeal from God's representative on earth—impressed perhaps, but not overwhelmed. She had no difficulty in translating the pope's Latin missive and was certainly flattered by his approach. To Diane, the Protestant threat was as abhorrent as it was to Henri, and both recognized that it constituted the real enemy.

It was Diane who helped Henri II see that the time had come to bring an end to the French kings' phantom of Italy and accept that Calais was a worthy substitute. For more than half a century, the rivalry between the house of Habsburg and that of Valois had not gained either any worthwhile prizes, and it had cost them many lives and much revenue. Consumed with their own obsessions, the two greatest Catholic monarchs of the time had inadvertently allowed the new heresy to spread. Diane was determined to direct The Most Christian King's energy toward conquering this foe. Henri could see that most of Germany and Switzerland, Scotland and Bohemia, had succumbed to heresy. It was even surfacing in Spain and the Italian peninsula. The cardinal de Lorraine maintained that two thirds of the inhabitants of France were "infected" during Henri's reign.

When the king left his meeting with the duchesse de Valentinois, he joined his council. Once Henri II made a decision—and it was clear he had been thinking about this one for some time—it was impossible to move him. Henri II had decided on peace at almost any price. There was still much to negotiate, but the price under discussion was indeed high. Henri declared himself willing to give up his territories in Luxembourg and Italy. He would keep only Calais and the three bishoprics of Metz, Verdun, and Toul. Henri ended by saying he had called the meeting to *announce* his decision, not to discuss it. Final negotiations with Philip were to begin.

That the king renounced all France's claims on Italy was a great blow to the Guises and to the queen. Catherine could not believe her husband would give up her heritage, so dearly won. Unable to blame Henri, in her fury, she blamed the Constable and inevitably also Diane. Henri firmly disagreed, telling her that the real culprits were those who had broken the truce with England, Spain, and Savoy—namely, the Guises.

There is a much-quoted story that when Diane came into the queen's apartment that evening to attend to her duties, she found Catherine sitting by the fire with a book. Possibly unaware of Catherine's fury over the loss of Italy, or perhaps choosing to ignore the queen's dismay, she asked what she was reading. It was one of the rare times when Catherine's hatred was not held in check. Announcing that her book was a history of France, the queen told a stunned Diane that in the annals of the kingdom she had found that "in every era there was a time when a whore dictated the affairs of state." For twenty years she had kept her peace with her husband's mistress, lying quiet and still in the grass. This time the serpent struck out. The insult traveled to all the palaces in France, all the courts of Europe. The truth was out, the mutual hatred of the rivals finally exposed.

Diane's revenge was subtle. Montmorency mentioned in passing how strange it was that only Henri's first child, the legitimized Diane de France, showed any resemblance to the king. This comment was also passed from one court to the next, and it was still a common rumor that Diane de France was the daughter of Diane de Poitiers. Henri fled from the fray and retired to the haven of Anet with his beloved "Lady."

Only the Guises did not profit from the truce with Spain. Their bellicose exhortation to war had caused the renewal of the hostilities that had cost France the dreadful defeat at Saint-Quentin. In order to pay the exorbitant ransoms for both Montmorency and Diane's son-in-law Claude d'Aumale, the king had to give both families money from the royal treasury. Once home, Henri gave Aumale a cavalry command serving under the Constable.

The religious issue was such a source of conflict among the two camps that Henri, Diane, and Montmorency formed a trio against the Lorrainers. All three sought peace. Since Montmorency's return, the cardinal, Diane's erstwhile protégé, was very aware of the Constable's growing ascendancy over the king, despite his sixty-five years. Diane, too, was consolidating her power base, and welcomed the marriage of her granddaughter, Antoinette de La Marck, to Montmorency's son, Damville. This would neutralize her own Guise connection through her daughter Louise's marriage to the duc d'Aumale. The Guise family was furious at the establishment of this new force against them and watched helplessly as the trio made decisions. The Guises' ace, yet to be played, was the seventeen-year-old dauphine, their niece Mary, who would surely tip the scales in their favor once again. The serpent still waited, but time was on her side and drawing near.

Final negotiations for the peace began on February 10, 1559 at Câteau-Cambrésis. There were two treaties—one between France and England, and one between France, Spain, and Savoy. In essence, France gave up all of her territories won over the past sixty-five years during the past four reigns. The king's great supporters—Montluc, Tavannes, Brissac, Saint-André—all echoed the Guises in their dismay at the humiliating terms to which Henri agreed. But the king wanted peace, whatever it might cost. The treaties were signed on April 3 and 4. Although the people rejoiced, the peace was not at all popular with the French military captains, who felt that so much blood had been shed to no purpose. Brantôme wrote that it was as if with one stroke of the pen, all the battles fought and French blood spilled throughout the century was for naught.

CHAPTER TWENTY

A Cruel Fate

*T*HE marriage of the queen of Scotland was the first of a series of moves designed to preserve the new balance of power by alliances forged within Europe's royal families. The dauphin's marriage had been followed by the wedding of Henri's daughter Claude de Valois to Charles II of Lorraine. The double nuptials of Henri's long-unmarried sister Marguerite, and of his fourteen-year-old daughter Elisabeth, were to take place a few months later, in June 1559. The French army was particularly distressed that Princess Marguerite was to marry their enemy Emmanuel Philibert, duc de Savoie, who had fought them with such brutality. Nor did they feel any more comfortable that their princess, Elisabeth, was to marry Philip II of Spain,[1] son of their old adversary, the emperor Charles V, and widower of Bloody Mary of England. But these were highly political unions brokered in the interests of peace in Europe, and the soldiery had no voice in politics.

---

1. This would be Philip's third marriage. His previous wives, Mary of Portugal and Mary Tudor, had both died. Next he had tried to marry Elizabeth I of England and failed. With Philip II's French marriage, peace in Europe was brought a step nearer.

Henri II displayed his joy and good humor in the weeks that followed the treaty. It was as if a great burden had been lifted from him, and the country reflected his mood. Despite the misery of the people, who had been stricken by endless wars, poverty, famine, and inflation, euphoria gripped the nation. The routes the procession would take were cleaned and the buildings were hung with banners, tapestries, and carpets. Workmen, carpenters, painters, and decorators labored to turn Paris into a suitable venue for the many international dignitaries who would come for the celebrations. Peace would mean prosperity, and the royal weddings were occasions to celebrate.

At the same time as the weddings were being arranged in the interest of peace, several highly respected councilors were arrested for denouncing the burning of people for invoking the name of Christ, whereas "adulterers, blasphemers and murderers" went unpunished. This accusation touched a raw nerve with Henri, and the councilors were sent to the Bastille. Not far from that prison, the residents of the rue Saint-Antoine once again saw the road's cobbles lifted and the ground prepared for a tournament—a traditional part of the celebrations in honor of a peace treaty and of royal marriages.

The three representatives of Philip of Spain all arrived in Paris on June 15 with so little pomp and splendor that the good and curious citizens felt cheated. Philip's dour entourage and lack of courtly display appeared in stark contrast to that of the other bridegroom, the duc de Savoie. He rode into a festive Paris at the head of two hundred knights in crimson velvet, their coats lined in cloth of gold, their pages dressed in black velvet. Philip II's three modest courtiers would jointly "marry" Elisabeth de Valois—by proxy, in his name. This wedding took place in Nôtre-Dame on June 22, in the presence of the entire court, including even Montmorency's Protestant nephews. The consummation following the nuptial Mass was purely symbolic: the Duke of Alba slipped his bare leg under the covers of the marriage bed and touched the naked bride. Thereafter, the French princess was legally queen of Spain. There was much ribald speculation among the population as to whether the Duke of Alba regretted his pleasure was so short-lived. The celebrations included banquets, dances, and masquerades held in the three Parisian palaces, Les Tournelles where Henri lived, the Louvre, and the Palais de la Cîté.

The betrothal of Henri's sister Marguerite and the duc de Savoie took place on June 28, and the marriage was to be celebrated on July 2. During the nine days between the two weddings, there would be five days of brilliant tournaments with jousting, the king's favorite sport, at which he excelled and intended to take part. The tourney ground in the rue Saint-Antoine had never looked so splendid with the royal arms of France, Spain, and Savoy draped over the timbers of the stands. Triumphal arches stood at either end with symbols of war and peace, and high galleries were erected on each side for the spectators.

On the first day of the tournament, the queen surprised her husband by seeking an early audience. It promised to be another glorious June day and Henri was excited by the prospect of some good sport in which he could shine before Diane and a large audience that would include many distinguished foreign visitors. The queen told her husband that she had had a dream in which she saw Henri's face covered in blood. Catherine had always been highly superstitious and became alarmed when her own astrologer, Ruggieri, warned her that the king would be killed in a duel. In her anxiety, she had sent for the great Nostradamus, who confirmed the prediction and foretold Henri's death. Some years earlier, Catherine had been warned by one of her Italian astrologers, Simeoni, never to allow Henri to compete at arms in an enclosed arena, as it would end in death, pierced through the eyes. He had foretold that the king's reign would begin with a duel and a death in an enclosed arena, and would end the same way in his forty-first year. Henri II's reign had begun with Jarnac's fatal duel and he had just turned forty.

Catherine was sincerely afraid, and would not be reassured by Henri that there was no danger, as he was not taking part in a duel. The purpose of jousting was, after all, to unseat the opponent, not to harm him. The king had often taken part in jousts and tournaments during his reign; why should today's event be any different? Henri did not believe in predictions—they were usually wrong—and he so enjoyed the thrill of jousting, especially against such excellent adversaries, and in the presence of Diane. In his mind, he was still *Le Beau Ténébreux*, and Diane the lovely Lady of his dreams.

Each morning of the tournament Catherine repeated her pleas and voiced her fears, but Henri merely laughed. He told Catherine and Diane that he intended to joust in an enclosed arena to teach the young knights raw courage, and Catherine trembled. Nostradamus' prediction went as follows:

> *The young lion will overcome the older*
> *On a field of combat in a single battle;*
> *He will pierce his eyes through a golden cage*
> *Two wounds made one, then he dies a cruel death.*

On the third day of the tournament, Vieilleville presented Henri with his armor as usual. The king entered the lists outside the Palace of Les Tournelles, wearing, as always, the black and white colors and the crescent moon emblem of his mistress. Since the birth and death of her twin girls in June 1556, Catherine had not completely recovered her health and the intense heat of June made her unwell. Such heat normally made the fat queen perspire and glow, but today she looked unusually pale. Nor was she pleased to have her wishes thwarted. Catherine was still smarting from the loss of her Italian heritage, and had become obsessed with her dark premonitions following the death of her twins. Distracted in her anxiety, she did not acknowledge her neighbors. On her left was the serene figure of the duchesse de Valentinois, in her habitual black and white. Next to her, Mary Stuart and her husband, the dauphin, who had both known and loved Diane all their lives, were their usual friendly selves.

Catherine and Diane watched the king ride into the lists, mounted on a splendid Turkish charger ominously named Le Malheur—The Disaster.[2] The horse was a gift from the duc de Savoie, soon to be his brother-in-law, with whom Henri "broke the first lance."[3] His next challenger was the duc de Guise, the great *Balafré*, but Henri failed to

---

2. Some biographers say the horse received his name only in retrospect.
3. If the opponent was not unseated by the blow of the lance, it would often snap and break. The invitation to joust was termed to "break a lance."

unseat him and that round ended in a draw. As Emmanuel Philibert de Savoie regained the stand, Henri publicly complimented him on the excellence of his gift horse, Le Malheur.

It was stifling hot on that June 30, 1559, and the queen, her face by now as flushed as her purple dress, begged the contestants, laboring in their heavy armor, to cease. But the king was buoyant with his success, and would not hear of it. Instead, he demanded to break his third and final lance with the twenty-nine-year-old comte de Lorge, Gabriel Montgomery, the noble captain of his Scottish Guard, who had unseated him on a previous day of the tournament.

Catherine's anxiety increased: she sent the duc de Nemours with yet another message begging Henri not to gallop any more "for love of her." Henri's ambiguous reply, that it was precisely "for the love of her" that he wished to break one more lance, has puzzled posterity ever since. A final warning came from the king's Master of the Horse, who advised him that his visor was not properly fastened. At times, Henri could be as stubborn as his grandmother, Anne de Bretagne. Ignoring the pleas of his wife and his household, Henri II spurred Le Malheur and charged Montgomery. The run was successful but ended in a draw as neither contestant was unseated. Vexed by scoring a second draw, on impulse, and against the laws of chivalry, the king challenged his brave captain, eleven years his junior, to break yet another lance with him.

A strange frisson of alarm made Montgomery attempt to decline, until his laughing, jubilant king ordered him to obey.

An uneasy stillness fell over the crowd, as if word of the queen's dream had spread. Two seasoned warriors, Vieilleville and Montluc, had also had premonitions of the king's death and watched anxiously. To a shout of "*Monjoie!*" (the French knights' traditional battle cry), both riders spurred their horses, the black and white plumes on the king's helmet flying like those on top of his horse's head. As always when he charged, Diane caught her breath. The impact of the lances simultaneously striking armor was tremendous, and both riders almost came down with their mounts, but they recovered and continued to the end of the lists. Once again, the run ended in a draw.

Annoyed with his performance, Henri grabbed another lance,

shouting to Gabriel Montgomery to come at him again. The captain just had time to turn his horse and none to change his lance as they began the run. As they lowered their weapons, Montgomery must have seen that the metal end securing the tip of his wooden lance was missing, but it was too late. Even if Montgomery did not notice, most of the spectators would have seen the unshod lance, so likely to split with the force of impact. The crowd held its universal breath and even the trumpeters, mesmerized, failed to sound the usual call. To the on-lookers, the charge seemed to pass in slow motion as the horses plowed through the sand, which flew with each stride. As the lances struck metal, the horses jarred violently on impact, rearing and screaming.

Both lances broke, Montgomery's splintering. The king was seen to reel from the force of the blow and slump forward, but through sheer willpower and the reflexes of an experienced rider, Henri managed to keep his seat. His horse continued on down the length of the lists with Henri holding on to its neck. Before he could fall from the saddle, the grooms caught Le Malheur and gently lowered their

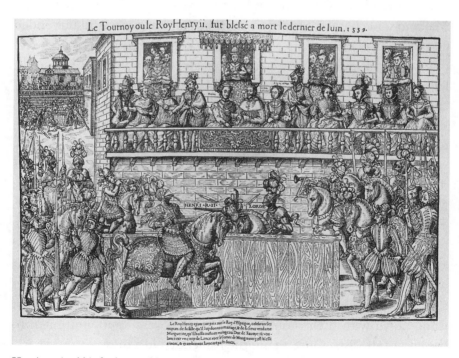

Henri received his fatal wound in a tournament on 30 June 1559.

wounded master. Before the run, Henri had opened his visor, the door of his "golden cage," as Nostradamus had called it, to mop his brow, and had failed to refasten it securely. As the gilded helmet was removed, the king fainted. All in the stands could see his face was covered in blood, and a cry of dismay rose from the crowd. The visor of the damaged helmet had been open a fraction; a large splinter from Montgomery's broken lance had entered the king's right eye, penetrating his skull and leaving the temple by the ear. Another thick splinter had pierced his throat.

While pandemonium broke out in the crowd, Henri was carefully carried to his pavilion, where he regained consciousness. His first thought was for the wretched Montgomery, who, kneeling, begged his king to cut off his hand and his head, and to pardon him. Despite excruciating pain, Henri assured the desperate man there was nothing to pardon: he had obeyed his sovereign and performed honorably and well.

In the stands, all was chaos; the queen was hysterical, the dauphin had fainted. Amid the mass of screaming spectators fighting to reach the ground, Diane struggled desperately to climb over the railings and force her way through, but the crush was too great. As she tried in vain to get word of the king's injury, Diane de Poitiers must have felt helpless for the first time since he had become her protector. Shock, panic, and resignation mingled with her fear—fear that her beloved might die, fear of living without him, fear of the queen's vengeance. Diane felt her power fading with the king's life. Without Henri, she had no authority. Her pleas to see him were left unanswered; no one would give her news—those were the queen's orders. Catherine was in charge at last. Distraught, Diane went back to her house nearby to wait for word from Henri.

The English ambassador, Sir Nicholas Throckmorton, watched as the king was taken back to the palace on a litter. "Nothing covered his face, he moved neither hand nor foot, but lay as one amazed." On reaching Les Tournelles, Henri regained consciousness again and tried to climb the stairs to his apartment. The king's own doctor, Jean Chapelain, washed the wound with vinegar and rosewater, and removed what he could of the splinters but did not dare touch the large piece of the lance embedded in the wound. Catherine, the duc de

Savoie, and the cardinal de Lorraine took the first shift by his bed until three in the morning, then François de Guise, Alphonse d'Este, and Anne de Montmorency took over until dawn. In his pain, Henri called out repeatedly for Diane, but no messenger was sent.

The next day, July 1, the king seemed better and was able to eat and drink a little and to sleep. All present noted his courage and stoicism. The following morning, Henri asked to see his captain Montgomery, but he was told that he had fled. Why? asked the king. He had done nothing wrong. But Montgomery was a Protestant who knew the temper of the queen and the Guise brothers. Meanwhile, the Guises had begun blaming the Constable, who was officially in charge of the king's armor and therefore responsible for the incorrect fastening of the visor.

Throughout Paris, votive processions of people chanting and praying wound slowly through the grieving city. In her house next to the palace, a frantic Diane waited for news; when none came, she humbly requested to see the king. Permission was coldly refused. Henri belonged to Catherine at last. One can only imagine Diane's suffering and her fear for the future.

When the accident took place, Emmanuel Philibert de Savoie immediately sent a fast courier to Brussels to fetch Andreas Vesalius, the renowned doctor of Philip II, and the queen called for the best surgeon in France, Ambroise Paré. Vesalius was the first to arrive, on July 3. He removed several splinters of wood and shattered bone from Henri's skull. The efforts of the king's doctor and the others had prevented his fever from rising throughout the 3rd and 4th, and for two days there was hope. The king asked for music and vowed, if he was cured, to make a pilgrimage on foot to Nôtre-Dame-de-Cléry. He also dictated a letter to the pope telling him of the arrest of several "Lutherans" in Paris and that he intended to use force if necessary to bring an end to the heresy spreading through the country.

Vesalius was not a surgeon and did not dare operate. Instead, he administered a mix of egg white, rhubarb, a special kind of tar from Egypt, and petroleum, all mixed into a paste to clean the wound. At last Ambroise Paré arrived. He was the most eminent surgeon of his

time and specialized in wounds to the head. It was Paré who had ex-
tracted piece by piece the broken weapon from the head of François de
Guise, who, despite a horrific scar, had survived the torture, to live and
prosper.

Henri remained conscious and never complained. Paré's success
with the duc de Guise did not give him enough confidence to perform
the same brutal operation on the king; he feared he lacked sufficient
practical knowledge. By July 5, the king had developed a fever, but the
surgeon still hesitated to operate. Vieilleville tells how, in her desperation, the queen ordered six condemned men to be decapitated in
prison, so that Paré could insert a similar long, thick splinter into their
heads to imitate Henri's injury and devise a strategy for surgery.

As nothing seemed to ease his pain, Henri asked for musicians to
play, a common request at deathbeds. Even if Henri was not soothed,
perhaps it helped those around him: the queen, the Constable, the duc
de Savoie, the Duke of Ferrara, the duc de Guise, the duc's brother the
cardinal de Lorraine. The only person missing was the one he loved
most in the world: Diane de Poitiers.

Blind and barely able to speak, Henri knew he was dying, but
wanted to ratify his Treaty of Câteau-Cambrésis and worried that his
sister Marguerite and Emmanuel Philibert de Savoie had missed their
wedding. Despite his pain and delirium, Henri ordered Catherine to
proceed with the marriage. Then he slipped into a coma. The small,
poignant wedding ceremony took place at midnight on July 8, in the
little church next to Les Tournelles. It was entirely draped in black, and
all parties were in floods of tears.

That same day, a messenger came from the queen to the duchesse
de Valentinois asking for the return of the crown jewels. "Is the king
dead?" Diane asked. She was told no, but that it would not be long.
Brantôme quotes Diane as refusing the request, saying: "So long as
there remains a breath of life in him, I wish my enemies to know I do
not fear them. As yet there is no one who can command me. I am still
of good courage. But when he is dead, I do not want to live after him;
and all the bitterness that one could wish me will be but sweetness beside my great loss." As Diane was so much older than Henri, naturally

At his death, Henri II was surrounded by all his family and important courtiers. The only person close to him missing from the scene was Diane de Poitiers.

she had expected to die before him. All her life she had planned for every eventuality but this. It was her tragedy that the situation was re-versed.

As he watched the infection progress, Ambroise Paré contem-plated trepanning the king's skull to drain the poison but decided to spare him the pain. The operation might have saved him.

On July 9, Henri asked for the Last Sacraments and to speak to his son. The king blessed the dauphin François, and just like Henri at the deathbed of his father, the dauphin fainted and was carried from the room. Still conscious, Henri dictated a letter to Philip II asking for his protection for the dauphin and for his people—in effect, an open invi-tation to his son-in-law of Spain to interfere in the affairs of France. It was the sort of political naïveté from which Diane de Poitiers and Anne de Montmorency had always protected him.

At one o'clock in the afternoon of July 10, 1559, twelve days after he had been wounded, Henri died. For most of the previous two days he had lain in a coma, his body paralyzed and swollen with infection. Henri II, king of France, had reigned for twelve years, three months, and eleven days.

On the orders of the queen, all his calls for "*Ma Dame*" had been ignored.

*I*N the preceding months, Catherine had been aware that she had won some measure of approval from Henri, especially during her regency and after her successful appeal for war funds. At sixty, Diane could not expect to live much longer and it is probable that, upon her death, Henri would have turned to his wife for guidance. After so many years of neglect, the Medici queen had felt herself on the brink of sharing the throne with her husband; but a cruel fate denied her this rightful place by his side. For all the twenty-five years of her arranged marriage, Catherine de' Medici had been robbed of her husband "by Diane de Poitiers in the sight and knowledge of everyone." Now the queen lost him to death.

Did Catherine love her husband? She was certainly devoted to him and his wishes, and her grief was terrible and sincere; but hatred of Diane was surely the stronger emotion. Was it *love* that had her deny him, on his deathbed, the sight of the person he cherished the most? Catherine had met Henri for the first time at their wedding and had fallen in love with him on that day. Known as a cold woman, she was said never to have shown warmth to friends or even to her children. Catherine was an intellectual who had learned from an early age to control her emotions. She had controlled her love by hating and waiting, and now it seems her *grande passion* had become jealousy and hatred, but not love. Can a woman in despair over her husband's suffering be thinking about the jewels he has given his mistress, and demand their return at such a time? A one-sided passion is almost impossible to sustain. Perhaps Catherine wept more for her lost future than her lost love. Of all her children, only the future Henri III became her obsession, and even he was said to have secretly called her "*La Serpente.*"

The next day at dawn, the queen's revenge began. She urged Mary, Queen of Scots, now queen of France, to send a messenger to the duchesse de Valentinois, the beautiful lady who was the first to befriend her when she had arrived at age six in France. Diane was to return the crown jewels[4] and the keys to Henri II's strong room and desk. The duchess de Valentinois, who was composed and prepared, returned everything in a casket, together with a meticulous inventory. She included a letter in which she humbled herself before Catherine, begging her pardon for her offenses and wishing her well. There is an entry in the Venetian diplomatic correspondence[5] which alleges that it was François II, and not Mary, who "sent to Diane that for reasons of her bad influence over his father the late king, she deserved great punishment, but in his royal clemency he would not trouble her further. However, she had to return to him all the jewels that his father the king had given her." He also banished Diane, her daughter Françoise, and her husband, the duc de Bouillon, from the court.

For the queen, the years of silent waiting were over. The new king, in awe of his responsibilities, asked his mother to rule in his place. Cleverly, Catherine declined, inviting the Guises to join with her in advising her son. The queen-dowager had learned from her rival how black and white flattered the older woman, and instead of the usual white mourning robes reserved for queens, she wore black velvet with a train, adding an ermine collar but no ornaments.[6] She was also wearing a black veil that covered her face. Accompanied by her son, the new king François II, and his queen in her white wedding dress, worn now in mourning, and Mary's triumphant Guise uncles, Catherine immediately left Les Tournelles for the Palace of the Louvre. Far from remaining in retreat for the traditional period of royal mourning in the place of the king's death, the queen-dowager urged the Guises to take control of the government before the deputation from the *Parlement* arrived. The takeover by the Guises was completed by installing the young king in the Louvre in apartments next to their own. Not to be marginalized, Catherine moved in as well.

The chancellor, Jean Bertrand, protégé and friend of Diane de Poitiers, was obliged to give up the royal seals of state, and François

4. Armond Baschet, *La Diplomatie vénitienne*.
5. Ibid.
6. Thereafter, the only time Catherine de' Medici put aside her black mourning and wore brilliant robes was for the weddings of her sons.

Olivier, who was close to the cardinal, was reinstated in his former position. The English ambassador noted: "The house of Guise ruleth and doth all about the French king."

At the Louvre, according to contemporary reports, Catherine sat "in a room that was entirely black; not only the walls but also the floor had been covered. There was no light except for two church candles burning on an altar that was covered by a black sheet. The queen's bed was covered in the same way. Her Majesty wore the most austere clothes. The queen of Scotland, now The Most Christian Queen Mary of France and Scotland, was in the same room, but wore entirely white. Also there was Marguerite, duchesse de Savoie, the dead king's sister; and then the daughters of France—the queen of Spain; the duchesse de Savoie; and their young sister, Margot, all dressed in white, and obliged to observe fourteen days of mourning." The queen mother spoke in the name of her group, but her voice was so choked and weak that no one could hear what she said no matter how hard they listened.

The Guise family, whom Diane had raised to power, turned against her. The duc de Guise claimed her apartments in the Louvre, while his brother, the cardinal, took over the Constable's. As Grand Master, Montmorency was obliged to remain with the body of the king at Les Tournelles, and was powerless. With only young and weak sons to inherit, the death of Henri II created a power vacuum which the Guise brothers rapidly filled. It was not long before Montmorency lost his post as Grand Master of the Household to François de Guise, ensuring that François and the cardinal now controlled the court.

Montmorency retired to his estates, but he was still Constable, as well as being the richest nobleman in France. Alienating him would not have served Catherine's purpose to control the Guise family. She had persuaded the Constable to relinquish the post of Grand Master by making his son, François, a marshal of France. Diane's nephew the bishop de Meaux had to resign his office as *grand aumônier*. The duc d'Aumale, husband of Diane's other daughter, Louise, almost lost his position as governor of Normandy, but he was spared—leaving him indebted to his Guise relations. No further move was made to interfere with Louise's inheritance.

Carefully, with the sharpest scalpel, Catherine began to pry Henri's

name away from that of his beloved mistress. The duchesse de Valentinois received no invitation to the funeral, and therefore watched the
procession from a window in her house near the Palace of Les Tournelles, noting with dismay the prominence of the assembled Guise
family. As the coffin passed by below her, she could see that the king's
effigy (once again the work of François Clouet) wore not black and
white but a crimson satin shirt, a tunic of purple satin covered in *fleur-
de-lys,* and a cloak of purple, not black velvet, decorated not with silver
crescents but with the *fleur-de-lys* of France. Nor was the king's rider-
less horse draped in the black saddlecloth with the silver "HD" cipher;
but the crescent was still there under Henri's initial "H" on the chariot
bearing the coffin.

Perhaps the cruelest of Catherine's petty acts of revenge was to de-
face the ciphers she could not remove so that they now read "HC";
there are many examples of this at Chenonceau, the Louvre, and other
royal châteaux.

Although Diane de Poitiers had sincerely tried to ease Catherine
de' Medici's difficult situation and had always shown her every respect,
she was fully aware of the intensity of Catherine's jealousy, and expected to be arrested. It did not happen. The duchesse de Valentinois
could not be treated like the duchesse d'Etampes; Diane had committed no crime, and had helped Henri rule wisely and well. During her
twenty-five years at the king's side she had formed many influential
friendships, and through the marriages of her daughters she had forged
links with Catherine's allies. The queen-dowager rightly judged that
she could not afford to alienate these great French families, and limited
her revenge to banishing Diane from the court, leaving her free to

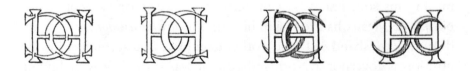

"HD" and "HC" ciphers showing how Catherine de' Medici altered the "HD" of Henri and
Diane to read "HC"—for Henri and Catherine.

live at Anet. This Diane did, according to all accounts, with exemplary dignity.

Perhaps it was inevitable, however, that in spite of all Henri's attempts to secure Chenonceau for Diane, Catherine would one day seize it, and out of feminine spite she did just that. Catherine knew she could not rule without the help of the Guises. Mindful of Diane's powerful alliances, the merchant-queen gave her Chaumont-sur-Loire in exchange for Chenonceau. The papers were signed on April 27, 1560.

No one would have appreciated better than Diane the irony of finding herself the châtelaine of Chaumont instead of Henri's coronation gift of Chenonceau. But when she visited Chaumont for the first time, she was appalled to find the disgusting evidence of the queen's necromancy in a room still full of alchemists' tools. Perhaps to frighten Diane, no effort had been made to destroy the proof of Catherine's pagan practices. A pentacle was clearly marked on the floor, and Greek, Egyptian, and Hebrew characters decorated an altar on which was placed a skull. All around the room, jars of powders, liquids, and pickled animal parts in bottles lined the shelves, as well as strange books, parchments, and the remains of animal sacrifices. Utterly repelled, Diane ordered everything to be burned and sent for a priest to exorcize the place.

The servants, when questioned, confirmed her worst fears, and the real horror of where Catherine's obsession had led her during the last years became clear. In the account by the historian Jehanne d'Orliac,

> one night when the moon was full over Chaumont, Queen Catherine sought to unveil the fates before giving up the château to Diane de Poitiers. With the help of Nostradamus, or—according to some—of Ruggieri, she invoked Elohim, Jehovah, Mihatron, Adonaï, by writing those names in the blood of a cock pigeon on the steel mirror. The magician traced a circle on the floor (according to the direction of Pope Honorius), after ranging around him a human skull, a shin bone, a lamp and a sleeping cat. Then, in response to the invocation, the queen, Catherine, suddenly saw her three sons appear in the mirror one after another. François turned about once, Charles fourteen times, Henri fifteen times, and lastly Henri de Bourbon [Navarre]

came and turned around once. She would not see more. All vanished. Thus she knew the length of her own and her sons' reigns, and also the coming of the new dynasty after the extinction of the Valois.

According to popular legend, it seems that the vision appeared on the forty-fourth night after the spell began. One wonders if Catherine waited there. In later life, the queen maintained that Henri had predicted the future of his dynasty and that she had indulged in sorcery because she wanted to know more for the sake of her sons. The story of the mirror and the four princes appears in a number of sources in connection with Catherine de' Medici, and is cited as the reason for her insistence on the marriage of her youngest daughter, Margot, with Henri de Navarre, the future Henri IV of France. Catherine de' Medici hoped that through their union, some Valois blood would remain on the throne of France. It was not to be. Margot was barren, and Henri IV subsequently married Marie de' Medici, increasing the Medici blood, not the Valois, on France's throne.

Diane ordered Chaumont closed. She never went there again. It was left in her will to the children of her daughter Françoise de Bouillon.

As the luckless Captain Montgomery was a Protestant, suspicion quickly spread that the king's death had been part of a heretic plot. Tensions between Catholics and Protestants rose to dangerous levels, which Catherine tried to ease by letting Montgomery go. Banished from France, the brave captain of Henri's Scottish Guard became a soldier of fortune. Fifteen years later, fighting as a mercenary for England, Montgomery was tricked into capture by the French—Catherine had always kept an eye on him. After a courageous defense of his stronghold, he and his ten thousand soldiers were promised their lives if they surrendered. Montgomery agreed, only to be arrested and brought to Paris for trial.

Catherine de Medici had never ceased to "Hate and Wait" for her husband's killer, who had caused her reversal of fortune. With Henri's death, she abandoned her emblem of a rainbow and adopted instead a broken lance. At last, she could avenge Henri's death and destroy the man who had taken him from her forever. Her face as expressionless as a mask, Catherine watched as the valiant Montgomery was tried for high treason, condemned, beheaded, and quartered in the Place de Grève.

$\mathcal{F}$RANÇOIS II reigned for less than one year. He died in Orléans on December 5, 1560, leaving Mary, Queen of Scots and France, a young widow. It was whispered that the royal physician Ambroise Paré had slipped some poison into his ear since Catherine de' Medici "saw no other way of assuring her authority."

As Catherine's next son, Charles IX, was too young to rule, she convinced the Princes of the Blood that she should act as regent. Nor was there any longer a place at court for the enchanting young queen-dowager of France, who, as a child, had dared to mock Catherine's origins. Ravishing in white, "*la Reine Blanche,*" as the French called Mary, remained in mourning for her husband in Orléans for the traditional forty days. There was an immediate diplomatic movement to find a new husband for Mary; even the new king of France, Charles IX, was mooted, as well as the feeble heir to the Spanish throne, Don Carlos. Catherine was not at all well disposed to an alliance of Scotland and Spain. How could it help her gentle daughter Elisabeth to reign as queen there if her contemporary, the ravishing Mary Stuart, was married to the *heir* to the throne? Comparisons would not favor her daughter, to whom she wrote, referring to Mary as "*le gentilhomme,*" urging her to do all in her power to hinder the union.

If Catherine genuinely felt grief at the death of her eldest son, she managed to set it aside for the moment. To deter the proposed marriage of Mary with the heir to Spain, the queen-regent of France offered Philip II the hand of her youngest daughter, Margot, for the stunted, crazy Don Carlos. After all, her sorcerer might have been wrong: her sons might produce heirs and Henry of Navarre might not become king of France. With serpentine cunning, Catherine maintained her mask of friendship toward her daughter-in-law Mary, and pretended no knowledge of the Spanish negotiations. The regent had never forgotten or forgiven Mary for her snobbish slight on her arrival in France so many years ago, and the tension between them had surfaced once Mary became queen of France.

The young queen-dowager, Mary, set out for a lengthy visit to her Guise cousins at their various properties, "to the spite" of Catherine and her "rigorous and vengeful dealing." According to Mary Stuart's envoy, Sir James Melville, Catherine alleged that "she was despised by her good daughter, during the short reign of king François her husband, at the instigation of the house of Guise." Melville goes on to allege that "the Queen-mother was glad at the death of King Francis her son, because she had no guiding of him, he being wholly counseled by the duc de Guise and the Cardinal his brother . . . so that the Queen-mother was much satisfied to be freed of the government of the house of Guise; and for this cause she entertained a great grudge at our Queen." As Mary saw her friends being disgraced, she withdrew from the court and traveled within the country. While staying with her relatives, Mary fell ill. She was unable to attend the coronation of Charles IX and only returned to the court after a crucial absence of three months.

According to Mary Stuart's marriage contract, Catherine's inner hostility could not deprive her daughter-in-law of the right to remain in France and maintain herself with her income from her marriage portion duchies. But being a woman of instinct, Mary sensed that there was not room for two dowager-queens in France. Rather than remain in a country where she was clearly not welcomed by the ruling house, she bravely decided to take the gamble and return to Scotland, to an unknown future in a Protestant country she had not seen for thirteen years. Although she had spent most of her life in France, various ambassadors noted that Mary was extremely eloquent in her own language. Then, to the surprise of everyone, Queen Elizabeth I refused her cousin a safe-conduct to cross the Channel. Nevertheless Mary set sail from Calais on August 14, 1561, accompanied by the four Marys— Mary Seton, Mary Beaton, Mary Livingston, and Mary Fleming—who had all come to France with her as children. Sharing her voyage was James, Earl of Bothwell, and the chronicler Brantôme.

"*Adieu, France! Adieu France! Adieu donc, ma chère France. . . . Je pense ne vous revoir jamais plus*" ("Good-bye, my dear France. . . . I fear I shall never see you again"), she cried, as she sailed toward her tragic destiny. In France it was said that without Diane de Poitiers and Mary, Queen of Scots, "the smile of the court disappeared." Many years later, during her imprisonment in Scotland, Queen Mary recalled her happy childhood experiences at Anet and Chenonceau, and worked Diane's famous symbols into her embroidery. With her heart always on her sleeve, a smile that lit up any room, the enchanting Mary of Scots was a slave of her emotions, seemingly drawn to misfortune. Neither her "crimes" nor her tragic end have diminished the admiration of succeeding generations.

AFTER Henri's funeral, Diane returned to her beloved Anet to reminisce on the fabled *douceur de vivre* they had shared in this enchanted château. Here Catherine could not erase the evidence of Henri's love, which had embraced Diane for twenty-nine years. She had her memories, and nothing else mattered. A number of historians maintain that Diane was isolated at Anet and that many of her friends were too afraid of the Medici queen's rage to comfort or console her. But her account books show that she often visited Paris and frequented the Montmorency, Bourbon, and Guise families as well as the Bouillons and the Nevers. Anne de Montmorency and his wife, Madeleine de Savoie, were regular visitors.

Directly after Diane's return to Anet, the villagers were unsure if the queen-regent would wreak her vengeance on them, but they soon proclaimed their love for their duchesse de Valentinois. Diane rewarded her people by building a small hospital in the village, as well as homes for unmarried mothers, orphans, destitute girls, and widows.

During the Wars of Religion, which devastated Normandy, Rouen was taken over by the Huguenots. When the Constable de Montmorency and Antoine de Navarre, who was the first Prince of the Blood, and their extensive suites arrived to relieve Rouen on September 24, 1562, all stayed at Anet for four days before mounting the siege. Diane had been at her house at Limours[7] and arrived just in time

---

7. She purchased Limours from Anne d' Etampes.

to receive the royal party. It is clear from the accounts showing the amount of food and hay ordered for the visit that the contingent was sizable. When the queen-regent and the young King Charles IX arrived with the army, the sojourn of the advance party with Diane at Anet at this critical time was made public, and demonstrated her continued close links with the establishment. Two months later, Diane's grandson was born at Anet, and the dukes of Montmorency and of Navarre both agreed to be godfathers. According to Brantôme, "Diane was wanted more than ever and returned to favor as I have seen."

On December 19, 1562, the Battle of Dreux was fought a few kilometers from Anet. Strange as it may seen, to be on opposite sides in a civil war did not necessarily damage family ties and friendships. The Huguenots were led by Louis, prince de Condé, and Gaspard de Coligny, while the royalists were commanded by Montmorency, François de Guise, and the maréchal de Saint-André. The Protestant prince de Condé, after leaving Paris with his army, spent several nights at Diane's house at Limours while she was in Paris, and, accompanied by the English ambassador and another courtier, spent the night before the Battle of Dreux at Anet during Diane's absence. The Protestants were beaten, with terrible losses on both sides. Montmorency was captured and a son of his killed; also killed was Henri's old friend Saint-André. Diane's son-in-law Aumale was seriously wounded. Ambassador Throckmorton took refuge with Diane's widowed daughter Françoise in her house nearby.

Diane hurried from Paris and arrived at Anet two days after the battle, but the signs of death and devastation were unmistakable. She was received by her daughter Louise d'Aumale and her granddaughter, wife of Montmorency's son Henri—more proof of Diane's enduring place in the center of life as it affected the court. In the 1660s, she succeeded in recommending Robert de Quesnel for the post of abbé de Conches in Normandy.

When Diane de Poitiers was in her early sixties, she was recorded as still being fit enough to ride throughout the night on horseback. At the age of sixty-four, however, she had a serious riding accident, badly breaking her leg. Brantôme wrote after visiting Diane at Anet:

"In spite of her fall and its attendant suffering, the charming and

Diane de Poitiers was buried in the chapel at Anet.

noble widow was still so lovely that I know not a heart, even one of rock, capable of resisting her . . . while her beauty, her grace, her majesty, were all the same as they have always been. I believe that should she live to a hundred years, she would have aged neither in face, so well was it made, nor in body, so excellent her constitution, so perfect her figure and her carriage." Perhaps Brantôme, like Henri, saw what he wanted to see. Surely this was Diane's triumph.

Two years later, on April 25, 1566, after a serious though brief illness and no pain, Diane de Poitiers, duchesse de Valentinois, died without any other family at Anet. She was the same age as the century.

After her death, Brantôme recalled that "Six months before she died she was still so beautiful . . . she was of the most perfect whiteness, without using any cosmetic though they do say that every morning she used a wash of liquid gold. It is sad that earth should hide that beautiful body."

Diane had always insisted that Henri burn all the letters she wrote him, perhaps fearing the use Catherine might make of them after her death. Few remain, but as Henri's death came unexpectedly before her own, she decided to preserve at Anet all of his letters and his simple, elegant poems. It was Henri's nature to love once and completely; it was Diane's privilege to be the recipient of that love, and to cherish and nourish it so that their names and their story would live on in the minds and hearts of future generations.

Diane had signed her will at Limours in January 1564 with a copy for the senior priest at Anet's chapel. She divided her vast fortune between her two daughters, but stipulated that should either become Protestant, the one would forfeit her inheritance to the other—"Never shall a Protestant have revenue from Diane de Poitiers." Even in death, Diane de Poitiers confirmed her position in the realm. She had gone to considerable trouble to ensure that her lands were secure for her two children's families, making an exact division between them.

Possibly fearing divine retribution for her own career, she left a bequest for masses to be said at a number of convents for fallen women. For her funeral procession, she wrote that one hundred poor from the villages surrounding Anet should be dressed in white and, carrying lit tapers, should follow her coffin chanting:

"Priez Dieu pour Diane de Poitiers."

Epilogue

DIANE was buried in the funerary chapel she had built next to Anet. But when French revolutionaries desecrated and opened her tomb in 1795, two small skeletons were found lying next to hers. For some time it was thought these were children she had borne the king. However, a manuscript belonging to the house of Guise in the Bibliothèque Nationale in Paris states that Diane's daughter Louise, duchesse d'Aumale, gave birth to three children at Anet. The youngest, Charles, died on May 7, 1568, and was "conveyed to Anet and buried there, and placed in the sepulcher with the late Mme Diane de Poitiers, duchesse de Valentinois, his grandmother, deceased at the Château d'Anet on April 25, 1566." If one of the "little girls" was a boy, perhaps the other existed only in the imagination. The despoilers of Diane's tomb cut her hair into small souvenirs and a later owner of Anet sold much of the château stone by stone. All that remains today are two beautifully restored wings. Goujon's great white marble sculpture *Diana and the Stag* is safe in the Louvre.

*W*HEN Henri II became king of France in 1547, the country's
situation was precarious. The Italian wars of François I had emptied the state's coffers; the people of Paris were in the throes of religious ferment; the outer French territories had collapsed almost
beyond redemption; and hundreds of Huguenots had been executed
in the Protestant persecutions of the final years of his father's reign.

The Peace of Câteau-Cambrésis, signed with Philip II of Spain in
1559, only a few months before the death of Henri II, brought a
much-needed break in the almost continuous foreign or civil wars in
which France was embroiled throughout the first half of the sixteenth
century. With peace came a dramatic improvement in the country's fi-
nances, which at that point were in better shape than they had been for
nearly three decades. Overall, the economy expanded gradually for a
number of years, and France's territories were extended. At home,
Henry II almost achieved the daunting task of balancing the opposing
factions at court.

Diane de Poitiers was deeply embedded in the fabric of French
public life by birth, by marriage, and then by her association with
Henri II. With or without the Reformation, that fabric was being constantly rewoven, and with it, the balance of power between rival groups
within the French nobility. The Guise family had risen with her—
Charles de Lorraine had been made a cardinal and François d'Aumale
became duc de Guise on the death of his father in 1550. With Diane's
initial support, they balanced the power of the Bourbon Princes of the
Blood, who had the backing of the Constable de Montmorency. With
the death of Henri, Diane's protectors, the Guises, threw their influence behind Catherine and turned against their patron. Her son-in-law
Claude d'Aumale tried to help, but was firmly told that he should be
grateful for the wealth his *mésalliance* had brought him. To be married
to the daughter of a former royal mistress could now "only bring
shame" on the Guise family. He should distance himself from his
mother-in-law and never forget the pain his association with Diane de

Poitiers caused Queen Catherine. But it would not take long before both families were frequenting each other's houses again.

Due to Diane's careful balancing of the two opposing camps, the reign of Henri II, though short, was very positive for France, and in its every aspect, the sure guiding hand of Diane de Poitiers was easily detected. François I had brought to his country the glory of the Renaissance; but it was under Henri II, with the help of Diane de Poitiers, that France developed to its full magnificence. Contemporary writers vied with one another in their search for superlatives to describe the glamour and *galanteries* of Henri II's court. Such luxury, elegance, and refinement existed nowhere else in Europe at the time. Yet it was Diane, not Henri, whose interest lay in the arts. It was Diane who encouraged a whole nation of craftsmen and artists, and who expanded on the enlightened patronage of François I and his School of Fontainebleau. Diane gloried in the High Renaissance and aimed, through her royal lover, to fulfill the ambition of his father: to create an intellectual and artistic climate that would rival the great courts and seats of learning in Italy.

The morals of the court of François I left very much to be desired, and the king was himself a formidable philanderer. According to the journal of Beatis: "The king is a great womanizer and readily breaks into others' gardens and drinks from many sources." Adultery was regarded lightly at court, and the courtiers' mistresses had marriages arranged to facilitate their *affairs*,[1] a reasonable solution accepted by all sides. The relaxed morality of François I's court should be seen in relation to the austerity of the two previous reigns, as well as to that of Emperor Charles V, the French king's contemporary.

Although Diane de Poitiers was the mistress of Henri II, his court had quite a different tone from his father's. Adultery was not condoned or encouraged, and although many came to know she was the king's mistress, Diane was officially his "Lady" and their relationship was portrayed as philosophical, not physical. As Grande Sénéchale, Diane had matured within the spirit and immorality of François I's

---

1. A mistress should be married as a cover lest she become pregnant with her lover's child.

court, but it was she who orchestrated the dramatic moral change in direction during Henri II's reign. It would be wrong to claim that Diane de Poitiers achieved this singlehandedly, but despite the attempts to smear her name—particularly following Henri's death—she retained the image of the "pure one" to the end of her life. It was claimed by Madame de La Fayette in *La Princesse de Clèves*, written a century later, that at no time in the history of France was the court so magnificent and so gallant as during the reign of Henri II.

Henri II continued the religious policies instituted by the *Parlement* during his father's last years; but the situation deteriorated severely. There is no doubt that following the Peace of Câteau-Cambrésis, persecution of the Protestants intensified as the Catholic monarchs of France and Spain united to stamp out heresy. Although Henri gave his sympathy and patronage to the Counter-Reformation Society of Jesus, court intrigues were aggravated by the religious issues.

Jean Calvin's enormous and growing influence in France led to a dramatic rise in converts, and as a result, the numbers of sentences against heretics increased. Diane certainly encouraged Henri in the persecution of those she saw as a direct threat to the old order of absolutism and Catholicism. Even in her will, a practical, meticulous document, and a tribute to her lucidity and pride, Diane de Poitiers remained steadfastly opposed to Protestants. Nonetheless, it is worth noting that by the standards of the Age of Faith, Henri II was not considered outstandingly brutal or even intolerant toward heretics.

After his death, the civil wars between Catholics and Protestants in France continued sporadically until the Edict of Nantes in 1598 granted them an *imperium in imperio*[2]—religious forbearance to all creeds. The French Wars of Religion were notorious for their brutality and mob violence, the most extreme example being the Massacre of Saint Bartholomew. This was carried out on the eve of the wedding of the Protestant king of Navarre, the future Henri IV of France, to Catherine's youngest child, Margot. Although ordered by the weakling Charles IX, the blame for this atrocity and the murder of countless thousands can be laid squarely at the feet of Catherine de' Medici.

2. Literally, "power within power" or "government within a government"—a double society, in this case religious, functioning on different levels.

*T*HE first half of the sixteenth century was an era of contradictions, a transitory period between medieval times and the Renaissance, a rebirth of the art, philosophy, and literature of the Golden Age of Greece. Henri was the very embodiment of these contradictions—medieval in his outlook and yet prepared to initiate quite modern changes in government and his army. Although a cold and largely indifferent husband to Catherine, he was a loving, cozy father to his many children. Henri was a loyal and generous friend and yet a vindictive and vengeful enemy. He could be easily persuaded, but once he had made up his mind, he refused to see that his argument was ill-founded. It was this obstinacy that made him insist on breaking yet another lance with Montgomery.

Diane de Poitiers was an intelligent though not strikingly original thinker. Nor was she an innovator. In outlook, she was a woman of her time, highly educated certainly, but passionately committed to the social hierarchy, and superb in her management of it. Perhaps Diane's iconographic legacy leads us to overlook her faults, but maybe her faults were exaggerated by jealous contemporaries, or those wishing to curry favor with her powerful successors.

Diane did not play a major part in forming French foreign or domestic policy, but she provided Henri II with all that her education at the hands of Anne de Beaujeu had taught her: in essence, a blueprint for living a worthy, romantic, and honorable life. It was her respect for that education that made her want to pass on such traditions. In fairness, the chroniclers all depict Diane de Poitiers as a reserved woman, thoughtful, who said little and kept her distance. Nor did anyone claim that there was a lascivious side to her extraordinary beauty. Diane never meddled in politics except in cases that touched Henri's personal affairs. She was his support, his comfort, his muse, his reason for living, and she valued this more than any desire for the political power and influence she could so easily have had. Diane was the queen of Henri's heart and would not have envied Catherine her role after his death. She had molded an awkward youth into a poet, a troubadour, a cavalier, and then a ruler. Henri and Diane looked to the Age of Chivalry for their values and behavioral code, a code that embraced "pure love." His father, François I, and aunt, Marguerite de Navarre, had both espoused the philosophy of Plato. Henri and Diane lived the legacy of that belief.

Their life together was an idyll shared by two people devoted to one another forever. Tragically but inevitably, Catherine de' Medici did all she could to destroy the memory of the love her husband shared with Diane. "Hate and Wait" had been her motto, and she had done both with the intelligence no one doubted she possessed. Her patience was superhuman, and it paid dividends, even if the price was the loss of her husband. Catherine de' Medici was the real ruler of France throughout the reigns of her three sons, François II, Charles IX, and Henry III's until her death. The negative and harmful image of Diane de Poitiers propagated in the literature of Catherine's time, and later, has convinced many historians to see Diane through a man's eyes, as a woman who takes advantage of a foolish young prince for profit and power. They forget her disciplined upbringing and the education to which she adhered all her life, and which she passed on to her children. They forget that she had only known a man more than forty years her senior, older than her father, and that the attraction of a virile, handsome, powerful young man is one few single women could resist. Why should she care how misguided history sees her? She alone knew the love of her king. She alone knew the truth.

Diane de Poitiers' legend lives on, not only because we see her today in the guise of her image as goddess created by the great masters of the French Renaissance, but because she was a woman of independent spirit who made an art of living the highest quality of life while preserving a youthfulness of spirit, body, and personality. She was an enchantress who inspired an unpromising youth to become a splendid king; that he loved her all his life, although she was twenty years his senior, is proof of her enduring mystique.

Omnium Victorem Vici—Diane the moon goddess truly conquered the King, Love, and Time.

Chronology

1499	Birth of Diane de Poitiers
1504	Treaty of Blois
1505	Marriage of Charles de Bourbon-Montpensier and Suzanne de Bourbon, daughter of Anne de Beaujeu
1509	Marriage of Marguerite d'Angoulême and the duc d'Alençon
1514	Death of Anne de Bretagne
1515	Marriage of Louis XII and Mary Tudor, sister of Henry VIII of England. Death of Louis XII Coronation of François I. Charles de Bourbon appointed Constable of France. Marriage of Diane de Poitiers and Louis de Brézé. Louise de Savoie named regent. Battle of Marignano. Concordat signed between François and Pope Clement VII
1516	Leonardo da Vinci comes to live at the court of France
1517	Birth of a son to Charles and Suzanne de Bourbon; he dies the same year
1518	Marriage of Madeleine de La Tour d'Auvergne to the pope's nephew, Lorenzo de' Medici, Duke of Urbino
1519	Birth of Henri d'Orléans, second son of François I and his queen, Claude. Birth of Catherine de' Medici. Death of her father and mother. Election of Charles V, Holy Roman Emperor. Death of Leonardo da Vinci
1520	Meeting between François I and Henry VIII on the Field of the Cloth of Gold
1521	Birth of Louise de Brézé, second daughter of Diane de Poitiers. Death of Suzanne de Bourbon. Seizure of her land by Louise de Savoie

1522 Death of Anne de Beaujeu. Contact made between Charles de Bourbon and the emperor Charles V. Henry VIII becomes the emperor's ally. Saint-Vallier involved in plot

1523 The Constable de Bourbon's lands confiscated by the *Parlement;* his subsequent treason. Louis de Brézé discovers plot involving Saint-Vallier, who is arrested

1524 Saint-Vallier sentenced to death, later commuted to life imprisonment. Death of Queen Claude

1525 Battle of Pavia. François captured and taken as a prisoner to Spain. Catherine de' Medici returns from Rome to live in Florence

1526 Treaty of Madrid liberating François I. Saint-Vallier freed and his property returned. Meeting between François and his future wife, Eleonore, sister of the emperor Charles V. Exchange of François I for his two eldest sons, the dauphin and Prince Henri, who leave for Spain. League of Cognac formed

1527 Anne de Montmorency installed as Grand Master. Anne de Pisseleu becomes the king's mistress. Marguerite d'Alençon marries the king of Navarre. Sack of Rome

1528 François' entry into Rouen

1529 Building starts at Fontainebleau. Peace of Cambrai, or "Peace of the Ladies," is signed

1530 The two royal hostages are freed. Coronation of the emperor Charles V in Bologna. Marriage of François and Eleonore of Portugal. Catherine de' Medici brought to live with Pope Clement VII in Rome. Marriage contract between Henri d'Orléans and Catherine de' Medici signed at Anet. Holy League of States formed

1531 Death of Louis de Brézé. Death of Louise de Savoie. Coronation of Queen Eleonore

1532 Brittany becomes part of France

1533 Marriage of Henri d'Orléans and Catherine de' Medici in Marseilles

1534 "Affair of the placards." Death of Pope Clement VII. Marriage of Anne de Pisseleu. Ignatius Loyola forms the Society of Jesus

1535 Persecution of Protestants

1536 Imperial invasion of France. Death of the dauphin François. Henri d'Orléans becomes dauphin and joins Montmorency's army

1537 Henri's encounter with Filippa Duci. Wedding of James V of Scotland and Madeleine de Valois. François cancels the treaties of Madrid and Cambrai. Probable year of the start of Diane and Henri's love affair

1538 Montmorency appointed Constable. A daughter born to Filippa Duci is put in the charge of Diane de Poitiers. Ten-year truce declared between Charles V and François I

1539 Marriage of Françoise de Brézé and Robert IV de La Marck. Death of Saint-Vallier. Meeting of Henri and Charles V at Bidassoa

1540 Entry of Charles V and François into Paris. Publication of the first French translations of *Amadís de Gaula* appear

1542 Treaty of alliance with Suleiman. Persecution of the Protestants by the king. Birth of Mary, Queen of Scots, and her recognition by François I

1543   Alliance between Henry VIII and the emperor Charles V. Philibert de l'Orme begins work at Anet

1544   Birth of Catherine de' Medici's first child, a son, François. Turks leave France. Henri's protest to the *Parlement* concerning his inheritance. Treaty of Gespy signed

1545   The duc d'Aumale, eldest son of the duc de Guise, receives the wound in battle that gives him the title *Le Balafré*. Death of Charles d'Orléans, younger brother of Henri

1546   Treaty of Ardes, making peace with England. Diane's second daughter, Louise, marries Claude de Mayenne, future duc d'Aumale. Death of duc d'Enghien

1547   Deaths of Henry VIII of England and François I of France. Coronation of Henri II. Diane de Poitiers is given Chenonceau. Diane de France legitimized by Henri II and betrothed to Horace Farnese. Duel between La Châtaigneraie and Jarnac

1548   Henri II's entry into Lyons. Diane becomes duchesse de Valentinois. Revolt over the salt tax. Anet becomes Diane's property in perpetuity

1549   Henri's entry into Paris and the coronation of Catherine de' Medici

1550   Henri's affair with Lady Fleming, governess of Mary, Queen of Scots. The king's entry into Rouen. Marie de Guise visits France

1551   Persecution of Protestants

1552   Montmorency occupies Toul. Henry secures foothold in Lorraine. Treaty of Passau

1553   Charles V retreats from Metz. Duchy and title of Etampes given to Diane de Poitiers. Building of Anet completed. Death of Edward VI of England. Coronation of "Bloody Mary"

1554   Regency of Catherine de' Medici. Coronation of Mary Tudor in England, who marries Philip II of Spain, heir to Charles V

1555   Settlement of Augsburg

1556   Abdication of the emperor Charles V. Truce between Henri II and Philip II of Spain

1557   Battle of Saint-Quentin. Edict of Compiègne

1558   The duc de Guise takes Calais from the English. Coronation of Elizabeth I of England. Deaths of the emperor Charles V and Queen Eleonore. Coronation of Philip II

1559   Wedding of Mary, Queen of Scots, and the dauphin François. Peace of Câteau-Cambrésis—ending hostilities between the Empire, France, and England. Marriages between Philip II and Henri's daughter Elizabeth de Valois; Marguerite de Valois, Henri's sister, and Emmanuel Philibert de Savoie; Claude de Valois and Charles de Lorraine. Mortal wounding of Henri during a celebration tournament. Banishment of Diane to Anet. Coronation of François II. Catherine confiscates Chenonceau

1560   Death of François II. The regent Catherine de' Medici forces Diane de Poitiers to exchange Chaumont for Chenonceau

1561   Mary, Queen of Scots, leaves France for Scotland

1562   Battle of Dreux

1566   Death of Diane de Poitiers at Anet

Bibliography

Adémar, Jean. "Documents and Hypotheses Concerning François Clouet." *Master Drawings* 18, 155–68.

Alberi, Eugène. *Vie de Catherine de Médicis.* Translated [into French] by Eugène Alberi. Paris: H.-L. Delloye, 1844.

Anselme, Père de la Vierge Maria. *Histoire généalogique et chronologique de la maison royale de France.* Paris: La Compagnie des Librairies, 1726–1733.

Antonio de Beatis. *The Travel Journal of Antonio de Beatis. Germany, Switzerland, the Low Countries, France, and Italy 1517–1518.* Translated by J. R. Hale and J. M. A. Lincoln. Edited by J. R. Hale. London: Hakluyt Society, 1979.

Arcenay, Jacques d'. *Diane de Poitiers et son temps.* Paris: Librairie illustrée, 1887.

Aubert de La Chesnaye-Desbois, François Alexandre, and François de Badier. *Dictionnaire de la noblesse.* Paris: Schlesinger frères, 1863–1877.

Aubespine, Claude de l'. *Histoire particulière de la cour du roi Henri II.* Paris: Beavais, 1835.

Balzac, Honoré de. *About Catherine de Medici.* London: Dent, 1840; reprinted 1911.

Bardon, François. *Diane de Poitiers et le mythe de Diane.* Paris: Presses Universitaires de France, 1963.

Baschet, Armand. *La Diplomatie vénitienne: Les Princes de l'Europe au XVIe siècle.* Paris: Henri Plon, 1862.

Batut, G. de la. *Les Amours des rois de France racontés par leurs contemporains.* Paris: Éditions Montaigne, 1929.

Baumgartner, Frederic J. *Henri II, King of France 1547–1559.* Durham, N.C.: Duke University Press, 1988.

Beaurain, Georges. *Anet. Diane de Poitiers et ses descendants.* Rouen: Imprimerie Commerciale de Journal de Rouen, 1933.

Bellay, Joachim du, Martin du Bellay, and Guillaume du Bellay. *Mémoires 1513–47.* Edited by Michaud and Poujoulat, 1837.

Belleforest, François de. *Chant funèbre sur trspas* [sic] *du trèscrestien roy des Gaules Henry deuxiesme de ce nom.* Paris: P. Gaultier, 1559.

———. *Les Grandes annales et histoire générale de France, des la venue des Francs en Gaule jusques au règne du Roy très-chrestien Henry III.* Paris: G. Buon, 1579.

Blunt, Anthony. *Philibert de l'Orme.* London: Zwemmer, 1958.

Bobbitt, Philip C. *The Shield of Achilles: War, Peace, and the Course of History.* New York: Alfred A. Knopf, 2002.

Brantôme, Pierre de Bourdeille, seigneur de. *Oeuvres complètes de Pierre de Bour-deille.* Edited by Ludovic Lalanne. Paris: Mme. V. J. Renouard, 1864–1882.

Buchot, Henri François Marie: *Catherine de Médicis.* Paris: Goupil et Cie, 1899.

Burnand Robert. *The Cambridge Modern History,* Vol. II. Cambridge: Cambridge University Press, 1934.

———. *La cour des Valois.* Paris: Hachette, 1938.

Calanio, P. *Traité excellent de l'entretènement de la santé.* Paris: F. Girault for J. Bon-fons, 1550.

Calendar of State Papers, foreign series of the reign of Edward VI, 1547–1553. London: W. B. Turnbull, 1861.

Capefigue, Jean Baptiste Honoré Raymond. *Catherine de Médicis, mère des rois François II, Charles IX et Henri III.* Paris: Amyot, 1856.

———. *Diane de Poitiers.* Paris: Amyot, 1860.

La captivité de François Ier. Paris: Champollion-Figeac, 1847.

Carroll, Stuart. *Noble Power During the French Wars of Religion. The Guise Affinity and the Catholic Cause in Normandy.* Cambridge: Cambridge University Press, 1998.

Castelot, André. *Cités et châteaux de la Loire.* Paris: S.F.E.L.T. (imprimerie De Clerc), 1951.

————. *François Ier.* Paris: Librairie Académique Perrin, 1983.

Castiglione, Baldassar. *Le Livre du courtesan.* Edited by A. Pons. Paris: Lebovici, 1987.

Cellini, Benvenuto. *The Life of Benvenuto Cellini Written by Himself.* Translated by John Addington Symonds. Edited by James Pope-Hennessy. London: Phaidon, 1947.

————. *Mémoires.* Paris: Le Grand livre du mois, 1997.

Chamberlin, E. R. *Everyday Life in Renaissance Times.* London: B. T. Batsford, Ltd. 1965.

Charles de Guise. *Lettres du Cardinal Charles de Lorraine (1525–1574).* Geneva: Librairie Droz, 1998.

Checksfield, M. M. *Portraits of Renaissance Life and Thought.* London: Longmans, Green and Co., Ltd., 1964.

Chevalier, M. l'Abbé C. *Archives royales de Chenonceau. Comptes des receptes et dépenses faîtes en la Chastellenie de Chenonceau par Diane de Poitiers Duchesse de Valentinois Dame de Chenonceau et autres lieux.* Paris: J. Techener, 1864.

————. *Archives du château de Chenonceau. Diane de Poitiers au conseil du roi, épisode de l'histoire de Chenonceau sous François Ier et Henry II, 1535–1556.* Paris: A. Aubry, 1866.

Cloulas, Ivan. *Diane de Poitiers.* Paris: Fayard, 1997.

————. *Henri II.* Paris: Fayard, 1985.

Constant, Jean-Marie. *La Vie quotidienne de la noblesse française aux XVIe et XVIIe siècles.* Paris: Hachette, 1985.

Correspondence of the Emperor Charles V and his ambassadors at the courts of England and France: from the original letters in the imperial family archives at Vienna; with a connecting narrative and bibliographic notices of the Emperor, and of some of the distinguished officers of his army and household; together with the Emperor's itinerary, from 1519–1551. Edited by William Bradford. London: R. Bentley, 1850.

Corson, Richard. *Fashions in Hair: The First 5000 Years.* London: Peter Owen, 1965.

————. *Fashions in Makeup from Ancient to Modern Times.* London: Peter Owen, 1972.

Cosmopolite, Eusebe Philadelphe. *Le Reveille-matin des français, et de leurs voisins, en forme de dialogues.* Paris: Editions d'historie sociale, 1977.

Cottrell, Richard D. *Brantôme: The Writer as Portraitist of His Age.* Geneva: Librairie Droz, 1970.

Cuisiat, Daniel, editor. *Lettres du Cardinal du Lorraine (1525–74)*. Geneva: Librairie Droz, 1998.

Defrance, Eugène. *Catherine de Médicis*. Paris: Mercure de France, 1911.

Delay, Florence. *Les Dames de Fontainebleau*. Milan: Franco Maria Ricci, 1987.

De l'Orme, Philibert. *Nouvelles inventions pour bien bâtir. Premier tome de l'architecture*. Reprint. Paris: L. Laget, 1988.

Dickens, A. G. *The Age of Humanism and the Reformation: Europe in the Fourteenth, Fifteenth, and Sixteenth Centuries*. Englewood Cliffs, N.J.: Prentice-Hall, 1972.

Dictionnaire de biographie française. Edited by J. Balteau et al. Paris: Letouzey et Ané, 1933–.

Dreux du Radier, Jean François. *Mémoires historiques, critiques, et anecdotes des reines et régentes de France*. Amsterdam: Michel Rey, 1776.

Duhamel, Jean. *La Captivité de François Ier et des dauphins*. Paris: Hachette, 1958.

Dycke, Paul van. *Catherine de Médici*. London: John Murray, 1923.

Elliot, Frances Minto Dickinson. *Old Court Life in France*. New York: G. P. Putnam's Sons, 1893.

Les Enseignements d'Anne de France, duchesse de Bourbonnais et d'Auverge, à sa fille Suzanne de Bourbon ... Edited by A.-M. Chazaud. Moulins: C. Desroziers, 1878.

Erlanger, Philippe. *Diane de Poitiers*. Paris: Librairie Gallimard, 1955.

————. *Diane de Poitiers: déesse de la Renaissance*. Paris: Librairie Académique Perrin, 1976.

————. "Diane de Poitiers—the Myth." *The Connoisseur* 163 (1966) 83–87.

————. *Henri III: le méconnu*. Paris: Librairie Académique Perrin, 1975.

Faria, Miguel A., Jr., M.D. "The Death of Henry II of France." *Journal of Neurosurgery* 77 (1992), 964–69.

Ferrara, Orestes. *Le XVIe siècle vu par les ambassadeurs vénitiens*. Paris: Éditions Albin Michel, 1954.

Ffolliott, Sheila. "Casting a Rival into the Shade: Catherine de' Medici and Diane de Poitiers." *Art Journal* (Summer 1989): 138–43.

————. "The Ideal Queenly Patron of the Renaissance: Catherine de' Medici Defining Herself or Defined by Others?" in *Women in Art in Early Modern Europe*. Edited by Cynthia Lawrence. University Park: Pennsylvania State University Press, 1998.

Fleuranges, Robert de la Marck, seigneur de. *Mémoires du maréchal de Florange dit le Jeune Adventureaux*. Edited by Robert Goubaux and P.-André Lemoisne. Paris: Renouard, 1913.

François de Guise. *Mémoires 1547–1561*. Edited by Michaud-Poujoulat. Paris: chez l'éditeur du Commentaire analytique de Code Civil, 1839.

Fraser, Antonia. *Mary, Queen of Scots*. London: Weidenfeld & Nicolson, 1969.

Gaillard, Gabriel-Henri. *Histoire de François Ier*. Paris: Saillant & Nuyon, 1769.

Gerard-Gailly, E. *Bussy-Rabutin: Sa vie, ses oeuvres et ses amies*. Paris: Librairie Ancienne Honoré Champion, 1909.

Germain, José. *Le roman d'Anet, ou les Amours de Diane de Poitiers*. Paris: Les Editions Nationale, 1936.

Le Grand triomphe fait à l'entrée du Trèschrestien et tousiours victorieux Monarche, Henry second de ce nom Roy de France, en sa noble ville et cité de Lyon et de la royne Catherine son espouse. Paris: B. de Gourmont, 1548.

Greengrass, M. "Property and Politics in Sixteenth-Century France: The Landed Fortune of Constable Anne de Montmorency." *French History* 2 (1988): 371–98.

Guerdan, René. *François Ier: Le Roi de renaissance*. Paris: Flammarion, 1976.

———. *Marie Stuart: Reine de France et d''Ecosse*. Paris: Pygmalion Gérard Watelet, 1986.

Guiffrey, Georges. *Chronique du roy Françoys I*. Paris: Jules Renouard, 1860.

Guiffrey, Georges, editor. *Lettres inédites de Dianne de Poytiers*. Paris: Jules Renouard, 1866.

———. *Procès criminel de Jehan de Poytiers, seigneur de Saint-Vallier*. Paris: Lemerre, 1867.

Guigne, G. *La Magnificence de la superbe et triomphante entrée de la noble et antique cité de Lyon au roi très chrétien Henri II*. Lyon: La Société des Bibliophiles Lyonnais, 1927.

Gwyn, Peter. "Wolsey's Foreign Policy: The Conferences at Calais and Bruges Reconsidered." *The Historical Journal* 23 (1980): 755–72.

Hackett, Francis. *Francis the First*. New York: Doubleday, Doran, 1935.

Haggard, Andrew Charles Parker. *Sidelights on the Court of France*. London: Hutchinson & Co., 1903.

Harding, Robert R. *Anatomy of a Power Elite: The Provincial Governors of Early Modern France*. New Haven, Conn.: Yale University Press, 1978.

Hauser, Henri. *Les Débuts de l'âge moderne*. Paris: A. Picard, 1906–1915.

———. *Les Sources de l'histoire de France au XVI siècle*. Vol. II. *François Ier et Henri II*. Paris: Presses universitaires de France, 1956.

Hay, Marie. *Madame Dame Dianne de Poytiers, la Grande Sénéchale de Normandie*. London: J. & E. Bumpus, 1900.

Henderson, Helen W. *The Enchantress; Being the Life of Diane de Poytiers, Mistress of King Henry the Second of France.* Boston and New York: Houghton Mifflin Company, 1928.

Héritier, Jean. *Catherine de' Medici.* Translated by Charlotte Haldane. London: George Allen & Unwin, 1963.

Higman, Francis. *"Farel et Luther dans la bibliothèque d'Anne de Montmorency?" Bibliothèque d'Humanisme de Renaissance* 3 (1991): 415–18.

Huffington, Arianna Stassinopoulos, and Roloff Beny. *The Gods of Greece.* London: Weidenfeld & Nicholson, 1983.

Hugo, Victor. *Le Roi s'amuse.* Paris: Renduel, 1832.

Jacob, P-L. *Les Secrets de beauté de Diane de Poitiers: Confessions archéologiques et cosmétiques.* Brussels: Alph. Lebègue, 1856.

Jensen, De Lamar. "Catherine de' Medici and Her Florentine Friends." *The Sixteenth Century Journal* 9ii (1978): 57–74.

Jouanna, Arlette, Jacqueline Boucher, Dominique Biloghi, and Guy le Thiec. *Histoire et dictionnaire des guerres de religion.* Paris: Robert Laffont, 1988.

Journal d'un bourgeois de Paris sous le règne François Ier 1515–1536. Edited by Ludovic Lalanne. Paris: J. Renouard et Cie, 1854.

Journal de Jean Barillon, secrétaire du chancelier Duprat, 1515–1521. [Edited by] Pierre de Vaissière. Paris: Renouard, 1897–1899.

Kelso, Ruth. *Doctrine for the Lady of the Renaissance.* Urbana: University of Illinois Press, 1956.

Kettering, Sharon. "The Patronage Power of Early Modern French Noblewomen." *The Historical Journal* 32 (1989): 817–41.

Knecht, R. J. *Catherine de' Medici.* London: Longman, 1998.

———.: *Francis I.* Cambridge: Cambridge University Press, 1982.

———. *French Renaissance Monarchy: Francis I and Henry II,* Longman, London, 1984.

———. *Renaissance Warrior and Patron: The Reign of Francis I.* Cambridge: Cambridge University Press, 1994.

Lalanne, Ludovic. *Lexique des oeuvres de Brantôme.* Geneva: Slatkine Reprints, 1970.

Langholm, Sheila. "Violent Conflict and the Loser's Reaction: A Case Study from 1547." *Journal of Peace Research* 2 (1965): 324–47.

Lebey, André. *Le Connétable de Bourbon.* Paris: Perrin et Cie, 1904.

Lefranc, Abel. *La Vie quotidienne au temps de la Renaissance.* Paris: Hachette, 1938.

L'Estoile, Pierre de. *Registre-journal du règne de Henri III.* Edited by Madeleine Lazard and Gilbert Screnk. Geneva: Librairie Droz, 1992.

Lettres de Catherine de Médici. Edited by H. de la Ferrière and G. Baguenault de Puchesse. Paris: Imprimerie Nationale, 1880–1885.

Lettres inédites de Henri II, Diane de Poitiers, Marie Stuart, François, Roi Dauphin, etc. Adressés au Connétable Anne de Montmorency. Paris: J.-B. Gail, 1818.

Lettres et Mémoires d'Estat des roys, princes, ambassadeurs . . . sous les règnes de François Ier, Henry II et Freançois II. Paris: G. Ribier, 1666.

Louise de Savoie. *Journal de Louise de Savoie Duchesse d'Angoulesme, d'Anjou et de Valois, mère du grand roi François Ier.* Paris: Guyot frères, 1851.

Mahoney, Irene. *Madame Catherine.* New York: Coward, McCann & Geoghegan, 1975.

Marguerite de Navarre. *L'Heptaméron.* Edited by Simone de Reyff. Paris: Flammarion, 1982.

———. *Lettres et nouvelles lettres.* Paris: F. Genin, 1841–1842.

Les Marguerites de la Marguerite des princess. Text of the edition of 1547. Introduction, notes, and glossary by Félix Frank. Paris: Librairie des Bibliophiles, 1873.

Marôt, Clément. *Les oeuvres de Clément Marot de Cahors en Quercy, valet du chambre du Roy.* Vol. 4. *À la Grande Sénéchale.* Edited by Georges Guiffrey and Jean Plattard. Paris: Schemit, 1929.

Martin, Graham. "The Death of Henry II of France: A Sporting Death and Postmortem." *ANZ Journal of Surgery* 71 (2001): 318–20.

Mary Queen of Scots. *Letters of Mary Stuart, Queen of Scotland, Selected from the "Recueil des Lettres de Marie Stuart," Together with the Chronological Summary of Events During the Reign of the Queen of Scotland, by Prince Alexander Labanoff.* Translated, with Notes and Introduction, by William Turnbull. London: Charles Dolman, 1845.

Maulde la Clavière, R. de. *The Women of the Renaissance: A Study of Feminism.* Translated by George Herbert Ely. London: Sonnenschein & Co., 1901.

McLeod, Glenda K., ed. *The Reception of Christine de Pizan from the Fifteenth Through the Nineteenth Centuries: Visitors to the City.* Lewiston, N.Y.: The Edwin Mellen Press, 1991.

Médicis, Catherine de'. *Lettres de Catherine de Médicis.* Paris: Imprimerie nationale, 1880–1943.

Melville, Sir James. *Memoirs of Sir James Melville of Halhill 1535–1617*. Edited and with an introduction by A. Francis Steuart. London: George Routledge & Sons, Ltd. 1929.

Michelet, J. *Histoire de France au seizième siècle*. Paris: Librairie classiques de L. Hachette, 1835.

Le Mythe de Diane en France au XVIe siècle. Actes du colloque, E.N.S. Bd Jourdan, Paris, mai 29–31, 2001. Edited by Jean-Raymond Fanlo and Marie-Dominique Legrand. Paris: Association des Amis d'Agrippa d'Aubigné, 2002.

Noëll, Henri. *Henri II et la naissance de la societé moderne*. Paris: La Nouvelle Edition, 1944.

Nostradamus. *Les Premières centuries ou propheties*. Edited by Pierre Brind'amour. Geneva: Librairie Droz, 1996.

Orieux, Jean. *Bussy-Rabutin: Le Libertin galant homme (1618–1693)*. Paris: Flammarion, 1958.

Orliac, Jehanne d'. *The Moon Mistress: Diane de Poitiers*. London: George G. Harrap and Co., Ltd., 1931.

Paillard, Charles. "The Death of François I and the First Days of the Reign of Henri II: after Jean de Saint-Mauris, Ambassador to Charles V in the French Court." *Revue Historique* (1877): 84–120.

Paré, Ambroise. *Oeuvres*. Edited by J. F. Malgaigne. Paris: J. B. Baillière, 1840–1841.

Petitot, M., editor. *Commentaires de messire Blaise de Montluc, maréchal de France*. Paris: Foucault, 1821.

Pisan, Christine de. *The Treasure of the City of Ladies; or, The Book of the Three Virtues ("La Trésor de la cité des dames")*. Translated and edited by Sarah Lawson. London: Penguin, 1985.

Poésies de François Ier, Louise de Savoie, Marguerite et correspondence intime du roi avec Diane de Poitiers. Paris: Champollion-Figeac, 1847.

Rabutin, François. *Commentaires des dernières guerres en la Gaule Belgique entre Henry second de ce nom, Très chréstien Roy de France, & Charles cinquiesme Empereur, & Phillipes son fils, Roy d'Espaigne*. Paris: Nicolas Chesneau, 1574.

Relations des ambassadeurs vénitiens sur les affaires de France au XVIe siècle. Edited and translated by N. M. Tommaseo. Paris: Imprimerie royale, 1838; together with the *Documents inédits de l'Histoire de France*. Edited in Italian by E. Alberi. Florence, 1839–1863.

Relations politiques de la France et de l'Espagne avec l'Ecosse au XVIe siècle. Paris: Alex Teulet, 1862.

Roberts, Jonathan. *Cabbages and Kings: The Origins of Fruit and Vegetables*. London: HarperCollins, 2001.

Roeder, Ralph. *Catherine de Médici and the Lost Revolution*. London: George G. Harrap and Co., Ltd., 1937.

Roelker, Nancy L. "The Appeal of Calvinism to French Noblewomen in the Sixteenth Century." *Journal of Interdisciplinary History* 2 (1972): 391–418.

Roussel, Pierre Desiré. *Histoire et Description du château d'Anet*. Paris: printed for the author by D. Jouaust, 1875.

Le sacre couronnement du Roy Henry deuxième de ce nom. Paris: de R-Estienne [n.d.].

Saul, Leon J. *The Childhood Emotional Pattern: The Key to Personality, Its Disorders and Therapy*. New York: Van Nostrand Reinhold Company, 1977.

Saulx de Tavannes, Gaspard de. *Mémoires*. Edited by Michaud. Paris: Guyot frères, 1851.

Scève, Maurice. *The Entry of Henri II into Lyon: September 1548*. Tempe, Ariz.: Medieval and Renaissance Texts and Studies, 1997.

Seeley, Grace H. *Diane the Huntress: The Life and Times of Diane de Poitiers*. New York and London: D. Appleton-Century, 1936.

Stevenson, Joseph. *Mary Stuart: A Narrative of the First Eighteen Years of Her Life, Principally from Original Documents*. Edinburgh: W. Paterson, 1886.

Stoddart, Jane T. *The Girlhood of Mary Queen of Scots from Her Landing in France in August 1548 to Her Departure from France in August 1561*. London: Hodder and Stoughton, 1908.

Sutherland, N. M. "Catherine de Medici: The Legend of the Wicked Italian Queen." *The Sixteenth Century Journal* 9ii (1978): 45–56.

Thierry, Adrien. *Diana de Poitiers*. Paris: La Palatine, 1955.

Thou, Jacques-August de. *Histoire de Monsieur de Thou, de choses arrivées de son temps*. Translated into French by P. Du Ryer. Paris: Augustin Courbé, 1659.

Tournon, Michel François. *Le Cardinal François de Tournon, Homme d'État, Diplomate, Mécène et Humaniste, 1489–1562*. Paris: E. de Boccard, 1951.

Turnbull, W. B. *Calendar of State Papers, Foreign Series, of the reign of Mary (1553–1558) preserved in the state paper department of Her Majesty's Public Record Office*. London: Green, Longman & Roberts, 1861.

Varillas, Antoine. *La Minorité de Saint-Louis avec l'histoire de Louis XI et de Henri II*. La Haye: Adrien Moetjens, 1687.

Viple, Joseph. *Les Enseignements d'Anne de France*. Moulins: Crépin-Leblond, 1935.

Voulté, Jean [Jean Visagier]. *Recueil de poésies*. Fond français no. 883, folio 38; *Hendescayllaborum* Libri III. Paris: S. de Colines, 1538.

Warshaw, J. "Recurrent Préciosité." *Modern Language Notes* 31 (1916): 129–35.

Watson, Francis Leslie. *The Life and Times of Catherine de' Medici*. London: Hutchinson & Co., 1934.

Wells, Charlotte. "Leeches on the Body Politic: Xenophobia and Witchcraft in Early Modern French Political Thought." *French Historical Studies* 22 (1999): 351–77.

Wiley, W. L. "Brantôme's Interest in Languages and Literature." *Modern Language Notes* 65 (1950): 331–36.

Williams, H. Noel. *Henri II: His Court and Times*. London: Methuen and Co., Ltd., 1910.

Young, George Frederick. *The Medici*. Vols. I and II. New York: E. P. Dutton, 1911.

Manuscripts in the Bibliothèque Nationale, Paris

Letter from Henri II to Diane, fonds français no. 2.991, folio 9.

Letter from Henri II to Diane, fonds français no. 3.143, folios 2, 4, 5.

Poems by Henri II to Diane, fonds français no. 3.143, folios 6, 7, 8.

Receuil de poésies, fonds français no. 883, folio 38.

"Testament de dame Diane de Poitiers, duchesse de Valentinois, facit le jour des Roys à Limours, l'an 1564," fonds français no. 3.902, folio 107.

Manuscripts at Saint-Germain-des-Prés

Letters, nos. 1781/2, from the Cardinal de Lorraine.

Index

Note: Page numbers in *italics* refer to illustrations. *Illus.* entries refer to color insert. Captions are indexed as text.

Illustration Credits

ILLUSTRATION CREDITS

page 31   *View of château d'Amboise,* by Charles Claude Pyne. (Victoria & Albert Museum, London, UK/The Bridgeman Art Library/www.bridgeman.co.uk)

page 32   The coronation sword of the kings of France, belonging to Charlemagne, shown with scabbard. (Musée du Louvre, Paris, France/Giraudon/The Bridgeman Art Library/www.bridgeman.co.uk)

page 33   The "hand of justice," from the Treasury of Saint-Denis. (Musée du Louvre, Paris, France/Peter Willi/The Bridgeman Art Library/www.bridgeman.co.uk)

page 34   *Marguerite de Navarre,* by Jean Clouet. (Private Collection)

page 35   *Mary Tudor and Charles Brandon, Duke of Suffolk.* (Private Collection/The Bridgeman Art Library/www.bridgeman.co.uk)

page 36   The royal Salamander, symbol of François I, from the château de Blois. (Private Collection)

page 39   *Louis de Brézé.* (Private Collection)

page 45   Homage to Louise de Savoie at Amiens in 1518, from *Les Chants Royaux,* engraving by A. Godard. French School, 16c. (Private Collection/The Bridgeman Art Library/www.bridgeman.co.uk)

page 51   The ermine of Brittany, symbol of Queen Claude. (Private Collection)

page 54   *Château de Blois,* by Thomas Shotter Boys. (© Yale Center for British Art, Paul Mellon Collection, USA/The Bridgeman Art Library/www.bridgeman.co.uk)

page 60   Fontainebleau: Galerie François I. (Château de Fontainebleau, Seine-et-Marne, France/Giraudon/The Bridgeman Art Library/www.bridgeman.co.uk)

page 61   Gold saltcellar, or *saliera,* made for François I by Benvenuto Cellini. (Kunsthistorisches Museum, Vienna, Austria/The Bridgeman Art Library/www.bridgeman.co.uk)

page 63   Antoine Macault Presents His Translation to François I (1494–1547) from "Books I, II and III" by Diodorus Siculus. c. 1532 (vellum). French School, 16c. (Musée Condé, Chantilly, France/Lauros/Giraudon/The Bridgeman Art Library/www.bridgeman.co.uk)

page 69   A jousting scene from *The Book of Hours,* Workshop of Gerart Horenbout and Simon Bening. (British Library, London, UK/The Bridgeman Art Library/www.bridgeman.co.uk)

page 72   *Henry VIII,* School of Hans Holbein. (Ackerman and Johnson Ltd., London, UK/The Bridgeman Art Library/www.bridgeman.co.uk)

page 74   Portrait presumed to be Charles de Bourbon, Studio of Clouet. (Musée Condé, Chantilly, France/Giraudon/The Bridgeman Art Library/www.bridgeman.co.uk)

page 77   Jean de Poitiers (d. 1539) Lord of Saint-Vallier (pencil on paper) by Clouet (16c.) (studio of). (Musée Condé, Chantilly, France/ Giraudon/The Bridgeman Art Library/www.bridgeman.co.uk)

page 81   *View of the château de Loches.* French School, 17c. (Bibliothèque Nationale, Paris, France/Lauros/Giraudon/The Bridgeman Art Library/www.bridgeman.co.uk)

page 88   Portrait of Queen Claude (1499–1524) (oil on panel 16c., French), by Corneille de Lyons (c. 1500–1575). (Pushkin Museum, Moscow, Russia/Giraudon/The Bridgeman Art Library/www.bridgeman.co.uk)

page 105   *Suleiman the Magnificent.* (Private Collection)

page 121   *View of the château de Saint-Germain-en-Laye,* by Israel Silvestre the Younger. (Musée de la Ville de Paris, Musée Carnavalet, Paris, France/Lauros/Giraudon/The Bridgeman Art Library/ www.bridgeman.co.uk)

page 122   *Henri d'Albret, King of Navarre, Presenting a marguerite to Marguerite, Sister of François I.* French School, 16c. (The Stapleton Collection, UK/The Bridgeman Art Library/www.bridgeman.co.uk)

page 135   *Marguerite de Navarre presenting the* Heptaméron *to Anne de Pisseleu, duchesse d'Etampes,* from *La Coche, ou le Débat d'Amour.* French School, 16c. (Musée Condé, Chantilly, France/Giraudon/The Bridgeman Art Library/www.bridgeman.co.uk)

page 143   Portrait of Catherine de' Medici (1519–1589), facsimile of a 16th century drawing appearing in *Portraits of the Most Famous Personalities of the 16th Century,* by P. G. Niel, Paris, 1848 (graphite on paper). French School, 19c. (Bibliothèque des Arts Décoratifs, Paris, France/Archives Charnet/The Bridgeman Art Library/www.bridgeman.co.uk)

page 145   *Ippolito de' Medici,* by Tiziano Vecellio (Titian). (Palazzo Pitti, Florence, Italy/The Bridgeman Art Library/www.bridgeman.co.uk)

page 154   *Dauphin François de France,* by Corneille de Lyon. (Musée Condé, Chantilly, France/Giraudon/The Bridgeman Art Library/ www.bridgeman.co.uk)

page 162   *Catherine de' Medici Riding Sidesaddle.* (Bibliothèque nationale de France)

page 164   *Anne de Pisseleu, duchesse d'Etampes,* Studio of Clouet. (Musée Condé, Chantilly, France/Giraudon/The Bridgeman Art Library/ www.bridgeman.co.uk)

page 175   A game of "real tennis": detail from *David and Bathsheba.* Flemish School, 16c. (Marylebone Cricket Club, London, UK/The Bridgeman Art Library/www.bridgeman.co.uk)

page 178   Quartering in the Place de Grève. (© ND/Roger-Viollet)

page 215   *"LeBalafré," duc de Guise.* (Bibliothèque nationale de France)

ILLUSTRATION CREDITS

page 222 *A Court Jester.* French School, 16c. (Bibliothèque nationale de France/The Bridgeman Art Library/www.bridgeman.co.uk)

page 244 Diane of France or of Valois (1538–1619), Duchess of Angoulême (oil on panel). French School, 16c. (Musée de la Ville de Paris, Musée Carnavalet, Paris, France/Lauros/Giraudon/The Bridgeman Art Library/www.bridgeman.co.uk)

page 245 Portrait of Cardinal Charles de Lorraine (1525–1574) c. 1555 (red chalk and pencil on paper). School of François Clouet. (Musée Condé, Chantilly, France/Giraudon/The Bridgeman Art Library/www.bridgeman.co.uk)

page 250 Diane's symbols with motto. (Private Collection)

page 252 Ceramic plate with "HD." (Private Collection)

page 256 Method of burning those condemned by the Inquisition. Flemish School, 16c. (Bibliothèque nationale de France/Giraudon/The Bridgeman Art Library/www.bridgeman.co.uk)

page 259 Crowned "H" resting on crescent moon. (Private Collection)

page 259 Diane's symbol. (Private Collection)

page 259 Diane's symbol. (Private Collection)

page 262 *François II as Dauphin,* by Léonard Limousin. (Musée du Louvre, Paris, France/The Bridgeman Art Library/www.bridgeman.co.uk)

page 268 Three intertwined crescent moons and the motto *"Donec totum impleat orbem."* (Private Collection)

page 269 Joint signature of Diane de Poitiers and Henri II. (Private Collection)

page 273 The Fountain of the Innocents, c. 1547 (photo) Jean Goujon (1510–1567) and Pierre Lescot (1515–1578). (Paris, France/Lauros/Giraudon/The Bridgeman Art Library/www.bridgeman.co.uk)

page 274 "HD" with *delta.* (Private Collection)

page 282 *Château de Chaumont.* (Private Collection)

page 284 Anet: Window catch with three entwined crescents. (Private Collection)

page 291 *Diane de Poitiers at Her Bath,* by François Clouet. (Kress Collection, Washington, D.C., USA/The Bridgeman Art Library/www.bridgeman.co.uk)

page 292 Diane de Poitiers (1499–1566) as Diana the Huntress (oil on canvas). Fontainebleau School, 16c. (Musée de la Venerie, Senlis, France/Giraudon/The Bridgeman Art Library/www.bridgeman.co.uk)

page 294 Anet: Existing façade. (Private Collection)

ILLUSTRATION CREDITS

ILLUSTRATION CREDITS

page 3   *François I,* by Tiziano Vecellio (Titian). (Musée du Louvre, Paris, France/Lauros/Giraudon/The Bridgeman Art Library/ www.bridgeman.co.uk)

page 4   *The Battle of Pavia,* by Ruprecht Heller. (Nationalmuseum, Stockholm, Sweden/The Bridgeman Art Library/www.bridgeman.co.uk)

page 4   Fontainebleau. (Private Collection)

page 5   *The Solemn Entrance of Emperor Charles V, François I, and Alessandro Farnese to Paris in 1540,* from the *Sala dei Fasti Farnese* (fresco), by Taddeo and Federico Zuccaro (Zuccari). (Palazzo Farnese, Rome, Italy/The Bridgeman Art Library/www.bridgeman.co.uk)

page 5   *François I* (1494–1547) *Receives the Last Breaths of Leonardo da Vinci* (1452–1519), 1818 (oil on canvas), by Jean-Auguste-Dominique Ingres (1780–1867). (Musée de la Ville de Paris, Musée du Petit-Palais, France/The Bridgeman Art Library/www.bridgeman.co.uk)

page 6   *Henri II as a Child,* by Jean Clouet. (Musée Condé, Chantilly, France/The Bridgeman Art Library/www.bridgeman.co.uk)

page 6   *Henri II on Horseback.* (Private Collection)

page 7   *Marriage of Henri II and Catherine de' Medici with Diane de Poitiers* (enamel), by Léonard Limousin. (Private Collection)

page 7   *Diana and the Stag,* by Jean Goujon. Made for Anet and now in the Louvre. (Private Collection)

page 7   *Catherine de' Medici* (enamel), by Léonard Limousin. (Private Collection)

page 8   *Catherine de' Medici.* French School, 16c. (Galleria degli Uffizi, Florence, Italy/The Bridgeman Art Library/www.bridgeman.co.uk)

page 8   *Catherine de' Medici,* by François Clouet. (Musée de la Ville de Paris, Musée Carnavalet, Paris, France/Lauros/Giraudon/The Bridgeman Art Library/www.bridgeman.co.uk)

page 9   *The Cortège of Drummers and Soldiers at the Royal Entry Festival of Henri II into Rouen.* French School, 16c. (Bibliothèque Municipale, Rouen, France/The Bridgeman Art Library/www.bridgeman.co.uk)

page 10   *The Drowning of Britomaris,* and detail. (The Metropolitan Museum of Art, gift of the children of Mrs. Harry Payne Whitney, in accordance with the wishes of their mother, 1942)

page 11   Equestrian portrait, presumed to be Dauphin Henri II, by François Clouet. (Menil Collection, Houston, Texas/The Bridgeman Art Library/www.bridgeman.co.uk)

page 11   *Henri II of France,* by François Clouet. (Musée Condé, Chantilly, France/Giraudon/The Bridgeman Art Library/www.bridgeman.co.uk)

page 12   *Catherine de' Medici, Wife of King Henri II of France.* French School, 16c. (Palazzo Pitti, Florence, Italy/The Bridgeman Art Library/ www.bridgeman.co.uk)

page 13   *Henri II.* French School, 16c. (Lobkowicz Collections, Nelahozeves Castle, Czech Republic/The Bridgeman Art Library/ www.bridgeman.co.uk)

page 13   *Diane de Poitiers, Mistress of Henri II, King of France.* French School, 16c. (State Collection, France/The Bridgeman Art Library/www.bridgeman.co.uk)

page 14   Portraits of Leo X, Cardinal Luigi de' Rossi, and Giulio de' Medici, by Raphael. (Galleria degli Uffizi, Florence, Italy/The Bridgeman Art Library/www.bridgeman.co.uk)

page 14   Portrait of Eleonore of Habsburg, Archduchess of Austria, Queen of Portugal, then Queen of France, and the second wife of François I, 1536 (oil on canvas), by Léonard Limousin (c. 1505–c. 1575). (Musée Nationale de la Renaissance, Ecouen, France/Roger-Viollet, Paris/The Bridgeman Art Library/www.bridgeman.co.uk)

page 14   *Anne de Montmorency, Constable and Marshal of France,* by François Clouet. (Musée Condé, Chantilly, France/Giraudon/The Bridgeman Art Library/www.bridgeman.co.uk)

page 15   *Diane de Poitiers in Her Bath,* by François Clouet. (Musée des Beaux-Arts, Rouen, France/Lauros/Giraudon/The Bridgeman Art Library/www.bridgeman.co.uk)

page 15   Portrait of Diane de Poitiers, by Cecchino Salviati. (Private Collection)

page 15   *Diane de Poitiers.* School of Fontainebleau, 16c. (Private Collection)

page 16   *Mary Stuart's Farewell to France,* by Henry Nelson O'Neil. (Phillips, The International Fine Art Auctioneers, UK/The Bridgeman Art Library/www.bridgeman.co.uk)

page 16   *Le Château de Chenonceau,* by Pierre-Justin Ouvrie. (Private Collection/Phillips, The International Fine Art Auctioneers, UK/The Bridgeman Art Library/www.bridgeman.co.uk)

1/06 (5) 6/05
3/07 (7) 1/07
10/18 (17) 7/17